Reading Hemingway's *A Farewell to Arms*

READING HEMINGWAY SERIES
MARK CIRINO, EDITOR
ROBERT W. LEWIS, FOUNDING EDITOR

Reading Hemingway's *The Sun Also Rises*
    H. R. Stoneback

Reading Hemingway's *Men Without Women*
    Joseph M. Flora

Reading Hemingway's *Across the River and into the Trees*
    Mark Cirino

Reading Hemingway's *To Have and Have Not*
    Kirk Curnutt

Reading Hemingway's *The Old Man and the Sea*
    Bickford Sylvester, Larry Grimes, and Peter L. Hays

Reading Hemingway's *A Farewell to Arms*
    Robert W. Lewis and Michael Kim Roos

Reading Hemingway's
A Farewell to Arms

GLOSSARY AND COMMENTARY

Robert W. Lewis and Michael Kim Roos

The Kent State University Press

KENT, OHIO

© 2019 by The Kent State University Press, Kent, Ohio 44242
All rights reserved
Library of Congress Catalog Card Number 2018055020
ISBN 978-1-60635-376-9
Manufactured in the United States of America

No part of this book may be used or reproduced, in any manner whatsoever, without written permission from the Publisher, except in the case of short quotations in critical reviews or articles.

LIBRARY OF CONGRESS CATALOGING-IN-PUBLICATION DATA
Names: Lewis, Robert W. (Robert William), 1930- author. | Roos, Mike, 1952- author.
Title: Reading Hemingway's A Farewell to arms : glossary and commentary / Robert W. Lewis and Michael Kim Roos.
Description: Kent, Ohio : The Kent State University Press, [2019] | Includes bibliographical references and index.
Identifiers: LCCN 2018055020 | ISBN 9781606353769 (pbk.)
Subjects: LCSH: Hemingway, Ernest, 1899-1961. Farewell to arms. | World War, 1914-1918--United States--Literature and the war.
Classification: LCC PS3515.E37 F35583 2019 | DDC 813/.52--dc23
LC record available at https://lccn.loc.gov/2018055020

23 22 21 20 19   5 4 3 2 1

For Robert W. Lewis
(1930–2013)

To live reasonably is not to live by reason alone—the mistake is easy, and if carried far, disastrous—but to live in a way of which reason, a clear, full sense of the whole situation, would approve.
 —I. A. Richards, *Poetry and Science*

The test of a first-rate intelligence is the ability to hold two opposed ideas in the mind at the same time, and still retain the ability to function.
 —F. Scott Fitzgerald, "The Crack-Up"

It is true that there is a heaven for the saint, but the saint leaves enough misery here below to sadden him even before the throne of God.
 —Emily Brontë, "The Butterfly"

Our deepest convictions—will Science upset them?
 —Ernest Hemingway, "Banal Story"

Que sais-je?
 —Montaigne

CONTENTS

Acknowledgments   xi
Introduction: Hemingway's Anxiety of Influence   xiii
Abbreviations for the Works of Ernest Hemingway Used in This Book   xxix
Series Note   xxxi
Front Matter   3
Book One
    Chapter 1   19
    Chapter 2   29
    Chapter 3   41
    Chapter 4   51
    Chapter 5   61
    Chapter 6   66
    Chapter 7   72
    Chapter 8   85
    Chapter 9   90
    Chapter 10   104
    Chapter 11   109
    Chapter 12   113
Book Two
    Chapter 13   121
    Chapter 14   124
    Chapter 15   127
    Chapter 16   130
    Chapter 17   134
    Chapter 18   138
    Chapter 19   143
    Chapter 20   153
    Chapter 21   159
    Chapter 22   170
    Chapter 23   174
    Chapter 24   183

Book Three
- Chapter 25   189
- Chapter 26   198
- Chapter 27   202
- Chapter 28   213
- Chapter 29   218
- Chapter 30   222
- Chapter 31   235
- Chapter 32   239

Book Four
- Chapter 33   243
- Chapter 34   248
- Chapter 35   259
- Chapter 36   269
- Chapter 37   273

Book Five
- Chapter 38   283
- Chapter 39   296
- Chapter 40   299
- Chapter 41   304

Works Cited   324

Index   336

ACKNOWLEDGMENTS

Illness prevented Robert W. Lewis from finishing the manuscript for *Reading Hemingway's* A Farewell to Arms before he died, and we all feel the loss. The *Reading Hemingway* series was his brainchild, and he served as the founding editor, shepherding into print the first two volumes, H. R. Stoneback's *Reading Hemingway's* The Sun Also Rises and Joseph Flora's *Reading Hemingway's* Men Without Women, volumes that set high standards for all the books to follow in the series. Regrettably, I never had the opportunity to meet Professor Lewis, but I am deeply grateful for his work in establishing this important series and providing a foundation for this manuscript upon which I have built. His daughter, Lisa Lewis, who has been generous, supportive, and kind throughout this process since Mark Cirino handed me the task of completing the manuscript in 2015, has told me her father would wish to acknowledge the able and invaluable assistance of Ursula Hovet, executive secretary of the English department at the University of North Dakota, who became Professor Lewis's right hand in all Hemingway-affiliated administrative duties and provided helpful comments as she typed his manuscripts. My fervent wish throughout my work on this project has been to help preserve Robert W. Lewis's important legacy and to produce a manuscript of which he would have been proud.

The completion of this project has been a collaboration far beyond the work of coauthors, however. I am deeply grateful to Series Editor Mark Cirino for having the confidence in me to take on the daunting task of completing a manuscript begun by such a luminary figure in Hemingway scholarship. Mark has been extraordinarily helpful and supportive throughout the three-year process of completing the book, and I have relied much on his wisdom and friendship. The Reading Hemingway Series is in excellent hands under his guidance.

I also greatly appreciate those, in addition to Mark, who have read previous versions of this manuscript, both Professor Lewis's early work and my drafts: Steve Trout, Lisa Tyler, Kirk Curnutt, and Don Daiker. Their astute and generous comments have helped to make the finished manuscript significantly better.

Additionally, I have benefited greatly from the friendship and advice of numerous Hemingway colleagues—especially Don Daiker, John Beall, Elizabeth Lloyd-Kimbrel, Ai Ogasawara, Clint King, Susan Beegel, Kirk Curnutt, Suzanne del Gizzo, Ellen

Andrews Knodt, Larry Grimes, Peter Hays, H. R. Stoneback, Kevin Maier, Mark Ott, and Verna Kale, all of whom have contributed in small and large ways to this volume.

During two separate weeks I spent at the John F. Kennedy Library in Boston, the staff—particularly Stephen Plotkin, Stacy Chandler, Maryrose Grossman, James DeMenna, Hilary Justice, and Susan Wrynn—provided congenial and professional assistance in reading and interpreting manuscript materials, scrapbooks, and letters, as well as in selecting appropriate photos for the book. The staff at the Harry Ransom Center, University of Texas—especially Kelly Kerbow Hudson, Richard Watson, and others whose names I have forgotten—provided equally friendly and valuable assistance during a week of research in the Hemingway family archives in Austin.

I have also received generous financial, scholarly, and emotional support for my Hemingway research from friends and colleagues at the University of Cincinnati Blue Ash College—Philip Luther, Marlene Miner, and Sue Sipple of the Department of English and Communications, Mark Otten of the Biology department (my consultant on scientific matters, especially those of evolutionary biology), Deborah Page of the foreign language department (my German translator), and deans Don O'Meara (a special friend) and Cady Short Thompson.

My son, Christopher Roos, and daughter-in-law, Kacy Hollenback, archeologists at Southern Methodist University, patiently provided valuable tutorial assistance in Adobe Illustrator, which I used to produce the five maps in the book.

Neuroscientist Olaf Blanke in Switzerland, cognitive scientist Glenn Carruthers in Australia, and psychologist Susan Blackmore in the United Kingdom contributed valuable expertise regarding Frederic Henry's out-of-body experience. Vincenzo Di Nardo in Italy provided important information about the Abruzzi region and Hemingway's friend Nick Nerone, as well as a possible source for the priest in the novel and found and translated some key Italian sources for me. An unexpected reward is that, as a result of our long-term contacts, Olaf and Vincenzo have now become my close friends and collaborators in spinoff projects.

I am also deeply grateful to the professional and supportive staff at Kent State University Press—Director Susan Wadsworth Booth, Acquiring Editor Will Underwood, Managing Editor Mary Young, Design and Production Manager Christine Brooks, Marketing and Sales Manager Richard Fugini, Marketing Associate Darryl Crosby, and my able and amiable copy editor, Erin Holman.

And finally I am deeply grateful for the friendship, bountiful love, and support of my wife and life partner, Minsun Kim Roos, who has been with me in body, mind, and spirit throughout the process, accompanying me twice on the fourteen-hour drive from Cincinnati to Boston for weeklong stints at the JFK Library, flying to Hemingway conferences in Venice and Paris, and tolerating the daily ups and downs of a long and arduous research and writing process. It is difficult to conceive how this project would have been completed without her.

M.K.R.
August 2018

INTRODUCTION

Hemingway's Anxiety of Influence

> [S]elf-appropriation involves the immense anxieties of indebtedness, for what strong maker desires the realization that he has failed to create himself?
> —Harold Bloom, *The Anxiety of Influence*

The decade of the 1920s was Ernest Hemingway's great period of self-education and self-appropriation, the time in which he grew from an apprentice to a master writer and, with the publication of *A Farewell to Arms*, joined an elite tier of novelists whose work continues to be read and esteemed nearly a century later. Upon graduating from high school in 1917, Hemingway momentously chose, against his parents' wishes, not to attend college, pursuing instead a career in journalism at the *Kansas City Star* and then seeking the education of experience through the adventure of war. However, a near-death experience in that war in Italy and the heartbreak of his hospital romance with nurse Agnes von Kurowsky produced a marked change in his writing goals soon after his return home. Now with a rich vein of writing material to mine, no longer satisfied with being a journalist, he meant to pursue a literary writing life. Yet he was perceptive enough to recognize that succeeding at such a pursuit would mean intensely studying the works of predecessors already firmly established in the canon. Thus, from 1919 to 1928, the year he began writing *A Farewell to Arms*, Hemingway would read at least five hundred books, averaging about a book a week, but closer to two books a week during the peak years of 1925, 1926, and 1927.[1] Although by the end of that period, Hemingway had published four volumes of fiction with two major publishers, none of these so skillfully combined Hemingway's biographical material with extensive historical research and the influence of his literary reading as would *A Farewell to Arms*.[2] Hemingway's third novel thus may be viewed as a kind of doctoral dissertation, a validation of his extensive self-education of the 1920s, guided, to be sure, by a committee of wise and well-read mentors—including Sherwood Anderson, Ezra Pound, Gertrude Stein, Ford Madox Ford, F. Scott Fitzgerald, and John Dos Passos.

But all that reading can be a double-edged sword for a writer. On the one hand, it certainly expands the mind, makes the writer aware of the creative possibilities of the literary art, and provides models of fine writing. On the other hand, as Harold Bloom has theorized, it is also almost certain to produce a high level of anxiety, for every writer knows that achieving greatness is no simple matter of imitating those who have gone before, not even for the greatest writers. As T. S. Eliot explains in "Tradition and the Individual Talent," the great works of the past must not be duplicated, but they must also not be ignored. The aspiring writer must necessarily measure his own works against those esteemed by the tradition, and such measurement inevitably produces anxiety. The writer reasonably questions his own ability to join the masters that he admires so much. This anxiety and self-doubt can be too much for writers without strength and fortitude, who allow themselves to be so intimidated that they either debase themselves by flaccid imitation of the masters or they give up the chase entirely. As Bloom says, only strong writers survive the test to produce works that offer something fresh to become a legitimate part of the ongoing tradition of great literature.

Hemingway seems to have been intuitively aware of the task he faced, and he chose his masters wisely. No one questions the literary status of the six writers on whom he seems to have been most fixated—three Russian, two French, one German—Ivan Turgenev, Leo Tolstoy, Fyodor Dostoevsky, Stendhal, Gustave Flaubert, and Thomas Mann. These imposing figures stood before him as he contemplated writing his next novel in the fall of 1927, and, initially, he seems to have been too intimidated to attempt the novel of love and war that his experiences had been pointing him toward at least since the end of the Great War. Instead, he embarked on a much different kind of story, one in the manner of a more distant and perhaps less intimidating predecessor, the eighteenth-century English satirist Henry Fielding. For several months, Hemingway intrepidly slaved over a *Tom Jones*–style picaresque that he was calling *A New Slain Knight*, a novel of a young boy named at first Jimmy Crane, then Jimmy House, then Jimmy Breen, who is traveling with his father by train from Michigan to New York toward revolutionary adventures in Europe. But after some twenty chapters, the writing bogged down and came to a dead stop. Ultimately, Hemingway had to admit to Maxwell Perkins, his editor at Scribner's, that he did not "know enough" to write a book in the *Tom Jones* manner (*Letters* 3 375).[3]

Thus, by January 1928, having failed at picaresque satire, Hemingway was facing an artistic crisis. If the Jimmy Breen story had mostly been an exercise in avoidance of the kind of novel he knew, in his heart of hearts, that he needed to write, he now had nowhere to turn except to face the anxiety head on. Although he was being hailed as a new master of the short story and his fame was growing to the point that parodies of his work were appearing in magazines like *The New Yorker* and *Vanity Fair*, he could not avoid that his place in the pantheon would only be granted if he proved his mettle as a first-rate novelist with the kind of work that had been produced by messieurs Turgenev, Tolstoy, Dostoevsky, Stendhal, Flaubert, and Mann.

Hemingway's biographers have extensively documented his experiential material that was waiting to be fully exploited in an extended work of fiction. To briefly summarize the relevant facts: Hemingway was the son of devoutly religious parents, including a father who was a doctor of medicine as well as a practitioner and teacher of science and a mother who was an artist in her own right, an operatic singer, who gave private music lessons in the Hemingway home. In such an environment, Hemingway became steeped in the inherent conflicts between reason and faith and between objective and subjective truth. Although part of him was inclined toward following his father in a career in the natural sciences, ultimately the artistic sensibility he inherited from his mother led him toward romantic adventures and a career in writing. When he graduated from Oak Park High School in suburban Chicago in 1917, like many young men, Hemingway was eager to serve in the Great War in Europe. However, the US military rejected him because of poor eyesight, so, after working for seven months as a cub reporter at the *Kansas City Star*, he volunteered to serve as an ambulance driver for the American Red Cross beginning in June 1918 and was assigned to duty on the Italian front. Disappointed with the lack of action in his sector, he volunteered to deliver candy and cigarettes to Italian soldiers on the front line near the Piave River, where there was still scattered fighting. At the town of Fossalta di Piave, on the night of 8 July 1918, he suffered serious wounds in his legs and feet from a trench mortar shell explosion and machine gun fire, and, after initial treatment at a field hospital, he was transported to the Red Cross hospital in Milan. There he met and fell in love with American nurse Agnes von Kurowsky, eight years his elder, and their romance continued until Hemingway sailed back to America in January 1919, a war hero, certain that Agnes intended to marry him as soon as he got a job and demonstrated his ability to support a wife. However, within two months, Agnes aborted their affair with a declaration that she was too old for him, besides being engaged to an Italian officer. These two serious scarrings—the physical one at Fossalta and the psychological one with Agnes—are generally considered essential elements that propelled Hemingway toward his pursuit of literary greatness.

While Hemingway certainly could have chosen to write an autobiographical novel that drew upon these central experiences, he elected instead to use only some of that material and to alter it in dramatically significant ways to produce a novel that has some biographical basis but is largely fictionalized. Part of his motivation might have been to avoid the kind of recrimination he had experienced following the publication of *The Sun Also Rises*, which relied heavily on real events from Hemingway's life in 1925 with thinly disguised actual people as its characters. Hemingway was also ten years older and vastly more experienced than the naive young man who had gone to Italy in 1918. He wanted his protagonist more closely to reflect himself as a twenty-nine-year-old rather than a nineteen-year-old, and, understandably, he wanted to avoid the issue of the age difference between the lovers. He thus presents the novel's romance as an affair between a man and woman of approximately the same age and experience. He also clearly desired his novel to be a tragedy, one where the movement of the love story is reflected in the movement of the war. Consequently, he shifted the timeline from the victorious year of 1918, the period of his own experiences, to one set in the context of the disastrous Italian defeat in the Battle of Caporetto in 1917. However, the alteration meant that the novel's action would have to occur in a time and place with which Hemingway was not familiar. Thus, he would have to add to his reading list extensive historical research on the Italian front during the years 1915 to 1917, a timeframe when he was still a high school student and then a cub reporter for the *Kansas City Star*.[4]

With the wealth of his experiences to build on, Hemingway could begin his period of education among the literary masters. In Paris, with help from his tutors, he soon identified as his most important role models Turgenev, Tolstoy, Dostoevsky, Stendhal, Flaubert, and Mann. Of the six, the German, Thomas Mann, the only author in the group still alive and working in 1928, would provide Hemingway with the needed impetus to overcome his anxiety. In February 1928, he borrowed Mann's most recent opus, *The Magic Mountain,* from Sylvia Beach's lending library at Shakespeare & Company (Reynolds, *Reading* 154), and in the novel's matrix of complex ideas and levels of meaning he must have recognized concepts that had already been percolating in his writing, including epistemology, objective and subjective truth, and the conflict between reason and faith. High in the Swiss Alps, Mann's protagonist, Hans Castorp, is caught between the rationalist materialism of Lodovico Settembrini and the radical faith-based ideology of Leo Naphta. Through most of the novel, spanning seven years, Castorp idles his time away passively in an Alpine sanatorium, possibly ill, possibly not, but surely suffering from love sickness and frustrated desire for a feline woman named Clavdia Chauchat, whose name implies the claws of a hot cat. When he is not thinking of ways to fulfill his desires, Castorp contemplates the mysteries of time and existence, subjectivity, objectivity, reason, and faith, without ever firmly establishing for himself a clear path to meaning—until finally at the end he abruptly decides that he must return to the world below, become fully engaged in the horrors of the Great War, and enlist as a soldier. For all its ambiguity, rather than a farewell, *The Magic Mountain* ultimately presents an embrace of the arms of war.

Mann's masterpiece seems to have crystallized in Hemingway's mind a way to use the fertile material gleaned from his own experiences during the war in Italy in 1918 as well as time spent in the Swiss Alps episodically from 1922 to 1927 and instilled in him the courage he needed to stare down his anxieties. In the novel Hemingway began writing in March 1928, he would construct his own triangle of reason and faith, with Frederic Henry torn between the rationalist materialism of the surgeon Rinaldi and the faith of the unnamed priest, but he would also fashion a narrative that would move conspicuously in a direction opposite that of Mann's novel. Hemingway would have his protagonist, after more than two years as an ambulance driver in the Italian army, desert, make a separate peace, and escape to an Alpine idyll in Switzerland with his own feline love, Catherine Barkley, who, until her tragic death, never frustrates him in the way Clavdia Chauchat frustrates Hans Castorp. In other words, Hemingway was taking the work of his master, turning it on its head, and reshaping it into something original and uniquely his own.

In fact, one of the most important themes of *The Magic Mountain* highlights an essential problem Hemingway had already absorbed from his father and then found strongly reinforced in certain readings of the other five key figures under examination here—specifically Turgenev's *Fathers and Sons,* Tolstoy's *War and Peace,* Dostoevsky's *The Brothers Karamazov,* Stendhal's *The Red and the Black,* and Flaubert's *Madame Bovary*—that is, the clash between religious faith and rational materialism, the contrast between subjective truth and objective truth, and the limits of human understanding. These five novels, more than any others in Hemingway's voluminous reading during the decade of the twenties, were the source of his anxiety of influence. He treasured them, to be sure, though they disturbed his thinking so deeply that they would be infused into the fiber of his final book of the decade.

Hemingway once described *Fathers and Sons* as "not [Turgenev's] best stuff by a long way," but Myler Wilkinson sees the comment as a revealing example of Bloom's "misprision," a misinterpretation by an aspiring author who is seeking to make room for himself alongside the precursor in the canon *(Letters 2* 445; Wilkinson 21–26).[5] Turgenev pits the rational materialism of his nihilist, the medical student Yevgeny Bazarov, against the faith and romanticism of the older Russian generation. Bazarov's chief antagonist from the previous generation, Pavel Petrovich, demonstrates the opposite frame of mind: "We are old-fashioned people," Pavel Petrovich says, "we imagine that without principles, taken as you say on faith, there's no taking a step, no breathing" (28). The Russian people, he insists, "cannot live without faith" (59). As a hardcore rationalist, Bazarov never finds a place for himself in this world and dies a brave but isolated and meaningless death from typhus. As he is dying, he declares to Anna Sergeevna, the woman who sees the world similarly yet denies him love, "Death's an old joke, but it comes fresh to every one. So far I'm not afraid . . . but there, senselessness is coming, and then it's all up!—" (220). Although Hemingway would admire such matter-of-factness in the face of death, and Catherine Barkley approaches death with much the same complexion as Bazarov's, Frederic Henry sits uneasily somewhere between Bazarov and Pavel Petrovich, entangled in a struggle between his essential faith in a transcendent creator and purpose—a loving interventionist God—and his innate rationalism, seeking a way to reconcile the suffering around him with what he has been taught of a compassionate divinity. In *A Farewell to Arms,* Frederic's friend Lieutenant Rinaldi is the pure rationalist materialist in the mold of Bazarov, while the priest represents the position of faith. Frederic's attempt to balance the two views through his true love with Catherine finally fails as it culminates in the meaningless deaths of Catherine and their child. An apparently unfeeling universe hammers the individual with one series of blows after another until everyone is broken. In the end, Frederic cannot find succor in faith, nor can he rationalize the state of things. All he can say with conviction is that he is not built the same way as the priest, whose faith never seems to waver. Yet Frederic never gives up his essential belief in God, and his conflict is never fully resolved. At the end, as angry as he clearly is with the deity, he still insists that the dead child should have been baptized.

The second great Russian icon on Hemingway's list, Count Leo Tolstoy, seems to have intimidated him more than any other novelist, yet there is no question that the influence of *War and Peace* can be felt throughout *A Farewell to Arms*. In April 1926, Hemingway wrote Maxwell Perkins, "After I read War and Peace I decided there wasnt any need to write a war book and I'm still sticking to that" (*Letters 3* 66). Yet Hemingway had some wonderful war material waiting to be shaped into a novel. What was he to do? To avoid a head-to-head competition with the Count, it seemed Hemingway would have to write a war novel that was not really a war novel—one with the war as a backdrop but with a real subject other than the war, an exploration of the conflict of reason and faith, for example. Yet even that subject would put him to some extent into competition with Tolstoy, whose grand epic seems to cover all topics.

At bottom, Tolstoy provided at least two essential lessons for Hemingway. First, Hemingway learned from the Count how to write an extended narrative that occurs in a time and place outside his own experience. Born in 1828 and writing his novel in the 1860s, Tolstoy was not even alive when the events of his novel took place, between 1805 and 1812. But, with assiduous historical research, he found a way to utilize his own experience of the brutal and senseless Crimean War (1853–56), and he produced some of the most vividly compelling scenes ever written of armies and individuals in battle and in retreat. Second, Tolstoy provided a model of a novel constructed upon an essential duality. Tolstoy's primary duality may reside in the title—*War and Peace*—but the novel also approaches the great questions of the meaning of life, testing religious faith with reason. Tolstoy's central figures Pierre Bezukhov and Prince Andrey Bolkonsky both struggle to find a rationalist understanding of God and the meaning of existence, as highlighted in a conversation between them in part 5, chapter 12, where Pierre, having found a measure of faith through his involvement with Russian freemasonry, tries to convince the agnostic Prince Andrey of the existence of a life after death, where there is a God and a "dominion of good and truth" (360). Prince Andrey, however, remains skeptical. He agrees that the suffering in the world calls for "the necessity of a future life," but he sees no evidence of the future life: When one goes hand-in-hand with some one [he says elliptically to Pierre], and all at once that some one slips away yonder into nowhere, and you are left facing that abyss and looking down into it. And I have looked into it" (360). Prince Andrey at this stage is in much the same frame of mind as Frederic Henry near the end of Hemingway's novel, when Frederic's meditation on the death of his child and Catherine's impending death leads him to a similar bleak conclusion.

However, in Tolstoy's novel, both Pierre and Prince Andrey work through the dark night of the soul and finally find comfort in a faith in a benevolent creator, thus, reflecting Tolstoy's own vision. Hemingway valued Tolstoy's descriptions of warfare above those of all other writers. He included three battlefield passages from *War and Peace* in his anthology of war writing, *Men at War*, published in 1942, but he nevertheless held reservations about the Russian master: "Actually 'War and Peace' would be greatly improved by cutting [Hemingway wrote in his *Men at War* introduction] not by cutting the action, but by removing some of the parts where Tolstoy tampered with the truth to make it fit his conclusions.... I learned from him to distrust my own Thinking with a capital T and to try to write as truly, as straightly, as objectively and as humbly as possible" (*Men at War* xvii). Hemingway may be referring to Tolstoy's theories of history, specifically the idea that individuals do not have the free will necessary to shape history, but he is also probably intending the sense that Pierre's and Prince Andrey's religious conversions are not earned, that they are forced tamperings "with the truth to make it fit [Tolstoy's] conclusions." Whether Hemingway's novel can stand next to Tolstoy's or not, there is no such tampering in *A Farewell to Arms*. It is a novel written "as straightly, as objectively and as humbly as possible."

In the third Russian novel centrally important to Hemingway, *The Brothers Karamazov*, which he had certainly read by November 1927, Dostoevsky provides one of the most intense and powerful studies of the conflict of reason and faith in all of literature.[6] It is nothing trivial to note that Dostoevsky and Hemingway were both the sons of medical doctors and spent more than a little of their creative energy trying to find ways to resolve the inherent conflict between science and faith. In *A Moveable Feast*, Hemingway makes it apparent that he found Dostoevsky fascinating, if mystifying: "In Dostoyevsky there were things believable and not to be believed, but some so true they changed you as you read them; frailty and madness, wickedness and saintliness, and the insanity of gambling were there to know as you knew the landscape and the roads in Turgenev, and the movement of troops, the terrain and the officers and the men and the fighting in Tolstoi" (133). He asked Evan Shipman, "How can [Dostoevsky] write so badly, so unbelievably badly, and make you feel so deeply?" (137). It was a puzzle neither he nor Shipman could solve.

However, Dostoevsky's power over Hemingway may have had something to do with the way the Russian's characters struggle so mightily to resolve the conflict of reason and faith. As Dostoevsky biographer Joseph Frank attests, "*The Brothers Karamazov* achieves a classic expression of the great theme that had preoccupied Dostoevsky since *Notes from Underground*: the conflict between reason and Christian faith" (848). In the novel, much as Hemingway does with Rinaldi and the priest in *A Farewell to Arms*, Dostoevsky contrasts the view of Ivan, the hard-bitten, passionate rationalist, so dramatically presented in the chapters "Rebellion" and

"The Grand Inquisitor," with that of Zosima, the pure spirited Christian cleric and teacher of Alyosha, Ivan's gentlehearted and religious brother. Ivan's struggles in his attempt to rationally understand the suffering in the world lead ultimately to his mental breakdown at the end. Although Dostoevsky's sympathies are clearly with the gospel of love as exemplified by Zosima and Alyosha, Ivan is such an eloquent and passionate spokesman for a rationalist view of things that the most gripping scenes in the novel focus on his predicament in a way that can lead readers to question whether Dostoevsky was able to resolve in his own mind the conflicts between science and faith. Ivan insists that he is a believer in God, but he chooses to rebel against a deity who has created a world full of suffering. He declares to Alyosha, "[I]f the sufferings of children go to swell the sum of sufferings which was necessary to pay for truth, then I protest that the truth is not worth such a price. . . . It's not God that I don't accept, Alyosha, only I most respectfully return him the ticket" (221–22). This sounds more than a little like the words of Frederic Henry, especially the powerful passage Hemingway intended for the start of chapter 40 of *A Farewell to Arms* but excised at the last moment:

> So if we want to buy winning tickets we can go over on the side of immortality; and finally they most of them do. But if . . . the first thing you loved was the side of a hill and the last thing was a woman and they took her away and you did not want another but only to have her; and she was gone; then you are not so well placed and it would have been better to love God from the start. But you did not love God. (302:21–30)

Frederic avoids Ivan's madness, at least as far as we know, but he shares the Russian rationalist's attitude toward a God who allows innocents to suffer in this world.

Hemingway's exploration of the Russians may have come primarily at his own initiative, but he had plenty of encouragement from his mentors, most importantly Ezra Pound, to explore the French too. Others have written about the influence of Stendhal's *The Charterhouse of Parma* on Hemingway's presentation of the Caporetto retreat, but *The Red and the Black*, Stendhal's *Bildungsroman* of the rise and fall of Julien Sorel with the backdrop of provincial France and Paris in the lead up to the July Revolution of 1830, may be an even more important influence on *A Farewell to Arms* as a whole.[7] Hemingway probably read it in early 1927 and followed it with a reading of Paul Hazard's biography of Stendhal published that year (Reynolds, *Hemingway's Reading* 136).[8] The title, like *War and Peace*, suggests a duality that resonated with Hemingway's thinking in the 1920s. Paul Fussell devotes a full chapter in *The Great War and Modern Memory* to a discussion of ways that the war to end all wars, with its almost stationary trench warfare, emphasized and magnified a "binary vision," a clearly demarcated "us versus them" attitude that influenced all kinds of thinking beyond the end of the war, what he calls the mode of gross dichotomy [that] came to dominate perception and expression elsewhere, encouraging finally what we can call the modern *versus* habit: one thing opposed to another, not with some Hegelian hope of synthesis involving a dissolution of both extremes (that would suggest "a negotiated peace," which is anathema), but with a sense that one of the poles embodies so wicked a deficiency or flaw or perversion that its total submission is called for. (86)

As we have seen, even before he went to war, Hemingway was well prepared for the "mode of gross dichotomy," having been raised in the bipolar environment of science and faith created and promoted by his (probably) bipolar father.

Although no one questions the dualistic nature of Stendhal's title, critics have strenuously debated the meaning of the colors red and black, having been provided little if any guidance by Stendhal himself. As Moya Longstaffe has written, the novel is infused with binary vision: "Everything in [*The Red and the Black*] is double: the slippery paths of worldly success and the arduous path of love, the Army and the Church, Jesuits and Jansenists, Chelan and Pirard on one hand and Maslon and Frilair on the other, Monsieur de Rênal and the obnoxious Valenod, the pastoral idyll of Vergy and the imbricated social and political comedy in Paris, cerebral love and passionate adoration, Mathilde and Madame de Rênal" (xxix). Some of these dualisms can seem related to the symbolism of red and black, and some not. The most common interpretation of the symbolism of the colors in Stendhal's novel is that red is the color of the military and black is the color of the priesthood, the only two realistic career options available to Julien if he wishes to rise from his humble beginnings to a level of greatness in the manner of his hero and exemplar, Napoleon Bonaparte.[9] It may be that Stendhal preferred ambiguity and had various interpretations in mind when he chose his title. However, one of those is surely the idea of red as the color of passionate earthly love. The book's content provides plenty of indications that the secular world of the heart, the body, *eros,* and passion is set in opposition to the realm of the spirit, of faith in God—red versus black. In addition, there is clearly an ambivalence in Stendhal's work about which path is the most likely to lead to happiness, that of earthly pleasures or that of spiritual purification, just as Frederic Henry struggles with the same ambivalence, recognizing that the priest's love of God makes the priest happy but that he himself is "not built that way" (302:11). The only sources of happiness he seems to be able to find, the "side of a hill" and the love a woman, reside in this world, not the next (25).

However, unlike Frederic Henry, from the beginning of *The Red and the Black,* Julien Sorel is presented as a nonbeliever. Yes, the kindly priest, the Abbé Chelan, has tutored him in Latin; he has, uncannily, memorized the entire New Testament in Latin, and he has knowledge of conservative Christian philosopher Joseph de Maistre's *du Pape,* a Counter-Enlightenment treatise promoting the authority of the Roman Catholic Pope, but, we are told, Julien "had as little belief in one as in the other" (2:32). His true Bible is Napoleon's self-glorifying *Mémorial de Sainte-Hélène*. Julien, of course, considers a career in the priesthood and wears a black jacket or cassock for much of the novel, but only because he believes that a military career like Napoleon's is impossible in Restoration France. However, he is most energized by the pursuit of romantic love, and fittingly, his two lovers, Madame de Rênal and Mathilde, present binary views of religious faith: Madame de Rênal is profoundly religious and lives a life steeped in faith, so much so that she is overwhelmed with guilt at committing adultery with Julien and insists on breaking off their affair, whereas Mathilde has little respect for traditional religion, is never troubled by guilt of any kind, and reads scandalous literature by the likes of Voltaire and works like *Manon Lescaut,* Rousseau's *Nouvelle Héloïse,* and *Letters of a Portuguese Nun,* all of which present a less-than-sympathetic view of traditional religion.

Julien's romantic movement in the novel is from Madame de Rênal to Mathilde and back to Madame de Rênal. At the end, in prison under a death sentence, Julien seems to find some kind of faith after Madame de Rênal survives his attempt to murder her for spoiling his scheduled marriage to Mathilde. However, Julien, much like Frederic Henry, is unable to place his complete trust in a benign and loving God. He wishes for a "good priest," one who "'would speak to us of God. But what God? Not the God of the Bible, a petty despot, cruel and filled with a thirst for vengeance . . . but the God of Voltaire, just, good, infinite. . . .' He was disturbed by all his memories of that Bible which he knew by heart. . . . 'But . . . how is one to believe in that great name of GOD, after the frightful abuse that our priests make of it?'" (2:340). Although Frederic may not share Julien's low regard for clerics, he does share a similar view of a cruel and despotic God. Like Frederic, Julien longs for "a just, good, all-powerful God, who is not wicked, not hungry for vengeance. . . . Ah! If he existed . . . alas! I should fall at his feet" (342). When Julien compares the human predicament to the confusion of ants whose anthill has been randomly disturbed by a hunter's boot, the passage may well have inspired Hemingway to include the powerful story of Frederic's memory of ants on a campfire log in the final chapter of *A Farewell to Arms* (341).[10] The ultimate point here is that neither Julien nor Frederic can find faith in a compassionate God when there is so much random and incomprehensible suffering in the world. Stendhal's fingerprints on Hemingway's novel are, thus, easy to detect. For both writers, there is no resolution to the conflict of reason and faith. For both writers, the ultimate questions remain unanswered. Hemingway seems to have believed that in *A Farewell to Arms* he fought Stendhal to a draw. Modern readers may be inclined to believe that he won a split decision.[11]

Gustave Flaubert, like Dostoevsky and Hemingway, was a son of a physician.[12] Although *Sentimental Education* was so much on Hemingway's mind in writing *A Farewell to Arms* that he considered titling his novel *The Sentimental Education of Frederic Henry* or simply *The Sentimental Education,* his anxiety of influence was probably more truly centered on *Madame Bovary,* since it more profoundly taps into the subject of reason and faith. Hemingway seems to have read *Bovary* early during his Paris years, at the urging of Ezra Pound. He came to consider it Flaubert's one truly great novel (*SL* 366). As Harold Hurwitz has pointed out, Pound preached to Hemingway the importance of developing the kind of discipline as a writer that Flaubert exhibited, to search for *le mot juste,* or as Hemingway expressed it in *A Moveable Feast,* "to write one true sentence. . . . the truest sentence that you know" (12).[13]

Emma Bovary, like Frederic Henry, is seeking happiness, and she is continually frustrated in her attempts to find it. Although she finds small measures of felicity in the early stages of her extramarital relationships with Rodolphe Boulanger and Léon Dupuis, both affairs end in frustration. Similarly, her indulgence in luxury items only increases her despondency. Like Stendhal's Julien Sorel, she is torn between the flesh and the spirit. Flaubert recognizes that the essential conflict of human existence lies between the rationalism of the material world and faith in God. Thus, Emma seeks help from and confides in both the parish priest, Bournisien, and the anticlerical man of science, the local pharmacist, Homais, much as Frederic Henry has close friendships with the priest and the atheistic materialist surgeon Rinaldi. Neither the priest nor the pharmacist provides satisfaction for Emma. She remains a lost soul on a path that leads inevitably to suicide by the arsenic she obtains, ironically, from Homais. Flaubert's satire of both faith and science reaches a culmination at Emma's wake, as Homais and Bournisien sit on opposite sides of her cold corpse and debate the efficacy of praying for her. "Read Voltaire! Read Holbach! Read the Encyclopedia!" Homais cries.[14] "Read the *Letters of Some Portuguese Jews!* . . . Read the *Proof of Christianity!*" Bournisien counters. The message of Flaubert's comedy in the scene is clear: neither of these bumptious fools has done anything to alleviate Emma's unhappiness.[15] More than any of Hemingway's other literary role models, Flaubert regarded both science and faith with the same level of skeptical cynicism.

The evidence of Hemingway's obsession with these six writers and these particular books is scattered across a number of published instances during the course of his career. Repeatedly over nearly thirty years, Hemingway revealed these six authors to be the pivotal influences on his novel writing and the targets of his competitive desires. Turgenev is given prominent mention in *The Sun Also Rises,* where Jake Barnes reads *A Sportsman's Sketches* and clearly treasures works by the Russian author (147–49). We can also measure Hemingway's esteem for Turgenev by the titles he borrowed from him: *The Torrents of Spring* (1926) and "Fathers and Sons" (1933). Tolstoy, Dostoevsky, Stendhal, and Flaubert get shout-outs in *Green Hills of Africa* (1935), in which Hemingway claims, in the manner of T. S. Eliot, that "a new classic does not bear any resemblance to the classics that preceded it. It can steal from anything that it is better than, anything that is not a classic" (*GHOA-HL* 16). A writer must have the discipline of Flaubert, he insists, and he claims that Flaubert, Tolstoy and Stendhal all learned to write by witnessing war or revolution (18). Similarly, he adds, Dostoevsky was made a writer by being sent to Siberia (46–48). In a pair of essays written for *Esquire* in 1935, Hemingway listed specific authors and works with whom or with which every aspiring writer should be familiar, including all six of our featured masters (*BL* 161–62, 189).[16]

Some years later, in 1950, when he was facing another intense moment of anxiety, just as *Across the River and into the Trees* was being published, Hemingway spoke effusively about his influences to Lillian Ross, in what would be published as her infamous *New Yorker* profile. Imagining writing as a series of boxing matches, he declared: "I started out very quiet and I beat Mr. Turgenev. Then I trained hard and I beat Mr. de Maupassant. I've fought two draws with Mr. Stendhal, and I think I had an edge in the last one. But nobody's going to get me in any ring with Mr. Tolstoy unless I'm crazy or I keep getting better" (42).[17] Later in the same piece, he elaborated further, identifying Stendhal's works as "the way I wanted to be able to write" and Flaubert as a writer "who always threw them straight, hard, high, and inside," baseball being another favorite Hemingway metaphor for writing (48). Only Dostoevsky and Mann are omitted from the *New Yorker* profile. In 1958, Hemingway used another sports metaphor, this time distance running, to explain himself to quiz show champion Edward Stafford: "What a writer has to do is write what hasn't been written before or beat dead men at what they have done. . . . It is like a miler running against the clock . . . rather than simply against whoever is in the race with him. Unless he runs against time he will never know what he is capable of attaining" (*Conversations* 166). Our Big Six were all included among eleven authors Stafford specifically identified on Hemingway's bookshelves.[18] About the same time, in the 1958 *Paris Review* interview, Hemingway listed for George Plimpton his literary forbears, and five of the first seven named were Flaubert, Stendhal, Turgenev, Tolstoy, and Dostoevsky (*Conversations* 118).[19]

In the posthumously published memoir *A Moveable Feast,* only Flaubert and Mann are not specifically named, but we certainly feel Flaubert's presence when Hemingway tells us of Ezra Pound's belief in the "*mot juste*—the one and only correct word to use," a phrase most commonly associated with Flaubert (134). Hemingway shares with us his discovery of the great Russian authors early in Paris at the bookstore of Sylvia Beach, who allowed him to read all the Russian literature he could hold. "At first there were the Russians," he declares, "then there were all the others. But for a long time there were the Russians" (134). At the same time, Ezra Pound, who is surprisingly unfamiliar with the "Rooshians," advises him to "keep to the French. . . . You've plenty to learn there," presumably meaning Stendhal and Flaubert, whom we know Pound greatly admired (135). Hemingway does not disagree with Pound's assessment of the French, even if he did not restrict himself to them. In short, in the midst of Hemingway's voracious reading in the 1920s, these six writers above all others left their deep mark on his mind. And the common thread that runs through their most important works was the focus on the central questions about the nature of existence—questions that may have been present in Hemingway's personality from a very young age—questions of objective and subjective truth, faith and reason, epistemology, and the meaning of human suffering.[20]

It is true that *A Farewell to Arms* would never have been written without Hemingway's biographical experiences in Italy in 1918. But it is also certain that the novel we know would not have been written without Hemingway's reading of Turgenev, Tolstoy, Dostoevsky, Stendhal, Flaubert, and Mann. Together, his past experiences and his reading prepared Hemingway to write what many readers regard as his most finely crafted, most focused, and most poetic novel. Ultimately, whether or not we can say he bested the authors who were the sources of his anxiety, in *A Farewell to Arms* Hemingway succeeded in producing not only a book that rose to the top of a gaggle of novels and memoirs of the Great War published at the end of the 1920s, pleasing both contemporary readers and reviewers, but also one that deserves to be included among the world's finest works of fiction.[21]

NOTES

1. For a catalog of Hemingway's reading between 1910 and 1940, see Michael Reynolds's *Hemingway's Reading*. The list is surely not complete, as Reynolds acknowledged, but the work is a monumental feat of scholarship. See also James Brasch and Joseph Sigman's *Hemingway's Library*, another massive undertaking, which carefully and apparently comprehensively catalogs the 7,368 books that Hemingway is known to have owned in his lifetime.

2. The four volumes are the short story collections *In Our Time* (1925), with Boni & Liveright, and *Men Without Women* (1927), with Scribner's, and two novels, *The Torrents of Spring* (1926) and *The Sun Also Rises* (1926), both with Scribner's.

3. For a thorough account of the drafting of Hemingway's picaresque manuscript, initially titled *A New Slain Knight,* but widely known among scholars as the Jimmy Breen novel, see Michael Reynolds, *American Homecoming* (145–57). The unfinished manuscript survives in the JFK Library, item 529b. Although parts of it were published in *The Complete Short Stories: Finca Vigía Edition* (1987), most of the manuscript remains closed to scholars. Reynolds received special permission to examine it.

4. Michael Reynolds and Robert W. Lewis have summarized the impressive extent of Hemingway's historical sourcing. Every serious student of *A Farewell to Arms* should read Reynolds's indispensable *Hemingway's First War,* which thoroughly explores the writing process and the historical and biographical underpinnings of *A Farewell to Arms*. The book is not flawless, as we will point out, but it is an essential guide to beginning study of the novel. Lewis provides important supplementary information in his essay "Hemingway in Italy: Making It Up."

5. This is not the only instance in which Hemingway seems to have wanted to deflect attention from his true influences. The same could be said in the ways he seemingly led scholars to believe Flaubert's *Sentimental Education* was a key influence on *A Farewell to Arms,* whereas *Madame Bovary* and *The Temptation of Saint Anthony* were probably more influential. He also made comments and considered alternative titles that suggest that Thomas Mann's *Buddenbrooks* and his short story "Disorder and Early Sorrow" were key influences, whereas *The*

Magic Mountain seems to have been most central to his thinking. See Roos, "Appendix A: Alternate Titles" for a discussion of alternative titles for *A Farewell to Arms*.

6. See Hemingway's 24 November 1927 letter to Maxwell Perkins, in which he refers to the "Karamazov boys" (*Letters* 3 326).

7. See Reynolds, *First War* 154–58, for an example of Stendhal's influence.

8. In a letter dated 30 September 1926, Hemingway ordered a copy of *The Red and the Black,* along with other books, from his friend Isidore Schneider, who worked as an editor at the book's American publisher, Boni & Liveright (*Letters* 3 124). He included payment for the book along with a letter mailed to Schneider on 14 February 1927 (208). Coincidentally, the 30 September 1926 letter also includes a sentence that anticipates the "world breaks everyone" passage of *A Farewell to Arms* (216:24–30) written almost two years later: "The world is so tough and can do so many things to us and break us in so many ways that it seems as though it were cheating when it uses accident or disease" (*Letters* 3 123).

9. The daily garb of priests and seminarians is black, but the uniform of the French army under the Bourbon Restoration of the 1820s was blue, not red. However, Stendhal may have had in mind the many early portraits of Julien's hero, Napoleon, depicting him wearing the red jacket of the first consul of France. In addition, four of the five versions of the famous heroic painting by Jacque Louis-David, *Napoleon Crossing the Alps,* swath Napoleon in a red cloak.

10. See entry 280:7–20 in this volume for a fuller discussion of the ant passage.

11. For a discussion of Stendhal as a source for Frederic Henry's name, see entry 34:3–4 in this volume

12. Stendhal was the grandson of a physician. In addition, Sinclair Lewis, Hemingway's contemporary, was the son of a physician, and Hemingway was surely aware, as he began composition of *A Farewell to Arms,* that Lewis's two most recent best-selling novels had focused separately on science and faith: the Pulitzer Prize–winning *Arrowsmith* (1925), a satire on the contemporary practice of medicine and scientific research, and *Elmer Gantry* (1927), a satire on evangelical Christianity. For insightful commentary on the relationship between Hemingway and Lewis, see Robert McLaughlin's "The Only Kind Thing Is Silence" and Mark Cirino's *Reading Hemingway's* Across the River (86–88).

13. In *The Green Hills of Africa* (1934), Hemingway claims a writer must have the talent of Kipling coupled with the discipline of Flaubert (18). A year later, in an article written for *Esquire* magazine, Hemingway lists Flaubert's *Madame Bovary* and *L'Education Sentimentale* among other classics as essential reading for aspiring writers (*BL* 189). In a 2 July 1948 letter to Lillian Ross, Hemingway named Flaubert as one of his heroes. The only other writer he included was James Thurber (*SL* 645). Finally, when George Plimpton asks him, in the 1958 *Paris Review* interview, to list his literary forbears—those he "learned the most from"—Flaubert comes second after only Mark Twain (Bruccoli, *Conversations* 118).

14. Paul-Henry Thiry, Baron d'Holbach (1723–1789), was an atheistic philosopher of the Enlightenment who wrote a number of antireligious works, including *Christianity Unveiled*.

15. Another Flaubert work that seems to have affected Hemingway is *The Temptation of Saint Anthony,* although it is not a novel in the conventional sense and thus should not be regarded as a work with which he felt the need to compete. For a discussion of the influence of Flaubert's *Temptation,* see entry 37:6–36 in this volume.

16. Although Thomas Mann's *The Magic Mountain* was not on Hemingway's list, his *Buddenbrooks* was. Mann receives less notice from Hemingway than the other five authors, no doubt because he was still living and working in Hemingway's time. Hemingway preferred to measure himself against dead writers, whose standing as classics was more or less secure.

For further commentary on Mann's influence on *A Farewell to Arms,* see Roos, "Appendix A: Alternate Titles."

17. Although we cannot be certain, in this comment Hemingway seems to indicate that *The Sun Also Rises* was written in competition with Turgenev and that his short story volumes were written in competition with de Maupassant, whom we will exclude from having significant influence on Hemingway's novel writing. What Hemingway calls the two draws with Stendhal would have to be *A Farewell to Arms* and *For Whom the Bell Tolls.* His remarks strongly suggest that he regarded *For Whom the Bell Tolls* as superior to *A Farewell to Arms,* although many readers would disagree with that assessment. While Hemingway did not explicitly mention Dostoevsky to Ross, any exploration of Hemingway's reading in the 1920s conclusively reveals how extensively he familiarized himself with Dostoevsky's works in the years prior to writing *A Farewell to Arms.* (See Reynolds, *Reading* 118.)

18. The eleven authors Stafford lists are Tolstoy, Dostoevsky, Stendhal, De Maupassant, Mann, Joyce, W. H. Hudson, George Moore, Stephen Crane, Turgenev, and Flaubert. Stafford adds that there were "several dozen others, similarly disparate as to era and nationality, having in common only their greatness" (166).

19. The other two names are Mark Twain and Bach.

20. For more discussion of the conflict of science and faith in Hemingway's childhood see Roos, "The Doctor and the Doctor's Son" and "Agassiz or Darwin."

21. The wave of excellent books published at the end of the decade treating the Great War as their primary subject included Edmund Blunden's *Undertones of War* (1928), Erich Maria Remarque's *All Quiet on the Western Front* (1929), Robert Graves's *Good-bye to All That* (1929), Frederic Manning's *Middle Parts of Fortune* (1929), and Siegfried Sassoon's *Memoirs of an Infantry Officer* (1930). For a summary of the critical and popular response to *A Farewell to Arms,* see Robert W. Lewis, A Farewell to Arms: *The War of the Words.*

ABBREVIATIONS FOR THE WORKS OF ERNEST HEMINGWAY USED IN THIS BOOK

ARIT *Across the River and into the Trees.* Scribner, 1950.
BL *By-Line Ernest Hemingway: Selected Articles and Dispatches of Four Decades,* edited by William White, Scribner, 1967.
DIA *Death in the Afternoon.* Scribner, 1932.
CSS *The Complete Short Stories of Ernest Hemingway: The Finca Vigía Edition.* Scribner, 1987.
DLT *Dateline: Toronto: The Complete* Toronto Star *Dispatches, 1920–1924,* edited by William White, Scribner, 1985.
DIA *Death in the Afternoon.* Scribner, 1932.
DS *The Dangerous Summer.* Scribner, 1985.
FTA *A Farewell to Arms.* Scribner, 1929.
FTA-HL *A Farewell to Arms: The Hemingway Library Edition,* edited by Seán Hemingway, Scribner, 2012.
FWBT *For Whom the Bell Tolls.* Scribner, 1940.
GOE *The Garden of Eden.* Scribner, 1986.
GHOA *Green Hills of Africa.* Scribner, 1935.
GHOA-HL *Green Hills of Africa: The Hemingway Library Edition,* edited by Seán Hemingway, Scribner, 2015.
IOT *In Our Time.* Boni & Liveright, 1925. Rev. ed., Scribner, 1930.
IIS *Islands in the Stream.* Scribner, 1970.
JFK Ernest Hemingway Collection, John F. Kennedy Presidential Library and Museum, Boston, Massachusetts.
Letters 1 *The Letters of Ernest Hemingway.* Vol. 1, *1907–1922,* edited Sandra Spanier and Robert W. Trogdon. Cambridge University Press, 2011.
Letters 2 *The Letters of Ernest Hemingway.* Vol. 2, *1923–1925,* edited by Sandra Spanier, Albert J. DeFazio III, and Robert W. Trogdon. Cambridge University Press, 2013.
Letters 3 *The Letters of Ernest Hemingway.* Vol. 3, *1926–1929,* edited by Rena Sanderson, Sandra Spanier, and Robert W. Trogdon, Cambridge University Press, 2015.

Letters 4	*The Letters of Ernest Hemingway.* Vol. 4, *1929–1931*, edited by Sandra Spanier and Miriam B. Mandel. Cambridge University Press, 2018.
MAW	*Men at War.* Crown, 1942.
MF	*A Moveable Feast.* Scribner, 1964.
MF-RE	*A Moveable Feast: The Restored Edition,* edited by Seán Hemingway, Scribner, 2009.
OMS	*The Old Man and the Sea.* Scribner, 1952.
Poems	*Complete Poems,* edited, with an introduction and notes by Nicholas Georgiannis, Rev. ed. University of Nebraska Press, 1992.
SAR	*The Sun Also Rises.* Scribner, 1926.
SAR-HL	*The Sun Also Rises: The Hemingway Library Edition,* edited by Seán Hemingway, Scribner, 2014.
SL	*Ernest Hemingway: Selected Letters, 1917–1961,* edited by Carlos Baker, Scribner, 1981.
TAFL	*True at First Light,* edited by Patrick Hemingway, Scribner, 1999.
THHN	*To Have and Have Not.* Scribner, 1937.
TOS	*The Torrents of Spring.* Scribner, 1926.

SERIES NOTE

All page references in this volume are keyed to the Hemingway Library Edition of *A Farewell to Arms* (2012), which begins on page 3 and ends on page 284.

Annotations are given a page and line number, separated by a colon. A reference to the third line of page 17, for instance, would be 17:3. A reference to the first three lines of page 40 would be 40:1–3.

Since Hemingway rarely used italicized words, consider words in italics to indicate major titles, a foreign language, or our emphasis.

When citing, we have appropriated the standard abbreviations for Hemingway texts used by *The Hemingway Review*, in concert with the Hemingway Letters Project (see "Abbreviations for the Works of Ernest Hemingway" above).

Reading *A Farewell to Arms*

FRONT MATTER

The Cover: The Hemingway Library edition reproduces the novel's original 1928 jacket cover art by Cleon, the pen name for Cleonike Damianakes Wilkins, who had also done the cover art for *In Our Time* and *The Sun Also Rises*. Her work has been described as "a typically arch Art Deco take on classical poses (togas, wreaths) filtered through the sensibilities of the Pre-Raphaelite era and rattled about in a chrome cocktail shaker" (Othen). As was typical for the time, Hemingway was not part of the cover art selection process, and, not surprisingly, he hated Cleon's drawing when he first saw it in a Paris bookshop after the book was published. In a letter to his editor, Maxwell Perkins, he complained about the female figure's "horrible legs" and "belly muscles," which he said resembled those of Wladek Zbyszko, a well-known Polish professional wrestler popular in America during Hemingway's teen years. Hemingway sarcastically called the male figure in the drawing "the big shouldered lad with the prominent nipples who is holding the broken axle (signifying no doubt the defeat of The Horse Drawn Vehicle)" (Bruccoli, *Only Thing* 117–18; *Letters 4* 108). Scribners apparently found the classical Greek theme as well as the suggestion of sadness and disenchantment in Cleon's drawings appropriate to the works they were publishing at the time, which also included F. Scott Fitzgerald's *All the Sad Young Men* (1926) and Zelda Fitzgerald's *Save Me the Waltz* (1932). Perkins shared some of Hemingway's concerns but defended the cover and Cleon, calling her "the best person in the market" and explaining,

> We were very nervous about the jacket because we did not want to bring out the book as a War book, that is as a combat book. Still less did we wish to after the appearance of "All Quiet" [Erich Maria Remarque's *All Quiet on the Western Front*]. We wanted no helmets or artillery, or any of that sort of thing. . . . I thought it did make the book stand out, and did have an emotional quality that was appealing. . . . And the main thing about a jacket is that it should give a book *visibility*. (Bruccoli, *Only Thing* 120)

The Hemingway Library edition reduces the size of the drawing by roughly one-third and slightly enlarges the font size for the title and Hemingway's name, as he wished. Cleon never did another cover for Hemingway.

Dedication (To G.A. Pfeiffer): In earlier editions of *A Farewell to Arms,* the dedication was given a page of its own after the title page and the copyright page. In the Hemingway Library edition, the dedication is easy to miss. It is at the top of the copyright page. Gustavus Adolphus (G. A.) Pfeiffer (1872–1953), affectionately called Uncle Gus, was the wealthy bachelor brother of Paul Pfeiffer, father of Pauline Pfeiffer Hemingway, Ernest's second wife, whom he had married on 10 May 1927. Hemingway sent directions for the dedication to Maxwell Perkins in a 26 July 1929 letter, explaining, "There couldnt be a less graceful name nor a much better man" (*Letters 4* 48). The dedication is apparently a gesture of gratitude for Uncle Gus's great generosity in supporting his niece's relationship and marriage to a divorced bohemian writer in Paris. Hemingway's first automobile, a yellow Ford, for example, was a gift from Uncle Gus, delivered to Ernest and Pauline upon their arrival in Key West in April 1928, as Hemingway was pushing full force through the writing of *A Farewell to Arms* (Baker, *Life Story* 191). Then he shipped them another new Ford in 1929, when they returned to Europe (*Letters 4* lxi). In 1931, Uncle Gus paid for their house on Whitehead Street in Key West, and in 1933–34, he funded their African safari. It is no exaggeration to say that G. A. Pfeiffer was Hemingway's most generous benefactor.

However, the dedication to Uncle Gus begs the question "Why not Pauline?" *A Farewell to Arms* was the second book Hemingway published since he had begun his relationship with Pauline in 1926. The first, the short story collection *Men Without Women* (1927), had been dedicated to poet friend Evan Shipman. *In Our Time* (1925) had been dedicated to first wife, Hadley, and *The Sun Also Rises* (1926) to Hadley and their son, John Hadley Nicanor. So logic would expect that a novel that deals so powerfully with love in a time of war would be dedicated to the central love of his life at the time, Pauline Pfeiffer Hemingway. Yet Pauline would have to wait until Hemingway's next book, *Death in the Afternoon* (1932), hardly a romantic piece of writing, before she would be honored with a dedication. The only reasonable explanation that Hemingway did not dedicate this book to her is that he wanted to avoid readers' identifying Catherine Barkley with her. Perhaps he wished to avoid any possibility of the novel's being read as straight autobiography. But we have to wonder whether Pauline felt slighted.

The Author's 1948 Introduction: Scribners released a new illustrated edition of *A Farewell to Arms* in 1948 and asked Hemingway to write an introduction for it. This piece is reproduced for the Hemingway Library edition. According to Carlos Baker, much of the piece was written in June 1848 during a ten-day voyage on the yacht of his wealthy Cuban friend Mayito Menocal, accompanied by his wife, Mary, and his sons Patrick and Gregory (*Life Story* 465–66).

vii:1–7 **This book was written . . . spring of 1929:** Hemingway's places and dates here are mostly accurate. According to Michael Reynolds, Hemingway began writing *A*

Farewell to Arms in early March 1928, and the editors of Hemingway's *Letters* date the beginning of the process as around 4 March 1928 (*American Homecoming* 166–67; *Letters 3* lxxix), somewhat later than the first winter months Hemingway claims, although he may have begun making notes toward the writing earlier, and certainly the autobiographical content had been in his mind since his wartime experiences in 1918. As Reynolds carefully explains in *Hemingway's First War,* the novel began as a short story and gradually developed into a much longer narrative than Hemingway originally intended. See appendix 1, pages 285–90, of the Hemingway Library edition for a reproduction of the first draft of the beginning of the novel, two chapters that eventually, with significant revision, became chapters 13 and 14 in the finished novel. Note that in this original beginning, Hemingway was presenting the story in the third person rather than the first person narration he would eventually use, and the protagonist's name was Emmett Hancock (the same initials as the author), not Frederic Henry. "Hancock" was the maiden name of Hemingway's maternal grandmother, Caroline Hancock Hall (Elder, Vetch, and Cirino 7).

vii:11–12 **the day it was published was the day the stock market crashed:** Hemingway's memory is flawed here. *A Farewell to Arms* was published in New York on 27 September 1929, about a month before the stock market crash, which began on Thursday, 24 October and peaked on Black Tuesday, 29 October 1929. Hemingway probably wished to suggest that the crash affected book sales, and it no doubt did, although it is impossible to say to what extent. The book sold 33,000 copies before the crash, putting it atop the best-seller lists, where it remained for months, as sales continued briskly. By Christmas 1929, it had sold over 65,000 copies. By Hemingway's death in 1961, it had sold 1,383,000 copies (Reynolds, *First War* 81).

vii:18–19 **making up what happened:** Hemingway is here emphasizing a point that was ticklish for him. Too many of his readers assumed that he always wrote autobiographically, that he did not truly "make things up" in his books. But even in his most autobiographical material, he was always fictionalizing to varying degrees. It is true that certain facts from Hemingway's experience in Italy during the Great War underpin *A Farewell to Arms:* his service as an ambulance driver, his wounding, and his falling in love with his nurse during his recuperation in a hospital in Milan. He also drew on memories of winter holidays in Chamby sur Montreux, Switzerland, with his first wife, Hadley. The book is, furthermore, true to historical facts of the Italian front in World War I, facts that were outside of Hemingway's direct experience, for which he relied on extensive historical research and did not make up (see Reynolds, *First War,* and Lewis, "Making It Up"). But beyond these key elements, the story he told was fictionalized, made up, and, as such an experience would for any writer of fiction, demonstrating to himself that he possessed the imaginative powers to create an epic story like this one was enormously pleasurable, as Hemingway here remembers. In *A Farewell to Arms,* Hemingway was a writer at the top of his game, and he knew it. More than any other, this novel was his ticket to greatness.

vii:24–25 **the book was a tragic one . . . life was a tragedy:** An important point that any reader should not forget. This is not a happy book. We must fully understand Hemingway's belief that life is a tragedy—not sometimes, but always—for everyone. *A Farewell to Arms* is designed to demonstrate this fact. Why did Hemingway view life as a tragedy? All indications in this novel and elsewhere in his work point to the inevitability of death administered by an uncaring, indifferent universe. It is this inescapable reality that makes it impossible for Frederic Henry ever to achieve the love of God that the priest in the novel has. In some tragedies, there may be spiritual growth in the protagonist, an "inner triumph . . . wrested from outer defeat" (qtd. in Williams 68). But not here. Frederic is as crushed by fate as is Catherine, and there is no sign of his redemption at the end, other than that he has learned how to love another person, in the form of Catherine.

viii:5 **I had published a novel previously:** *The Sun Also Rises* (1926). Hemingway is obviously discounting his short satire, *The Torrents of Spring,* also published in 1926.

viii:13–14 **how I felt about illustrations and having a book illustrated:** The 1948 edition of *A Farewell to Arms* was illustrated with twenty-eight monochrome watercolors by Daniel Rasmussen. Hemingway felt only marginally better about these illustrations than he did about Cleon's jacket cover artwork for the original 1929 edition. In an 18 September 1947 letter to his publisher, Charles Scribner, he complained: "They [the illustrations] are not the way I would do it: any of it. But they are a damned sight better than haveing the book out of print and some are excellent and some have an excellent feeling that comes through" (*SL* 627). His chief complaint concerned the depiction of Catherine Barkley, who had been given what he termed a "sort of Mother Superior face" (627). In his own memory, he claimed that Catherine resembled the young Marlene Dietrich. For a description of each of the illustrations, see Roos, "Appendix C: 1948 Illustrations."

viii:21 **Winslow Homer:** American landscape painter (1836–1910), whose many stark seascapes have been commonly interpreted as depicting individuals struggling for survival in an uncaring, impersonal, Darwinian universe. In 1884–85, Homer spent time in what would become Hemingway territory—Florida, Cuba and the Bahamas—yielding some of his most striking work. See, for example, *The Gulf Stream* (1899), completed the year of Hemingway's birth. Homer's most famous Darwinian painting is *The Fox Hunt* (1893), in which a fox foraging for food in the snow is about to be attacked by a flock of huge crows. In spite of the imagery in Homer's paintings, Charles Colbert insists that he was a "reluctant modern," that he maintained a belief in God and the afterlife and saw no conflict between scientific progress and religious faith. In other words, although Hemingway obviously did see a conflict between science and faith, he may have recognized in Homer an artist exploring some of the same themes he did in his own work.

viii:23 **Guy de Maupassant:** French author (1850–1893), master of the short story, much admired by Hemingway, who recommended that aspiring writers should read "all the good de Maupassant" (*BL* 189). Six books by de Maupassant were in Hemingway's Key West library (Reynolds, *Hemingway's Reading* 157).

viii:25 **Toulouse Lautrec:** Henri de Toulouse-Lautrec (1864–1901), French post-impressionist painter and illustrator.

viii:26 **Renoir . . . Norman landscapes:** Pierre-Auguste Renoir (1841–1919), French impressionist painter, many of whose landscapes treated scenes from Normandy as their subject.

viii:30 **Max Perkins:** Maxwell Perkins (1884–1947), Hemingway's editor at Charles Scribner's Sons, for whom he had great love and respect. They had been working together since early 1926, when Hemingway left his original publisher, Boni & Liveright, and signed with Scribner's, who published in America *The Torrents of Spring, The Sun Also Rises,* and every book Hemingway published thereafter. Perkins first read the manuscript of *A Farewell to Arms* during a visit with Hemingway in Key West in the winter of 1929, and he immediately recognized the book's high quality. He intended to do whatever he could to increase Hemingway's audience and, to that end, proposed that the manuscript be submitted to *Scribner's Magazine* for serialization. Although he and Hemingway disagreed over certain words of profanity (*shit, balls, cocksucker*), they eventually compromised, and suitable substitutes or dashes replaced the three offending words (See entry 29:2 for a discussion of the censored words). Perkins also edited the works of F. Scott Fitzgerald and Thomas Wolfe, among others. When Perkins died of pneumonia in 1947, it was a severe blow to Hemingway and nearly everyone who knew him. See A. Scott Berg's National Book Award–winning *Max Perkins: Editor of Genius* for an excellent account of his life.

viii:30–31 **the other people that died last year:** Besides Max Perkins, Hemingway grieved over the deaths of a number of other good friends in 1947. Katy (Smith) Dos Passos, the sister of his friend Bill Smith, wife of John Dos Passos, and friend of Hemingway since his teen years at Horton Bay in Michigan, was killed in a violent car wreck on 12 September (*SL* 628; Baker, *Life Story* 463). Hemingway blamed Dos Passos, who was driving the vehicle, for her death, and the friendship of the two writers, who had already fallen out during the Spanish Civil War, never recovered. The character of Kate in the posthumously published short story "Summer People" (written in 1924) is based on Katy Smith. Two generals whom Hemingway had worked with during the Spanish Civil War also died—Hans Kahle of natural causes and Karol Swierczewski by political assassination (Baker, *Life Story* 463). A heart attack also claimed the cook at the Hemingway home in Cuba (463). Another good friend lost his wife in childbirth "when the doctor didn't show up in time," and an Idaho friend, Taylor Williams, lost his daughter. At the end of the year, Hollywood producer Mark Hellinger, who had made a film of Hemingway's "The Killers" and was arranging a lucrative deal for further films of Hemingway's work, also died suddenly, at the age of forty-four (463). Perhaps less traumatic but surely jarring nevertheless were the deaths of Gertrude Stein on 27 July 1946 and Zelda Fitzgerald on 10 March 1948. In addition, Hemingway may also have been thinking of recent near-death experiences of two of his most loved ones. His fourth wife, Mary Welsh Hemingway, would have died of an ectopic pregnancy in August 1946 if not for Hemingway's own intervention in giving her a blood transfusion (456–57). And Patrick, his second son, suffered a severe concussion in a minor auto accident in April 1947 and was not immediately treated. As a result, Patrick descended into fever and delirium. Here again, Hemingway nursed him back to health (460–61). In a subsequent letter to Lillian Ross, Hemingway listed among his heroes both Mary, for "when she fought on the operating table and wouldn't die," and Patrick, "old Mousie," who, "when he was delerious, def[ied] Satan and all fiends and all local devils" (*SL* 645).

viii:35 **Sun Valley, Idaho:** A ski resort in central Idaho, which wealthy financier and later diplomat Averill Harriman established in 1936. The resort invited celebrities like Hemingway and provided them with free use of the facilities if they permitted their names and photos to be used in publicity. Hemingway began going there in 1939 with Martha Gellhorn, even before he was divorced from his second wife, Pauline. The resort is less than two miles from Ketchum, where Hemingway purchased a home with fourth wife, Mary, in 1959, the home where he killed himself on 2 July 1961.

ix:2 **Ingrid Bergman:** Well-known Swedish actress (1915–1982), who starred opposite Humphrey Bogart in *Casablanca* (1942) and then played Maria in the 1943 film of Hemingway's novel *For Whom the Bell Tolls*. Hemingway first met Bergman in January 1941 at a lunch in San Francisco when she was being considered for the role. Since she would have to have her hair cut short for the film, Hemingway asked to see her ears. They met his approval, and she got the job (Baker, *Life Story* 359). Bergman was one of several beautiful Hollywood stars whom Hemingway counted as friends, including Marlene Dietrich, Ava Gardner, and Lauren Bacall.

ix:2 **Daughter:** Always wanting a daughter but never having been blessed with one, Hemingway took to addressing young women that he liked as "Daughter."

ix:14–18 **Scott Fitzgerald . . . Tom Wolfe . . . Jim Joyce . . . John Bishop:** All of these writers suffered what can be regarded as premature deaths. F. Scott Fitzgerald, author of *The Great Gatsby, Tender Is the Night,* and other important novels of the Jazz Age, died of a heart attack on 21 December 1940, at the age of forty-four. Thomas Wolfe, author of *Look Homeward, Angel* and *Of Time and the River,* died of tuberculosis on 15 September 1938, at thirty-seven. James Joyce, Irish author of *Dubliners, Portrait of the Artist as a Young Man,* and *Ulysses,* died of a perforated ulcer on 13 January 1941, at fifty-eight. John Peale Bishop, American poet, died on 4 April 1944, at fifty-one. In his 1936 essay "Homage to Hemingway," Bishop said Hemingway possessed "the most complete literary integrity it has ever been my lot to encounter. . . . He could not be bought" (38). Bishop also credited Ezra Pound with leading Hemingway to the discipline of Flaubert (40). Hemingway had met and befriended Fitzgerald, Joyce, and Bishop in Paris in the twenties. He met Thomas Wolfe in New York in 1933 at a lunch with Max Perkins, their mutual editor, but Hemingway regarded Wolfe as immature, and they never developed a friendship (Baker, *Life Story* 236).

ix:19–21 **hung upside down . . . German towns:** Hemingway is referring first to the killing of Italian fascist dictator Benito Mussolini. Coincidentally, Mussolini and his mistress, Clara Petacci, were caught near Lake Como in northern Italy, trying to escape to Switzerland, in the manner of Frederic Henry and Catherine Barkley. They were shot on 28 April 1945, days before the end of World War II. Their bodies were then transported to the Piazza Quindici Martiri in Milan, where they were kicked and spat upon and then hung upside down from the roof of an Esso gas station for public display. At the conclusion of World War II, Allied soldiers executed many Nazi German war criminals by hanging or firing squad. Ten of the most prominent, convicted following trials at heavily bombed Nuremberg, were hanged one by one on 16 October 1946. The executions, which used a standard drop method of hanging rather than a long drop, have been described as "botched," resulting in several of the guilty "strangling to death for as long as 25 minutes" (Shnayerson 141).

x:14 **June 30, 1948:** This is a slight misdating by Hemingway; the package in which he mailed the introduction to Scribner's was postmarked 29 June 1948, the day Carlos Baker says he finished it (*Life Story* 648).

Foreword by Patrick Hemingway: Patrick Hemingway has written a brief, quirky foreword for each of the books published so far in Hemingway Library editions (*The Sun Also Rises, A Farewell to Arms, Green Hills of Africa, The Short Stories,* and *A Moveable Feast Restored Edition*), but this one must have felt special to him. As Hemingway's second son, he was born during the writing of the novel, on 28 June 1928, following eighteen hours of very difficult labor for his mother, Pauline Pfeiffer Hemingway, culminating in a caesarian section, an experience, as Patrick here suggests, that surely helped his father formulate the tragic ending of the novel. At birth, Patrick weighed nine pounds eight ounces, too large, it seems, for his small-framed mother, and the effects on her were such that doctors cautioned her not to get pregnant for three years. Three years and five months later, his brother, Gregory, Hemingway's third and final child, was born, on 12 November 1931. For a full account of Hemingway's marriage to Patrick's mother, see the excellent 2012 biography *Unbelievable Happiness and Final Sorrow: The Hemingway-Pfeiffer Marriage*, by Ruth A. Hawkins.

xi:6 **Erwin Schrödinger:** (1887–1961) German-born Nobel Prize–winning physicist, known as the father of quantum mechanics. The *AFTA* passage to which Schrödinger's biographer, Walter Moore, refers is taken from the first page of chapter 2 (5:4–13). Schrödinger served as an Austrian artillery officer on the Italian front, including time spent in Gorizia, where important early scenes in Hemingway's novel take place. Patrick's injection of such a prominent scientist into a discussion of his father's novel is particularly fascinating, given the way the novel explores the conflict between science and faith, through the characters of Rinaldi and the priest. As a scientist, Schrödinger leaned toward atheism, but in his personal statement of belief, *Meine Weltansicht* (My Worldview), which Moore calls "a cry of spiritual pain of a soul torn between a need for religious belief and an inability to accept such a belief without treason to his intellectual standards," Schrödinger declares himself a believer in Vedanta, a version of Hinduism (123–29). As we shall see, *A Farewell to Arms* can also be read as the same kind of "cry of spiritual pain." Schrödinger's best known work, *What Is Life?* (1944), speculates on the possibility that genetic information could be encoded in complex molecules, and it inspired James Watson and Francis Crick to research DNA, culminating in their 1953 discovery of the double helix molecule, for which they were awarded the Nobel Prize in Medicine in 1962.

xii:4–5 **the Dasein thoughts of Heidegger:** We will not attempt an in-depth explanation of why Patrick Hemingway was moved to insert this phrase and reference to German philosopher Martin Heidegger (1889–1976), considered an important figure in the movements of phenomenology and existentialism. *Dasein* is a German word normally translated as "being there," and Heidegger's definition of the term lies at the heart of his magnum opus, *Being and Time,* published in German in 1927, not long before Hemingway began writing *A Farewell to Arms*, in the spring of 1928. However, *Being and Time* was not translated into English until 1962, so Hemingway would not have read it.

xii:12 **teenage illness:** Patrick here refers to the aftereffects of a severe concussion he suffered in an auto accident with his brother Gregory in April 1947. See entry viii:30–31.

Introduction by Seán Hemingway: Seán Hemingway, the editor of all the books published thus far in the Hemingway Library series, is the third son (of eight children) of Gregory Hemingway, Ernest Hemingway's third son. He has a PhD in classical art and archaeology from Bryn Mawr College and works as a curator at the Metropolitan Museum of Art in New York. His archeological thriller, *Tomb of Alexander,* was published in 2013. Seán's introduction serves as a satisfactory, if brief, overview of the novel. It helpfully acknowledges other important previous introductions, especially those by Ford Madox Ford (1932) and Robert Penn Warren (1957). Ford's comments are especially noteworthy in that he authored one of the great novels of the twenties, *Parade's End,* actually a tetralogy of novels about Britain during the Great War, including large sections that take place with the British army on the French front. Hemingway, however, was not fond of Ford when they worked together on the literary journal the *transatlantic review.* In both *The Sun Also Rises,* in which Ford appears as the character Braddocks, and later, the memoir *A Moveable Feast,* Hemingway presented very unflattering portraits of him.

In spite of its good qualities, Seán Hemingway's introduction here would be greatly improved if it had included an explanation of the principles and methodology followed in editing the text. He and his Uncle Patrick should be lauded for generously sharing Ernest Hemingway's manuscript material for *A Farewell to Arms,* which sheds light on the novelist's creative process and Hemingway's intended meanings in the book. However, it is unfortunate that this new edition not only misses the opportunity to fix serious flaws in the original text, but, in fact, inexplicably introduces egregious new errors, which we will point out in the context of our notes and commentary. There was also the missed opportunity to replace the censored words that Hemingway fully intended to use, words commonly used in many books published since 1929.

xiv:17–18 **General George S. Patton Jr.:** (1885–1945) commander of the US Seventh Army in North Africa and Europe during World War II. In Hemingway's *Across the River and into the Trees,* the protagonist, Richard Cantwell, refers to General Patton disparagingly, as "Georgie Patton who possibly never told the truth in his life" (116). Hemingway seems to have shared this opinion of the flamboyant general. In a 1948 letter to his friend General R. O. "Tubby" Barton, Hemingway said that color photography can get "more balled up than one of Georgie Patton's columns held up by two burp guns" (*SL* 639). In a 1950 letter to Charles Scribner, Hemingway shares a scurrilous but unsubstantiated account of Patton raping the daughter of a friend when she was a child (714). The title role in the Academy Award–winning film *Patton* was portrayed by George C. Scott, who went on to play Thomas Hudson in the film of Hemingway's *Islands in the Stream.* See Mark Cirino's comments on Patton in *Reading Hemingway's* Across the River and into the Trees (109).

xiv:28 **Euripides's *Medea*:** Ancient Greek dramatist Euripides (c. 480–c. 406 B.C.) is noted for his great tragedies; *Medea* is probably the best known of more than 90 works. In the play, Medea is abandoned by her husband, Jason, when he is invited to marry the daughter of Creon, the king of Corinth. Medea gets revenge on Jason by murdering his new wife and her own two children. In the C. A. E. Luschnig translation, Medea declares, "I would rather stand three times / in the line of battle than once bear a child" (ll. 249–50). As a sentence that conjoins war and childbirth, the passage bears special pertinence to *A Farewell to Arms*.

Epigraphs (Unused): Although Hemingway had not used epigraphs for either of his previously published short story collections, both of his two previous novels begin with epigraphs. Hemingway readers are very familiar with the twin epigraphs for *The Sun Also Rises*—Gertrude Stein's quote, "You are all a lost generation," and the "earth abides forever" passage from Ecclesiastes, from which the title of the novel is taken. As an epigraph for *Torrents of Spring,* Hemingway chose several lines from Henry Fielding's preface to his novel *Joseph Andrews,* which finishes with the statement that "life everywhere furnishes an accurate observer with the ridiculous." Although *A Farewell to Arms* has no epigraph, Hemingway apparently considered using one, and it is worth looking at the passages he seems to have considered for what they might tell us about his thinking. As Michael Reynolds has pointed out, the original holograph manuscript has an unnumbered page with two separate typewritten passages on it in the midst of chapter 34, when Frederic is reunited with Catherine after his desertion (*First War* 60–62). By this point in the writing, as Reynolds attests, Hemingway must have had a clear sense of his novel's ending with Catherine's death. One of the typed passages is the statement "The position of the survivor of a great calamity is seldom admirable," apparently Hemingway's own words, which provide us with an accurate assessment of Frederic Henry's predicament at the end of the novel. Had this been used as an epigraph for the novel, it would have highlighted Frederic's culpability in the death of Catherine Barkley and their child and made plain the depth of Frederic's tragic awareness. By the time Hemingway typed that sentence, he was certainly aware that his protagonist could not be regarded in heroic terms. Nevertheless, Hemingway probably decided that he did not wish to state a theme for the novel so baldly.

The second typed passage comes from Henry James, who was quoted in a 21 March 1915, *New York Times* article in conversation with Preston Lockwood:

> One finds it in the midst of all this [The Great War] as hard to apply one's words as to endure one's thoughts. The war has used up words; they have weakened, they have deteriorated like motor car tires; . . . and we are now confronted with a depreciation of all our terms, or otherwise speaking, with a loss of expression

through increase of limpness, that may well make us wonder what ghosts will be left to walk. (qtd. in Reynolds, *First War* 60–61)

Reynolds has an accurate assessment of Hemingway's consideration of this passage as an epigraph. As he says, "[t]he polite and decorous language of [a Jamesian novel] was no longer a useful tool to the post-war writer. The novel of the American in Europe, James's forte, had to change after the war; *A Farewell to Arms* is that change. . . . Hemingway's novel is an answer to James's question about what language will remain" (61). Hemingway's famous passage in chapter 27, in which Frederic expresses his embarrassment over abstract words and asserts that "finally only the names of places had dignity" can be interpreted as a direct response to Henry James (see entry 161:13–27). There Hemingway effectively places the concrete in opposition to the abstract, the objective in opposition to the subjective. Thus, the James quotation can effectively prepare us for the central theme of the book—the clash of reason and faith. Ultimately, however, Hemingway chose to use no epigraph for this novel, perhaps out of frustration with the many readers who misunderstood his use of the two epigraphs for *The Sun Also Rises*. Rather than risk readers' misunderstanding of his intentions, he chose instead to allow the novel to speak for itself.

The Title: Manuscript materials preserved at the JFK Library in Boston indicate Hemingway considered more than forty possible titles before settling on *A Farewell to Arms*. For a complete listing, see appendix 3 in the Hemingway Library edition (323–24). For comments on the most interesting of the alternate titles, see Roos, "Appendix A: Alternate Titles."

Anyone with a general acquaintance with Hemingway's writing knows he had a penchant for highly allusive titles (*In Our Time, The Sun Also Rises, The Torrents of Spring, For Whom the Bell Tolls,* "In Another Country," "The Light of the World," "Fathers and Sons," among others), and the allusions in these titles add significant layers of meaning to the works. In some cases, those from Turgenev, for example, the title may primarily function as a tribute to an author Hemingway admired. Whatever his motives in selecting them, Hemingway's titles almost always are carefully chosen signifiers of his intentions. And given his iceberg methodology of composition (see entry 3:1–5), we ought to give serious thought to allusions and meanings in his titles, used or unused, as part of the submerged portion of the novel's iceberg.

A Farewell to Arms: *Farewell,* of course, derives from *fare thee well* or *fare you well,* now a rather formal synonym for *goodbye,* which is itself a condensed imperative sentence meaning "God be with you," a plea, or even a demand, denoting an intention beyond the colloquial *goodbye* that it became. In contrast, *farewell* has no sense of an imperative. It is instead an expression of good wishes, a hope that the recipient of the message meets with good fortune in the time of separation between the two parties. As such, it connotes a greater sense of peace than *goodbye* does. Robert Graves titled his own fine memoir of World War I *Goodbye to All That,* which, like *A Farewell to Arms,* was also originally published in 1929. Given its title, it should be no surprise that Graves's book has the tone, as he describes it in its prologue, of a "bitter leave-taking." Hemingway, however, thought seriously of titling his novel *A Separate Peace,* a phrase Frederic Henry uses to describe his own circumstances following his desertion. As a title, *A Farewell to Arms* has some of that sense of peace, certainly more so than *A Goodbye to Arms* would have had. Perhaps that sense of peace is what makes the title seem more poetic to us. Note that Hemingway decided to use *good-by,* not *farewell* in the last paragraph of the novel (see entry 284:3–5).

As Hemingway was surely aware, the dual meanings of *arms,* the military sense and the anatomical sense, function perfectly for a novel in which the protagonist both deserts from his military service in wartime and then must part from the warm embrace of his lover, who dies at the end. The twin meanings of the English word originate from different source languages: the military meaning comes from Latin via French, while the anatomical meaning comes from German (*Oxford English Dictionary Online*). Thus, ironically, Hemingway's title unites two of the Great War's chief antagonists, France and Germany.

Since Philip Young in 1952, scholars have recognized that Hemingway's source for the title was George Peele's poem "A Farewell to Arms," composed in 1590 and included in the *Oxford Book of English Verse* (Quiller-Couch 142–43). Bernard Oldsey, however, was the first to note that "A Farewell to Arms" was an addendum at the end of Peele's longer poem "Polyhymnia" (1590), which commemorated a jousting tournament to celebrate the birthday of Queen Elizabeth I as well as the retirement of Sir Henry Lee from service as the Queen's Champion. Whether Hemingway was aware of "Polyhymnia" or not is unknown. Only the longer poem identifies the retiree as Sir Henry Lee, so we cannot be sure that Hemingway named his protagonist, Frederic Henry, after Sir Henry. Without the addendum, it is unlikely that "Polyhymnia" would have been of much interest to him or to very many people outside of its original audience. Only the "Farewell to Arms" sonnet is included in the *Oxford Book of English Verse,* but those eighteen lines, dedicated to the Queen, resonate with the key themes of Hemingway's novel:

> His golden locks Time hath to silver turn'd;
> O Time too swift, O swiftness never ceasing!
> His youth 'gainst Time and Age hath ever spurn'd
> But spurn'd in vain; youth waneth by increasing:
> Beauty, strength, youth, are flowers but fading seen;
> Duty, faith, love, are roots and ever green.

His helmet now shall make a hive for bees;
And lovers' sonnets turn'd to holy psalms,
A man-at-arms must now serve on his knees,
And feed on prayers, which are Age's alms.
But though from court to cottage he depart,
His Saint is sure of his unspotted heart.

And when he saddest sits in a homely cell,
He'll teach his swains this carol for a song:
Blest be the hearts that wish my Sovereign well,
Curst be the souls that think her any wrong.
Goddess, allow this agéd man his right
To be your beadsman now that was your knight.

Critics have long argued about how Peele's poem relates to Hemingway's novel, and their disagreements have lain at the heart of disputes that remain unresolved between those who see Frederic moving toward redemption and spiritual love and those who see development only in his disillusionment regarding any eternal truths in this world. Focusing on line 6, the eternal verities of duty, faith, and love, Clinton Keeler has argued that Frederic learns only that there is no constancy in any of these abstractions in the modern world. Frederic "does not become *Croyant*," Keeler insists (625). Others take the opposite view. What we can say with certainty is that the title is supremely apt because questions surrounding duty, faith, and love are at the heart of this novel, along with the issue of time, the brevity of life. All readers agree that there is no real irony between Peele's bow to time and the novel's presentation of it. Peele's "Time too swift" lends a sense of urgency to Frederic and Catherine's love and their efforts to capture as much life as time will allow them. As the novel will prove, that allowance is maddeningly brief. However, Peele's first stanza does more than simply express the trite and the obvious, that "Beauty, strength and youth are flowers but fading seen." It contrasts the mutability of the material world with what it sees as the eternal verities, the "evergreen" abstractions of duty, faith and love, which Peele calls "roots" as opposed to the "flowers" of beauty, strength and youth. The latter three are all caught in what Frederic refers to in the novel as the "biological trap" (see entry 121:11). The question is whether duty, faith, and/or love can provide an escape from that trap, and this is where differences among readers arise. Which side we join will depend greatly on how we interpret the treatment Hemingway gives to duty, faith, and love in the text. Whether he wanted his novel's tone to be one of despair or of hope, Hemingway must have smiled when he came across Peele's lovely, poetic title, "A Farewell to Arms," and read through its eighteen lines. He must have known his search for the perfect title had ended.

BOOK ONE

CHAPTER 1

It is not surprising to learn from manuscript materials at the JFK Library how extensively Hemingway revised this brief but powerful opening chapter to improve its effects (JFK item 64). Not in spite of its brevity but in part because of its brevity, we may read the chapter as having the compression and economy of poetry. Indeed, throughout this novel, his prose is poetic in its intensity. In lieu of a standard prose introduction, Hemingway composed a prose poem to make us both see and feel. Many of the details function as geographic opposites and, as we will learn, as foreshadowings of a world and lives in it that are also opposed, for the novel is structured around a series of dualities—like *boulders* and *pebbles,* the *dry* and the *water,* the *white* and the *blue.* The dualities prepare us for the central conflict of the novel between reason and faith—the objective and the subjective.

Also, given our understanding of the novel's title, we might expect to hear an active authorial voice of a fighter and lover, expressed in strong verbs of action, but instead we find vagueness and passivity: *lived, looked, were, was.* This tone continues throughout the chapter: the troops, for example, do not militarily *march* but merely "went by."

3:1–5 In the late summer of that year . . . blue in the channels: The chapter's first two sentences seem entirely peaceful, with nothing to indicate a war going on. The narrator, in fact, seems deliberately vague as to the date and locale and thus, probably intentionally, establishes a sense of universality as we begin the novel. In these two sentences, we could be anywhere, anytime in recorded history. However, subsequent details enable us to identify the setting and time as the eastern sector of the Italian front during the summer of 1915, the first months of Italy's involvement in the Great War, as the First World War was known until the commencement of the Second World War.

The river is the Isonzo, which today flows through northwestern Slovenia and northeastern Italy before emptying into the Adriatic Sea near the Italian city of Monfalcone. Michael Reynolds makes a convincing case that the village described here is Gradisca (*First War* 88). Gino Speranza, an Italian American journalist in Italy to cover the war for the *New York Post,* describes Gradisca in his diary: "In front lay the Isonzo, with fields running down to its banks, across it, a low livid red mountain, the Carso, and farther away to the left (north), under the protection of the Austrian mountains, Gorizia!" (Speranza 233). Gradisca lies about six miles downriver from Gorizia.

Hemingway's "craft of omission" (see Beegel) leaves out the historical background for the beginning of the novel. One of the tasks of this book is to fill in information of which Hemingway was fully aware as he was writing but chose to omit. This tactic is known as his "iceberg theory" of writing fiction, as first explained in *Death in the Afternoon* (1932), the book Hemingway wrote after *A Farewell to Arms*: "If a writer of prose knows enough about what he is writing about he may omit things that he knows and the reader, if the writer is writing truly enough, will have a feeling of those things as strongly as though the writer had stated them. The dignity of movement of an iceberg is due to only one-eighth of it being above water" (192). In chapter 1, a significant portion of the subsurface iceberg is the historical background. At the start of the Great War in August 1914, Italy remained officially neutral, courted by both sides: the Central Powers (Germany, Austria-Hungary, and Turkey), on the one hand, and the Triple Entente (Great Britain, France, and Russia), on the other. Somewhat Machiavellian in pursuing its own best interests, the Italian government, attracted by a better offer of territorial rewards after the war, eventually joined the Triple Entente, declaring war on Austria-Hungary on 23 May 1915, and fifteen months later, in August 1916, on Germany.

During the summer of 1915, the Italians and Austrians fought two separate battles on the Isonzo front, with the Italians on the attack in both cases—the first from 23 June to 7 July, the second from 18 July to 3 August. Italy's first important objective was to capture Gorizia on the eastern side of the river, but these initial battles, though inflicting heavy casualties on both sides, ended in stalemate. All of this Hemingway omits, leaving it beneath the surface of the iceberg as background to chapter 1. The unnamed narrator does go on to describe, indirectly and passively, additional fighting during the autumn. In actuality, these were the Third and Fourth Battles of the Isonzo (the battles were numbered only after the war by historians), from 18 October to 4 November and from 10 November to 2 December 1915, which also, to the great demoralization of both sides, ended with no significant gains for either the attacking Italians or the defending Austrians. Gorizia, as Hemingway's chapter 1 implies, remained in Austrian hands at the end of 1915.

The blue waters of the Isonzo are well known. Benito Mussolini, upon his arrival as a soldier at the Isonzo river in September 1915, is said to have been "struck by its extraordinarily blue waters" (Gooch 99). He later claimed that he dipped his hand for a drink "with sacred devotion" (99).

3:5–10 Troops went by . . . except for the leaves: After the entirely peaceful and universal first two sentences, in the third sentence, the war abruptly obtrudes:

troops animate the peaceful setting and introduce the first of a series of symphonic foreshadowings, in which trees, virtually universal images of life and growth, are covered with the dust of mortality: "and the leaves fell early that year and we saw the troops marching along" in the dust. The repetition of *leaves* in lines 6, 7, 8, and 10, with the near-rhyme of *breeze,* stirring those leaves, in line 9, poetically emulates the rhythm of the marching. Both the sound and the sense of the five paragraphs of this chapter convey the movement of mechanized warfare.

During the period of his writing apprenticeship some six years prior to the composition of this chapter, Hemingway attempted to capture this same tone in a piece of journalism he wrote for the 22 July 1922 *Toronto Star,* "A Veteran Visits the Old Front":

> It was the same old road that some of the same old brigades marched along through the dust of June of 1918, being rushed to the Piave to stop another offensive. Their best men were dead on the rocky Carso, in the fighting around Goritzia, on Mount San Gabrielle, on Grappa and in all the places where men died that nobody ever heard about. In 1918 they didn't march with the ardor that they did in 1916, some of the troops strung out so badly that, after the battalion was just a dust cloud way up the road, you would see poor old boys hoofing it along the side of the road to ease their bad feet, sweating along under their packs and rifles and the deadly Italian sun in a long, horrible, never-ending stagger after the battalion. (*DLT* 178)

Hugh Dalton's *With British Guns in Italy,* one of Hemingway's important historical sources, provides a more romantic, less cynical description of the Isonzo valley around Gradisca:

> What a country! The white houses, the white roads, the masses of fresh green foliage, chiefly acacias, the tall dark cypresses, the cool blue water of the Isonzo, the blue-grey mountains in the distance, and on their summits the sunshine on the snow, which is hardly distinguishable from the low-lying cloud banks in an otherwise cloudless sky.
>
> Italian troops, dusty columns marching along the road, throw up at me an occasional greeting as the lorry goes by. Long lines of transport pass continually. "Sempre Avanti Savoia!" "Sempre Avanti Italia!" (35)

3:11–16 The plain was rich with crops . . . not the feeling of a storm coming: Yet again we have a sense of opposition: the crops and orchards contrast with the "brown and bare" mountains—more of the dualities that we shall see repeatedly in this novel. The plain here is associated with the fullness of living, whereas the starkness of the mountains, where there is fighting, reveals the barrenness of death. Hemingway had previously used this same kind of duality in the setting of his brilliant and widely anthologized short story "Hills Like White Elephants." Here, the "flashes from the artillery," if a viewer could lose awareness of the present, might even be a pleasant reminder of "summer lightning," a harbinger of life-giving rain to a field of crops, but, as the narrator reminds us, the nights are too cool to be summertime, and thus there is no welcoming anticipation of a summer rainstorm. These flashes are harbingers only of death.

3:17 **Sometimes in the dark:** Even the word *sometimes* temporally continues the contrasts between the richness and fertility and the fear and dying. Contingency and uncertainty seem to govern life, both in nature and in human effort and desire, and even without the presence of the title word *farewell,* its shadow looms over all the story.

4:1–4 **There were big guns . . . over the tractors:** The lovely irony and dualism of the "green leafy branches," symbolic of the vitality of spring and summer, the fullness of nature, here used to camouflage the mechanistic man-made instruments of death, the tractors, are nearly perfect examples of Leo Marx's "machine in the garden," emblematic of the human propensity for corrupting and destroying the Edenic qualities of nature. Hemingway's carefully rhythmic repetition of "green branches and green leafy branches," alliterative and assonant, not only highlights the corruption and disruption of the natural order but also conveys the sonic effect of the rhythmic noise of a mechanized army on the move. In fact, Hemingway reminds us of "branches" four times in the paragraph. Even though in the first two references, the branches are green, they are, in fact, ironically more dead than the branches that are referred to as "bare"—stripped only temporarily for the hibernation of winter, whereas the "green leafy branches" used for camouflage have been cut and killed in the prime of their lives, just as will be the soldiers who are marching to the battlefront.

4:4–7 **To the north . . . but it was not successful:** The forest of chestnut trees to the north of Lucinico is still there today. The mountain described is certainly Monte Sabotino, scene of savage fighting during these early battles on the Isonzo front, although it is actually only about two thousand feet high. Hemingway was probably relying on British Red Cross ambulance commander G. M. Trevelyan's description of this area, as he wrote it in *Scenes from Italy's War* (1919). Trevelyan vividly describes the chestnut woods below the slopes of Monte Sabotino and the "fruit-laden hills" that slope down to the plain that Hemingway includes in his own tableau (49).

As Mark Thompson also explains in his widely praised history of the Italian front, *The White War,* Gorizia was sheltered on three sides by a series of mountains and hills, all of which were held by the heavily entrenched Austrians, affording them excellent views of the valley and Italian movements. Monte Sabotino and the hill of Podgora were north and west of the Isonzo. Monte Santo and Monte San Gabriele lay to the east, and San Michele rose above the southern limits of the town.

Here as elsewhere, Hemingway relies on elegant understatement in describing the fighting for Monte Sabotino: "but it was not successful" (4:7). That is one way to put it. The Italians suffered 15,000 casualties (2,000 dead, 11,500 wounded, and 1,500 missing) in the First Battle of the Isonzo (Thompson 111; Gooch 109). This was bad enough, but things grew almost three times worse in the Second Battle, in which the Italians lost 42,000 in dead, wounded, and missing, in the first of a series of bloodbaths on this front. The Italian commander in chief, General Luigi Cadorna, believed in full frontal attacks, but under the conditions on this front, with the Austrians entrenched in well-fortified defenses and holding all the higher ground, the Italian soldiers, most of whom had not yet even been supplied with helmets, were systematically slaughtered, many by machine gun fire, even while inflicting heavy casualties on the Austrians. The Italian losses, though a little lower than the Austrian, represented more than 5 percent of the Italian fighting force at the time, an enormous cost for a period of less than two months (Thompson 111). No wonder the narrator later tells us that "only 7,000" died of cholera.

4:7–11 **and in the fall . . . dead with the autumn:** The unsuccessful fighting is followed by a deadening rain (not the life-giving rain of summer), which strips the trees bare of leaves and blackens the trunks to the color of mourning. Likewise, the vineyards, source and symbol of vitality in the summer, now seem skeletal. So we are left with a world that is "wet and brown and dead."

4:11–18 **There were mists . . . six months gone with child.** In this single eighty-five-word compound sentence, Hemingway belies his reputation for short, simple declarative sentences. The content continues to shower us with the dense and deadening moisture, in the "mists over the river and clouds on the mountain," the "splashed mud," the troops "muddy and wet in their capes," with their wet rifles. Again, the twin agents of death seem to be the machines of war (in the form of the trucks) and nature (in the form of the rain). Then Hemingway concludes the sentence with perhaps his most striking image of the chapter, in a long string of details that link the ammunition of death (worn in the leather cartridge boxes on the front of the soldiers' belts) bulging forward in the men's capes so that they appear "six months gone with child." Much as he did in his short stories "On the Quai at Smyrna" and "Indian Camp," Hemingway paradoxically couples childbirth with death and thus presents us with what we ultimately realize is the grimmest piece of foreshadowing in the novel, for not only are these men marching toward their death, most of them in the full bloom of youth, but, by the end of the novel, the war will also bring conjoined pregnancy and death to the protagonist and his lover.

The phrase *gone with child*, a gloomy old colloquialism, is a curious choice of words. It may have been passed down from a time when many women and infants did not survive the rigors of childbirth, and Hemingway may have heard his obstetrician father use it. The phrases *with child* and *to get with child* go back at least to Middle English, according to the Oxford English Dictionary. However, the earliest usage cited in the *Oxford English Dictionary* for *gone with child* is 1765, from *The Midwife's Pocket Companion*: "If a miscarriage happens when a woman has been long gone with child . . . the danger is great." The King James Bible uses the phrase *with child* frequently throughout, but never *gone with child*. However, commentaries on the Bible are another story. It is worth noting that the exact phrase as Hemingway uses it, *six months gone with child,* turns up in at least three such commentaries. It appears in Charles Fell's *Lives of the Saints,* first published in 1729, in its explanation of the Catholic Church's celebration of the Feast of the Annunciation to Mary, when the Archangel Gabriel reveals to her that she will be the mother of God, as written in the Gospel of Luke (1:26–36): "The Divine Messenger [the Angel Gabriel] then proceeded to tell [Mary] the miraculous Manner, in which this glorious Work was to be effected, and, as a Proof that God can do what seems impossible to Man, told her that her Cousin Elizabeth, though old and barren, was then six Months gone with Child" (xxv). The same phrase, in the same context, appears also in John Gill's *Exposition of the Entire Bible* (1746–1763) as well as in Charles Butler's *A Continuation of the Reverend Alban Butler's Lives of the Saints to the Present Time,* published in 1823. In the King James Gospel of Luke, Gabriel says to Mary, "And, behold, thy cousin Elisabeth, she hath also conceived a son in her old age: and this is the sixth month with her, who was called barren. For with God, nothing shall be impossible" (1:36).

We know Hemingway was very familiar with the Bible, but was he familiar with Fell's, Gill's, or Butler's texts? They do not appear in Reynolds's *Hemingway's Reading: 1910–1940,* but there are, however, other books we know Hemingway read that Reynolds neglected to include. If Hemingway had not read any of these texts, his devoutly religious obstetric physician father may have and passed the phrase on to his son. Was Hemingway, in conjoining this image of pregnancy with the imminent deaths of soldiers, consciously evoking this scene from the Gospel of Luke and its assertion of God's omnipotence—a biblical passage that leads, of course, to Mary and Elizabeth's mutual acknowledgement of being "with child," as one of these women will bring forth the precursor of the Messiah and the other the Messiah himself, children destined to die as martyrs in their young manhood? And then, do the soldiers depicted in chapter 1 of the novel as appearing "six months gone with child" serve as precursors of the fate of Catherine Barkley and her child? And, if we accept all this, should we see the allusion as an emblem of Hemingway's piety and the eventual redemption of Frederic Henry? Or should we see it as bitterly ironic commentary on the wasteland of the modern world, wherein the soldiers may indeed be precursors of Catherine's fate, but their millions of dead would not, in fact, be a sacrifice that would open any gates of heaven for anyone, but a meaningless waste of human lives, like burying "the meat of the Chicago stockyards"? Interpreting Hemingway can be a minefield (see entry 161:13–27).

Note also that the mountain San Gabriele, named of course for the Angel Gabriel, is one of those heavily contested mountains in the series of battles of the Isonzo (see entry 4:4–7). In the spirit of vagueness and universality, the mountain is unnamed in chapter 1 but will be clearly identified later in the narrative. See entry 27:30. The name of the mountain was not Hemingway's doing, of course, but he may have found it convenient to his purposes.

In addition, if we acknowledge that the phrase "six months gone with child" can be an allusion to the Annunciation and the Angel Gabriel, then we have to consider the possibility of an allusion to the poet, novelist, warrior Gabriele D'Annunzio, whose name means, of course, Gabriel of the Annunciation. Furthermore, in another perverse connection to the Annunciation, D'Annunzio has been called, fairly or unfairly, "the John the Baptist of fascism" (Woodhouse 1). Hemingway based a character in one early short story, "The Mercenaries," on D'Annunzio (Casillo and Russo 415). And in another, "The Passing of Pickles McCarty or The Woppian Way," he created an Italian American named Nick Neroni, a boxer who fought under the name Pickles McCarty and served heroically for the Italian Arditi on Monte San Gabriele in World War I, who is on his way to join D'Annunzio in the invasion and takeover of the Dalmatian city of Fiume in September 1919. On 11 November 1919, Hemingway wrote his mother from Petoskey, Michigan, "Wish I were at Fiume" (*Letters 1* 211). In 1920, he gave a copy of D'Annunzio's lush Venetian novel *The Flame* to his Toronto friend Dorothy Connable, and in 1921 he gave another to his fiancée, Hadley Richardson (Reynolds, *Young Hemingway* 212–13). Yet, also during this same period, he wrote a short poem entitled "D'Annunzio," which reads, in its entirety: "Half a million dead wops / And he got a kick out of it / The son of a bitch" (*Poems* 28). In March 1924, he was still mentioning D'Annunzio in a letter to Ezra Pound, remarking on Mussolini's bestowing upon D'Annunzio the honorary title "Principe di Monte Nervosa": "Well he rates it. It's damn late coming. Probably too late for him to get the kick out of it." Then he added in postscript, "After Renouncing Italy and all its works I've gotten all ~~homesick and~~ nostalgique about it" (*Letters 2* 103). Hemingway's fascination with D'Annunzio is clear, but his feelings were complex. Late in his career, Hemingway was still drawing inspiration from D'Annunzio. *Across the River and into the Trees* is set in Venice, as is *The Flame,* and the heroine's name, Renata, is taken from the character of D'Annunzio's daughter in his prose poem *Notturno.* The protagonist, Colonel Richard Cantwell, like his creator, has very complicated feelings about D'Annunzio. See Mark Cirino's comments on the numerous D'Annunzio connections to *Across the River and into the Trees* in *Reading Hemingway's* Across the River and into the Trees. For further discussion of Hemingway's "D'Annunzio obsession" see also John Paul Russo.

4:19–25 **small gray motor cars . . . probably the King:** In this paragraph, the emphasis shifts somewhat, from wetness to smallness—first the small automobiles and then a particular one with an especially small passenger, the King, who was in fact Italy's King Victor Emmanuel III. The image is not intended to flatter the leader of the country, yet it is apparently an accurate description:

> Very short in stature and ill-favoured, he did not cut a regal or martial figure. One of his cruel nicknames was *sciaboletta,* or "little sabre"; he could not wear a full-length sword, and cartoonists drew the tip of his scabbard resting on a little trolley. When the war started, he wanted to cut the figure of a soldier king, but really preferred coin-collecting and photography.... Insecure and naïve, he was easily led by forceful personalities. (Thompson 19)

Hemingway conveys this sense of the King being "easily led" by placing him in the middle of larger officers, undoubtedly General Luigi Cadorna, the Italian commander in chief, and another of his generals. There is a dark comedy in this image of recklessness, the portrait of a powerful yet somehow ineffectual leader, akin to the Keystone Cops, whose antics Hemingway would have enjoyed in silent films of his day. The machines of death, propelled by the men in charge of the government and the military, are small but nevertheless splash more mud than the camions.

4:25 **He lived in Udine:** Udine is the one detail in this first chapter, coming near the end of it, that identifies the part of the world we are in—northeastern Italy. Now, given the motor cars, the trucks and tractors, and the long guns, we can guess that we are on the Italian front during the First World War. The King and his commander in chief, General Luigi Cadorna, established their wartime headquarters in Udine, about twenty-five miles from the front lines, and from there they made frequent visits to the front. Cadorna took over the archbishop's palace and grandiosely labeled it the Comando Supremo (Supreme Command). The King set up residence in Villa Linussa (renaming it Villa Italia), an unpretentious mansion just outside of the town. Baedeker's *Italy: From the Alps to Naples* 1928, one of Hemingway's many source books in composing the novel, describes Udine, a place Hemingway never visited, as

> a town of 55,700 inhabitants.... Among the chief buildings are the Cathedral, with a hexagonal campanile, and the Archbishop's Palace, containing fine frescoes by G. B. Tiepolo and Giovanni da Udine (1487–1564).... Above the picturesque Piazza Vittorio Emanuele, with a clock-tower resembling that at Venice..., rises the Castello, which contains the Museo Civico, a collection of antiquities and paintings. [Also] Numerous palaces of the Friulian noblesse. (87)

"Friulian" refers to the Friuli region in Northeast Italy, where Friulian, a Romance language, is still spoken by as many as six hundred thousand people. See entry 170:26–27.

4:27 things went very badly: Action in chapter 1 encompasses the Third and Fourth Battles of the Isonzo, which as the narrator casually states, for the Italians went very badly indeed. The Third Battle of the Isonzo, another of General Cadorna's blunt, full-frontal attempts to take Gorizia, lasted from 18 October to 4 November 1915, with the shocking loss of 67,000 dead, wounded, or missing Italians and "only" 25,000 Austrians. Even in the face of such numbers, General Cadorna ordered another attack just six days later. This battle raged from 10 November to 2 December, with results only slightly less devastating than the previous battle—49,000 Italians and 42,000 Austrians lost (Thompson 134–35). According to military historian Cyril Falls in *The Battle of Caporetto*, the defeats were not the result of cowardice on the part of the Italian infantrymen, who "showed splendid courage in hopeless tasks" (9). The fault, Falls claims, lay in the persistence of Cadorna, whom he describes as the "arch-attritionist," staging frontal attacks on nearly impregnable positions (7). In total, the Third and Fourth battles of the Isonzo resulted in 66,908 dead and 48,967 wounded for the Italians (Gooch 118). Although these numbers were greater for the Italians than for the Austrians, proportionately, the Austrians suffered more. They lost 40 percent of their personnel in these battles, compared to 23 percent for the Italians (118). Either way we look at it, the carnage is mind-boggling.

4:28–30 At the start of the winter . . . only seven thousand died of it in the army: Although the chapter begins in the fruitful "late summer," it soon brings the autumn rains, connoting the end of natural life, an end that arrives in the last brief, two-sentence paragraph with its controlled explosion: "At the start of the winter came the permanent rain." And this permanent rain (only a slight exaggeration for Northern Italy at that time of year) now brings an even greater certainty of death, if not in battle, then by the disease of cholera, spread by unsanitary conditions in the trenches of the battlefront. The real power of Hemingway's expression here is conveyed in the word *only*. Yes, if we place this information in the context of a total loss of well over 100,000 Italian lives in the first six months of the war, 7,000 may seem a small number. But in saying these cholera deaths were "in the army," the narrator sardonically implies that there were additional, unnumbered cholera deaths among civilians. The war's destructive effects leave nothing and no one untouched.

Hemingway's number, probably drawn from contemporary news accounts and war histories, is accurate: in *The Italian Army and the First World War*, John Gooch claims that by the beginning of August 1915, 21,000 Italian soldiers had caught cholera and typhus and 4,300 had died (112). The 1915 cholera epidemic was so severe it required Italian commanders to "isolate whole units" (Gilbert 204). Hemingway's important source G. M. Trevelyan, serving with the British Red Cross on the Italian front, also provides a vivid account of the horror of the cholera epidemic, which he says peaked in November 1915:

> The cholera ... was at its worst, the victims dying in agony often in forty-eight or twenty-four hours, and the battle was raging all the time.... I remember entering the door of a church, and finding myself alone in company with twenty men lying on the bare ground in various attitudes of despair. On looking more carefully, I saw that fifteen were dead, and the remainder just dying of cholera, too far gone even to roll an eye asking for aid. The symbols of religion looked down on this silent section of the floor of hell. (56–57)

Trevelyan's phrase "too far gone" may remind readers of Hemingway's use of "gone with child" (4:17–18). In Mark Thompson's *The White War*, a British private serving in Italy describes "a field of filth" in the Italian trenches: "I had never seen such a disgusting sight and wondered what kind of epidemic was being bred amidst the excreta" (151–52). Benito Mussolini, who became the fascist prime minister of Italy in 1922, was a victim of the typhus epidemic while serving on the Isonzo front. "Rain and lice, these are the two enemies of the Italian soldier," he wrote in his diary. "The cannon comes after" (qtd. in Gilbert 204).

Understandably, morale of the soldiers suffered greatly under these conditions and was not helped by the callousness of their commanders. For example, one of the Italian superior officers, General Vincenzo Garioni, believed that the slaughter of Italian soldiers in en masse attacks was "a necessary holocaust." Their sacrifice, he said, was "therapeutic, a purgative that strengthened the army for future battles, rendering it fit for victory" (qtd. in Thompson 151). Military scholar Jonathan Fennel has suggested that "incidences of sickness ... [are] one of the best indicators of morale problems in an army" (qtd. in Wilcox, "Morale and Battlefield Performance" 842). If so, then 7,000 deaths from cholera must have correlated with seriously damaged morale along the Isonzo front.

CHAPTER 2

5:1 The next year there were many victories: The next year is 1916. The narrator is still being coy about time and place, stretching the sense of universality as far as possible. The tone here may seem sunnier, but only if we completely erase memories of chapter 1. We will discuss later whether the reference to victories is hyperbole or not. We already know we are in northeast Italy in World War I, and, if we consult a history of the war, the "many victories" help us to guess the year.

5:1–3 The mountain . . . and the hillside . . . was captured: A subject-verb agreement error here (with the compound subject of *mountain* and *hillside*, the verb should be *were captured*) seems to have survived all editions of the novel—one of numerous opportunities lost in the Hemingway Library edition to correct some inadvertent errors in the original text. Beyond that, the narrator is reminding us of the setting in chapter 1, where we identified the mountain as two-thousand-foot Monte Sabotino. See entry 4:4–7. The victories described here occurred historically in the Sixth Battle of the Isonzo, which took place in August 1916. Hemingway has glossed over the abortive Fifth Battle, which took place earlier that year, 9–17 March, and resulted in no territory gained for the Italians and another 13,000 dead and wounded (Thompson 157–58). At that point, after five bloody battles, General Cadorna apparently recognized at last that he needed more heavy artillery to be able to make any progress against the Austrians' fortified positions on the high ground surrounding Gorizia. As a result, there was a lull in fighting on the Isonzo for several months as the Italians manufactured more big guns.

However, in May, the Austrians mounted an attack in the Dolomite Mountains of the Trentino area of northern Italy and very nearly broke through the Italian lines. This too, Hemingway chooses not to mention, presumably because the protagonist was not involved in the action there and, although they were severely strained, losing almost twelve miles of territory, the Italians held on in the end and retook a third of the Austrians' gains. The Trentino battle lasted through June and part of July, with enormous casualties: 286,000 for the Italians alone (Falls 13). Meanwhile, for our narrator, the months between March and August must have been relatively quiet in Gradisca with his unit, waiting for the next big action on the Isonzo.

The Sixth Battle of the Isonzo began on 6 August and ended on 17 August. In that push, the Italians caught the Austrians in a weakened condition, having moved some men and equipment to other fronts. As a result, the Italians gained an average of three to four miles along the front and crossed the river, as the narrator tells us, to achieve the important goal of capturing Gorizia, as well as the elevations of Monte Sabotino and the hills of Podgora to the north of the town and Monte San Michele to the south, which gave them a foothold on the Carso, the plateau to the south of Gorizia. It was the biggest territorial gain of the war for the Italians until the final weeks in 1918. Nevertheless, in the fighting, despite what Frederic calls "many victories," the Italians lost at least another 100,000 men, more than twice as many as the Austrians lost—another dark detail beneath the surface of the iceberg.

5:4 **we:** The first person plural collectives *we* and *us*, which characterize the first chapter, continue here through the first paragraph, with one notable exception. By the second paragraph, the narrator shifts to the first person singular *I* and will remain in that mode essentially for the remainder of the novel, except for occasional significant instances, which we will note.

5:5 **Gorizia:** This detail enables us to identify with certainty not only the location but the year of the action. Historical accounts tell us the precise details of the capture of Gorizia by the Italians in the Sixth Battle of the Isonzo in August 1916, as explained in entry 5:1–3. Having never been to the town, Hemingway no doubt relied on descriptions provided by the memoirs of Hugh Dalton and G. M. Trevelyan, as well as the following passage in Baedeker's 1928 edition of *Italy: From the Alps to Naples:*

> Gorizia (295 ft.), a town of 26,400 inhab[itants], and the seat of an archbishop, lies near the left bank of the Isonzo, in a fertile plain enclosed on three sides by mountains.... The old Castello of the Counts of Gorizia crowns the castle-hill, at the foot of which lies the Cathedral, dating from the 14th but altered in the 17th century. A tramway runs [north] to the ... Piazza Edmondo de Amicis, on the [west] side of which is the Palazzo Attems, containing the Provincial Museum. (87–88)

Because the surrounding mountains protect the town from cold winds that affect much of the nearby terrain, Gorizia has a year-round mild Mediterranean climate and, as a result, was and remains a popular tourist resort. Today the Italian border with Slovenia skirts the eastern edge of the city.

As Dalton and Trevelyan both explain, a civilian population remained in the town, as Hemingway describes, even in the midst of artillery fire on both sides (5:13–14). Trevelyan talks of "several hundred" children attending school daily at the local convent, under the tutelage of a Sister Matilda (116). The Italian military supplied civilians with food and transportation to the market in Udine.

H. G. Wells may have provided Hemingway with another source here. Wells visited Gorizia soon after its capture in 1916 and described what he saw in a chapter of his report *War and the Future:*

> I found [Gorizia] very little injured—compared, that is, with such other towns as have been fought through. Here and there the front of a house has been knocked in by an Austrian shell, or a lamp-post prostrated. But the road bridge had suffered a good deal; its iron parapet was twisted about by shell bursts and interwoven with young trees and big boughs designed to screen the passer-by from the observation of the Austrian gunners upon Monte Santo. Here and there were huge holes through which one could look down upon the blue trickles of water in the stony river bed far below. (chap. 1)

5:7–8 **Now the fighting was . . . not a mile away:** The next mountains are San Daniele, San Gabriele, and Santo, none of which the Italians were able to take in the Sixth Battle of the Isonzo. There were three more relatively brief battles in the fall of 1916, none of which produced any additional gains for the Italians: the Seventh (14–17 September), the Eighth (10–12 October), and the Ninth (1–4 November). The battle lines indeed were not far outside of Gorizia at the foot of these mountains. Historians Cyril Falls, Mark Thompson, and John Gooch all fault General Cadorna for not pushing aggressively following the gains achieved in the Sixth Battle. Instead, he waited a month, allowing the Austrians to regroup and retrench and thus prevent any further gains that year.

5:11–13 **I was very glad . . . only a little in a military way:** For the first time, the narrator steps forward as an individual voice to express a personal opinion about a town that he obviously likes very much. After the gloom of chapter 1, in this chapter the narrator seems not deeply touched personally by the general horrors of the war. Here, there are many pleasures of life in Gorizia, where surprisingly there are still some citizens living and going about their daily lives, even as the battles rage on nearby. The description of the town here is consistent with that of Hugh Dalton, the British artillery officer who was stationed in Gorizia in 1916:

> Gorizia lies in a salient of hills, with the Austrians looking down upon it from the tops of most of them. But, still hoping to win it back, they do not shell it heavily or often. . . . Gorizia is a sort of Austrian Cheltenham, whither Austrian officers retire in large numbers to pass their last years in villas which they take over from one another's widows. So the Austrian officer class has a sort of vested interest in the preservation of the place. (56)

5:15 two bawdy houses, one for troops and one for officers: Hemingway curiously uses a rather archaic term, *bawdy house,* for a brothel or house of prostitution. The Italian term is *case di tolleranza,* literally "houses of tolerance." Military historians have remarked that Italian soldiers, under the severe regulations of General Luigi Cadorna, had only two officially sanctioned forms of recreation away from battle: alcohol and the military brothels (Gooch 164). Although prostitution certainly contributed to sexually transmitted diseases that took men out of action, authorities also believed that masturbation was a "threat to the race" and that long periods of sexual abstinence could lead to "homosexuality, rape and sadism" (166). So establishing government-sanctioned and regularly inspected sexual outlets for soldiers was deemed a matter of practicality. To provide a sense of the level of the demand: just one of the brothels served between seven and nine hundred customers every day (166). Hemingway would have been familiar with these government-established institutions from his own period of service on the Italian front in 1918.

5:20–6:1 the King ... beard like a goat's chin tuft: The narrator again presents a somewhat comic image of the Italian king, Victor Emmanuel III, who ruled Italy from 29 July 1900, following the assassination of his father, King Umberto I, until abdicating in a futile effort to save the Italian monarchy in 1946. Although the King did indeed have a small body, being only five feet tall, we have not located any photos of Victor Emmanuel III with a beard. In all extant photos, he is depicted with a long handlebar moustache, but his chin is always clean-shaven. Hemingway may have confused him with his grandfather, King Victor Emmanuel II, the first monarch of a unified Italy, who was always depicted with a long goatee.

6:4 going well on the Carso: The Carso is a stark limestone plateau southeast of Gorizia, on which the Italians gained several kilometers of territory and seized several villages from the Austrians during fighting there in the autumn of 1916, as Hemingway here implies. H. G. Wells visited the Carso in 1916 and described it thus: "The Carso itself is a waterless upland with but a few bushy trees; it must always have been a desolate region, but now it is an indescribable wilderness of shell craters, smashed-up Austrian trenches, splintered timber, old iron, rags, and that rusty thorny vileness of man's invention, worse than all the thorns and thickets of nature, barbed wire" (*War and the Future,* chap. 1).

6:7–17 The forest of oak trees ... latrines behind the trenches: This powerful piece of descriptive writing conveys the profound effects of the war on the environment. The machines have severely scarred the garden. Yet the cycles of nature continue unabated, as if to say that war's effects are only temporary. Nature reigns supreme and will renew itself, no matter how badly damaged it becomes from the war. The rain of chapter 1 has turned to snow that covers everything, the guns and the stumps of dead trees the guns have produced. The paragraph concludes with the sardonic reminder of how nature calls the soldiers "to the latrines behind trenches." During the early years of the war, the location of the latrines so close to the trenches contributed to the spread of diseases like cholera and typhus.

Unlike the rain that frequently accompanies foreboding events in this novel (see entry 110:1–2, for example), the snow at the wintry end of the year denotes a welcome pause in most of the fighting for the year, given that both armies lacked resources to engage in battle during harsh winter conditions, especially in the hills and mountains of northern Italy.

The narrator tells us he "was out where the forest had been," and he saw the change in the weather coming, but he does not tell us what he was doing there. We still do not know what his role in this war is. Hemingway deftly builds our curiosity about him with small bits of information in this chapter.

6:19–20 **the bawdy house, the house for officers, where I sat with a friend:** We learn more about the narrator here. He is an officer, or he would not be allowed in the officers' bawdy house. He seems comfortable, implying that he spends a lot of time there in pursuit of sexual pleasure. The friend is most likely the officer we come to know later as Lieutenant Rinaldi, the atheistic surgeon, who serves as counterpoint to Frederic Henry's other good male friend, the priest.

6:20 **a bottle of Asti:** The first of many references to alcoholic drinks in the novel. Asti, also known as Asti Spumante, is a sparkling white wine named for the province of Asti in northwestern Italy, one of the several well-known wine regions of the country. Most commonly served with dessert, it is low in alcohol content and sweet. In this instance, since no women seem to be joining the two men, Asti is probably being consumed post coitum, that is, after sex in the bawdy house.

6:24–28 **My friend saw the priest . . . shook his head and went on:** If we are correct in assuming that the narrator's friend is Lieutenant Rinaldi, then this is the first instance where Hemingway pairs Rinaldi and the priest and contrasts their influence on Frederic Henry, the as yet unnamed narrator. The friend's invitation for the priest to join the men in the bawdy house is, of course, meant to be a joke. This priest, here and throughout the novel, is incorruptible. With his smile of recognition, he is presented as kindly and gentle, without a touch of the irony or cynicism that pervades the world of most of the officers. Frederic Henry, as we shall see, is at ease with both sides. This brief appearance of the priest prepares for the scene in the mess hall that follows, in which the officers cruelly bait the priest for his lack of sexual experience.

The central conflict in the novel between the rationalism of Rinaldi and the faith of the priest recalls a dialogue in the first novel of John Dos Passos, *One Man's Initiation: 1917* (1920), in which a rationalistic captain debates a man of faith, an *aumonier* (chaplain for the French army), on the power of religion or the lack thereof among soldiers on the battlefield (*Novels* 61–62).

6:28–36 That night in the mess . . . picking on the priest: The paragraph concludes with another sentence that is atypical for Hemingway, a very long one with a lengthy subordinate clause spread between the two parts of the main clause. The middle of this sentence is something of a sensual grammatical tour de force, further characterizing the narrator's relationship among his comrades as well as emphasizing the importance of food and drink throughout the novel.

6:37 The priest was young and blushed easily: The priest's youthful innocence is an important part of his character, contrasting him starkly with the officers and their worldly cynicism.

6:39–7:1 pidgin Italian for my doubtful benefit: The captain is speaking a combination of Italian and English, providing an instance of the ongoing theme of language. The narrator's noting that the pidgin Italian is for his "doubtful benefit" underscores his ambivalent position between the priest and the officers. As he is positioned between Rinaldi's atheism and the priest's faith, doubt and uncertainty are essential traits of his character. The phrase also identifies him as a nonnative speaker of Italian.

7:12 "every night five against one": If this is not obvious, the captain is accusing the priest of masturbating nightly, with five fingers against one male sex organ. Italian authorities frowned upon masturbation as a "threat to the race." See entry 5:15.

7:15 "The Pope wants the Austrians to win the war": The major, the highest ranking officer present, joins in the baiting with a more serious accusation against the priest: an implication of treason. Pope Benedict XV, who was elected in September 1914 in large measure because of his opposition to the Great War, had declared the Vatican's neutrality in the war between Italy and Austria-Hungary, both heavily Roman Catholic. In the process of Italian unification between 1861 and 1870, the Vatican had lost territorial control of the Papal States, which comprised much of central Italy, including Rome, and it maintained close ties to the Catholic monarchy of Emperor Franz Joseph in Austria-Hungary, traditionally referred to as His Apostolic Majesty. As it became clear in the spring of 1915 that Italy intended to pull out of its alliance with Austria-Hungary and Germany and join the Triple Entente, Pope Benedict tried and failed to broker a peace among all factions. Thus, Roman Catholic clergy in Italy were treated with some suspicion regarding their support for the war and the irrendentist movement to recapture territories with large ethnic Italian populations.

7:16 **"He loves Franz Joseph. That's where the money comes from":** Emperor Franz Joseph was ruler of the Austro-Hungarian Empire, also referred to as His Apostolic Majesty. See entry 7:15. In the manuscript, Hemingway wrote and crossed out "Cecco Beppe," replacing it with "Franz Joseph." Cecco Beppe is a shortening of the Emperor's name as rendered in Italian, Franchesco Giuseppe. The major is implying that the Vatican had economic reasons for not supporting Italy against Austria-Hungary.

7:16–17 **"I am an atheist":** With this proud declaration by the major, Hemingway draws the battle line for the most important war in the novel—that between reason and faith. The major wants all to understand his opposition to the Church, and while other officers seem content simply to poke fun at the priest, the major defies him, as if he wishes to draw the priest into a debate on the existence of God. Ultimately the surgeon, Lieutenant Rinaldi, will be the novel's chief spokesperson for the position of reason, though his attitude toward the priest will be noticeably more tolerant than what the major exhibits here. In this scene, it seems that all the Italian officers support an essentially atheistic position against the priest, the lone proponent of religious faith. Frederic Henry, the narrator, remains neutral, though his neutrality does not prevent him from joining the other officers in pursuit of sensual pleasures.

7:18–26 **"Did you ever read the 'Black Pig'?" . . . "I will get it for you":** The lieutenant is addressing the narrator, Frederic Henry. While various commentators have correctly identified the book in question as Umberto Notari's *Il maiale nero: Rivelazioni e documenti* (*The Black Pig: Revelations and Documents*), published in Italy in 1907 or 1908, Miriam Mandel has produced the most thorough study of the content of the book (see "Reading and Not Reading"). Mandel reveals that later editions were titled *Dio contro Dio* (*God versus God*), with the original title kept as a subtitle. By the time of *The Black Pig*'s publication, Notari was already a popular author of journalism, biography, fiction, drama, and polemical essays. *The Black Pig* is a nonfictional polemic designed to reveal that "the Church is hypocritical and its clergymen despicable" (101). Notari claims that *black pig* is a common term for Catholic clergy, and his first chapter "proceeds to attack the texts, ceremonies, and precepts of the Catholic Church, finding them to be not divine revelation but plagiarized from other cultures and religions" (101). The lieutenant, whom we will come to know as Frederic Henry's surgeon friend, Rinaldi, admits here that *The Black Pig* "shook [his] faith," and he is clearly eager to share it with Frederic, assuring him that he "will like it."

After passively submitting to the officers' taunts, the priest, for the first time, responds aggressively to the lieutenant's challenge, calling the book "filthy and vile" (7:20). He insists that Frederic will not really like it. Frederic's smile at the priest in response is significant, as if to ease any worries the priest may have. Seemingly reassured, the priest smiles back and commands Frederic, "Don't you read it." Although the lieutenant insists he will get the book for Frederic, it is never mentioned again. Most important, however, is that Hemingway, in this first spate of dialogue in the novel, establishes the central focus of the novel's conflict. Frederic lies between the diametrically opposed worldviews of Lieutenant Rinaldi and the priest. Without ever stating it directly, Frederic will seek to find some kind of healthful balance or resolution between these two warring factions.

7:27 **"All thinking men are atheists":** The major connects atheism to rationality, a key to understanding the conflict in the novel. He is arguing that if we think, if we reason, the logical conclusion is that there is no God. No one present in the mess challenges this position, but various points in the novel make clear that Frederic Henry is testing the truth of this claim. He is a thinking man, a man of reason, as we shall see, but is he an atheist?

7:28 **the Free Masons:** An anticlerical organization founded by guilds of actual stonemasons in medieval Europe who were craftsmen for many churches and other monuments. By the time of the Enlightenment, the Freemasons had become secretive organizations heavily influenced by Enlightenment rationalism and thus were perceived as a threat to organized religion. Though the Freemasons tended to be deistic, they did not require members to profess religious beliefs. The Catholic Church, however, has traditionally forbidden its members from becoming Freemasons. In the 1917 Code of Canon Law, issued the year after this discussion takes place in the novel, Pope Benedict XV declared that membership in the Freemasons would result in automatic excommunication from the Church. In Tolstoy's *War and Peace,* the protagonist Pierre Bezukhov, in the midst of a spiritual crisis, joins the Freemasons, which seems to have had a more strongly religious element in nineteenth-century Russia than elsewhere at that time. The major's denial here of belief in the Freemasons may suggest he is not as strongly atheistic as some of his comments appear to be. In contrast, the lieutenant, we should note, declares in the following line that he believes in the Freemasons.

7:36 **Amalfi:** The lieutenant, the same one who has recommended that Frederic should read *The Black Pig* (see entry 7:18) and who is later identified as Rinaldi, the surgeon, is from Amalfi, a coastal city in the region of Campania, about twenty-one miles southeast of Naples on the Tyrrhenian Sea. In the Middle Ages, as one of the four most powerful Italian maritime republics (with Genoa, Pisa, and Venice), it was a flourishing maritime center noted for establishing the maritime codes (the Amalfian Laws) and for its schools of law and mathematics. In other words, it is an appropriate place of origin for Lieutenant Rinaldi, who will represent the worldview of science and reason in contrast to the priest's worldview of faith and religion. Notably, just as earthquakes have played an important role in the history of the priest's home region of the Abruzzi (see entry 8:1–2), so too have they in the history of Amalfi. In 1343, an earthquake and tsunami devastated the city, which had a population of seventy thousand at the time, and the city never fully recovered. Today, the Amalfi population is only about five thousand. At the same time, although the Vesuvius volcano is only fifteen miles to the northwest of the town, Amalfi is protected by mountains from any eruptions.

The lieutenant's offer to make arrangements for Frederic to stay with his family, who, he says, will "love you like a son," parallels the priest's later offer for Frederic to visit his family in Capracotta. See entry 8:1–2. Rinaldi will later refer to Frederic as his "war brother" (58:15–16; 150:3).

7:38 **Palermo:** The capital city and center of culture on the island of Sicily, noted for its architecture and fine food.

7:39 **Capri:** The Isle of Capri, mentioned here as another potential destination for Frederic (as well as several times later in the novel as a source of wine), is twenty miles south of Naples and twenty-two miles west of Amalfi in the Tyrrhenian Sea. A small island, just four miles long and two miles wide, with two towns, Capri and Anacapri, it has been popular as a resort since the ancient Roman emperors. When Hemingway and his first wife, Hadley, were making plans to move to Europe following their wedding in 1921, they considered living on Capri for a few months through the winter of 1921–22 and then moving to the Abruzzi in the spring (see *Letters 1* 290). These plans changed when they decided, on the advice of Sherwood Anderson, to live in Paris. There is no evidence that Hemingway ever visited Capri.

8:1–2 **Abruzzi ... Capracotta:** The Abruzzi is a mountainous region in central Italy. In 1915, the full name of the region was Abruzzi e Molise, but in 1963, it was split into two regions, Abruzzo and Molise. Capracotta today is in the northern sector of Molise near the border with Abruzzo. At 4,662 feet above sea level, it is among the highest villages in Italy. In 1916, the population was approximately forty-five hundred but has since declined to roughly a thousand.

Hemingway biographers have attempted to identify the source for the character of the priest in the novel, and most have concluded that the prototype is Don Giuseppe Bianchi, a priest from Florence (Baker, *Life Story* 44, 183; Mellow 346; Meyers, *Biography* 32, 184–85), possibly the priest who Hemingway claimed administered the sacrament of Extreme Unction to him shortly after he was wounded near the Piave River in 1918. However, Vincenzo Di Nardo, a native of Capracotta (the hometown of the priest in the novel), disagrees. He has identified a priest from Capracotta, Don Rodolfo d'Onofrio, who served as a soldier priest in the Ninth Health Company of the Italian Army, stationed in Bassano when Hemingway spent time there in the fall of 1918 following his convalescence from his wounding. The priest took the name "Padre Placido," and Di Nardo believes his personality corresponded to that of the priest in the novel. While it is possible that Hemingway may have met Padre Placido, there has been no evidence, as of this writing, that Hemingway actually crossed paths with him (see Di Nardo and Roos).

At the same time, it is possible the prototype for the priest and the description of the Abruzzi came from completely different sources. Di Nardo is convinced that the details the novel provides of the Abruzzi and Capracotta could have only come through firsthand knowledge of the region, and we know that Hemingway, like Frederic Henry, never visited the Abruzzi. We do know, however, that he was well acquainted with someone who was born in the Abruzzi and had family there during and after the war. This person was Nick Nerone (Hemingway spelled it *Neroni*), an Italian captain and war hero, whom Hemingway met in Italy in the fall of 1918 during their mutual convalescence from war wounds. Nerone's first name initially appears in a Hemingway letter to his family on 11 November 1918, the day of the armistice to end World War I:

> After my treatments are finished I've been invited by an Italian officer to take two weeks shooting and trout fishing in the province of Abruzzi. He wants me to spend Christmas and New Years at his country home and guarantees fine quail, pheasant and rabbit shooting. Abruzzi is very mountainous and is in the south of Italy and will be beautiful in December. There are also several good trout rivers and Nick claims the fishing is good. So I'll take my permission there. (*Letters 1* 150)

The letter makes clear that Nerone has been providing Hemingway with significant details about his place of origin. With his avid interest in hunting and fishing, it is easy to understand why spending the Christmas holidays there would have appealed to Hemingway. Although he repeated his intentions to his family on 28 November, a visit to the Abruzzi never happened. Hemingway instead took up an offer from his Red Cross associate James Gamble to spend time with him in Taormina, Sicily.

Hemingway would meet Nick Nerone again, however, back in America. In 1920–21, Nerone served at the Italian consulate in Chicago, and Hemingway renewed a close acquaintance with him. They became sparring partners, frequently boxing on the roof of the apartment building where Hemingway shared rooms with Y. K. Smith. When Hemingway became engaged to Hadley Richardson, the two of them planned to live in Italy as early as November 1921, with Naples and the Isle of Capri on their itinerary till the weather warmed in spring, at which time they planned to go up into the Abruzzi:

> Capracotta probably [Hemingway wrote in a letter to Grace Quinlan on his twenty-second birthday, 21 July 1921]—there's a fine trout stream there—the Sangro River—and tennis courts and it's 1200 meters above sea level—most wonder-

ful place you ever heard of. I've gotten all the dope on prices and so on from my best pal, Nick Neroni who's just come to this country, we were together in the war, and he's been staying around with me and given me all the dope. He's going back in the fall and will arrange everything for us. (*Letters 1* 290)

However, these plans also did not work out, since the newlywed Hemingways chose to live in Paris instead of Italy (see entry 7:39). Thus, Hemingway's relationship with Nick Nerone likely not only provided him with the details he used to describe the idyllic world of the Abruzzi in the novel, but also the idea of Frederic Henry's unfulfilled desire to go to the Abruzzi.

Hemingway may have attempted to repay Nerone by modeling the character of the obnoxious war hero Ettore Moretti, after him. See entry 104:23. Nerone eventually returned to Italy and joined the Fascist party under Benito Mussolini. Although Nerone and Hemingway seem not to have had any contact after 1921, Nerone's nephew claims that his uncle attempted to contact Hemingway during the latter's 1948 visit to Italy by asking his brother-in-law Ugo De Iorio to deliver a letter to Hemingway (Di Nardo, "Nick Nerone"). However, no trace of such a letter has been found.

8:16–19 "soto-tenente. . . . soto-colonello": The captain's finger games now make a joke about the effects of excessive sexual activity during Frederic's leave, using ranks in the Italian army. Hemingway misspells *sotto,* which means *sub* or *under.* Thus, a *sottotenente* corresponds to a second lieutenant in the American army, the lowest rank of a commissioned officer. Beginning with his thumb and ending with his little finger, the captain ascends the ranks thus:

Thumb: *sottotenente* (second lieutenant)
First Finger: *tenente* (lieutenant)
Next Finger (Middle Finger): *capitano* (captain)
Next to the Little Finger (Ring Finger): *maggiore* (major)
Little Finger: *tenente colonello* (lieutenant colonel)

The captain jests that Frederic will begin his leave as a *sottotenente* (second lieutenant) and return a *sottocolonello* (second colonel). To be consistent with the labeling of his fingers, he would mean that Frederic would return a *tenente colonello* (lieutenant colonel). The captain may be too drunk to keep his words straight, or it could be an undetected error on Hemingway's part. Regardless, the captain intends to imply that there is an inverse ratio of the size of a man and his rank. As Frederic Henry's size diminishes, presumably through all his sexual exertion, his rank in the army will increase. See Mark Cirino's "You Don't Know the Italian Language Well Enough" for a list of Hemingway's errors in rendering Italian words and Cirino's proposed changes for future editions of the novel (59).

8:27 **Caruso:** Enrico Caruso, Italian operatic tenor (1873–1921), along with Gabriele D'Annunzio, was one of the two most famous Italians in the world in the period prior to World War I. Between 1902 and 1920, he made more than 250 commercially released recordings. The officers' debate over the quality of his singing underscores the subjectivity of their experiences. Some like it; some do not. The reference also introduces the motif of music, specifically opera, that makes occasional appearance in the novel through the characters of the singers Ralph Simmons and Edgar Saunders. See entry 104:26.

8:37–38 **"Good-night" . . . "Good-night":** Frederic's ambivalent position between the officers' atheistic sensuality and the priest's faith is perfectly conveyed here, as Frederic, while heading to the brothel with the officers for sex, acknowledges the priest as he leaves. However, the priest's idea of a good night may not be the same as Frederic's at this point.

CHAPTER 3

9:1–3 When I came back . . . spring had come: Hemingway has elected not to provide us details of the still unnamed narrator's leave over the winter. For now, he holds us in suspense, wondering whose advice the narrator took for places to visit in Italy. We know immediately, however, that he has been gone for months, having left soon after the first snows of winter and now arriving with the coming of spring. The gap provides a historical sense of the degree to which the fighting shut down over the winter months. The armies remained in their defensive positions, but neither side attempted an offensive. It is now 1917, a pivotal year in the war historically and a very eventful year for Frederic Henry, as we shall see. The action will remain in 1917 until the final three chapters of the novel. The town is still Gorizia, as nothing has changed, except that the lull in the fighting has allowed both sides to fortify themselves with more guns. In other words, the imminence of great violence expected with the resumption of intense warfare has overshadowed the normal optimism that characterizes the onset of spring. As do chapters 1 and 2, chapter 3 begins with a detailed descriptive paragraph that helps convey the irony of spring and impending doom.

9:8–9 You met British men and sometimes women: This is one of the novel's few historical inaccuracies, but Hemingway needed to take this liberty in order to set up the beginning of the relationship between Frederic Henry and Catherine Barkley. The British Red Cross had been serving in Italy since early in the war, September 1915, but, as Michael Reynolds points out, there were no British nurses or VADs (Voluntary Aid Detachments) in Gorizia in 1916–17 (*First War* 95). Nor was there a Red Cross hospital in Gorizia. There was only one British Red Cross ambulance unit stationed there, made up of male drivers and mechanics. British soldiers and artillery did not arrive at the Italian front until the summer of 1917 (see Dalton 10). But Hemingway needed a way for Frederic to meet Catherine before he is wounded in chapter 9. Thus, Frederic's mentioning that he "sometimes" met British women on the street helps foreshadow her appearance in chapter 4.

9:18–21 the major sitting at his desk . . . I decided to go on upstairs: Presumably this is the same major who in chapter 2, recommended that the narrator should go to centers of culture and civilization—Rome, Naples, and Sicily—as opposed to the priest's primitive but idyllic homeland in the Abruzzi. The major's adamant rationalism and atheism was opposed to the priest's faith. As we learn on the next page, Frederic basically followed the major's advice during his leave and traveled to the centers of culture, never having visited the Abruzzi. Yet he here seems to be avoiding contact with the major. He decides instead that he needs to "clean up" first, an indication perhaps that he is returning with something of a guilty conscience.

10:1 **the lieutenant Rinaldi:** While the priest is the first character the reader sees in the novel (6:24–25), Rinaldi is the first character in the book who is given a name, one that seems to have held some fascination for Hemingway. Hugh Dalton's *British Guns in Italy* may have provided it. When Dalton's artillery tractor breaks down during the Caporetto Retreat, he gets help from a young mechanic:

> We went along at a fine pace for several miles and then our tractor stopped and wouldn't start up again. Whereupon there came to our assistance a young man named Rinaldo Rinaldi, a skilled and resourceful mechanic, who was driving a tractor in rear of us. He patched up our engine and got us going again. But we kept on breaking down after intervals never very long. Time after time Rinaldo Rinaldi came running up, smiling and eager to help. He patched us up and got us going six times. But at last he had to pass us and go on. For he, too, was drawing guns. I shall never forget Rinaldo Rinaldi and the cheerful help he gave us. (118)

At different times, Frederic, the priest, and Rinaldi himself refer to Rinaldi as Rinaldo, presumably as his first name. However, for this theory to be true, Hemingway would have to have read Dalton's book virtually as soon as it was published in 1919, the year he wrote a short story called "The Mercenaries," in which the narrator is named Rinaldi Renaldo (see Griffin 104–12). Hemingway used the name again in the chapter 6 vignette of *In Our Time*, written in 1923, in which Nick Adams and his fellow soldier, Rinaldi, have both been wounded. Nick jests, "Senta Rinaldi. Senta. You and me, we've made a separate peace" (*CSS* 106). For a different suggestion for the source of Rinaldi's name, see Linda Wagner-Martin (60).

Henry Villard believes that the character of Rinaldi (not the name) is based on Captain Enrico Serena, who was a frequent visitor at the American Red Cross Hospital in Milan during the time Hemingway was a patient there in 1918. Agnes von Kurowsky, the nurse with whom Hemingway fell in love and upon whom Catherine Barkley's character is partially based, accepted a dinner invitation from Captain Serena on the evening of 10 August 1918, the date of Hemingway's second operation on his wounded knee. Villard reports that the captain had "engaged a private dining room, complete with couch and piano," but Agnes resisted seduction on the grounds that she had to report back for duty by midnight (Villard and Nagel 33). Villard also courted Agnes during the summer of 1918. Michael Reynolds believes Captain Serena provided Hemingway with many stories of war experiences during their acquaintance at the Red Cross Hospital (*First War* 161).

10:11 **"Ciaou!"** A misspelling of *ciao,* the informal Italian word of greeting, used for both *hello* and *goodbye* (see Cirino, "You Don't Know" 59). The error also occurs at 63:19, 67:2, 107:27, 107:28, 157:34, and 157:35. Hemingway frequently repeated this error in his early letters, attempting to impress his readers with his knowledge of Italian (see, for example, *Letters 1* 187, 218). The *Oxford English Dictionary* credits *A Farewell to Arms* as the first use of the word in the English language.

10:16 **"You're dirty.... You ought to wash":** Frederic's dirtiness may be taken to imply more than being physically unclean. Ironically, the sensualist Rinaldi calls our attention to the fact that Frederic's lifestyle during his leave may have been immoral. Frederic's need for a bath may remind readers of *The Sun Also Rises,* in which the sexually promiscuous Brett Ashley expresses frequent desires to bathe and Jake Barnes tries and fails to draw a bath after serving as facilitator for her sexual affair with the matador Pedro Romero.

10:18–19 **I went everywhere. Milan, Florence, . . . Taormina:** Frederic, of course, has not gone everywhere, just the places that matter the most to him. Milan, Florence, Rome, and Naples are important Italian cities and centers of culture, major tourist draws and places with plenty of night life. The last three—Villa San Giovanni, Messina, and Taormina—indicate that he spent a substantial part of his time on the island of Sicily. Villa San Giovanni is the terminal port on the Italian mainland, across the Strait of Messina from the Sicilian city of Messina. Taormina is a beach resort further south from Messina on the eastern coast of Sicily. Hemingway would have visited these places when he spent a week at Taormina at the invitation of James Gamble in late December 1918, just before leaving Italy and returning to the United States (Baker, *Life Story* 55–56). The list excludes both the priest's hometown of Capracotta and Rinaldi's hometown of Amalfi.

10:27–28 **the Cova:** The Caffè Cova was founded in 1817 as a "literary café" and pasticceria (bakery) on the piazza of the grand La Scala opera house in Milan and therefore was celebrating its centennial at the time of the novel's action. Artists, intellectuals, politicians, journalists, and the upper crust of the city gathered to enjoy liquor, wine, espresso, cappuccino, and fine pastries in its lavish interior, noted for its "polychrome" floor, mirrors, and crystal chandeliers ("History of Excellence"). Later in the novel, after Frederic is wounded and sent to recuperate at the American hospital in Milan, the Cova will be within easy walking distance of the hospital. The Cova is also prominently mentioned in Hemingway's short story "In Another Country," where it is described as being "next door to La Scala" and a place "where it was rich and warm and not too brightly lighted, and noisy and smoky at certain hours, and there were always girls at the tables and the illustrated papers on a rack on the wall" (*CSS* 207–08). Hemingway would have had firsthand knowledge of the Cova, since he recuperated from his war wounds at the American Red Cross Hospital in Milan not far from the café. Baedeker's *Italy: From the Alps to Naples 1928* describes the Cova as a "smart establishment with a confectionary department and a pretty garden" (25). The Cova is still in business today, but at a new location. The building sustained heavy damage during World War II bombing of Milan and in 1950 moved a few blocks to the northeast of its original location.

10:31–34 **"Here now we have beautiful girls." . . . "You don't believe me?"**: Rinaldi's enthusiasm, in response to Frederic's terse description, has his little joke, the girls' newness, implying that they are virgins. Frederic's response, "Wonderful," must be sarcastic, since Rinaldi takes it as an expression of disbelief.

10:35 **English**: *British* would be a more accurate term than *English,* since at least one of the women, Miss Ferguson, is Scottish. There may also have been Irish, Welsh, and Canadian women among those serving in the British Red Cross on the Italian front.

10:35–37 **"I am now in love. . . . I will probably marry Miss Barkley"**: Rinaldi's talk of love and marriage is comical, since his character most fully represents the hardened, objective, materialist perspective. His feelings never truly rise above the level of lust. Of course, at this stage neither do Frederic's.

The other point to make here is the emphasis on the name of Miss Barkley, the second character to be named, while the narrator, Frederic Henry, still has not been named. Hemingway, through Rinaldi here, makes certain we learn Miss Barkley's name quickly and do not forget it, repeating it five times in the space of twenty-five lines. We do not learn of her first name, Catherine, until page 21, when Helen Ferguson addresses her (21:37). Two potential sources have been identified for "Barkley." One is Hemingway's friend the writer Barklie McKee "Buzz" Henry, sometimes cited, first by Henry himself, it seems, as the source for both characters' last names. Three years younger than Hemingway, Barklie Henry was a Harvard graduate whose one novel, *Deceit,* was published in 1924. That same year, he also married wealthy heiress Gertrude Vanderbilt Whitney and attended Balliol College, Oxford University, for a year. He probably met Hemingway in Paris sometime during this period. When *A Farewell to Arms* was published in 1929, Henry kidded Hemingway about using both his names for his characters. Hemingway responded jocularly, "By god I did name all the characters after you didnt I. McKee was the only one left out—I'll get that in next time" (*Letters 4* 182).

The other potential source, suggested by Peter Hays, is British philosopher Bishop George Berkeley, whose name is properly pronounced "Barkley." Hays speculates intriguingly that Berkeley's immaterialist philosophy, in which things only exist in our thoughts, is "adapted by Catherine in her relationship with Henry: she believes in their love, and so creates it" (105). If Hays is correct, then Catherine's last name adds to the conflict of reason and faith in a peculiarly ironic way. As we shall see, Catherine is an atheist, who does not believe in an afterlife and claims she has no religion, yet, in seeming contradiction to these traits, she is willing to explore supernaturalism with Frederic and seems to draw spiritual nourishment from her love for Frederic. See entry 99:13–16. It is possible that Hemingway is using her name to highlight one side of the polar opposite views of rationalist materialism and religious faith.

10:39 **chilblains:** A medical condition of tissue damage that is sometimes confused with frostbite. Its symptoms of redness, itching, and inflammation of the skin, especially toes, fingers, ears, and nose result from excessive exposure to cold and dampness.

11:1–2 **hard and soft chancres:** These are sexually transmitted ulcerated sores. Hard chancres, associated with the first stage of syphilis, have a hardened base and are painless. Soft chancres, also called chancroid, are a different bacterial infection from syphilis but are also spread through sexual contact and, in contrast to hard chancres, are painful. To summarize Rinaldi's list of diseases and the source of his work throughout the winter, the primary health issues are exposure to the harsh winter weather, hepatitis (jaundice), and sexual contact.

11:3–4 **Next week the war starts again:** On the Italian front, the fighting, much of which took place at higher elevations, was often controlled by the seasonal weather. When the snow arrived, the armies shut down for the winter, to renew again at the spring thaw. Frederic has arrived back at the front just in time, it seems, for the Tenth Battle of the Isonzo, which began on 12 May 1917 and lasted until 6 June. It is during the initial stage of this battle that Frederic will be seriously wounded.

11:13: **He loved being a surgeon and we were great friends:** Frederic here highlights Rinaldi's role as rationalist—the medical doctor/surgeon—who will assume the position as primary spokesperson for the rationalist worldview in the novel. As indicated by his phrase *we were great friends,* Frederic's attachment to Rinaldi is certainly at least equal to his attachment to the priest, who serves as the spokesperson for the opposing worldview, that of religious faith.

11:17 **fifty lire:** Given an exchange rate of 7.51 lire for one US dollar in 1917, fifty lire would have equaled $6.66, which would have the purchasing power of $127 in 2017 (the most recent year for which data is available). All determinations of exchange rates and relative worth are taken from Samuel Williamson's website *Measuring-Worth.com,* and tools provided there.

11:24 **"Go to hell":** Frederic's response should be taken as good-natured, considering he has loaned Rinaldi money without hesitation. This exchange also helps set up Frederic's comparable relationship to the priest, which is highlighted in the immediately succeeding paragraphs.

11:25–26 **the priest . . . not gone to the Abruzzi:** As we have already pointed out in reference to Hemingway's relationship with Nick Nerone (see entry 8:1–2), there is significant autobiographical experience behind Frederic's unfulfilled desire to go the Abruzzi. It is unknown whether Hemingway had to explain uncomfortably to Nerone why he never went to the Abruzzi, as Frederic Henry must to the priest, but certainly his reasons would not have been the same as Frederic's.

The Abruzzi region is a nearly perfect selection for the home country of the novel's primary exemplar of religious faith, who is presented in contrast with Rinaldi, the exemplar of science and reason. Though most commentators have accepted at face value the priest's idealization of his home country in the Abruzzi (and Capracotta native Vincenzo Di Nardo confirms that the area is truly idyllic), they fail to take into account that the region is also a distinctly harsh representation of a destructive and irresolvable duality. The region, which includes the central range of the Apennine Mountains running down the length of Italy, sits atop the conjunction of two tectonic plates—the Adriatic and the Tyrrhenian. These two colliding plates are the forces that have not only produced the peaks of the Apennines, the highest of which exist in the Abruzzi, but have also created a series of fault lines that have produced periodic dramatically violent and very deadly earthquakes. Although the 1920s were relatively quiet, with no major earthquake recorded in the region between 1920 and 1930, a ferocious 6.7-scale earthquake hit the region in January 1915, only four months before Italy's entrance into the Great War, essentially wiping out the Abruzzi city of Avezzano and killing thirty thousand people. Avezzano is only forty-five miles as the crow flies from the priest's hometown in Capracotta. The death toll places it as the ninth deadliest earthquake in the world since 1900, the second deadliest ever in Italy. Sudden natural disasters such as this always bring the clash of science and faith to the fore and raise the question of God's benevolence. See, for example, Voltaire's satiric treatment in *Candide* of the Great Lisbon Earthquake of 1755, and its death toll of between thirty and forty thousand.

The 1915 Avezzano quake made headlines in newspapers around the world. Hemingway was enough of a scientist to have plausibly known something of the geology of Italy and its history of earthquakes. Certainly, the region was, and remains to some extent even today, relatively isolated and unspoiled by corrupting influences of the modern world. Population, especially in the mountains, has declined in the past hundred years, and poverty is widespread. Its isolation, no doubt, would help to keep religious faith relatively untainted by the forces of the modern world. However, the prevalence of deadly earthquakes must be reckoned with. In fact, as this entry was being written (late January 2017), another series of powerful quakes, of magnitude from 5.2 to 5.7, had just struck the Abruzzo region, causing an avalanche that killed twenty-nine people in a hotel in Farindola, forty-eight miles north of Capracotta as the crow flies. While we cannot be certain that Hemingway was aware of this history of earthquakes in the region or whether he had any knowledge of the causes of earthquakes, it is noteworthy that the clash of tectonic plates in central Italy appropriately resonates with the novel's emphasis on the clash of dualities—especially the irreconcilable conflict of science and faith.

At the very least, the Abruzzi represents the past, the old world that the modern world has left behind. As a man of the modern world, Frederic cannot go back to that simpler past. He is stuck in the much more complicated modern world. Henry Adams, one of Frederic Henry's possible namesakes, articulated this reality in his great works *Mont Sainte Michele and Chartres* and *The Education of Henry Adams* as well as his lesser-known novel *Esther*.

11:32 **afterward coffee and Strega:** Strega (a trade name meaning *witch* in Italian) is a yellowish herbal liqueur from the Campania region of Italy, which includes Naples, Capri, and Amalfi, Lieutenant Rinaldi's hometown (Greene 271). See entry 7:36. Typically 80 proof (40 percent alcohol), Strega is normally considered a digestif—that is, an after-dinner drink, as opposed to an aperitif, or before-dinner drink. In Italy, especially northern Italy, where the novel takes place, it is customary to follow a meal with coffee and a liqueur like Strega or grappa. See entry 15:15. Intended to dull the taste or caffeine effect of the coffee, the liqueur may be served in its own glass or used to rinse the coffee cup. The Italians call it *ammazzacaffè*.

12:10 **sometimes a dispute about the cost:** This highly charged swirl of erotic excitement—"so exciting that you must resume again"—delivers an abrupt "jolt," as we suddenly realize that Frederic must pay for these experiences (Wagner-Martin 58–59). What he is describing is certainly lust, not love. Later, after he has fallen in love with Catherine (see entry 81:24–26), he informs us he "had not wanted to fall in love with any one." At this starting point in his development, Frederic, from all indications, does not know how to look for real love.

12:14 **the difference between the night and the day:** In the context of this novel, the night represents the realm of the subjective (and, by extension, faith) and the day the realm of the objective (rationality). At this stage, Frederic prefers the night because it frees him from the harsh realities of the day, which brings with it disputes about the cost (and other painful details). The night, which is "all unreal," is strangely exciting and carefree. As he says, the night is better "unless the day was very clean and cold," that is, unless the objective reality was easy to identify and understand. The problem is that objective reality is rarely so clear.

12:15–17 I could not tell it. . . . But if you have had it you know: This passage and the more famous one a few lines later beg the question of when this story is being written or told to us and how much Frederic Henry has changed since the time of his conversation with the priest. In other words, when is the "now" of 12:16? Frederic insists to the priest that there is an important difference between the night and the day and that the night is better unless the day is very clean and cold. As discussed in entry 12:14, the night seems to represent the realm of the subjective, the realm of irrationality and religious faith, whereas the day seems to represent the realm of the objective and reason. For Frederic, the night is the time where he escapes from the brutal realities of the day—the world of pain, suffering, and death—where he escapes with the help of the short-term pleasures of the flesh: alcohol and sex. In addition, and somewhat conversely, the night later, after his wounding, becomes the time when he fears God—the only time he seems to admit that he has any faith. Because the realm of the night is so subjective, to "tell" about it, using his rational mind and language, is difficult, if not impossible. That Frederic cannot tell the priest about it and feels as if he cannot tell it now to us, his readers, suggests that in this elemental attitude toward the night Frederic has not changed. In other words, considering the use of the time reference *now* and the verb tenses in these two sentences, this difference between the night and the day seems to exist still as Frederic is writing this passage and conveying it to us years after the fact. He thus suggests that nothing he has learned through the entirety of the experiences of the novel seems to have contradicted what he knew then about the difference between the night and the day. "If you have had it," he tells us, "you know." This, naturally, falls under the category of subjective knowledge, based solely on personal experience. However, that does not mean we should not take him seriously. Considering all the times in the novel that Frederic says he does not know, we should pay attention anytime he tells us he knows something, even if it comes out of subjective rather than objective experience. The priest, he reminds us significantly, "had not had it" and therefore cannot possess this kind of subjective knowledge, though he does have other kinds of subjective knowledge, for which Frederic clearly values their friendship.

12:17–18 he understood that I had really wanted to go to the Abruzzi: Frederic's insistence that he "had really wanted to go to the Abruzzi but had not gone" tacitly admits to a duality in his character, for it would be naive and foolish to think that, even if he genuinely wanted to go to the Abruzzi, he did not also wish to visit the places he did, the cities of the flesh, Milano, Roma, Napoli—places quite different from the clear cold pure environment of the Abruzzi. Thus, these places are yet another kind of representation of the dichotomy of subjectivity and objectivity, faith and reason, the night and the day.

12:19–22 **He had always known . . . although I learned it later:** How we interpret these two challenging and important sentences depends entirely on how we define the verb *to know* and to identify the antecedents of the pronouns *what, it,* and *that.* This is more complicated than it might seem at first glance. First, with *to know,* we need to recognize that there is objective knowledge and there is subjective knowledge. Objective knowledge pertains to verifiable facts upon which we can all agree—what epistemology calls a "justified true belief" (Dew and Foreman 24). Two plus two equals four. The earth is the third planet from the sun. Ernest Hemingway was born on 21 July 1899. Subjective knowledge, though, is much more slippery. It consists of thoughts that we may regard as truths but that only our own unique experiences, not anything outside of ourselves, can establish. We may still hold these to be justified true beliefs and cling to them fiercely, although these truths may well contradict other people's subjective knowledge. Sometimes we can only trust in these truths by a kind of leap of faith. There is no way of knowing in an objective sense if our subjective knowledge agrees with the subjective knowledge of anyone else. And, indeed, with some people, it may not even matter.

In this instance, since Frederic refers to knowledge that, when he learned it, he "was always able to forget," he must necessarily be speaking of subjective knowledge. In the process, he is acknowledging that the priest is able to make a leap of faith that he, Frederic, was unable to make in the past. This is the "what" of the first sentence of the passage, which can be translated thus: "He, the priest, had always had faith in the truth of his own experiences." For the priest, in other words, there is no difference between subjective truth and objective truth. For Frederic, it seems, in contrast, the truth of each individual experience was soon lost and had to be relearned, only to be forgotten again. In that stage, he, too, cannot know the difference between subjective and objective truth, and because he is unable to make the leap of faith that the priest makes, he has to relearn these truths with each new experience, only to forget them again. It is also possible that Frederic is just being disingenuous as an unreliable narrator, who, when he says he was "always able to forget," really means he was "always able to ignore."

Now we come to the ambiguity of the pronouns *that* and *it* in the passage's second sentence. Most commentators assume that the second sentence means that Frederic eventually learned what the priest has always known and has not forgotten it—that is, he has not forgotten what he had previously always been able to forget. For some interpreters, it simply means that Frederic has eventually reached (by the time of his writing of the novel) the kind of faith that the priest has (see Stoneback, "Lovers' Sonnets Turn'd to Holy Psalms"; Nickel). That may indeed be one legitimate way to interpret the second sentence, but it is not the only way to interpret it. It is just as legitimate to say that what Frederic did not know then but has since learned is that the priest has always had that kind of faith in the truth of his subjective experience. In these terms, what Frederic has learned is not the ability to have faith but instead the difference between subjective and objective truth. From this perspective, Frederic still does not have the kind of faith the priest has. He simply recognizes that the two realms of knowledge—the subjective and the objective—are different. He also still recognizes, according to this reading, that he and the priest are different. Frederic's awareness of this difference is highlighted in a passage that Hemingway excised from the beginning of chapter 40. See entry 262:1. In that passage, Frederic acknowledges that he and the priest are not "built" in the same way. Once we establish these two variant readings of this passage, the next goal is to consider carefully which of these the rest of the novel supports.

For Joyce Wexler, the meaning of the passage is simpler: what the priest has always known and what Frederic has always been able to forget when he learned it is the difference between lust and love (120). In this interpretation, Frederic knows the true meaning of love because Catherine Barkley has taught it to him. Wexler also argues that passages like this one, where Frederic is clearly speaking in the present, at the time of the writing, years after the events of the novel, are important to the work's theme because they show us how much Frederic has grown and matured as a character (121). Thus, in Wexler's view, the novel should be read as a eulogy to Catherine, to honor her for what he has learned from her. As Wexler recognizes, the priest sees the potential for love in Frederic, but Catherine is the one who "enables him to realize" the potential (120).

12:30–35 **"The priest wants us never to attack."** . . . **"He's all right"**: The captain here renews the charge that the priest is not loyal to the Italian cause. See entry 7:15. The priest is a pacifist and seems less content when the war is going strongly and soldiers are full of fighting spirit. The captain, who declares vehemently, "Must attack. Shall attack!" is clearly a patriot in the mold of Gabriele D'Annunzio. Later, when the soldiers are demoralized about the war, the priest gets more sanguine, with optimism that the war may end soon. Curiously, the major, who in chapter 2 is defiant and aggressive in declaring his atheism against the priest's faith, here seems more gentle and comes to the priest's defense.

CHAPTER 4

13:1 **battery:** A fortified emplacement of several artillery guns, which can be fired together in salvo fashion or serially one after another. Frederic is awakened by their firing. This is another detail that Hemingway likely found in G. M. Trevelyan's *Scenes from Italy's War*. As Trevelyan explains, "Gorizia and its pleasant villa suburbs were honeycombed with batteries that barked and roared night after night. The guns were packed so closely that they were often near enough to the hospitals and dressing-stations to offer some excuse for the destruction by enemy bombardment of one after another of the sanctuaries protected by the Red Cross sign" (111).

13:2–9 **the sun coming through . . . motor truck starting on the road:** Frederic again notes features of the natural world around him and the machinery of war—death in the midst of life (or the paradox of the function of ambulances and their crews to preserve life)—another emblem of Leo Marx's *The Machine in the Garden*. Hemingway may also be reminding us of Frederic's lustful lifestyle, with the phallicism of the firing guns, which cause the front of his pajamas to flap.

Italian field artillery in World War I ranged from 65 millimeters to as large as 305 millimeters in caliber (Gooch 50–51, 79–80). However, the most common cannon size was 75 millimeters, and, given Frederic's description, it seems likely these are 75 millimeter guns, plenty large enough, with their proximity, to wake up forcefully anyone who happens to be sleeping in the building next door.

13:13 **blunt-nosed ambulances:** In this chapter, for the first time, we learn the still unnamed narrator's role in the war. He is an English-speaking lieutenant attached to the Italian army in charge of an ambulance group.

13:17 **"Signor Tenente":** Literally, Italian for "Sir Lieutenant," as for example on 170:9 but more naturally in English "Lieutenant, Sir."

13:20 **"on permission?"** Frederic has been on official leave, meaning he had permission to be absent. The word *permission* also implies the recurrent problem the Italian army had with deserters, men who left the front lines without permission.

According to the army's official archives, 11,598 Italian soldiers were charged with desertion in the war zone between June and December 1916 (Gooch 170). As a result, Supreme Commander General Luigi Cadorna declared that his commanders were to resort to decimation, that is, to draw lots for summary executions. In 1916, there were 83 summary executions and 242 standard executions without a trial. Another 761 soldiers who had deserted received death sentences in absentia (170). Questioned by the Italian parliament, Cadorna defended the policy of decimation, insisting that "Modern mass armies 'with improvised officers and soldiers' were less solid than in the past; modern wars, which were longer and harder than in the past, 'inevitably provoke[d] acts of indiscipline'; and finally soldiers came from backgrounds which for many years had educated them to indiscipline" (qtd. in Gooch 171). The situation did not improve the next year, the year of the Caporetto Retreat and Frederic Henry's desertion. If anything, it worsened. Mark Thompson, in *The White War*, calls 1917, the year of this chapter and all but three that follow, "the year of decimation" (263). So it is certain that Frederic and his mechanics in this exchange are aware of what would probably happen to any of them if they were to leave the front lines without permission. Here and elsewhere, Hemingway uses expressions in stilted or non-idiomatic English to suggest the speech of characters who are not bilingual. The Italian word for *leave* is *permesso*, so *permission* is as close to a literal translation as possible.

14:1–2 **"You have a good time?" The others all grinned too:** This remark not so subtly reveals how class or rank distinctions may be subverted. The soldiers would not ask a superior officer if he had had sex during his leave, but the question and Frederic's response, "Fine," tell them what they want to know and evoke their grins.

14:18–19 **Evidently it did not matter whether I was there or not:** This sentence effectively conveys Frederic's sense of detachment from his surroundings and his lack of central purpose.

14:23 **gasoline park**: A refueling and servicing site, not a place of recreation.

14:26 **bowl of coffee:** In this case, a *bowl* is a multipurpose dish, probably without a handle, not uncommon among the lower classes. As is typical with Hemingway, Frederic provides sensuous description of the appearance ("pale gray") and taste ("sweet with condensed milk") of the drink.

14:31 **The whole thing seemed to run better while I was away:** This also underscores the degree to which Frederic Henry is peripheral to the events in the war. He is a true outsider.

14:34 see about the posts for during the attack: The major orders Frederic to check out places to post the ambulances during the attack, presumably a well-protected spot that would enable the drivers to get to the wounded in a timely fashion. The details of the planned attack correspond to the historical Tenth Battle of the Isonzo, which consisted of two main thrusts by the Italians: one on the Carso plateau to the southeast of Gorizia, with hopes of creating a breakthrough to Trieste, and the other to the north of Gorizia, with the aim of capturing Monte San Gabriele. Frederic will be part of the northern thrust. Below Monte San Gabriele, the Austrians still controlled the western shore of the Isonzo River. As Frederic states, the attack would "cross the river up above the narrow gorge and spread up the hillside," the slopes of San Gabriele.

14:39 false feeling of soldiering: Frederic knows that the infantry commanders, with greater senses than he has of battle plans and what will be needed during the attack, will actually decide where the ambulance posts will be located. But working on the project at least makes Frederic feel somewhat like a soldier, even with certain delusions.

15:1 I was very dusty and dirty and went up to my room to wash: This reminds us again of Frederic's spiritual condition at this stage in the novel, prior to meeting Catherine Barkley. See entry 10:16.

15:2–3 Hugo's English grammar: This text is part of the pervasive theme of language, its uses and abuses in the novel, even when, as here, Rinaldi is intent on improving his language proficiency. Hugo's Language Institute has long published textbooks for learning many different world languages.

15:14 Not Strega: Probably still hungover from the night before, Frederic may be associating Strega with the unpleasant experience he had in trying to explain to the priest why he had not visited the Abruzzi during his leave. See entry 11:32.

15:15 Grappa: Instead of Strega, they drink grappa, the generic name for an Italian brandy distilled from pomace—the skins, pulp, seeds, and stems of grapes left over from the process of winemaking (Greene 270). Often harsh in flavor, grappa can vary from 35 to 60 percent alcohol in content. Like Strega, it is normally a digestif, an after-dinner drink, designed to aid digestion. Since Frederic describes the grappa as "very strong" (15:18), we can assume it is in the high range of alcohol content. In spite of its strength, Frederic agrees to a second glass.

15:17–18 first fingers extended: The touching of glasses with first fingers extended is an Italian way of saluting one's companion.

15:23–24 The British hospital . . . built by Germans before the war: Not everything in the novel is historically accurate. This detail is an example of how Hemingway thoroughly researched his story for accuracy but fictionalized some details when it suited his purposes. As Michael Reynolds has pointed out, there was no British hospital in Gorizia in 1917 (*First War* 95). When the Italians took Gorizia, the British Red Cross hospital remained in Cormons, approximately nine miles to the west, on the other side of the Isonzo. Only one British Red Cross ambulance unit was moved to Gorizia. Hemingway would have found this detail in Hugh Dalton's memoir, *With British Guns in Italy,* published in 1919. The drivers of that unit stayed in an old boardinghouse on the Via Ponte Isonzo "with a large untidy garden behind" (56). There would not have been British Red Cross nurses in Gorizia in 1917, but, since Hemingway needed to bring Frederic and Catherine Barkley together, he created the fiction that the British converted one of the old German villas (which Dalton describes) into a hospital.

15:24 Miss Barkley was in the garden: This initial meeting of the protagonist and the woman who will become his paramour is set, romantically, among trees "in the garden" of a villa. We will not suggest that Frederic and Catherine are Adam and Eve, but it seems likely that this first announcement of Catherine's appearance is intended to associate her with an Edenic quality. Of course, the paradise of the Book of Genesis ends with a fall. Hemingway would ultimately apply the Genesis story to his posthumously published novel *The Garden of Eden,* an ironic exploration of some of the darker corners of human sexuality. To amplify the inference, we should note that Rinaldi later identifies himself as the "snake of reason." See entry 149:15. In other words, the layers of potential meaning here are numerous and difficult to sort out, and they depend a great deal on whether we read Hemingway's words as ironic.

15:26 I saluted too but more moderately: Italian officers in the Great War were stereotyped for their fashionable, even operatic uniforms and sometimes their accompanying manners. Here Frederic makes a little joke about Rinaldi's undescribed salute.

15:27–28 "You're not an Italian, are you?" Catherine Barkley's first words may sound oddly antagonistic for an initial meeting, but they immediately address what will be one of the central motifs of their many exchanges of thoughts and desires: Who are we, you and I? The question of identity. In addition, we should put Catherine's question in the context of Rinaldi's later expression of what it means to be Italian, that is, "all fire and smoke, with nothing inside." See entry 57:20–23. To be an Italian in Rinaldi's terms is to be wholly invested in reason, rejecting the realm of faith. So, Catherine may be intuitively aware that Frederic differs significantly from the Italian Rinaldi, in a way she finds appealing. These issues of reason and faith, objectivity and subjectivity, are the central focus of the novel and, in addition to the question of identity, will help define the relationship of Frederic and Catherine.

15:32 **"not really the army. It's only the ambulance"**: Frederic is highlighting the fact that he is not really a soldier—that he is not fully invested in the rationale for fighting this war.

15:33–36 **"Why did you do it?" . . . "I was brought up to think there was"**: This exchange is one of many that highlight the question of what can be known and what cannot be known, and, as such, it introduces the epistemic theme of the novel. Frederic here readily admits his lack of self-knowledge, his lack of subjective knowledge. He cannot provide a reasonable explanation for why he joined the Italians in the war. Yet Catherine seems to disagree or at least to assert that she was taught that there is a reason for everything, implying that Frederic should know himself well enough to be able to explain his behavior in this case. Nevertheless, he is unwilling to pursue the topic, an indication that he is not interested in self-examination at this point. The epistemic theme will remain a central focus throughout the novel.

16:2–4 **quite tall . . . gray eyes:** Frederic's description of Catherine Barkley seems quite close, except for the hair color, to the description Henry Villard provides for Agnes von Kurowsky, the Red Cross nurse with whom the eighteen-year-old Ernest Hemingway fell in love in the hospital in Milan after he was wounded. Villard and Nagel describe Agnes as a "tall, slender, chestnut-haired girl with friendly blue-gray eyes" (3).

Catherine Barkley is essentially a conglomeration of three or even four women: Agnes von Kurowsky; Hadley Richardson Hemingway, Ernest's first wife, with whom he shared romantic times in Switzerland and in Italy; Elsie Jessup, another nurse at the hospital, who, similar to Catherine Barkley, carried a cane and was in love with a soldier who had been killed (Reynolds, *First War* 174); and Pauline Pfeiffer Hemingway, Ernest's second wife, who was pregnant with his child as he began writing the book and experienced a difficult labor and caesarian section as he was roughly halfway through the first draft.

16:5 **a thin rattan stick like a toy riding-crop:** Catherine is probably holding a swagger stick, a short stick carried especially by officers in the British army as a symbol of authority. Rattan is a climbing palm tree with long thin branches, which are used in the making of swagger sticks. So why does Hemingway not just call it a "swagger stick," a term with connotations of authority and self-confidence? Given the stick's phallic nature, that Hemingway (Frederic) compares it to a "toy riding-crop" (even Catherine calls it a "little stick"), and that it is a memento of Catherine's previous lover would all seem to imply the sexual immaturity of that love, a condition borne out by the fact that Catherine and the boy (note that he is repeatedly referred to as a "boy") apparently never consummated their eight-year relationship and engagement. In other words, Catherine, we should understand, is a virgin. Carrying her dead fiancé's "little stick" around reminds her constantly of what she denied him.

16:10 **the Somme:** Catherine's fiancé was killed in a horrific battle that took place on the Western Front near the Somme River in France in the summer of 1916. Therefore, as this meeting with Frederic takes place, it is now less than a year since her fiancé was killed. The battle was indeed a "ghastly show," as Frederic asserts, possibly unwittingly attempting to imitate stereotypical upper-class British language, rather than describe it as an objective American might otherwise, as a battle. On 1 July 1916, the British and French armies attacked the Germans along a twenty-five-mile front near the Somme. The cost in casualties was the highest of any single day of battle in World War I. On the British side alone, 20,000 men were killed and 25,000 more were wounded. The fighting continued till November 1916. All totaled, nearly 100,000 British and 50,000 French soldiers lost their lives on the Somme. The Germans lost more than 160,000.

16:19–20 **"And why didn't you marry?" "I don't know. I was a fool not to":** An epistemic turnabout is fair play. Frederic has his own "why" question for Catherine, and she reveals a similar lack of self-knowledge, although she seems to have learned something. If she had it to do over again, it is clear she would have married him.

16:20–21 **"I could have given him that anyway":** Here, Catherine could be referring to marriage or only to sex. Either way, she seems to believe it would have required little effort on her part, compared to the sacrifice of her fiancé's life.

16:21 **"I thought it would be bad for him":** Catherine does provide a feeble reason here for not marrying her fiancé, one that she now recognizes does not hold up. Her reasoning, however, reminds us of Rinaldi's previous insistence that he intends to marry Miss Barkley, "after the war, of course" (11:5). Some people argue that soldiers should not make widows by marrying before going off to war. In Hemingway's brilliant short story "In Another Country," which is related in theme to *A Farewell to Arms,* an Italian major, who is recuperating from a war wound and had been careful not to marry until he was permanently disabled out of the war, grieves for the sudden, completely unexpected death of his wife from pneumonia and concludes, as a result, that "a man must not marry" (*CSS* 208). Catherine's reasoning, of course, inverts the wisdom of not marrying to avoid making widows—unless she is not being truthful and in fact refused to marry in order to prevent herself from becoming a widow, a case that would explain her level of guilt. Recall that Hemingway seems to have considered as an epigraph for his novel the following sentence: "The position of the survivor of a great calamity is seldom admirable." See the entry Epigraphs (Unused). While the statement applies to Frederic Henry at the end of this novel, Catherine seems to be dealing here with a similar kind of guilt.

16:23–24 **"Have you ever loved any one?" "No":** It is important to note Frederic's own inexperience in matters of true love. He is remarkably honest in this respect. He says something similar in conversation later with the priest. See entry 62:26.

16:26 **"You have beautiful hair":** This may appear an unoriginal pickup line, but the novel will show that Frederic Henry does have a thing about hair, as Carl Eby has carefully explored in *Hemingway's Fetishism*. Most important, Frederic's comment emphasizes how his attraction to Catherine at this point is based primarily on her appearance.

16:29 **"I was going to cut it all off when he died":** As both Carl Eby and Marc Hewson have suggested, Catherine's cutting her hair off after the death of her fiancé would have been a form of penance for refusing to give up her virginity to him (Eby 84; Hewson 58). That she apparently thought better of it and did not cut her hair may indicate that she is open to new relationships in the future.

16:32 **"the other thing and he could have had it all":** The other thing is, of course, sex. Given what we know about Frederic Henry's pursuit of sexual pleasures, we can assume this acknowledgement from Catherine stirs his desire.

16:34–37 **"I know all about it now. . . . I didn't know about anything then":** This is another admission by Catherine that she was ignorant in the past, suggesting, therefore, that she has learned a valuable lesson from the loss of her fiancé. In consequence, she is a phase ahead of Frederic Henry in her personal development, since he has not yet experienced such a loss. The sentence "But then he wanted to go to war and I didn't know" is not in the manuscript and was added later (JFK item 64).

16:39 **"killed and that was the end of it":** Catherine means that there is no afterlife following death. She has no hope of seeing her fiancé again and being able to make up to him what she withheld.

17:1 **"I don't know":** This is one of the novel's key moments, an exchange that gets at the epistemic crux of the conflict in the narrative. As Frederic does so often (twenty-three times, to be exact), he expresses his inability to know something. In this most important case, there is even some lovely ambiguity in what he is referring to. Is he suggesting that the death of Catherine's fiancé is not the end of the possibility of love and sex? Or is he questioning whether death is the end of human existence? Hemingway probably took pleasure in the thought that his readers could not *know* with certainty what Frederic is thinking. Both meanings apply. If he means the former, it suggests that Frederic is thinking of seduction, seeing Catherine as little more than an object for his sexual pleasure and insinuating to her that he would be more than happy to stand in for her dead lover if she should like to share her previously withheld sexual favors. But the novel is concerned with far more than the consummation of sexual desire.

If Frederic is to win any kind of sympathy from us here, we should not ignore the possibility that when he says, "I don't know," he is referring to his inability to know about the continued existence of the soul after death. Thus, interpreted this way, his response would suggest agnosticism on the subject. He does not know enough to have reached a conclusion concerning whether there is life after death. As we have said, there are things we can know and things we cannot know. There are also objective truths and subjective truths: truths that can be verified by others and beliefs that we hold to be true without being able to prove them to others. The existence or nonexistence of an immortal soul must necessarily fall under the category of subjective truth: something that cannot be proven or disproven. Frederic will continue to ponder that basic question throughout the novel.

17:2 **"Oh, yes. . . . That's the end of it"**: In contrast to Frederic, Catherine is certain, and there is no ambiguity in what she means. In this case, she knows what she knows. She is referring to the existence of an immortal soul, and she is clearly not agnostic. Of course, it is impossible for us to know how she knows this, and she makes no attempt to explain to Frederic how she does. It is subjective, an article of her kind of faith.

17:15 **"Since the end of 'fifteen. I started when he did"**: Catherine establishes the length of time she has been serving as a nurse, having entered the service at the end of 1915, at the same time her fiancé entered the British army. The beginning of their service, then, was a little over a year after the war began.

17:19 **"This is the picturesque front"**: The irony of Frederic's statement may be unintentional. The massed artillery, suicidal frontal attacks, poison gas, and desperate trench warfare in France also characterized the Italian front, which most assuredly had its share of carnage, as both Frederic and Catherine will learn in the months ahead. With its mountainous landscape and the blue waters of the Isonzo, the Italian front may have been visually beautiful, but as Mark Thompson has attested, it was the scene of "some of the most savage fighting of the Great War" (1). In just over three years of warfare, the Italians suffered more than nine hundred thousand dead and wounded, with a similar number on the Austrian side, all for Italy to gain about thirty kilometers of territory, hardly numbers that suggest the picturesque (4–5). So Frederic's comment says more about what he has to learn than it does about the nature of the war in Italy. Thus, he may still be under the same kind of romantic delusions that Catherine Barkley was before her fiancé was so brutally killed on the French front. In *The Sun Also Rises,* Jake Barnes refers to the Italian front as a "joke front," but his comment is a sardonic attempt to make light of his war wound, the emasculating loss of his penis, as he piloted a plane over a battlefield (31). As Richard Cantwell says in *Across the River and into the Trees,* "The hell with picturesque" (34).

17:21–22 **"He didn't have a sabre cut. They blew him all to bits":** Catherine seems to have taken a scene from romantic novels for her imagination of how her fiancé would be wounded—something "picturesque," as she calls it. However, the reality of modern warfare has not only blown her fiancé's body to bits; it has also blown her romantic notions to bits, with the side effect of destabilizing her psyche.

17:23 **I didn't say anything:** Eight times in the novel, Frederic tells us that he "didn't say anything." Each instance occurs following a remark by another character, and Hemingway leaves it to us to interpret Frederic's silence. In this case, it could mean that he simply does not know how to respond to such a blunt and brutal description of her fiancé's death.

17:27–33 **"It will crack somewhere" . . . "Anybody may crack":** Hemingway provides seven "cracks" in seven lines. Something is going on here. Frederic begins with "*It* will crack," presumably meaning there will be a weak spot in the battle front and one side will exploit it for a breakthrough that will lead to an end of the war. Catherine, however, as the more emotionally and psychologically fragile character at this stage, is the first to apply a personal pronoun, "*We'll* crack," implying that the cracking has a psychological component, a break*down* by one side that leads to a break*through* by the other. She attaches the idea of cracking to the horrors that occurred during the battle of the Somme, where her fiancé was killed in 1916. Her logic is that so much trauma must lead inevitably to a crack-*up,* as it apparently has for her. Frederic, the detached and more psychologically secure, if flawed, person here, is confident that there will not be such a breakdown on the Italian front. As we will learn in Book 3, he is spectacularly wrong about this. During the Battle of Caporetto, the Italians will "crack" in a very big way. Catherine, thus, is more insightful when she says, knowing from experience, "Anybody may crack," though she retreats somewhat in considering the Germans, who were generally regarded as the most militaristic pro-war nation involved in the conflict. For an account of a personal breakdown, see F. Scott Fitzgerald's "The Crack-Up," published in 1936.

18:1 **"Abbastanza bene"**: Frederic's Italian translation means "Pretty good" in English, not as enthusiastic as Ferguson's insistence that she loves Italy "Quite well." The language gets garbled throughout this exchange.

18:7 **"But Scotland is England"**: Rinaldi demonstrates that his knowledge of British geography is no better than his knowledge of the English language. Scotland and England are separate parts of the United Kingdom (along with Wales and Northern Ireland) that share a common language (Gaelic and Scots speakers in Scotland notwithstanding).

18:9 **"Pas encore"**: Presumably searching for a language she and Rinaldi can mutually understand, Ferguson here speaks French, meaning "not yet," which Rinaldi shows that he essentially understands.

18:11 **"We do not like the English"**: Scottish enmity for the English dates at least to the Middle Ages, with a long history of religious, political, social, and economic rivalry between England and Scotland.

18:12–13 **"Not like the English?"** . . . **"mustn't take everything so literally"**: It is clear from this exchange that Rinaldi and Ferguson both understand Catherine to be English, whereas Ferguson is Scottish. We make this point because Catherine's nationality gets confusing later in the text. Whether Hemingway was confused about Catherine's region of origin is debatable. See entries 99:32 and 110:8–10.

18:16 **"the little Scotch one"**: In another bit of evidence that Catherine Barkley and Helen Ferguson are not of the same nationality, Rinaldi distinguishes between the two women, implying that Ferguson is Scotch and Catherine is not.

18:17–18 **"Very"** . . . **"No," said Rinaldi**: These last two lines are not in the manuscript. Instead there is the line "I felt I had been talking a part in a bad play."

CHAPTER 5

19:2 She was not in the garden: It is not clear why Frederic should think that Catherine would be in the garden again in the middle of the afternoon during working hours, but the phrase is perhaps an indication that his notion of paradise at this point is a delusion.

19:4–5 "there's a war on, you know." I said I knew: After establishing the novel's epistemological theme in the previous chapter, Hemingway reminds us of the centrality of this issue with this exchange between Frederic and the head nurse. The existence of the war, of course, is an objective fact. But the head nurse is reminding Frederic not just of something obvious, but also that the existence of a war has its consequences. There will be wounded and sick for a nurse to care for. Since Frederic is in the same line of work as the nurse, he should not need to be reminded of this, but, under the circumstances, his clear attraction for Catherine Barkley may be clouding his reason. The head nurse, thus, puts him in his place.

19:10 "I don't know": We move from the area of objective truth to the area of subjective truth, and we have another expression of Frederic's uncertainty. Once again, the matter pertains to his self-knowledge.

19:11–13 "Why did you join up with the Italians?" . . . "and I spoke Italian": Frederic's answer to the head nurse's query may be rational, but is not convincing, probably not even to himself, suggesting that there is little or no rationale to his decisions. He is living a directionless life.

20:1–2 "A rivederci, Tenente." . . . "A rivederla": The nurse practices her Italian on Frederic with a more formal *goodbye* than the colloquial *ciao*. Both *a rivederci* and *a rivederla* essentially mean "until we meet again," but *a rivederla* denotes more formality. See Cirino, "You Don't Know the Italian Language Well Enough" (57).

20:6 Plava: This small village lies on the right (western) bank of the Isonzo River, about twelve miles north of Gorizia. Today located in the Republic of Slovenia, the village has a population of fewer than four hundred.

20:6–20 It was there ... in plain sight: Frederic's description of the geography and military dispositions correspond with the facts prior to the beginning of the Tenth Battle of the Isonzo, which would start on 12 May 1917. As Frederic states, the Italians had established a bridgehead there and held a mile and a half of ground on the eastern (Austrian) side of the river. However, to get there, Frederic cannot follow the river all the way from Gorizia to Plava, both because the Austrians still hold a significant area on the western side of the river there and because even the areas held by the Italians are too exposed to Austrian fire. Thus, Frederic must take a back route through the mountains on the western side of the river and come down out of them to Plava, as he describes. Hemingway likely took these details from British historian G. M. Trevelyan, the officer in charge of the British Red Cross station near Cormons. Here, for example, is Trevelyan's description of the road down to Plava:

> A further weakness of the Italian bridgehead position lay in the fact that only one narrow road ran down from Verhovlje Pass to Plava bottom; and it was overlooked at the distance of a kilometer by the Austrian artillery and machine gunners on Monte Kuk, across the Isonzo. Yet everything that the mules could not bring down to Plava through the forest tracks had to come down the exposed road. (72)

Trevelyan's service on the Italian front from August 1915 to December 1918 parallels that of Hemingway's Frederic, and he was probably the model for the unnamed English character of that service who appears later in the novel.

21:12 carabinieri: Italian policemen. In Italy, the Carabinieri (properly capitalized) are the national police force, charged with policing both military and civilian populations. Because part of their duties entailed enforcing military discipline, there were natural tensions between them and other troops. For example, the elite Arditi nicknamed the Carabinieri *aeroplani* (airplanes) because of their distinctive headgear, large tricornered hats that looked like wings (Nicolle 39). Their appearance here foreshadows chapter 30, where they participate in the summary executions of presumed deserters at the Codroipo bridge over the Tagliamento River during the Caporetto Retreat.

21:13 seventy-sevens: Relatively small artillery cannon with a caliber of 76.5 millimeters. The Austrians deployed several different types of these during the war. For comparison, the largest artillery cannon deployed by Austria had a caliber of 305 millimeters.

21:23–24 sitting on a bench in the garden: Frederic once again finds Catherine in the garden of the converted villa, accompanied by Miss Ferguson, who we learn is named Helen.

21:32 **Mr. Henry:** This marks the first use of the narrator's last name. We are still awaiting his first name. Miss Ferguson's use of it here confirms to us that he must have introduced himself and given his name to the women on their first meeting, the previous evening, a fact he left out of his narration. For a discussion of the potential sources of Frederic Henry's first and last names, see entry 74:3.

21:33 **bother the censor:** During the war, all communications from the front lines were heavily censored to prevent the enemy from intercepting any valuable information.

21:37 **Catherine:** This is the initial appearance of Catherine Barkley's first name. In the manuscript, Hemingway initially wrote "Frances," then crossed it out and replaced it with "Catherine," although he debated whether to spell her name "Katherine" or "Catherine," ultimately deciding on the latter (JFK item 64). There is good reason to believe that Hemingway drew the name from Catherine Earnshaw in Emily Brontë's classic novel, *Wuthering Heights*. See entry 99:36 for a full discussion of the implications of the Brontë connection to the novel, first explored by Lisa Tyler.

22:2–4 **"She's a nurse. . . . I'm something called a V.A.D."** Helen Ferguson is a nurse, having gone through a more formal education to be licensed and certified, whereas Catherine is a "Voluntary Aid Detachment" (VAD), a designation in the British Red Cross for a nurse's aide. As Catherine explains, a VAD's training is significantly shorter than a nurse's, which she compares to a doctor's. Because of a shortage of trained nurses, the British Red Cross relied increasingly on VADs in all theaters of the war. In *The Sun Also Rises*, Brett Ashley also served as a VAD and nursed Jake Barnes as he recuperated from his war wound in Italy. Thus, Hemingway invites us to compare the characters of Brett and Catherine. Both are British and beautiful, each lost a lover to the war, and, significantly, both are atheists. In contrast, Brett has been twice married and is sexually promiscuous, whereas Catherine, as we have seen, is a virgin. Another interesting distinction: Brett has very short hair, like a boy's, and Catherine's is long. Although Catherine is at least partially based on the American nurse Agnes von Kurowsky, with whom Hemingway fell in love in 1918, there were no American nurses on the Italian front in 1917, only British. American nurses did not arrive in Italy until 1918.

22:23–28 **put my arm around under her arm . . . slapped my face hard:** Frederic's physical aggression here is clearly premature, and he ignores Catherine's "No," trying to force a kiss. Her violent reaction is swift.

22:31–35 **"I'm so sorry" . . . "I did hurt you, didn't I?"** While feminists understandably complain of Catherine's easy compliance here after she has initially been firm in resisting Frederic's advances, her apologetic reflex after inflicting pain upon him surely arises out of the guilt she still has over her fiancé's death.

22:36–37 I was angry . . . like the moves in a chess game: Frederic's behavior, however, is less worthy of our sympathy. His thought process, which, to his credit, he fully shares with us in his narration years after the fact, reveals his single goal: sexually conquering Catherine Barkley. He intuitively understands immediately that he has an advantage in this contest, which he envisions as a game of chess, where he can see all the moves ahead that lead to his goal.

Hemingway may be alluding to T. S. Eliot's *The Waste Land,* in which the second section is titled "A Game of Chess" (*Complete Poems* 39–42). There, Eliot focuses on two women in unsatisfactory relationships with men, one of whom has had an abortion, and he includes allusions to the rape of Philomela in Greek mythology. The section begins with an allusion to Shakespeare's Cleopatra and concludes with an allusion to his Ophelia, both women who have been compromised by men and who take their own lives in consequence.

22:38 "You did exactly right. . . . I don't mind at all": This is clearly a lie, since Frederic has given us access to his angry thoughts and chess maneuvering.

23:1 "sort of a funny life": This too is essentially a lie, designed to further manipulate Catherine's emotions, but, of course, there is some truth in it. Frederic *has* been leading an odd life in its lack of direction and purpose and its general irresponsibility.

23:4 "a lot of nonsense": Catherine is perceptive enough to see through the pose, although her recognition of his disingenuousness does not mitigate her guilt enough to prevent her from giving in to his advances, as she grants him permission to kiss her.

23:7–8 I watched her face: This seems to have been added later to the holograph manuscript (JFK item 64). The sentence is an indication that Frederic is paying close attention to her emotions, to read them so as to gain an advantage in the game he is playing.

23:13–17 I kissed her hard . . . and then she was crying on my shoulder: The still angry Frederic callously forces a French kiss past her initial resistance until she fully acquiesces and breaks down with the conflicting emotions she must be feeling.

23:18–22 "Oh, darling, . . . we're going to have a strange life": Again, sensitive readers may groan in dismay at how pliable Catherine is here, but her response is understandable and deserves our sympathy if we understand the depths of her grief over her dead fiancé and her guilt over having denied him her physical love. In offering herself and her future to Frederic, she is clearly projecting her previous love and current guilt onto him, who ("What the hell") is happy to reap the benefits. In the holograph manuscript, at the end of this passage, Hemingway wrote, "I did not know what it was all about," then crossed it out (JFK item 64).

23:26–36 **"So you make progress. . . . Good-night, little puppy":** As Frederic returns to his room with an apparent swaggering air, Rinaldi is quick to recognize a change in him. Rinaldi speaks here in Italian, and his phrase "a dog in heat" perplexes Frederic who does not "understand the word." Hemingway may have been thinking of and imagining a medical doctor like Rinaldi using technical or abstruse words for what is commonly and simply "a dog in heat." A basic literal rendering of the phrase in Italian would be *cane in calore,* which should not be difficult to understand for someone as fluent in Italian as Frederic seems to be. Since Frederic uses the word *dog* in his response, the context indicates that he understands *cane,* and it is *in calore* that puzzles him. It is unclear whether Hemingway intended the dash after "a dog who—" to be a censored obscenity in Frederic's response to Rinaldi or an instance where Rinaldi simply interrupts Frederic before he can complete his sentence. The holograph manuscript completes the sentence, "a dog who takes no interest due to an operation" (JFK item 64). At any rate, Rinaldi concludes the exchange by appropriately calling Frederic "little puppy," in keeping with the dog metaphor but also underscoring Frederic's immaturity at this stage.

23:37–39 **I knocked over his candle . . . went on reading:** This might seem an insignificant detail. However, as Frederic retaliates, even if good naturedly, for Rinaldi's "puppy" remark, he extinguishes the candle and puts himself in the dark, literally, just as he is figuratively at this point in the narrative. Rinaldi's relighting the candle and resuming reading emphasizes his power of reasoning and relative enlightenment compared to Frederic, the "little puppy."

The holograph manuscript adds, "In bed I lay awake a long time. I did not know what it was all about but it was something to do" (JFK item 64).

CHAPTER 6

24:2–3 She was not in the garden: Again, by stating the unsurprising fact that Catherine is not in the garden when Frederic comes to call on her, Hemingway highlights Frederic's essentially fallen condition. His callousness toward Catherine and their relationship is indicated by his not having told her that he was going away for two days.

24:4 many marble busts: In a setting that foreshadows the novel's final scene (see entry 284:3–5), in which Frederic tries to say goodbye to Catherine's corpse and compares it to a statue, Frederic, in the hospital office, part of a former German villa, is surrounded by marble busts that remind him of a cemetery. These images of death contrast with the vernal lushness of the garden outside.

24:9–10 one fine cemetery . . . at Pisa: Frederic is apparently referring to the Camposanto Monumentale (Monumental Cemetery) in Pisa, Italy, constructed between the thirteenth and fifteenth centuries. Its foundation is reported to be numerous shiploads of soil from Golgotha, the hill on which Christ was crucified, brought to Pisa in the thirteenth century by Ubaldo Lanfranchi, the city's archbishop, after the Fourth Crusade to the Holy Land. Baedeker's *Italy: From the Alps to Naples* 1928 claims there were "fifty-three shiploads of earth brought from Jerusalem in 1203" (165). Since we learn later that Frederic has been an architectural student in Italy, he would probably have visited the site and been aware that the marble cloister that enclosed the ground was designed in 1278, by Giovanni di Simone (architect of Pisa's famous Leaning Tower). In addition, inside the cloister are striking religious frescoes, including *The History of Creation* and *The Triumph over Death* (165–66). The cemetery was the chief resting place for Pisa's upper classes until the late eighteenth century.

24:10–11 Genoa was the place to see the bad marbles: The exact reference is uncertain. However, Genoa's most famous cemetery with numerous marble sculptures is the Cimitero monumentale di Staglieno, and Baedeker's *Italy: From the Alps to Naples* 1928, which we know Hemingway consulted as he wrote the novel, calls the monuments "sumptuous, if inartistic" (159). Having opened in 1851, the Staglieno was also much more recently constructed than was the medieval Camposanto in Pisa, so it is possible Hemingway wished to indicate a preference for the medieval over the modern.

24:20–21 **English gas mask . . . a real mask:** Italian gas masks were notoriously ineffective. Germans first used gas on the French front in April 1915. The Austrians first used gas, a mixture of chlorine and phosgene, against the Italians more than a year later, on 29 June 1916. At that point, the Italian soldiers had only been issued primitive gas masks, "cotton-wool pads impregnated with alkaline solution, and separate goggles," and they were ineffective against phosgene (Thompson 173). That day, two thousand Italians died and another five thousand were injured in the battle. At the start of the Battle of Caporetto in October 1917, the Germans used a mixture of phosgene and diphenylchloroarsine, against which the Italian masks were completely ineffective (301). The British army, in contrast, had developed a full gas mask with a respirator, introduced in the summer of 1916 and standardized by early 1917. These proved far more effective in preventing deaths from poison gas on the battlefield. Frederic somehow has been able to obtain one of these. After the disaster at Caporetto, the Italians adopted the British model, and their deaths from poison gas were significantly reduced for the remainder of the war.

25:1 **sanitary officers:** Soldiers engaged in such activities as waste disposal, insect control, and supply of pure water.

25:5 **Astra 7.65 caliber:** A semi-automatic pistol manufactured in Spain by Astra Unceta y Cia, a weapons supplier for the French and Italian armies. Frederic follows orders and carries "a real" pistol that makes him feel like a real, not a pretend, "gunman," until he tries to shoot with it and discovers it is so poorly designed that it is very difficult to hit a target with it. He loses this gun when he is wounded and replaces it by buying another at a gun shop before returning to the front. See entry 130:22.

25:12 **vague sort of shame:** Frederic's shame at carrying a weapon indicates his lack of commitment to the war, though he seems to have more desire to be a soldier than does Rinaldi, who does not carry a gun at all but instead stuffs his holster with toilet paper.

25:16–17 **Any frescoes were good when they started to peel and flake off:** Frescoes are murals painted on wet plaster, so that the paint penetrates the plaster and becomes an integral part of it as it dries. Peeling and flaking of old frescoes is a common problem. Frederic's statement may be facetious, but it may also be taken as another indication of his preference for things of antiquity as opposed to the modern.

In other words, similar to his possible namesake Henry Adams, Frederic seems to long for a simpler time, when it was easier to have an unblemished religious faith, the kind exemplified in the artists' work on the frescoes. After this sentence, the holograph manuscript adds this rather nihilistic passage, "[T]hey were like smashed houses. Smashed houses were the best looking. But these frescoes weren't peeling much yet" (JFK item 64).

25:25 **out into the garden:** This is their third visit to the garden, as Frederic Henry continues his hot-blooded pursuit of paradisiacal ecstasy. Catherine, however, is decidedly cool toward him after he did not tell her he would be away for two days.

25:37 **"This is the third day. But I'm back now":** Frederic tries to make a bad joke, in which he compares himself to the risen Christ. Catherine shows no sign of appreciation for the attempt.

25:38–26:2 **"And you do love me?" . . . "Yes," I lied. "I love you":** Frederic is simply telling her what he believes will get him what he wants—a sexual conquest. The idea of lies between lovers will be revisited later in their relationship, in chapter 16 when Catherine will explore Frederic's sexual history. See entry 91:21–36. The manuscript adds, "I did not love her of course" at the end of this passage (JFK item 64). Again, note that Frederic is including these unflattering details about himself as he is telling the story years after the fact.

26:3 **"And you call me Catherine?"** Modern readers may miss the point here, of an earlier, more formal time. Catherine is seeking reassurance that their relationship has advanced beyond the stage of formality, during which they would address each other as Miss Barkley and Mr. Henry. The original manuscript has "Then you won't call me Miss Barkley any more?" "No." "You'll call me Catherine" (JFK item 64).

26:6 **"Say, 'I've come back to Catherine in the night'":** Catherine is clearly acting out a romantic fantasy here, a dramatic love story in which two passionate lovers have been reunited after a painful absence. More specifically, she is undoubtedly projecting her dead fiancé on to Frederic, for it is her dead fiancé, at this point, whom she truly wishes to return to her. Frederic, naturally, as a lustful man on the make, is happy to play along, if it gets him what he is after. But his words are all lies, betrayals. Rather than the Garden of Eden, this is more like the Garden of Gethsemane, in which Judas Iscariot betrayed Jesus with a kiss.

26:14–15 **I kissed both her shut eyes:** Catherine's shut eyes are emblematic of her momentary blindness to Frederic's true nature here, allowing him to have his way with her. The act of kissing her shut eyes demonstrates his awareness of the advantage her blindness bestows on him.

26:15–19 I thought she was probably a little crazy . . . trips upstairs with brother officers: The original manuscript omits the sentence "It was all right if she was" (JFK item 64). Obviously, not only does Catherine's apparent "craziness" not bother Frederic, but he is probably thinking it is advantageous to him. It is likely to make the sexual conquest easier. As he admits, sex with a woman like Catherine would be better than sex with the prostitutes in the officers' bawdy house, where the women are shared with many others and there is always the risk of sexually transmitted diseases, with which Rinaldi will later have to contend. See entry 153:6–10. Craziness is also one form of irrationality, and it prevents us from being able to recognize the truth, as it does Catherine here, at least for the time being. The novel revisits the subject again later. See, for example, entry 79:24, among others.

26:20–24 This was a game, like bridge. . . . It was all right with me: Another rendition of the game motif, first raised during Frederic's previous meeting with Catherine, when he thinks of "the moves in a chess game." See entry 22:36–37. Now the game is bridge, a strategic card game. In this instance, Frederic includes the element of gambling. As in bridge, where the excitement of the game is heightened if players pretend to be playing for money, here, in the game of seduction, he has to pretend that there are emotional stakes involved, although, as he shares with us, "Nobody had mentioned what the stakes were." That is fine with him because he is naively unconcerned about consequences. Hemingway probably had Dostoevsky's novel *The Gambler* in mind as he wrote this passage.

26:26–27 the masculine difficulty of making love very long standing up: Frederic wishes to push their physical relationship to the next level. At this point, they are merely kissing, standing up in the garden. Do not be confused by the phrase *making love,* which in contemporary times has come to be used only in reference to sexual intercourse. When Hemingway was writing, the usage of the term was much broader, to include any form of physical affection between lovers.

26:28–29 She came back from wherever she had been: Catherine's romantic fantasy has been shattered, and she now recognizes the relationship for what it is, or, more specifically, she recognizes that Frederic's actions are driven by nothing more than physical desire. The phrase *came back* foreshadows Frederic's similar wording when he has his out-of-body experience during his wounding in chapter 9. See entry 47:12–17. In both cases, they return from a subjective realm back to objective reality.

26:32 **She would not let me put my arm around her:** The original manuscript adds, "I supposed my whorehouse manners were a strain" (JFK item 64).

26:36 **"rotten game":** Catherine is no longer blind to the reality of gamesmanship in Frederic's interactions with her. She no longer wishes to play that game. She would prefer a relationship built on honesty.

26:37–27:10 **"What game?" . . ."It's only a little sometimes":** Frederic attempts to maintain the lie, but Catherine can see through him and quickly disarms him, calling him "a nice boy," just as Rinaldi, in the previous chapter, called him "little puppy" and later "baby." It is also worth noting that in her breakup letter to Hemingway, Agnes von Kurowsky addressed him as "Ernie, dear boy" and "still Kid to me, & always will be" (Villard and Nagel 163). Here Catherine has trumped Frederic's card, and she uses the same ironic British word, *show* (which soldiers used to understate murderous battles), to describe her brief diversion into the mad deceits of courtly love—that is, a false love based on old but mad conventions. In *The Great War and Modern Memory,* Paul Fussell discusses how it was only British soldiers, out of the British flair for theatricality and charades, who referred to the horrors of war as "shows" (213–15).

Some readers may think Catherine is too easy on Frederic, but, just as the priest sees something in him that is worth redeeming, Catherine too must see something in him that is worth hanging on to, but it will be on her terms from now on. Thus, in this exchange, Hemingway lays the foundation for presenting Catherine as the emblem of balance between reason (Rinaldi) and faith (the priest), and she will be his exemplar in learning how to love. Catherine's admitted craziness is no permanent condition. It is not madness or insanity. As she says, "It's only a little sometimes." She is probably suffering from some kind of post-traumatic stress disorder, but she is healing and will get better with time.

27:12–13 **"It sounds very funny now. . . . You don't pronounce it very much alike":** This statement clarifies for us how Catherine has been projecting her feelings for her dead fiancé onto Frederic. Now that she is back to objective reality, she can hear the difference. Frederic, with his American accent, does not pronounce her name the same way that her British fiancé did. Frederic is *not* her dead fiancé, a fact she has apparently not fully absorbed till now.

27:30 **I watched the flashes on San Gabriele:** Monte San Gabriele is a mountain northeast of Gorizia, where at this moment in the novel there is artillery fire producing the flashes that Frederic sees. Its capture would be one of the primary objectives of the Italian offensive during the Tenth Battle of the Isonzo, which would begin on 12 May 1917. See entry 4:11–18. Frederic's relationship with Catherine has just experienced a major turning point, which will enable it to progress later into a full expression of true love. Just as the angel Gabriel announced to the Virgin Mary that she was to be the Mother of God, these flashes can be seen as a kind of annunciation to Frederic, although he does not yet seem to recognize their full import.

27:31 **the Villa Rossa:** This is the officers' bawdy house, previously unnamed. Frederic's pause in front of the house reminds him of what he could have been doing instead of engaging in his frustrated attempts to seduce Catherine Barkley. In the chapter 7 vignette in *In Our Time,* which explores the question of religious faith under the extreme stress of battle, the soldiers' bawdy house in Mestre is also named the Villa Rossa.

27:34 **"Baby is puzzled":** The perceptive Rinaldi again uses an appropriate epithet, "Baby," which emphasizes Frederic's immaturity and inability to appreciate the value of a love relationship with Catherine—not that Rinaldi has any desire to encourage such a relationship. He is thankful now he did not get involved with "the British" as Frederic has.

CHAPTER 7

28:2 **smistimento:** A misspelling of *smistamento,* Italian for *sorting,* that is, a place where wounded soldiers could be transferred from the ambulances, processed, and sent on to hospitals. G. M. Trevelyan explains that the *smistamento* at Plava was originally near the village railway station, but it proved to be too exposed to Austrian fire. For the 1917 offensive, it was moved across the river to a more sheltered spot beneath the Plava hill. There, wounded were sorted and carried across the river on a pontoon footbridge and then loaded onto waiting ambulances for the journey to field hospitals (74).

28:6 **Fiat:** Most of the Italian ambulances were manufactured by the well-known Italian automotive company Fiat in Turin. Then, as now, it was the largest Italian automotive company.

28:7 **thought about nothing:** This may remind experienced Hemingway readers of his well-known short story "A Clean Well-Lighted Place," published in 1933, which is dominated by the English word *nothing* and the Spanish word for *nothing, nada.* Two waiters in a Spanish café watch over a drinking old man, who tried to commit suicide the week before:

> "Why?" [asks one waiter.]
> "He was in despair."
> "What about?"
> "Nothing."
> "How do you know it was nothing?"
> "He has plenty of money." (CSS 288)

The older waiter is probably punning on *nothing,* which has dual meanings as he is using it: he means either that the man had no reason to commit suicide or that he attempted suicide because of his thoughts of nothingness, meaninglessness. The story concludes with the thoughts of the older waiter, who sympathizes with the attempted suicide because he is afflicted with the same disease: "It was a nothing that he knew too well. It was all a nothing and a man was nothing too.... *nada y pues nada y nada y pues nada* [nothing and then nothing]. Our *nada* who art in *nada, nada* be thy name" (291). It is one of Hemingway's grimmest stories, written out of a dark night of the soul. Here, it is certainly possible that Frederic's mind may truly be empty, numbed by the drudgery of his job and the aftereffects of being rebuffed by Catherine. However, given the novel's overarching questions about the meaning of life, it is also possible that he is contemplating the prospect of nothingness, meaninglessness, or the aimlessness of his own life.

The passage also recalls the nihilism of Yevgeny Bazarov in *Fathers and Sons*, by Ivan Turgenev, one of the novelists who most influenced Hemingway: "'A nihilist,' said Nikolai Petrovich [referring to Bazarov]. 'That's from the Latin *nihil, nothing*, as far as I can judge; the word must mean a man who . . . who accepts nothing?'" (28).

28:10 **Most of the helmets were too big:** As Mark Thompson explains, Italian soldiers had to do without steel helmets for a long time, and when the helmets finally arrived, they were not well designed (149).

28:12 **brigata Basilicata:** Probably a historical inaccuracy on Hemingway's part. The Basilicata Brigade, consisting of the Ninety-first and Ninety-second Infantry regiments of the Italian army, seem only to have fought on the Trentino front rather than the Isonzo front during World War I ("Brigata 'Basilicata'"). Hemingway probably saw members of the brigade when he was stationed in the Dolomites in 1918.

29:2 **"—— the war":** In Hemingway's original holograph manuscript, the missing word is represented "F——" (JFK item 64). It is the first instance of many in the novel in which profane words were deleted and marked by dashes. Hemingway apparently held no illusions about being able to print the word *fuck* in the book, only writing it twice in other places before scratching it out. He never made an issue about it with Maxwell Perkins, his editor at Scribner's. When the publisher deleted the *F* before printing, Hemingway did not protest. He did object, however, to the censorship of *shit, cockersucker,* and *balls* in other instances in the book. None of these were allowed to be printed. Hemingway complained in a 7 June 1929 letter to Perkins that such language had appeared in Shakespeare and more recently in Erich Maria Remarque's best-selling war novel: "[Y]ou will find them in a book called All Quiet on The Western Front which Scott gave me and which has sold in the 100s of thousand copies in Germany and is around 50,000 copies in England with the word shit, fart etc. never dragged in for coloring but only used a few times for the thousands of times they are omitted" (*Letters 4* 19). However, Hemingway was probably looking at the British edition of Remarque's novel, published in March 1929. The US edition, published in June, was heavily expurgated, and, even so, it was banned in Boston for obscenity. Perkins, aware of the existing strict postal prohibitions against profane language, anticipated that, with these three words, the novel's serial version scheduled to be published in installments over the summer of 1929 in *Scribner's Magazine,* would almost certainly be banned by the Watch and Ward Society in Boston, which was founded for the suppression of vice. Of course, sophisticated American readers would likely have little trouble understanding what Hemingway intended in the blanks. As it turned out, the second installment of the serialization, the June issue of *Scribner's Magazine,* was banned anyway, in spite of the cleaned up language, the rationale being the perceived immorality in the relationship between Frederic and Catherine. As so often happens in such instances, the banning probably only increased sales when it was published in book form.

Fortunately, for Hemingway, the standards for language changed considerably by the late 1930s; he was able to include most of these words in his next novel, *To Have and Have Not.* Nevertheless, the blanks have remained in all subsequent editions of *A Farewell to Arms.* Since at least 1964, critics have been arguing for the publication of a definitive edition of the novel that fills in all the blanks in the text with Hemingway's intended meanings (see Meriwether, "Blanks in Hemingway's 'A Farewell to Arms,'" and Reynolds, "Words Killed, Wounded, Missing in Action"). In the Hemingway Library edition, Scribner's has missed an excellent opportunity to publish such a definitive text that carefully takes into account Hemingway's intentions in the manuscript.

For the full discussion between Hemingway and Maxwell Perkins concerning these censorship issues, see Matthew Bruccoli's *The Only Thing That Counts: The Ernest Hemingway / Maxwell Perkins Correspondence, 1925–47.* See also Scott Donaldson's "Censorship in *A Farewell to Arms*" for a discussion of the impact of the Boston banning on the final version of the book. In his introduction to volume 4 of Hemingway's letters, Donaldson points out that US Customs had recently banned the British edition of *All Quiet on the Western Front,* forcing Little, Brown to "bring out a sanitized version" in the United States (lviii). For a discussion of Hemingway's continued rage over the censorship, as late as 1951, see Rose Marie Burwell's *Hemingway: The Postwar Years and the Posthumous Novels* (195n17).

30:1–3 **"Don't I talk Italian good enough?"** . . .**"Another American"**: The relaxed diction in the dialogue between Frederic and the man with the hernia probably indicates that they are speaking colloquial English rather than Italian. Aldo's "Another American," in Italian, adds a sardonic twist.

30:5 **"lootenant"**: Likely a typographic convention to suggest the hernia man's colloquial English. Having the ruptured Italian's oral *lootenant* switch to *lieutenant* may be an editorial oversight (30:25, 30:38).

30:7–8 **"I threw away the goddam truss so it would get bad"**: Such behavior, of course, is liable to lead to a court-martial and severe punishment under the harsh rule of General Luigi Cadorna's army. The man takes Frederic into his confidence only because he must sense that Frederic is not a strict enforcer of the military law and is more likely to sympathize with a fellow American.

30:22–23 **"get a bump on your head and I'll . . . take you to a hospital"**: The bump on the head, a person's center of reasoning ability, becomes a motif in the novel, as Frederic will get a severe bump on the head, possibly a skull fracture, when he is wounded and again during his flight following his desertion (see entries 51:5–9 and 198:14–15). Though we might sympathize with Frederic's offer to help the hernia man get out of the war, to a certain extent it contradicts his later statements in support of the war effort, specifically when he speaks of the necessity to win it. See entry 43:18. The man's self-inflicted wound, on Frederic's advice, was not historically uncommon on the Isonzo front, where the general morale was low, under the strain of General Cadorna's insistence on full frontal attacks against almost impregnable Austrian defenses. Such low morale contributed to the collapse of the army during the Battle of Caporetto a few months later, in the fall of 1917.

31:1 **When I got back to the villa:** Previous editions of the novel all had an extra space before the start of this paragraph, typically an indication of the passing of an indeterminate amount of time before continuing with the story. Since the space in this case coincides with a page break, the standard practice would be to insert a series of asterisks at the top of the page before the new paragraph to indicate the break.

One distinct flaw in the Hemingway Library edition of *A Farewell to Arms* is the removal of all of these extra spaces, twenty of them in total. We will identify each of these locations as we come to them, since they are important to the novel's meaning. In this case, the meaning lost is relatively minor. We should understand that Frederic continued to work the rest of the day following his last encounter with the hernia man but that nothing of importance happened to him.

In the holograph manuscript, Hemingway actually indicated a chapter break here. He first wrote the words "chapter VII Seven," crossed them out, and then wrote "Chapter Eight" (JFK item 64). In the later typescript, there is no chapter break, but a horizontal line to indicate extra space needed (JFK item 65).

31:4 **In two days the offensive was to start:** Since the Tenth Battle of the Isonzo began on 12 May 1917, this detail enables us to date the action here as 10 May 1917.

31:7–8 **There was nothing to write about:** This is the first indication in the novel that Frederic is estranged from his family. His excuse that it has been such a long time since he last wrote to them that "it was almost impossible to write now" only reinforces the point. Certainly, he would have had many experiences he could share with his family if he wanted to, but he clearly does not want to. This distance from his family is another way Frederic is essentially alienated from life at this point.

31:8–9 Zona di Guerra post cards, crossing out everything except, I am well: These postcards, with optional generalized items to ignore or check off, were common among all armies during the Great War. They were designed to control the kind of information that might leak from the front lines and to prevent enemies from gathering compromising knowledge of military positions and plans, while allowing families to be reassured that their loved ones were all right on the front lines. A British example, probably very similar to the Italian one Frederic uses, had instructions on the top, reading: "NOTHING is to be written on this side except the date and signature of the sender. Sentences not required may be erased. *If anything else is added the post card will be destroyed.*" Then below that were the following options:

> I am quite well.
> I have been admitted into hospital (sick wounded) and am going on well and hope to be discharged soon.
> I am being sent down to the base.
> I have received your (letter telegram parcel) dated _____.
> Letter follows at first opportunity.
> I have received no letter from you (lately for a long time).
> Signature only: _____
> Date: _____ ("British Field Service Postcard")

Frederic tells us he crosses out everything except "I am well," commenting, "That should handle them." For further discussion of Frederic's relationship with his family see entry 135:6–13.

31:13–14 The Austrian army was created to give Napoleon victories; any Napoleon: Frederic is sardonically referring to both Napoleon Bonaparte and Napoleon III. Napoleon Bonaparte (Napoleon I) soundly defeated the Austrians, conquering most of the Italian peninsula, in 1796. The army of Napoleon III defeated the Austrians, again in Italy, in 1859.

31:15 Il Generale Cadorna, fat and prosperous: Instead of a Napoleon, the Italian army of the Great War was led by the unpopular supreme commander, General Luigi Cadorna, whose tactics were criticized for leading to senseless slaughter. For example, he ordered full frontal assaults without adequate artillery support, leading to enormous casualties, and he positioned too many troops on the front lines, making it easier for them to be cut off by breakthroughs like that at Caporetto in 1917 (Keegan 347). He also carried himself with "aristocratic hauteur," distancing himself from the soldiers, whom he frequently blamed for lacking fighting spirit. Historian John Keegan's description of him captures the essence: "He not only stood on his constitutional rights of supreme authority—independent of King and Prime Minister—over the army once war began; he exercised that authority with a brutality not shown by any other general of the First World War" (227). In 1917, during the Caporetto Retreat, Cadorna ordered the summary execution of all retreating officers separated from their troops, as Hemingway describes in Book Three (see entry 193:25–26). See also Mark Thompson's *The White War* for a full discussion of Cadorna's failures as a military leader. *Aloof, heartless,* and other similarly pejorative adjectives have been frequently applied to Cadorna; oddly, however, *fat* has not. Nor do photos of him in any way indicate that he was overweight (Gooch 187). Perhaps Hemingway simply meant *fat* as in *well off.*

31:15–16 Vittorio Emmanuele . . . goat beard: The king's name correctly spelled in Italian is Vittorio Emanuele. He is King Victor Emmanuel III of Italy, whom Frederic has previously inaccurately described with these same terms. See entry 5:20–6:1.

31:17–20 Duke of Aosta . . . the third army: The Duke of Aosta, also known as Prince Emanuele Filiberto, who commanded the Italian Third Army, was actually a cousin of King Victor Emmanuel III (not his uncle). The Third Army was positioned on the right (or southern) side of the Isonzo front (from the Italian perspective). Mark Thompson describes the duke as "an imposing figure. Tall, handsome, melancholy, he was not given to airing controversial views or large conceptions" (257). During the disastrous Caporetto Retreat, the duke was credited with holding the Third Army together, unlike the scattered Second Army, but he was forced to retreat as the Austrians were eviscerating the Second Army in the northern sector. The Third Army survived the retreat virtually intact and helped the Italians stop the Austrian advance at the Piave River. Thus, the Third Army was regarded as undefeated during the war.

31:20–21 We were in the second army: Significantly, Hemingway places Frederic in the Second Army, which would be routed in the Caporetto Disaster in October 1917. The Second Army was commanded by General Luigi Capello, who goes unmentioned here. Capello was frequently ill and absent from the front during key periods prior to the Caparetto disaster, a fact that certainly contributed to the defeat, although low morale among the soldiers was probably more important. Though intellectual, Capello, like Cadorna, preferred frontal assaults in battle. He was "notorious for devising an exhausting routine of exercises and fatigue duties for troops out of the line"

(Thompson 235). As a result, soldiers often returned to the front in worse shape than they left it, especially in terms of morale. Instead of enthusiasm, Capello's men felt "mounting hatred" toward him (236).

31:21–22 **British batteries up with the third army:** Hemingway obtained this information by reading Hugh Dalton's *With British Guns in Italy.* Dalton's battery was stationed on the Carso with the Italian Third Army (43).

31:28–30 **I knew I would not be killed . . . war in the movies:** This reveals Frederic's detached naivete and immaturity. His knowledge, in this regard, is highly subjective and will be proven wrong. In chapter 9, his attitude will change dramatically. In his introduction to *Men at War,* published in 1942, Hemingway wrote, "When you go to war as a boy you have a great illusion of immortality. Other people get killed; not you. . . . Then when you are badly wounded the first time you lose that illusion and you know it can happen to you" (xii).

31:32–33 **Maybe the Austrians would crack . . . other wars:** Frederic refers again to the perceived weakness of the Austrian army, "created to give Napoleon victories" (31:13). The term *crack,* used here twice as he and Catherine have used it before (see entry 17:27–33), lends a mental aspect to the outcome of military conflicts. In other words, the loser is the army that mentally breaks down first.

31:34–35 **Rinaldi said that the French had mutinied and troops marched on Paris:** Rinaldi's information is essentially accurate. Mutinies among French soldiers began with scattered outbreaks in April 1917, in the aftermath of a disastrous and unexpected defeat at the Second Battle of the Aisne. The mutiny eventually involved nearly half the French army and peaked in June before being repressed (Keegan 329–30; Gilbert 333–34).

31:37 **Black Forest:** A large mountainous forest region in southwestern Germany, the Schwarzwald. In Hemingway's short story "Cross-Country Snow," Nick Adams speaks of going through the Schwarzwald with his skiing buddy George (*CSS* 145). Donald Daiker contributed to this note.

31:37–38 **Hartz Mountains:** Frederic surely means the Harz Mountains, the tallest mountain range in northern Germany, the highest peak being 3,744 feet above sea level. There are Hartz Mountains on Baffin Island in Canada and twin mountains in Tasmania called Hartz Mountains, but it seems unlikely Frederic would be referring to these.

32:1 Carpathians: A long mountain range that arcs across central and eastern Europe. Austrian and Russian armies were fighting in the Carpathians along the eastern border of the Austro-Hungarian Empire.

32:2 I could go to Spain if there was no war: Hemingway here works in his own fondness for the nation; he began traveling regularly to Spain in 1923.

32:5 Cova: See entry 10:27–28.

32:6–7 Via Manzoni . . . canal . . . hotel: Frederic later identifies the hotel to which he imagines taking Catherine along the Via Manzoni as the Hotel Cavour (see entry 134:30), which Baedeker describes as "prettily situated opposite the *Giardini Pubblici* [Public Gardens]" (*Italy* 1928 24). The hotel remains in essentially the same location today, about an eleven-minute walk from the Milan Cathedral. The canal, however, is no longer there. Milan once had an elaborate system of canals for transportation, called *navigli,* including one created out of the moat around the old walls of the city. This formed the Inner Ring canal, which would have been the one Frederic dreams of crossing to get to the Hotel Cavour. However, Benito Mussolini's Fascist government covered over the canal in 1929–30 to build a ring road around the city center. For Via Manzoni, see entry 103:26–27.

32:17 capri bianca: Correctly *Capri bianco,* a white wine from the isle of Capri. See entry 7:39.

32:23 small bats hunting over the houses: This detail of Frederic's fantasy foreshadows chapter 16, when a bat enters Frederic's hospital room, where he and Catherine are resting after making love. See entry 88:1–89:3.

32:27 I would eat quickly and go and see Catherine Barkley: Frederic has excited himself with his highly detailed and erotic fantasy about a hot night in a Milan hotel with Catherine. At this stage, his feelings for her still do not extend beyond the physical.

32:30 Archbishop Ireland: Archbishop John Ireland (1838–1918) was a leading progressive American Roman Catholic cleric in the late nineteenth and early twentieth centuries, who fought against injustices to Irish Catholic immigrants to the United States. A friend to US presidents William McKinley and Theodore Roosevelt, he was opposed to racial inequality and worked to improve access to education.

33:3–4 The priest was good but dull. . . . The wine was bad but not dull: A reference that highlights the priest's shortcomings for Frederic, who remains interested in little besides Catherine's body. The bad wine, however, mitigates the general dullness, causing him to forget even Catherine until it is too late.

33:6–11 **"And the priest was locked up . . . quite evident he had stolen the bonds":** In a continuation of the baiting presented in chapter 2, Rocca, presumably one of the officers, tells the story of a corrupt priest.

33:12 **"I don't believe a word of this":** Rinaldi's declaration reinforces his position as a person of reason, who will not take anything on faith, but it also helps to suggest his essential fairness in that he is refusing, in this instance, to participate in any baiting of the priest.

33:20–21 **"'Bless me, father, for you have sinned'":** A parody of the conventional opening statement of a penitent making confession to a priest: "Bless me, father, for I have sinned. It has been [amount of time] since my last confession."

33:26–27 **the story about the English private soldier who was placed under the shower bath:** This paragraph contains a series of references to obscure jokes or stories. This one by Frederic may be a subtle Hemingway jest at the expense of Ford Madox Ford, a writer and editor with whom Hemingway worked on the *transatlantic review* literary journal in 1924. Hemingway had already presented an unflattering portrait of Ford through the character of Braddocks in *The Sun Also Rises* and would be far more brutal in *A Moveable Feast* (81–88). In Ford's fine tetralogy, *Parade's End,* the phrase "pulling the strings of shower baths" is coined by Sylvia Tietjens, the troublesome wife of the protagonist, Christopher Tietjens, who serves as an officer in the British army on the French front in World War I.

33:28–34 **the story of the eleven Czecho-slovaks . . . when the mistral was blowing:** The sources of the four stories—the eleven Czecho-slovaks and the Hungarian corporal, the jockey who found the penny, the duchess who could not sleep at night, and the traveling salesman who arrived at five o'clock in the morning at Marseilles when the mistral was blowing—are all undetermined. Frederic tells the stories of the jockey and the traveling salesman, and the major tells the other two. The holograph manuscript adds that the duchess "could not sleep at night without internal bathing" (JFK item 64). The mistral is a strong cold wind that blows southeasterly through the Rhône Valley of southern France to the Mediterranean Sea, chiefly in winter.

33:36 **Bacchus:** The Roman god of wine, known in Greek mythology as Dionysus, is also associated with ritual madness and religious ecstasy and thus contributes to the motif of craziness in the novel and the conflict between the irrational and the rational. Throughout this scene, of course, the excessive consumption of wine is severely compromising Frederic's powers of reason.

33:38–34:3 **Bassi . . . what was his name anyway?** The major arranges for a drinking contest between Frederic and a man named Fillipo Vincenza Bassi, though Frederic is so drunk that he cannot keep Bassi's name straight. Mark Cirino points out that Bassi's first name should be correctly spelled "Filipo" ("You Don't Know" 59).

34:3–4 **Frederico Enrico or Enrico Federico:** In the holograph manuscript, it is "Frederico Enrico or Enrico Frederico" (JFK item 64). In the midst of this confusion about names and the inversion of them, Hemingway chooses for the first time to provide us with at least an Italian rendition of Frederic Henry's full name, though Bassi cannot figure out which is the first name and which is the last. For his part, Frederic provides him with no help. Only once in the novel does Frederic Henry pronounce his own full name. See entry 74:3. In writing *A Farewell to Arms*, Hemingway may have been influenced by Marcel Proust, whose protagonist in *In Search of Lost Time* (known in Hemingway's day as *Remembrance of Things Past*) also provides a retrospective first-person narration and never provides his name to the reader. There are certainly Proustian elements in Hemingway's novel, and the narrative provides numerous instances in which Frederic's identity is confused or ambiguous. However, unlike Proust, Hemingway does provide his narrator with a definite name, even if it is seldom used in the novel, and it is a name both parts of which have interesting potential sources.

Consider first the several possibilities for *Frederic*. It is not out of the question that Hemingway was paying tribute to Captain Frederick Marryat, whose novels of adventure on the high seas Hemingway loved and extolled in letters to friends in the 1920s. *Peter Simple* was one of his favorites, and Peter, like Frederic, falls in love with a woman, Celeste, who nurses him after a battle wound. They are separated, reunited later, and marry. Michael Reynolds, however, seems convinced that "Frederic" came from Frederic Stendhal, but, although Stendhal was certainly a powerful influence on the novel, Stendhal (real name Marie-Henri Beyle) rarely used a first name in his nom de plume. Only his obscure little volume *The Privileges* is signed "Frederic Stendhal," and there is no evidence Hemingway was familiar with it. Sheridan Baker, amid a strange and unconvincing argument that Frederic Henry is a feminine name, believes that Frederic Manning may have contributed Frederic Henry's first name. Again, although Hemingway later had high praise for Manning's *The Middle Parts of Fortune*, in his introduction to *Men at War*—calling it "the finest and noblest book of men in war that I have ever read"—Manning's book was published in a limited edition of 520 copies in 1929, the same year *A Farewell to Arms* was published, and there is no evidence that Hemingway had any familiarity with Manning's work prior to that (xiv). The character of Frederick Winterbourne in Henry James's *Daisy Miller* has also been suggested, but Frederic Henry would seem to have little in common with the staid Winterbourne. H. R. Stoneback, seemingly in jest, considers that Frederic could be named after the Martini rifle, invented by "Frederic Martini and A. Henry," although he is not quite precise about Martini's name ("Lovers' Sonnets Turn'd to Holy Psalms" 37). It was Friedrich von Martini, a Swiss designer. Alexander Henry was a Scotsman. The British army used the rifle in the late nineteenth century.

While these examples have their merits, some more than others, Gustave Flaubert is the most likely source for Frederic Henry's first name. A look at Hemingway's list of potential titles suggests that Flaubert's *Sentimental Education* was much on Hemingway's mind as he wrote *A Farewell to Arms,* and there are good reasons for that. Hemingway seriously considered titling his novel *The Sentimental Education* or *The Sentimental Education of Frederic Henry.* The protagonist of Flaubert's *Sentimental Education* is named Frederic Moreau, who shares with Frederic Henry an essentially passive and aimless nature. Both stories focus on their education in matters of love, and both have a backdrop of social turmoil: whereas Flaubert's has the French Revolution of 1848, Hemingway's has the Great War. That Hemingway eventually chose a different title does nothing to diminish Flaubert's influence on the novel.

Henry, however, has so many possible and very reasonable sources that we can wonder whether there was any way Hemingway could have avoided using the name for his main character. Reynolds (more reasonably this time) suggests Stendhal once more, taken from his real name, Marie-Henri Beyle. And we know Hemingway had identified the great French novelist as a key influence, an author with whom he was competing in writing *A Farewell to Arms.* We also know that Hemingway held Stephen Crane's *The Red Badge of Courage* in high regard, and its protagonist is Henry Fleming. Psychologically, however, Fleming has little in common with Frederic Henry. Flaubert is a possible influence here as well. His first version of *Sentimental Education,* completed in 1845 with a completely different set of characters and narrative from the version eventually published in 1869, has two protagonists, one of whom is named Henry. However, the book was not published until the eve of the First World War, and not translated into English until 1972. Although Ezra Pound, with his deep affection for Flaubert, would surely have known of it and may have spoken of it to Hemingway, there is no reason to believe Hemingway would have read it in French. There is also a quartet of writers with *Henry* in their names, all of whom were important to Hemingway: Henry James, Henry Adams, William Henry Hudson, and Henry Fielding. James, of course, in a series of novels, had explored themes of Americans in Europe, and he provided a quote about the effects on language of the Great War that Hemingway considered using as an epigraph for *A Farewell to Arms.* See entry Epigraphs (Unused). Henry Adams is a more likely source than James. His influence on Hemingway has been underrated, although George Monteiro has written persuasively on the Adams connection. Patrick Hemingway has insisted that Nick Adams's last name came from Henry Adams (foreword, *The Short Stories,* Hemingway Library edition vii). It was certainly no accident that Hemingway gave Nick Adams's father the name Henry Adams, after the author who wrote so movingly in *Mont-St.-Michel and Chartres* and *The Education of Henry Adams* about the ways modern science and industry had demolished the religion and art of the past. H. R. Stoneback notes that Hemingway's considered title *The Sentimental Education of Frederic Henry* is as much an allusion to Adams as it would be to Flaubert ("Lovers' Sonnets Turn'd to Holy Psalms" 63). As Stoneback writes, both *The Education of Henry Adams* and *A Farewell to Arms* are studies of "Twentieth-Century Multiplicity," which is the subtitle of the Adams work: "Both works," Stoneback asserts, "deal with the historical 'broken neck' of modern man. Both contrast the chaotic forces of the twentieth century with an age and place of faith" (63). William Henry Hudson is even more underrated as a Hemingway influence. Most Hemingway critics (including Stoneback) are misled by the apparent disparagement of Hudson in *The Sun Also Rises,* where Jake Barnes critiques Robert Cohn's infatuation with Hudson's *The Purple Land.* But Hemingway genuinely loved Hudson and listed his *Far Away and Long Ago* among his must reads for aspiring writers (*BL* 161, 189). To Isidore Schneider in 1926, Hemingway wrote, "Hudson writes the best of anyone, I think" (*Letters 3* 91). Perhaps most pertinently, in "Loss and Gain," the concluding chapter of *Far Away and Long Ago,* Hudson wrote achingly of the way he came to accept, reluctantly and with much pain and anguish, the truth of Darwinian evolution, and how it destroyed his belief in an afterlife. Later, Thomas Hudson, the protagonist of Hemingway's posthumously published novel *Islands in the Stream,* is almost certainly named after W. H. Hudson. Hemingway was also fond of Henry Fielding's eighteenth-century satires, using a passage from Fielding's preface to *Joseph Andrews* as an epigraph to *Torrents of Spring* and then attempting to write a Fielding-esque picaresque novel he tentatively titled *New Slain Knight* in 1927 before giving up on it and writing *A Farewell to Arms*. In addition, we cannot dismiss the possible influence of French novelist Henri Barbusse, whose *Le Feu* (*Under Fire*) was one of the first realistic accounts of trench warfare, published in 1917, which Hemingway read and refers to in chapter 35 of this novel (see entry 225:33). We also know Hemingway read, as they were first published in the 1924, Ezra Pound's *Cantos,* specifically Cantos VIII–XI, which explored the life and times of Sigismundo Malatesta in fifteenth-century Italy. In Canto X Hemingway would have found the names of Federico d'Urbino, a rival to Malatesta, and Enricho de Aquabello, a steward to Malatesta. The names conceivably gave Hemingway the idea to use them in the jesting confusion about whether Frederic's name is "Enrico Frederico or Federico Enrico." And then there is the case of Barklie McKee Henry, a friend of Hemingway and author of the novel *Deceit,* published in 1925. When *A Farewell to Arms* was published, Henry joked with Hemingway in a letter about naming his two main characters after him. See entry 10:35–37. Thus, considering all of these possibilities, whichever source we wish to pick (and it is really not possible to pick just one), Hemingway, it would seem, had no better option than to provide his protagonist with the name Henry, first or last. The natural conclusion is that Hemingway drew on some of his most important sources (Flaubert, Stendhal, Adams, Hudson) that suggested to him a conflict between the rationality and science of the modern world and the security of a faith in a higher purpose and meaning from an older age. Frederic Henry's name highlights that theme in all its ramifications.

34:21 **"baby":** Here and again at 34:22 and 34:33, with the nickname "baby," Rinaldi emphasizes Frederic's essential immaturity. Rinaldi's genuine love for him is evident, as he is concerned that if Frederic appears drunk to Catherine Barkley, it will have negative consequences for the progress of their relationship.

35:14 **feeling lonely and hollow:** This is the first small sign of growth in Frederic Henry, a recognition that his profligate lifestyle is a road to nowhere. This is also the first indication that his attraction to Catherine Barkley is more than sexual desire. His lonely and hollow feeling is a positive sign that he is beginning to understand that Catherine might be able fill the hollowness inside him. The phrase may also be an allusion to T. S. Eliot's poem "The Hollow Men." See entry 93:1–8. The holograph manuscript highlights the epistemological theme, adding, to conclude the chapter, "Something I did not know about was going on all right" (JFK item 64).

CHAPTER 8

36:7–8 the junction of the road to Cormons: The junction lies about five miles west of Gorizia, across the Isonzo River. To travel north to Plava without crossing Austrian lines, it was necessary to travel first west to Cormons and then north so as to approach Plava from the West. See entry 20:6–20.

36:19 "And you're all right?" This is a sign of growth in Frederic, as he expresses concern for Catherine's well-being.

36:21 "a show up above Plava": Frederic uses the British term *show* to describe what is to be the beginning of the Tenth Battle of the Isonzo. See entries 11:3–4 and 26:37–27:10. The date is 11 May 1917, the day before the battle is to begin.

37:6–36 Saint Anthony . . . dressing stations: A full understanding of the richness of this allusion is essential. Catherine gives Frederic what she has been told is a "very useful" Saint Anthony medal for his protection, even though she is an apparent atheist. See entry 16:39. That is, Hemingway presents Catherine as someone between a religious believer and a strict atheist/materialist. Even without a belief in an afterlife, Catherine has a mystical side, which manifests itself here as well as at other points in the novel. As such, her mysticism helps underscore the notion that Frederic and Catherine's love is a religious feeling.

This passage, with its reference to Saint Anthony, can also serve as an excellent example of what Susan Beegel calls Hemingway's "craft of omission," also known as his iceberg principle. See entry 3:1–5. In alluding ambiguously to a "Saint Anthony," Hemingway coyly neglects to inform us that there is not just one Saint Anthony in Catholic theology; the *Book of Saints* lists no fewer than twenty different saints named Anthony (Benedictine Monks). However, only two of these, as far as we can determine, are found as icons on medals worn for protection: Anthony of Padua and Anthony of Egypt. Both are relevant to what Hemingway is presenting in *A Farewell to Arms;* Hemingway was surely aware of both Saint Anthonys, and, since he does not identify which one is referenced here, the ambiguity is probably fully intended. Most critics, Reynolds and Stoneback included, automatically assume the saint intended is Anthony of Padua (1195–1231 A.D.), since Padua, in northeast Italy, is within the geographic locus of the novel, and Anthony of Padua is the patron saint for the return of lost items, for the protection of pregnant women, and for the protection of travelers (see Reynolds, *First War* 239; Stoneback, "Lovers' Sonnets Turn'd to Holy Psalms" 50). Reynolds, however, confuses Saint Anthony of Padua with Saint Jude, the patron of lost causes.

There should be little difficulty in understanding the relevance here of the patron saint of lost items, Anthony of Padua. Catherine wants to ensure the safe return of her love, to guarantee that he is not lost. Though at first reluctant to wear the medal, Frederic follows the advice of his ambulance driver, puts it around his neck under his shirt, and forgets about it. He wears the icon until he is wounded, a fact he chooses to reveal here rather than to wait until it happens in chapter 9, when he loses the medal. In keeping with the novel's general level of ambiguity, Frederic cannot say how the medal is lost. He figures, "Some one probably got it at one of the dressing stations" (37:35–36). The irony of losing the object designed for the return of lost items would not have been *lost* on Hemingway. Given the novel's concern with matters of faith, naturally, we are left to wonder whether the medal does any good in protecting Frederic as traveler and ensuring that he is not lost to Catherine. Yes, Frederic is returned to Catherine alive, but not without having been seriously wounded. The traveler, in other words, has not been fully protected.

In addition, although Frederic and Catherine have not yet consummated their relationship, eventually she will become pregnant, and thus, if she were religious, she would have reason to call on Saint Anthony of Padua to protect her and her unborn child. The Saint Anthony of Padua medal depicts him holding an infant, actually the Christ child. So, in the larger context of the book, as Stoneback indicates, the loss of the medal foreshadows the disastrous end to her pregnancy ("Lovers' Sonnets Turn'd to Holy Psalms" 50).

Stoneback is so good at explaining the relevance of Saint Anthony of Padua that it is unfortunate he misses the other relevant Saint Anthony, who, it can be argued, is as equally important to Hemingway's text as Anthony of Padua, if not more so. Saint Anthony of Egypt lacks the geographic connection of Padua, but is, nonetheless, very pertinent for reasons that should become obvious. Miriam Mandel is the only scholar we have found to identify him as a potential source for the icon on Frederic's medal (*Reading Hemingway* 116–17). However, she apparently confuses Anthony of Egypt with Anthony of Padua, quoting Stoneback that Saint Anthony "is chiefly invoked for the return of lost property," without realizing, apparently, that these are two different Saint Anthonys. Saint Anthony of Egypt, also known as Saint Anthony the Abbot (ca. 251–356 A.D.), is regarded as the father of monasticism. An Anthony of Egypt medal typically depicts the saint with a long beard, bearing a staff and a book, facing a lion. Although he is regarded as the protector against infectious skin diseases, most often Catholics pray to Saint Anthony of Egypt to help them persevere in their faith, because Anthony, according to his biography, persevered mightily against repeated demonic temptations ("Saint Anthony the Abbot").

Actually, few icons of Catholic sainthood have preoccupied artists of various media more than Saint Anthony of Egypt. His life story, colorfully written by one of his contemporaries, Athanasius of Alexandria (a saint in his own right), became one of the best known and widely read pieces of Latin literature in the Catholic Church through the Middle Ages. The highlight of the biography is the account of the temptations of Saint Anthony, a series of sometimes bizarre supernatural encounters with demons, who repeatedly challenge Saint Anthony's faith in God. Hemingway may not have read Athanasius, but by 23 January 1923, he had some familiarity with Saint Anthony of Egypt, because he alludes to him in a letter to Ezra Pound: "I have laid off the barber in order that I wont be able to take a newspaper job no matter how badly St. Anthonied" (*Letters 2* 6). Since poverty is not associated with Saint Anthony of Padua, who was born to a wealthy Portuguese family, there can be no doubt that Hemingway was referring here to Saint Anthony of Egypt. The reference also suggests that Pound, the devotee of Gustave Flaubert, had already introduced Hemingway to the best known contemporary literary treatment of Saint Anthony of Egypt, Flaubert's *The Temptation of Saint Anthony*.

Although well-known paintings of the Temptation of Saint Anthony were on display in museums across Europe, including those in Paris, Madrid, and Genoa, with which Hemingway was familiar, Flaubert offers the kind of extended detailed account of the saint that would have captured Hemingway's sustained attention. In addition, it would have come to him with the endorsement of writers whom he greatly respected: not only Pound, but also John Dos Passos and F. Scott Fitzgerald, both of whom reference Flaubert's *Anthony* in their works. There is also an extended reference to Saint Anthony of Egypt in Samuel Butler's *The Way of All Flesh*, which Hemingway read. Furthermore, Hemingway's friend and correspondent Isidor Schneider published a long narrative poem called "The Temptation of Anthony," about a man undergoing a crisis of faith, which appeared in *The American Caravan: A Yearbook of American Literature* (1927) along with Hemingway's short story "An Alpine Idyll" and was published separately as a book in 1928.

Space precludes a detailed discussion here of Flaubert's *Temptation*. It is enough to say that central to its theme is an unresolved conflict between science and faith, an attempt to find a kind of balance between the two. As Flaubert scholar Mary Orr explains, "[i]n the end, Antoine's personal expression of belief remains precisely that of the religious or anti-religious reader, since neither religion nor science has adjudicated finally on first things. . . . His final epiphany is then not so much pantheistic as pan-creational, to bring the wonders of natural science and the ecstatic experience of mystics into one work, a modern *mystere*" (228). Like Anthony, Frederic is in the midst of a crisis of faith that he ultimately cannot resolve, and the Saint

Anthony medal, deep within Hemingway's iceberg, is, thus, more intricately tied to the theme of the novel than has been previously appreciated.

37:22 His right hand left the wheel: A subtle joke by Hemingway/Frederic that suggests the dualities at play in the novel.

37:35 After I was wounded: It is notable that in one sentence Frederic shifts from the present narrative to skip ahead to an event in the next chapter. These indications do not occur often in the text, but when they do, they remind us that he is a retrospective narrator—that is, one who, like Proust's narrator in *In Search of Lost Time* (or, as Hemingway would have known it *Remembrance of Things Past*), is telling us a story that happened at some time in the past. He has the entire story in his mind as he is telling it to us.

38:8–9 a long column of loaded mules: While this may allude to Saint Anthony of Padua's Miracle of the Mule, in which a mule kneels before the saint in recognition of his Godly authority, the allusion could also just as well be to Saint Anthony of Egypt. In Flaubert's *Temptation of Saint Anthony,* "mules loaded with baggage" are part of the procession in prelude to the entrance of the Queen of Sheba, who represents the temptations of the flesh, like those that have tempted Frederic often (83). The mules can thus be seen as precursors of the fact that Frederic's faith is about to be severely tested, in his wounding and all that surrounds it. In John Dos Passos's *Three Soldiers*, read by Hemingway, John Andrews is composing music inspired by the entrance of the Queen of Sheba in Flaubert's narrative (*Novels* 386). See entry 37:6–36.

38:9–10 the drivers walking along beside the mules wearing red fezzes: The last three words comprise a misplaced modifier. Of course, the drivers, not the mules, are wearing red fezzes.

38:10 bersaglieri: These are elite Italian infantrymen specially trained as highly mobile sharpshooters. (The name, which should be capitalized, means *marksmen*). Their most distinctive headgear was a plumage of cockerel feathers on the right side of their broad-brimmed hats. In parades, Bersaglieri distinctively keep at a fast jog to demonstrate their swiftness and endurance. Because of their high visibility, the ostentatious feathers were removed in the front lines in 1915, but they were brought back for morale reasons in 1917. The red fez with a long, blue tassel was the Bersaglieri undress headgear (Nicolle 22). Benito Mussolini, fascist prime minister of Italy from 1922 to 1943, was a sergeant in the Eleventh Bersaglieri Regiment during World War I and, like Frederic, was wounded on the Isonzo front in 1917. However, Mussolini's wounding was the result of an accidental explosion of an Italian mortar bomb in his trench on 22 February (Gilbert 310). When he was released from the hospital in August, he returned to his prewar occupation of journalism.

38:11–39:5 **Beyond the mule train . . . beside the river:** As we read this long, vividly descriptive passage that is comparable in detail to some of the best descriptive writing in *The Sun Also Rises,* we should recall that, in this instance, unlike in his descriptions of Spain, Hemingway was working entirely through his research and imagination. G. M. Trevelyan was likely helpful. See entry 38:27. The road trip from Gorizia to Plava via Cormons is about thirty-four miles over some very hilly and mountainous terrain, so it is likely that it took more than an hour for Frederic's ambulance crew to drive it.

38:27 **rough new military road:** Hemingway likely got this detail from G. M. Trevelyan's *Scenes from Italy's War,* which mentions this new "more sheltered road," cut down to Plava in preparation for the May offensive of 1917 (72–73). Trevelyan calls it the road of "thirty-two hairpins. . . . a wonderful piece of engineering but slow work for a car with a bad lock" (129). Since the roads permitted traffic in only one direction, ambulances and trucks came down by the new road and returned by the old. The new road, in other words, doubled the traffic that could be sustained in each direction and dramatically reduced the amount of time for wounded to be taken to hospitals. Frederic would later benefit from this speed.

CHAPTER 9

On this page in the manuscript, Hemingway wrote, "Read August 12. Seems fine so far" (JFK item 64).

40:1–3 screens of cornstalk . . . entrance of a circus or a native village: The cornstalk and straw matting help conceal the Italian troop movements from the Austrians in this mountainous terrain. Giovanni Cecchin's *Americani sul Grappa* (*Americans on the Grappa*) contains photos of the same kind of road matting and camouflage on the Trentino front (272).

40:9 Austrian observation balloons: Giovanni Cecchin's *Americani sul Grappa* contains photos of these huge observation balloons (264–65). The Austrians generally had the advantage of higher ground, looking down on the Italians, but they augmented these advantages with observation balloons filled with hydrogen, outfitted with a man in a suspended wicker basket below the balloon, with a wireless radio, binoculars, and a long-range camera. The balloons could be shot down but only with great difficulty, because they were protected by fighter planes as well as antiaircraft guns and long-range machine guns on the ground. In addition, the balloons were tethered to the ground with a motorized winch and could be drawn down within a minute if they spotted an enemy fighter in the area (M. Duffy).

40:17 It was a one-road show: Frederic's description contradicts Trevelyan's explanation that the return journey for the ambulances was to take the old road. See entry 38:27.

41:3 the war in Libya: The major refers to the Italo-Turkish War, fought in Libya between Italy and the Ottoman Empire of Turkey from 29 September 1911 to 18 October 1912. The Italians sought their own African colonies, as Britain, France, Belgium, and Germany had done. The war was an important precursor to World War I, because the Italians' relatively easy capture of Tripoli, Benghazi, and Turbruk stirred Balkan aggression against the Turks also. The war was the first in which aircraft were used to drop bombs. See Gooch for an account of the Italian army during the war in Libya (38–50).

41:13 when I came in they stopped: The drivers' behavior is a natural expression of the difference in status between an officer and the men who serve under him. Although Frederic seems an unusually democratic leader who respects his subordinates, he has been away for several months on leave, and they are clearly not yet entirely comfortable in his presence.

41:14 Macedonias: A brand of cigarettes sold in Italy, with highly aromatic Turkish tobacco typically grown in Macedonia. Once the nation of Alexander the Great, Macedonia is now a region made up of parts of Greece, Bulgaria, and Yugoslavia.

41:17 Fiat radiator: The shape of the lighter imitates the shape of the radiator of a Fiat automobile. See entry 28:6. The Italian ambulances for which Frederic and his drivers are responsible are Fiats and representative of an increasingly industrial, mechanistic culture.

41:22 "They'll shell the —— out of us": Probably spoken by Passini. The dash replaces the word *shit*, which Hemingway wrote in the holograph manuscript (JFK item 64). This is one of several omissions Hemingway's publisher forced on him, but still it adds to the characterization of Passini, the most outspoken and aggressive of the drivers. His words carry a bitter irony when it is he who is then killed by the enemy shelling (48:1–8). See entry 29:2 for a discussion of censorship issues in the novel.

41:34–35 They were all mechanics and hated the war: Another reason for the drivers' silence in the presence of Frederic is that in the Italian army at that time officers were generally drawn from the middle and upper classes, whereas the enlisted men came from the peasant classes, with whom officers were not expected to socialize away from the front lines. The middle and upper classes generally supported Italy's entry into the war, but the peasants, never clear about the motives for a war that put their lives at risk, tended to oppose it, as suggested here.

In this chapter, Frederic's men come to recognize him as a sympathetic foreigner, whom they undertake to convert to their antiwar sentiments. Having been unified only since 1871, Italy was still just a loose union of disparate provinces, and its major hope was to claim or reclaim the border regions to its north and east (the setting of this novel), where Italian was, had been, or should be (in the view of irrendentists) the dominant language and culture.

42:4 Bersaglieri: See entry 38:10.

42:18 granatieri: The Italian word for grenadiers. The *Granatieri di Sardegna* were an elite brigade of grenadiers, chosen for their height (Nicolle 21). Hugh Dalton, in *With British Guns in Italy,* describes a unit of *Granatieri* thus:

> Just before we entered Gradisca, we passed a Battalion of the Granatieri, the Italian Grenadiers, all six foot tall, with collar badges of crimson and white, coming up from reserve to fight a rear-guard action. . . . And in their march that night and in their faces was scorn for fugitives and contempt for death. The Major said to me, as they swung past us, that that Battalion could be trusted to fight to the end. And they did. (109)

Such a description does not seem to apply to the drivers' discussion here, in which the *Granatieri* appear to be a joke that everyone understands. The reference is to an earlier incident on the Isonzo front, where some *Granatieri* refused an order to attack.

42:23–24 "They . . . took every tenth man. Carabinieri shot them": The practice of executing every tenth man is known as decimation, a measure used to instill discipline out of fear. See entry 13:20. Usually lots are drawn to select those to be killed. The practice was initially instituted in the ancient Roman army. Italian Supreme Commander Luigi Cardona approved of the harsh measure as incidents of mutiny among the army, like that of the *Granatieri* discussed in entry 42:18, became more common as the war wore on. For *Carabinieri* see entry 21:12.

42:39–43:3 "Now they have a guard . . . take their property": In addition to execution of the cowardly or mutinous soldier, the soldier's family also faced severe punishments as Passini describes here.

43:4–5 "If it wasn't that that happens . . . nobody would go to the attack": It is unclear who speaks this line, but it argues that the punishment of the families was a greater inducement for soldiers not to rebel than was the threat of execution.

43:6 Alpini: The Alpini were a special infantry class recruited from the mountains of northern Italy and especially adept at mountain fighting.

43:6 V.E. soldiers: As Hemingway explained to Maurice Coindreau, his French translator, these were "shock troops," who in 1917 would become known as the Arditi (*Letters 4* 382). *VE* is the monogram of King Victor Emmanuel III, which they wore on their left arm band. Here, as in most respects in the novel, Hemingway is historically accurate. This monogram was created in 1916 to honor especially brave soldiers in any unit. Not until June 1917 were these men gathered together in select units, which were officially designated *reparti d'assalto,* shock troops, although they would come to be known as the Arditi, "bold ones" (Nicolle 23). At this point in the narrative, May 1917, VE soldiers would still be specially recognized men of courage scattered among different units in the Italian army. In Hemingway's "A Very Short Story," an earlier attempt to convert into fiction the autobiographical material of his wounding and love affair with his nurse during recuperation, Luz, a nurse, falls in love with the major of a battalion of Arditi, ending her relationship with the American (*CSS* 108). Also, in Hemingway's story "In Another Country," one of the narrator's companions undergoing rehabilitation from war wounds is a lieutenant in the Arditi (207). Donald Daiker contributed to this entry.

43:8 **"Evviva l'esercito":** "Long live the army," spoken sarcastically by Passini. The drivers are surprised that Frederic allows them to speak so critically.

43:18 **"Defeat is worse":** Frederic is expressing an opinion that Hemingway held and expressed often in his career. In a 1938 essay for *Ken* magazine, he declared, "War is a hateful and dirty business but when one has become involved in a war there is only one thing to do: win it" ("Treachery in Aragon" 26). In 1942, in the introduction to the *Men at War* anthology, he wrote, "But once we have a war there is only one thing to do. It must be won. For defeat brings worse things than any that can ever happen in a war" (xi). Later in the same essay, he added, "But there are worse things than war; and all of them come with defeat. . . . You have to win it and get rid of the people that made it and see that, this time, it never comes to us again" (xxvi–xxvii). Finally, in *Across the River and into the Trees,* Colonel Cantwell claims, "If you ever fight, then you must win it" (286).

43:31 **Tchecos:** This is an alternate spelling for Czechs, soldiers from Czechoslovakia, which was part of the Austro-Hungarian Empire until 1919. Passini cites the Czech soldiers as an example of Manera's assertion in the previous lines that an army cannot make conquered soldiers fight.

43:36–37 **"When people realize how bad it is . . . they go crazy":** This is another reference to the motif of insanity in the novel. Passini understands the complete irrationality of the war and the complete inability of the objective human mind to understand it rationally.

44:5 **San Gabriele:** See entry 27:30.

44:6 **Carso . . . Monfalcone . . . Trieste:** For the Carso see entry 6:4. Monfalcone is a coastal industrial town near the mouth of the Isonzo River. Its mention here by one of the drivers as a so far uncaptured objective is a rare historical error by Hemingway. The Italians, in fact, captured Monfalcone quickly at the start of the war, on 9

June 1915, during the First Battle of the Isonzo, and they held it until the Caporetto Retreat in October 1917. The capture of Monfalcone was the first significant Italian victory. Trieste is an important seaport just eighteen miles down the coast of the Adriatic from Monfalcone, with a predominantly Italian population, living under Austro-Hungarian rule during the time of the novel. Its capture was a major goal of the Italian irredentists, who wished to bring under Italian rule all regions where the Italian language was dominant. Italian speakers made up 60 percent of Trieste's population in 1911. The city remained under Austrian control until the Italians captured it on 3 November 1918, just days before the war's end. Irish writer James Joyce, who befriended Hemingway in Paris in the 1920s, was a resident of Trieste from 1904 to 1915, when he moved to Zurich, Switzerland, because of the war. In Trieste, Joyce befriended and tutored the native Triestine Ettore Schmitz, another novelist, who wrote under the pseudonym Italo Svevo. Hemingway owned a copy of Svevo's modernist novel *La Coscienza di Zeno* (1923) in Italian (Reynolds, *Hemingway's Reading* 179). Svevo's novel is set in Trieste and Lucinico in the period just prior to and during the opening days of the war.

44:13 **"We think. We read"**: Passini describes a growing class of educated and skilled workers in an evolving Italy. Literacy—which might seem a given in most of Europe—was a new factor in Italian politics. According to Robert Casillo and John Paul Russo, illiteracy, which in the nineteenth century had been far higher in Italy than in most of the rest of Europe, had been virtually eliminated by 1914, and nationalistic, fascistic, socialistic, and conservative forces, chief among them the omnipresent Catholic Church, struggled with each other as the nation waged war with Austria-Hungary and Germany.

45:10 **"Savoia," said the major:** *Savoia* is an Italian war cry that dates at least to the nineteenth century, abbreviated from *Avanti Savoia!* meaning *Go Savoia!* It was used to exhort soldiers in the Italian army into battle in support of the King and the Royal Family, which was known as the House of Savoy, established by Humbert I, Count of Savoy, in 1003. The Savoyard kings who ruled a unified Italy from 1861 to 1946 were Victor Emmanuel II (1861–1878), Umberto I (1878–1900), Victor Emmanuel III (1900–1946), and Umberto II (9 May–12 June 1946). Umberto II was deposed following Italy's constitutional referendum in 1946. The major here seems to utter the battle cry mechanically, without any enthusiasm. In *The White War*, Mark Thompson describes the use of the cry by Italian officers:

> The countdown was excruciating; after fixing bayonets and draining the double tot of grappa, the men had to get through endless minutes before their officer shouted "Avanti Savoia!" and led them into the smoking din. . . . The men knew an attack was imminent when the military police mounted their machine guns

behind the trench, ready to shoot at soldiers who lingered when the cry of "Savoy!" went up. (226–27)

In Hemingway's short story "A Way You'll Never Be," Nick Adams, clearly suffering from PTSD, recalls a moment in his own battle experience very similar to what Thompson describes: "Do you think they'll go over? If they don't, shoot two and try to scoop the others out some way. Keep behind them, sergeant. It's no use to walk ahead and find there's nothing coming behind you. Bail them out as you go. What a bloody balls. All right. That's right. Then, looking at the watch, in that quiet tone, that valuable quiet tone, 'Savoia'" (*CSS* 310).

As a measure of Savoia's significance in Italian military lore, the Italian army maintained a cavalry regiment called the Savoia Cavalleria, which is known for perhaps the last cavalry charge in history, against a Russian regiment in World War II. The skirmish is called the Charge of the Savoia Cavalleria at Izbushensky, where seven hundred Italian cavalry attacked a Russian force of twenty-five hundred. In "A Way You'll Never Be," Nick also recalls having once seen the "Terza Savoia cavalry regiment riding in the snow with their lances. The horses' breath made plumes in the cold air" (*CSS* 314–15). John Beall and Mark Cirino contributed to this note.

45:17 **pasta asciutta:** Plain pasta, cooked but without any sauce.

45:27 **something was set down beside the entrance:** A wounded man has been brought to the first aid station. Hemingway/Frederic's choice to describe the wounded man as "something" highlights the necessary inhumanity of warfare. Frederic cannot pause to consider the man's condition. His immediate task is getting food to his drivers so they have the energy and alertness to do their very important job as well as they can. A short time later, Frederic will himself become a wounded "something."

45:32 **and brought him in:** The holograph manuscript adds much more detail: "His head hung on one side and his tongue was out. There was dirt blown into his face and dirt in his eyes and as he breathed a very light red ['scarlet' crossed out] foam made bubbles where his tunic was ripped and torn along his chest as though it had been rubbed against an emery wheel" (JFK item 64).

46:19–20 **"Start in to eat, Tenente." . . ."Put it on the floor. We'll all eat":** For Hemingway, eating and drinking are essential rituals, to be carefully and mindfully savored communally. Here as elsewhere in this novel, even a simple meal has the effect of a secular communion rite. Frederic's initiative in obtaining the simple food is extended by his democratic leadership in sharing it with his men, as he declines to eat first. Normally, the subordinates would defer to their officer, allowing him to eat before them.

46:35–36 Something landed outside that shook the earth: A verbal echo of Frederic's use of *something* to refer to a wounded man. See entry 45:27. In this case, the *something* is an artillery shell that could make of Frederic and his men *something* that would require medical attention.

46:37 "Four hundred twenty or minnenwerfer": "Four hundred twenty" means a 420 millimeter diameter artillery shell. These were used by super heavy howitzers. Frederic is correct that these were too large and difficult to move for use in mountain fighting. A "minnenwerfer" (correctly spelled *Minenwerfer*, German for *mine launcher*) was a short-range mortar cannon that came in three sizes, the largest of which was 260 millimeters in caliber, but only put into service near the end of the war in 1918.

47:1–2 "Skoda guns. I've seen the holes." . . ."Three hundred fives": Gavuzzi is challenging Frederic's knowledge of Austrian artillery, but Frederic knows what he is talking about. The Austrians indeed used the Skoda 305 millimeter guns on the Italian front.

47:6 "big trench mortar": Again, it is Frederic who identifies this, who seems to have more knowledge of Austrian artillery than any of his men. A trench mortar shell could possibly be a 225 millimeter *Minenwerfer*. It is probably a shell of this size that wounds Frederic soon after this. On 8 July 1918, more than a year later than the setting of this moment in the novel, Hemingway was wounded by a similar weapon while delivering chocolate and cigarettes to Italian soldiers in the trenches along the Piave River near Fossalta. Although Carlos Baker says that the mortar that wounded Hemingway was probably 420 caliber, that is highly unlikely, since the largest Austrian trench mortar was 260 caliber, put into service in March 1918 (Baker, *Life Story* 44; Ortner 480).

47:12–17 I tried to breathe . . . and I was back: As Allen Josephs has observed, Frederic Henry, at the moment of his wounding, describes an out-of-body experience (OBE) combined with a near-death experience (NDE), phenomena that have received considerable attention in neurological and psychological research. In fact, this passage is one of four (or possibly five) known instances—two fictional and two (or three) ostensibly nonfictional—in which Hemingway described such an experience. Whether what is described is autobiographical (and there are reasons to be skeptical), for Frederic Henry, such an experience is, naturally, significant. Often, an OBE and/or an NDE can provide a person with subjective evidence of an afterlife. It can turn blind faith into a justified true belief, something that can count as knowledge (Dew and Foreman 24). We have seen that the atheism of the officers at the mess and of Catherine Barkley (see entries 7:16–17 and 17:2) have forced

Frederic to consider his own beliefs in an afterlife. Here, as if in response, Frederic asserts, "I knew I was dead and that it had all been a mistake to think you just died" (47:15–16). However, we should be careful not to regard the question as settled.

As is so often the case here, we should ask what it means *to know,* a question at the heart of the novel's epistemic theme. The entire experience is presented necessarily subjectively by the first-person narrator, making it more difficult to determine what objectively happens. The key verbs in the passage are *felt* and *knew,* but both express subjectivity in this instance. Frederic claims that he feels himself "rush bodily out of" himself and "out and out and out and all the time bodily in the wind. I went out swiftly, all of myself" (47:13–15). Frederic's *feelings* lead him to conclude that he *knows* he is dead, but that claim is almost immediately refuted by the objective fact that he does not die from the explosion of the mortar shell. He "float[s] and instead of going on [he feels himself] slide back" (47:16–17). The whole experience seems very brief, only a few seconds, though the wording makes it difficult to know precisely how much time passes. When it is over, the most Frederic can conclude, based on the description he provides us, is that perhaps he has had a glimpse of an afterlife, some tenuous subjective evidence of the existence of an immortal soul. But how can he truly know with certainty? Frederic's reticence here and in the rest of the novel adds to our challenge. About the only thing we can say for sure at this point is that Frederic now knows this war can kill him, a realization in itself enough to produce significant change in anyone's character. Nevertheless, it is curious that Frederic apparently never shares this experience with anyone else in the novel—not his close friends Rinaldi or the priest and not even the person of whom he comes to think as his twin, Catherine Barkley. For studies of the characteristics and effects of OBEs and NDEs, see Blackmore, Blanke and Dieguez, and Carruthers.

For Hemingway, the writing of this passage marked the fourth and perhaps final time, that we know of, in which he described an OBE or NDE relating to his own or a fictional character's wartime wounding. The previous three were a speech he delivered to an Oak Park High School assembly soon after he returned from the war in 1919, then in the writing of the Nick Adams short story "Now I Lay Me" in late 1926, followed by a conversation with his journalist friend Guy Hickock during a ten-day road trip through northern Italy in March 1927. The two ostensibly nonfictional accounts are certainly interesting but problematic. To the Oak Park High School assembly, Hemingway claimed, "When the thing exploded, it seemed as if I was moving off somewhere in a sort of red din. I said to myself, 'Gee! Stein, you're dead,' and then I began to feel myself pulling back to earth. Then I woke up" (qtd. in Hemingway, *My Brother* 47). We might be more inclined to accept this as fact if Hemingway had not also spiced his story with the blatant lie that he was serving in the Italian Sixty-ninth Regiment of Infantry when he was wounded and with the certain falsehoods that he was awarded the highest decoration given by the Italian government, which was "conferred personally by the King of Italy" (47–48). Much like his character Harold Krebs in "Soldier's Home," Hemingway apparently felt the need to lie about his war experiences so people would listen to him (*CSS* 111).

Hemingway's second ostensibly nonfictional account of an OBE is the tale that Guy Hickock relates in a 1927 article for the *Brooklyn Eagle*:

> "We were in a hole with sand bags around," [Hemingway] says, not for publication. "There was one of those big noises that sometimes occur on fronts. I died then." And he laughs a big tough laugh. "I felt my soul or something coming right out of my body, like you'd pull a silk handkerchief out of a pocket by one corner. It flew all around and then came back and went in again and I wasn't dead any more." (qtd. in Trogdon 190)

Once again, this account is accompanied by verifiable falsehoods that make it impossible to accept this version at face value. Besides the OBE, Hemingway claims to Hickock to have been "an honest to Jerry Italian officer in command of Italian troops" at the time of the wounding and that he has a metal kneecap and a grafted bone in his foot as a result of the experience (190). In reality, Hemingway only served as a noncombatant ambulance driver in the American Red Cross. He never served in the Italian army, least of all as a commanding officer, and the details about the kneecap and foot are refuted by reproductions of X-rays of Hemingway's knee and foot published in Villard and Nagel's *Hemingway in Love and War* (218). Even Hemingway's wording in describing the OBE/NDE to Hickock seems to have been a bit of self-plagiarism. In a typescript draft of the fictional OBE passage in "Now I Lay Me," composed some five months earlier, Hemingway had written that Nick's soul leaving his body was "something like a red silk handkerchief being pulled out of your pocket if your pocket was your body" (JFK item 620).

Getting the words right, finding the Flaubertian *mot juste*, in describing an OBE was challenging to Hemingway. He went through several drafts of the few OBE lines in "Now I Lay Me" (JFK items 619–22), and his final description, the passage in *A Farewell to Arms*, is one of the most heavily revised pages in the holograph manuscript preserved at the JFK Library (item 64). In the first draft, the description is much longer than the published version, 119 words versus 78. A transcription of the original draft is reproduced in appendix 1 of the Hemingway Library edition, page 291, no. 3–4, which includes the sentence "I knew I was dead and that it had all been a mistake to think you just died." Hemingway did not alter this for the published novel. In other words, he was confident about making the point that Frederic sees this as proof that death is not the end. He seems to have been less certain, however, about referring to the soul. In the original, Frederic feels as though there is "a long thin wire through the center of my soul," a phrase Hemingway scratched for publication. However, the word *bodily* does not appear in the original draft. Hemingway removed the soul and added the body to his final version. With all this in mind, we can conclude that Frederic Henry does have an OBE, leading him to believe, at least for the time being, that he has crossed over into death and come back.

Perhaps the least reliable report of a Hemingway OBE/NDE did not surface until a 1978 *National Enquirer* article. There, after a summary of the previous four accounts, all of which the article takes as autobiographical fact, Hemingway's brother Leicester claims that Ernest said to him in 1934,

> I've died once already, and since then I've no longer been afraid of death. . . . I felt myself high up in the air. Suddenly I had a feeling of deep inner peace. I felt my soul slipping from my body and flying free. I knew with absolute certainty that I had died—and yet, strangely, I felt no fear. . . . When I was in the hospital, they came and gave me a medal for bravery. I didn't tell them I'd gained more than any medal from that experience with death. (Wright 37)

However, Leicester later told Allen Josephs that the *Enquirer* reporter took "certain liberties with what he said," while acknowledging that it was "partially true," leaving us to wonder what was true and what was not (Josephs 14). Given the reputation of the *National Enquirer* for "fake news" and that Leicester Hemingway's comments to Josephs came just a few months before Leicester committed suicide in September 1982, there is every reason to be skeptical of this account. In addition, we should note that none of these five stories of OBEs, fictional or nonfictional, has nearly the level of detail that typical accounts of an OBE contain—most importantly, details of what the subject saw from an elevated perspective, including the subject's own body. See, for example, Robert A. Monroe's extensive accounts of his many OBE experiences in *Journeys Out of the Body* or Susan Blackmore's description of her own OBE in "An Out-of-Body Experience."

Nevertheless, a surprising number of Hemingway biographers seem to assume that Frederic's description of an OBE is autobiographical (Griffin 74–75; Meyers 30–36; Mellow 60–61; Hutchisson 27; Dearborn 63; Paul 154–60). Even though most of them point out Hemingway's great propensity to distort his war record, not even the most respected biographers, Reynolds or Baker, ever questions the veracity of the OBE claim—perhaps because such a claim is, admittedly, impossible to disprove. No one but Hemingway can know whether he had an OBE on the night of 8 July 1918, when he was wounded. However, scholars need to be consistent in avoiding the biographical fallacy in this instance and elsewhere. With Hemingway, there is almost always too much ambiguity present not to be skeptical about the details of his life.

One final note: without treating the OBE passage in *A Farewell to Arms* as autobiographical, Mark Cirino has perceptively pointed out the way Hemingway presents Frederic's experience "in a decidedly ambiguous way": "[T]he bombing transcends a moment of life and death and exists as a dramatic moment of transfiguration or conversion—in which a person's identity is at stake, his psychological self, and not just his biological self. In this way, readers are invested in the transformation of the protagonist, and the bombing has a psychological and spiritual impact, not just a physical one" ("Supreme Moment" 255). The ambiguity that Cirino recognizes does not make our job as interpreters any easier, but it is certain that Hemingway wants us to recognize the wounding as a transfigurative moment for Frederic. And we will see the quality and the extent of that transfiguration most clearly in his subsequent interactions with Rinaldi, the priest, and Catherine over the remainder of the novel, even without his ever mentioning the OBE to them.

47:25 **"Mama Mia":** This is Italian for *My mother* but also a call for Maria or Mary, the mother of Christ, a common Catholic plea of a supplicant. Cirino points out that the correct Italian spelling should be *Mamma* ("You Don't Know" 59).

47:32 **"Dio te salve, Maria":** Correctly, as Cirino points out, the phrase should be "*Dio ti salvi, Maria*," which translates literally as "God save you, Mary" ("You Don't Know" 59). This and other calls to Jesus and God are examples of human desire for an interventionist divinity, one who can ease human suffering. One of Frederic's persistent concerns, as it is for Dostoevsky's Ivan Karamazov, is God's relationship to the suffering that exists in the world.

47:37 **"Porta feriti!"** Mark Cirino corrects this to "*Portaferiti!*" meaning *bearer* ("You Don't Know" 59). Frederic is calling for stretcher bearers to carry off the wounded.

48:8 **I made sure he was dead:** The original manuscript has "His teeth were relaxed from his arm and his lips were drawn back and when I touched him I knew he was dead" (JFK item 64).

48:13 **My knee wasn't there:** Whether or not Frederic's out-of-body experience is autobiographical, his fictional wounding is similar in some respects to Hemingway's actual wounding, which occurred about fourteen months later than Frederic's and at a much different location, near the town of Fossalta on the Piave River about seventy-five miles west of Plava, where Frederic is wounded. There are also other significant differences. According to X-rays that have survived, Hemingway's knee, unlike Frederic's, was intact following the wounding (Villard and Nagel 218). Although Hemingway led some people (Guy Hickock, for example) to believe that he had an artificial metal knee cap implanted after the wounding, no more surgery was required beyond removing a machine gun bullet lodged behind his kneecap (see Trogdon 190). Neither is such surgery necessary for Frederic, in spite of the seriousness of his knee damage. Frederic is only wounded by an exploding trench mortar shell, whereas Hemingway was wounded by both a trench mortar and machine gun fire. Although some accounts of Hemingway's wounding report that he carried a wounded man after the trench mortar explosion and then was hit by machine gun fire, the most plausible explanation is that Hemingway was hit by machine gun fire as *he* was being carried by stretcher bearers out of the dugout where the explosion occurred.

48:16 **Oh, God, I said, get me out of here:** Frederic prays for the intervention of God. The question of God's intervention in the affairs of the world is central to the novel's theme.

48:16–17 **I knew, however, that there had been three others:** Dropping the prayer and moving out of the subjective realm of faith into the objective realm of reason, Frederic shows both remarkable awareness and remarkable concern for his men, considering his own pain and fear. Even under duress, he thinks of himself as just one among several wounded.

50:11 **"medical wallahs":** *Wallah* is an Anglo-Indian term for a person with any particular occupation, in this case medical personnel. The usage may indicate the British officer has spent time in India but at least suggests British internationalism, as does his "voluble and perfect Italian," which he uses to get Frederic prompt treatment (50:8).

50:26 **"the legitimate son of President Wilson":** The US president in 1917 was Woodrow Wilson, highly respected around the world as a leader of democracy and a skillful diplomat. At the time of Frederic's wounding, in May 1917, the United States had just declared war on Germany, an act that lifted the Allies' hopes. Thus, the British officer is using the president's name, if only jokingly, to get Frederic more prompt treatment among the Italians. He may not have been aware that Woodrow Wilson had three daughters but no sons. A little later, the officer repeats the joke in another form by calling Frederic the "only son of the American Ambassador" (50:33).

50:30 **"Ça va bien?"** Frederic, probably jokingly, addresses the Italian major surgeon, whom he knows, in French, asking him if things are going well. The major's response, likewise in French, "Ça va," means *It's okay*, but his furious look at them when they bring Frederic inside the dressing station indicates the extreme stress of the moment and his displeasure at seeing another patient that needs attention.

51:5–9 **"Multiple superficial wounds . . . line of duty":** The description of Frederic's wounds corresponds reasonably closely to the description of Hemingway's own wounds with the exception of the head wound, which is diagnosed preliminarily as a skull fracture (51:35), a diagnosis that is later contradicted by Rinaldi. See entry 56:8. The best research into Hemingway's wounding in Italy has been published by Henry Villard and James Nagel in *Hemingway in Love and War* (1989). See entry 48:13. He makes no mention of a head wound. However, Andrew Farah, in *Hemingway's Brain,* assumes that Hemingway would have experienced at least a concussion, even if he did not have a visible headwound (28–30). Hemingway may have decided to include Frederic's head wound after he himself suffered a severe gash to his head and probably a concussion in March 1928, when he accidentally yanked a skylight down onto his head (30). The gash required three interior and six exterior stitches, and all the bleeding probably reminded him of his war wounding (Reynolds, *American Homecoming* 166–67). It was about this time that he decided to abandon the "American Tom Jones" novel he had been working on and to switch to the one that would become *A Farewell to Arms*. Frederic's head wound, in other words, may be Hemingway's private joke to honor the moment of inspiration that produced this novel.

51:31 **"Better not drink too much brandy then"**: This line foreshadows the event later near the end of Frederic's treatment in Milan, when the antagonistic nurse Miss Van Campen accuses him of deliberately drinking too much alcohol in order to induce a case of jaundice that would get him out of returning to the front. See entry 125:4–9. However, it turns out that Frederic does not have a skull fracture, so it seems his drinking will not need to be curtailed so drastically (see entry 56:8).

51:33 **Sweat ran all over me:** The original manuscript adds, crossed out, "I knew I had never felt pain before. I hoped there would be a limit" (JFK item 64).

52:2–3 **"I always thought he was French":** This is one of several instances in the novel where Frederic's nationality is mistaken and is part of the general theme of Frederic's search for identity. As Mark Cirino has pointed out, in addition to this instance, Frederic will be mistaken for an Austrian officer by a barber in the hospital (79:39); for an Italian from North or South America by an Italian sergeant (170:13–14); for a German in disguise by battle police at the Tagliamento River (194:1); and for a South American by a bartender (206:12) ("You Don't Know" 43).

52:8 **"What class?"** Class refers to the year of a soldier's birth. The Italian army labeled those men born in 1899, for example, as the "Class of 1899." Young men were called up for service upon turning eighteen, so the Class of 1899 was eligible to be drafted in 1917.

52:22 **I lay still and let the pain ride:** In the original manuscript, after this sentence Hemingway wrote "End of Chapter" but then crossed it out (JFK item 64). Thus, what follows regarding the death of the man in the stretcher above Frederic was added as an afterthought.

52:32–35 **The stream kept on . . . it was warm and sticky**: This chilling description helps to amplify the terror of Frederic's near-death experience. Frederic must lie in the dying man's blood and be reminded, in no uncertain terms, that he could be the one dying and, if not now, then one day in the future. After this, Frederic will no longer believe that the war has nothing to do with him. See entry 31:28–30.

52:38–39 **settled more comfortably:** The man's death may remind readers of Hemingway's short story "Indian Camp" and the death of the father, who slits his throat to commit suicide in the top bunk, as Nick Adams's father performs a caesarian section on the man's wife in the lower bunk (*CSS* 67–70). The hemorrhage of the man above Frederic foreshadows the death of Catherine Barkley from hemorrhage after her own caesarian section. The word *comfortably* also figures prominently in the final chapter of *The Sun Also Rises,* echoing its earlier use in Burguete by Bill Gordon. Donald Daiker contributed to this note.

53:4 **It was cold in the car in the night as the road climbed:** The coldness that Frederic feels is more than literal. In its highly understated form, the sentence powerfully conveys Frederic's overwhelming sense of the presence of death.

CHAPTER 10

Chapters 10 and 11 present parallel visits to Frederic in the field hospital by his counterpart friends, first Rinaldi, the atheistic man of science, and then the priest, the avatar of religious faith. Such scenes will continue through Book Three, after which we do not see them again. Until then, Hemingway always presents these two opposing characters in balanced, parallel scenes, providing us the opportunity to understand the conflict within Frederic's character and to judge the ways his wounding has affected him.

In the manuscript, the chapter begins with an odd paragraph that Hemingway crossed out:

> There are only three people of any importance in this story, although my life was full of people, all of whom were important at the time, and I did not see any of the three for over three months. During this time I was at hospitals first at Dormans, then at Mestre and finally in Milan. I saw them all three before I left the first hospital at the front and all three of them wrote me. (JFK item 64)

The three people are apparently Rinaldi, the priest, and the major, all of whom will visit Frederic before he is sent to Milan. It would seem that the phrase "of any importance in this story" refers only to this section of the story, thus the exclusion of Catherine Barkley. The other confusing detail, "Dormans," is unidentified as a location in northeastern Italy. Hemingway surely meant to write Cormons. G. M. Trevelyan directed a Red Cross field hospital just outside Cormons at Villa Trento (103–6). Mestre is the mainland borough of the City of Venice and a train stop between the front and Milan. Apparently, Hemingway decided not to include a hospital stay at Mestre for Frederic.

55:1 **cognac:** A variety of brandy produced in the region of France around the city of Cognac, about seventy-five miles north of Bordeaux in the southwestern part of the country. As Philip Greene explains, "All cognacs are brandies, but not all brandies are cognac" (29). Cognac must be distilled twice from white wine made from grapes grown in the area of Cognac.

55:3 **"medaglia d'argento but perhaps they can get only the bronze":** Rinaldi is referring to two of the three levels of the Italian medal for bravery, the *medaglia al valore militare*, which came in three classes: bronze, silver, and gold, with gold being the highest. Rinaldi explains that to get the silver medal (*medaglia d'argento*) Frederic must have performed some "heroic act." His wounding alone would merit the *medaglia di bronzo* (bronze medal). Hemingway received the *medaglia d'argento*, which supports the idea that he performed some feat of bravery in his actions when wounded—carrying a wounded man, for example. However, his citation makes no mention of carrying any wounded (see Lewis, "Making It Up" 224).

In Hemingway's masterful short story "In Another Country," the narrator, possibly Nick Adams, has received medals whose citations contain words like *fratellanza* (brotherhood) and *abnegazione* (abnegation, self-sacrifice) "but which really said, with the adjectives removed, that I had been given the medals because I was an American" (*CSS* 208). Thus, Frederic might expect to receive a higher order of medal than he deserves, simply because of his status as an American volunteer in the Italian army, especially at a moment in the war when America was just entering and Italy was eager to attract more American soldiers to its front.

55:23–24 **"Look at your valorous conduct":** Despite Frederic's humble downplaying of his actions, Rinaldi is correct that he has displayed at least admirable conduct. When wounded, he is willing to have others treated before him (50:22–23).

55:26–27 **"Did they cross the river all right?" . . . "a thousand prisoners":** Rinaldi's response to Frederic's question about the success of the battle distorts the reality of the Italian offensive in the Tenth Battle of the Isonzo. Yes, the Italians succeeded in establishing a new bridgehead above Plava and captured Monte Santo, but they did not achieve the objective of capturing Monte San Gabriele and instead suffered enormous casualties, far outnumbering those of the Austrians. In three weeks of fighting, 36,000 Italians were killed and another 115,000 were wounded, while the Austrians suffered 7,300 dead (Thompson 254). Of course, as Rinaldi is speaking to Frederic, the fighting in this battle is still only a few days old, so his optimism may be justified, but more likely he is simply trying to present his wounded friend with as positive a report as possible.

56:1 **The Lancet:** Founded in the early nineteenth century by a British surgeon, the *Lancet* is one of the world's oldest and most respected medical journals ("Best Science"). The reference helps to establish Rinaldi not only as a skillful battle surgeon but also as a man of science, working to advance knowledge in medicine. Hemingway, who, as a boy, thought seriously of following his father into a career in medicine, naturally had great respect for the field of medical science (see Sanford 134). Following his wounding, his letters to his father frequently provided details of his treatment and sought his father's professional opinion. Hemingway's interest in the sciences was an important facet of his character. In Hemingway's story "Indian Camp," Dr. Adams contemplates submitting to a medical journal an account of his caesarian section on an Indian woman with a jackknife and fishing line (*CSS* 69). Donald Daiker contributed to this note.

56:8 **"I looked at your papers. You haven't any fracture"**: Rinaldi tells Frederic that he does not have a skull fracture, an important piece of medical information, since it places fewer restrictions on Frederic's drinking during his recovery.

56:13 **fifteen lire:** The bottle of cognac Rinaldi brings would have cost, at the 1917 exchange rate, $2.12, which would be $40.50 in 2017 (Williamson). A typical good quality 750 ml bottle of Hennessy or Courvoisier cognac currently (2018) costs around $25 or $30, while Remy Martin VSOP starts at around $40. So Rinaldi is not exaggerating that he has brought Frederic good quality liquor, an indication of how much he values their friendship.

56:19 **"Have you seen Miss Barkley?"** Frederic's question makes it clear that she remains a central concern of his, perhaps now more than before his wounding. It may also betray some insecurity on his part, fear that Rinaldi may be pursuing her in his absence.

56:21 **"How are the girls?"** Rinaldi's offer to bring Catherine seems to allay any jealousy that may be stirring in Frederic, but he would rest more easily if Rinaldi assured him he was still visiting the prostitutes at the Villa Rosa.

56:22–23 **"For two weeks now they haven't changed them":** Rinaldi's complaint underscores his purely materialist view of life and love. For Rinaldi, there is no real love. Females mean little more to him than short-term sexual satisfaction. Two weeks with the same girls has not generated any emotional attachment, only resentment; even a friendship with one of them is "disgraceful."

56:26–27 **"They all ask for you":** This line helps us understand the degree to which Frederic was a regular and very popular customer at the Villa Rossa.

56:38–39 **"when you lie here . . . don't you get excited?"** Rinaldi, of course, means sexually excited. His two chief interests in life are his work and sex, although he genuinely cares for Frederic and regards him as a close friend.

57:9 **"If you must have a priest have that priest":** Hemingway is careful to portray Rinaldi as a religious skeptic, but a kind hearted one. He distinguishes himself from the captain's cruel baiting of the priest. For all their differences, Rinaldi likes the priest and acknowledges the priest's friendship with Frederic.

57:12–13 **"a little that way"**: As a man who sees sexuality in almost all human relationships, Rinaldi is jokingly implying homosexuality between Frederic and the priest. Scribner's wished to cut this passage (including lines 57:12–17), but Hemingway argued forcefully for its retention, and the passage was retained (Bruccoli, *Only Thing* 94–96).

57:15–16 **"like the number of the first regiment of the Brigata Ancona"**: The Brigata Ancona was an infantry brigade in the Italian army composed of two regiments—the Sixty-ninth and the Seventieth. Therefore, the number of the first regiment of the brigade was sixty-nine, a fact Hemingway confirmed in a letter to his French translator, Maurice Coindreau (*Letters 4* 382). Rinaldi is thus referring to the sex act of mutual oral gratification, jokingly implying that Frederic and the priest have been engaging in sixty-nine. Hemingway was delivering candy and cigarettes to members of the Sixty-ninth Regiment on the Piave River at the time of his wounding. According to the *Oxford English Dictionary*, the first documentation of the term *sixty-nine* being used to mean a sex act was 1888, by P. Perret, in *Tableaux Vivants* (xiii, 109): "In familiar language this divine variant of pleasure is called: *faire* soixante *neuf* (literally, to do '69')."

57:20–23 **"just like me . . . All fire and smoke and nothing inside"**: Here Rinaldi weighs in on the question of Frederic's identity, insisting that Frederic is just like him in nature. This might have been more true before the wounding, but Frederic is quick to disagree now. They are still friends, but the gap between them has widened. Rinaldi also reinjects the notion of "nothingness" into the novel. See entry 28:7. To be Italian, in Rinaldi's terms, is to have "nothing inside," to be soulless. After his out of body experience, Frederic may not regard himself as soulless.

57:29 **"Your lovely cool . . . English goddess"**: Rinaldi's sexless description of Catherine Barkley leads to a trading of insults between the two friends that seems more than simple jesting. It also reemphasizes Catherine's Englishness. See entry 18:12–13, an emphasis repeated with "Englishwoman" in 57:31.

57:32 **dago**: A disparaging term for a person of Italian, Spanish, or Portuguese descent.

57:34–35 **wop**: Another disparaging term for an Italian or person of other southern European origin. Rinaldi uses it also against Frederic, but his pause before saying the word suggests that he may not know what it means. According to the *Oxford English Dictionary*, the term had only come into usage in the United States not long before

1914, when it appears in L. E. Jackson and C. R. Hellyer's *Criminal Slang*, defined as "an ignorant person; a foreigner; an impossible character."

57:37 **"stupid from inexperience"**: Frederic's insults of Rinaldi would seem to indicate that in his hospital bed Frederic has already been meditating on the possibility of love as opposed to the loveless sex in which he and Rinaldi have indulged at the Villa Rossa. In his view, Rinaldi is ignorant of love because he has never experienced it. Frederic has not yet either, but, unlike Rinaldi, he must be thinking of the possibility and must believe in its existence.

57:39–58:2 **"There is only one difference. . . . That's all I know"**: Rinaldi crudely suggests that, whether a woman is a virgin or not, for the man the experience is still only about receiving sexual satisfaction. In the process, he perhaps unwittingly acknowledges his inexperience at love.

58:4–16 **"Don't get angry." . . ."Kiss me good-by"**: At this point, Frederic realizes that Rinaldi is getting genuinely angry, and, since he values their friendship, in spite of their differences, he makes a peace offering before Rinaldi leaves, and Rinaldi accepts.

CHAPTER 11

59:8 It made me feel very young: The first paragraph here certainly sets a new mood, beginning, as many have before, with comforting references to the natural world and food, the treetop, the breeze, even the flies, recalling happy evenings of Frederic's youth. These details help emphasize Frederic's rebirth after his wounding, the opportunity for him to start afresh.

59:13–16 some packages ... the chair that had been brought for Rinaldi: Hemingway connects the priest's visit with Rinaldi's in the previous chapter, comparing and contrasting the important thematic relationships Frederic has with his two friends. As did Rinaldi, the priest brings gifts (mosquito netting, English newspapers, and vermouth, compared to Rinaldi's cognac) and sits in the same chair.

60:3 "I am so glad you are all right": Prior to this paragraph, in the holograph manuscript, Hemingway included the following intriguing passage and then struck it out:

> "My Saint Anthony." I pulled the metal capule out from where it lay on my chest. "You see my Saint Anthony?" He looked at the thin gold chain.
> "Perhaps he saved your life."
> "Passini saved my life," I said. "He was between me and the burst."
> "Poor Passini. You might remember him in your prayers."
> "All right."
> "I don't want to make you sad," he said. (JFK item 64)

Hemingway later decided to have Frederic lose the medal at some point in the process of his wounding and treatment at the dressing station. See entry 37:6–36. This excised passage, however, shows Frederic clearly in his rationalist materialist mode, even while agreeing to remember Passini in his prayers, in contrast to the committed faith-based perspective of the priest, who is inclined to believe that the medal saved Frederic from death.

60:9 **vermouth:** This wine is fortified with extra alcohol and flavored with various other dry ingredients, depending on the brand. The priest's offering is more humble than Rinaldi's cognac.

60:16 ***The News of the World:*** A British tabloid weekly newspaper published between 1843 and 2011, highlighting sensational reportage of crime and vice. At the time of the novel, its circulation was between 2 and 3 million.

60:20 **Mestre:** The mainland borough of the City of Venice.

60:33–34 **Sometimes we talked . . . but to-night it was difficult:** In spite of Frederic's apparent pleasant mood, with the sense of a new spiritual beginning in the novel, he and the priest are not quite in sync during this conversation.

60:35 **"You seem very tired":** The word *tired* is applied to the priest six times in the space of a page.

61:4 **"You do not mind it. You do not see it":** The priest recognizes a difference between his attitude toward the war and Frederic's. The priest is feeling low presumably because of the enormous casualties the Italians are suffering in the new attack (the Tenth Battle of the Isonzo). See entry 55:26–27. In his position, he would be very aware of the number of casualties, and there is no prospect of an end to the war. His essential pacifism and hatred of warfare in the face of these facts have undoubtedly led to his depression.

62:21–22 **"You understand but you do not love God." "No":** Just as in the previous chapter Hemingway made certain we understand the differences between Frederic and Rinaldi, here too, he makes certain we understand the difference between Frederic and the priest. Frederic's attitude toward God is not the priest's, and the rest of their conversation will further amplify our understanding of their differences. This does not diminish their friendship, but they are not the same in their religious faith.

62:23–24 **"You do not love Him at all?" "I am afraid of Him in the night sometimes":** The priest seems taken aback by Frederic's insistence that he does not love God. But Frederic's second response, while still refraining from an expression of love for God, indicates a change in his attitude from what we have seen before he was wounded. In chapter 3, when Frederic attempts to explain to the priest "the difference between the night and the day," he insists the night is better "unless the day is very clean and cold." See entry 12:14. At that point, Frederic seems to have no fear of God or anything in the night. So this is our first indication that Frederic's wounding has produced a profound psychological change in him. It is important to understand that Frederic does not deny faith in God here, but his wounding seems to have made him aware that God has the power to take his life at any time, and that awareness produces his fear. The fear comes at night, because, as we pointed out in entry 12:14, the night is the realm of subjectivity, when the mind's ability to hold on to an objective reality is at its most fragile. Frederic now recognizes that death is a reality for him, and he does not want to die.

62:26 **"I don't love much"**: Frederic's declaration is similar to one returning war veteran Harold Krebs makes in the Hemingway short story "Soldier's Home." When Krebs is asked by his mother if he loves her, he replies, "No. . . . I don't love anybody" (*CSS* 116).

62:27–29 **"Yes. . . . You do. . . . You wish to serve"**: This is one of the novel's most often quoted passages for the priest's definition of love as an act of sacrifice and service. The priest recognizes that Frederic has the capacity to love, even though he has not expressed it much to this point. The priest's definition applies to his own love of God, but it also clearly applies to secular love. The definition will stand throughout the rest of the novel as a yardstick for measuring Frederic and Catherine's love.

62:33 **"You cannot know about it unless you have it"**: This line is another that highlights the novel's epistemic theme. The priest's antecedent for "it" is love. He knows that Frederic's skepticism about love comes from a lack of experience, which, as we have seen, mirrors the accusation Frederic makes against Rinaldi in the previous chapter (57:37). But, of course, the priest has his own lack of experience in matters of secular love. See entry 62:37–39.

62:37–39 **"If I really loved some woman" . . ."I don't know about that"**: Frederic's question again reveals that he has been thinking about where his relationship with Catherine Barkley might lead. The priest's response, however, is another indication of the way he differs from Frederic. He cannot offer advice about secular love, because he lacks the empirical evidence to draw any conclusions.

63:5–7 **"You are a fine boy" . . ."But you call me father"**: Frederic searches for words during an awkward moment as they both recognize the important difference between them. In the realm of human relationships, the priest remains immature compared to Frederic, in spite of what he has to teach him about an abstract definition of *love*.

63:10 **"You do not want me for anything?"** The priest apparently hopes Frederic might want to make a confession, but Frederic declines—another illustration of the difference between them.

63:19 **"Ciaou"**: See entry 10:11.

63:22 **I hoped he would get back to the Abruzzi some time**: Frederic generously wishes the priest well, but he does not say anything about wanting to visit the Abruzzi himself.

63:25–26 **forbidden to play the flute at night**: According to Vincenzo Di Nardo, a native of Capracotta, there is no word for *flute* in the dialect of Italian spoken in Capraccotta. Instead, the word *fife* is used ambiguously to suggest sexual relations that may lead to unwanted pregnancies. In other words, the priest has probably tried in delicate terms to suggest to Frederic that the village takes special precautions to protect the chastity of its virgins ("Hemingway"). Hemingway may have heard this story from his friend Nick Nerone, who grew up in the Abruzzi. See entry 8:1–2.

63:28 **The peasants all called you "Don"**: *Don* is an honorific; in English the equivalent is addressing a person who has been knighted as *Sir*. The implication is that life in the Abruzzi is a throwback to a simpler, almost medieval time.

63:30 **stopped to eat at the houses of peasants**: This line is reminiscent of one of Hemingway's favorite books, the Russian Ivan Turgenev's *A Sportsman's Sketches,* in which an upper-class huntsman relates encounters with peasants and their stories as he hunts through the countryside on foot. In *The Sun Also Rises,* Jake Barnes reads *A Sportsman's Sketches* appreciatively (147).

63:32–33 **Gran Sasso D'Italia**: At 9,554 feet, the Gran Sasso is the highest mountain in the Appenines, the mountain range that runs north and south through the length of Italy. The mountain is more than a hundred miles from Capracotta by automobile and would have been difficult to get to.

63:33 **Aquila**: Today, L'Aquila is the capital city of the province of Abruzzo, sitting in an earthquake-prone valley about twenty miles southwest of the Gran Sasso (see entry 63:32–33). Though the region is among Italy's most picturesque, the city's history has been marked by periodic major and tragic earthquakes, which have killed thousands of people. The most recent occurred in 2009, with a magnitude of 6.3 on the Richter scale, killing 309 and leveling thousands of residences and businesses in the area. See entry 11:25–26. The legend of L'Aquila's origin is that there were ninety-nine lords from castles in the region who joined together to found the city, and each built his own piazza with a fountain and a church. However, the actual number is no more than eighty ("L'Aquila"). The town is also famous for its fountain with ninety-nine spouts, ninety-three of which seem to be original. Citizens added another six in an adjacent lower location to make the fountain fit the town's mythology.

CHAPTER 12

64:6–14 If any one were going to die . . . took it away: The dominant image of this first paragraph is of death and dying, indicating death is one of Frederic's chief concerns as he lies in his hospital bed slowing recuperating from his wounds and waiting to be transferred to a bigger hospital away from the front lines.

64:20–21 see the new graves in the garden: Yet another reminder to Frederic of the nearness and ever-presence of death.

65:7 mechano-therapy: This is treatment of disease or injury by mechanical means. See Hemingway's short story "In Another Country" in his collection *Men Without Women* (1927), in which a wounded American soldier receives mechanotherapy in a Milan hospital for a leg wound similar to Frederic Henry's (*CSS* 206–10). For a discussion of the story and its connections to *A Farewell to Arms,* see Joseph Flora's *Reading Hemingway's* Men Without Women (31–41).

65:9 needed for the offensive, when it should start: This may be an oversight on Hemingway's part, since it confuses the timeline of the story. From all indications, Frederic's wounding occurs as the offensive is beginning, which would situate it chronologically at 12 May 1917. Frederic has only been in the field hospital a few days, and the fighting is surely continuing with huge numbers of Italian casualties that would need immediate treatment in this field hospital. With wounds similar to Frederic's, Hemingway spent five days in the field hospital before being transferred to Milan, but that was during a relatively quiet time in the conflict along the Piave River. The fighting in the Tenth Battle of the Isonzo continued from 12 May through 8 June 1917, after which there was a lull of two months before the launch of the Eleventh Battle of the Isonzo, on 19 August 1917.

65:12 an American hospital in Milan that had just been installed: Hemingway is deliberately bending history in order for Frederic and Catherine to continue their relationship. As Michael Reynolds has pointed out, there was no American Red Cross Hospital in Milan or anywhere in Italy in May 1917; Hemingway was the first patient at the new American Red Cross Hospital in Milan in July 1918 (*Hemingway's First War* 23). Hemingway could have had Frederic transferred to the Hospital Maggiore in Milan, where Hemingway received mechanotherapy in 1918, but he was not familiar with the regular routine and layout of the hospital, and it would be unlikely for a British nurse like Catherine, who does not speak Italian, to be transferred there. So Hemingway's best option was to tweak history to fit his purposes. It is only barely plausible, given that the United States had just declared war on Germany on 6 April 1917.

65:17–67:5 **The Italians were sure . . . but went to sleep:** The next three long paragraphs are a fascinating stylistic blend of dialogue and stream of consciousness between Frederic, Rinaldi, and the major from the mess, effectively conveying the trio's increasingly inebriated camaraderie.

65:19–21 **They asked me . . . only a matter of days:** The United States, through the efforts of President Woodrow Wilson, who had the majority of public support, had maintained official neutrality between the war's beginning in August 1914 and April 1917. Eventually, however, the sinking of American ships in the North Atlantic by German submarines turned the tide of opinion, and with congressional approval, Wilson called the country to arms. However, it would take nearly a year for American soldiers to be battle ready in very big numbers, and then almost entirely on the French front, not the Italian front. Frederic's estimate of how long it would take the United States to declare war on Austria is no doubt influenced by the conviviality of the moment with Rinaldi and the major. The United States would not declare war on Austria for another eight months, not until 7 December 1917.

65:24–25 **Turkey . . . was our national bird but the joke translated so badly:** The Italian word for turkey (the bird) is *tacchino*, but the Italian word for Turkey (the country) is *Turchia*, so Frederic would have difficulty making the joke work in Italian. Adding to the confusion here is that, of course, the turkey is not the national bird of the United States. As most people know, the bald eagle is. The turkey became associated with the major national holiday of Thanksgiving, established by President Abraham Lincoln in 1863. In World War I, the United States never declared war on Turkey, Bulgaria or Japan.

65:33–34 **Nice and Savoia:** The County of Nice, of which the city of Nice on the Mediterranean coast is the capital, is a region of southeastern France on the border of Italy. The region of Savoia ("the Savoy" in English), is north of the County of Nice, extending to the border with Switzerland. The two areas were previously part of the Kingdom of Sardinia, ruled by the House of Savoy, but in 1860, through a treaty with Sardinia during the wars for Italian independence and unification, France annexed the County of Nice and Savoia. In exchange for France's military assistance for Italy to regain territory in northeastern Italy from Austria, France would get the County of Nice and Savoia. Italy would keep Liguria and the Piedmont. The King of Sardinia from the House of Savoy in 1860 was King Victor Emmanuel II, who became the ruler of a unified Italy. His grandson, King Victor Emmanuel III, ruled Italy during World War I. Thus, there was some historical justification for Italians to hope to regain the County of Nice and Savoia, although it never happened.

65:34 **Corsica:** An island in the Mediterranean Sea, west of Italy, and a region of France. Until the mid-nineteenth century, Italian was the language of culture on the island, but there was little reason for Italy to believe it could convince France to give up the island to the Italians.

65:34–35 **all the Adriatic coast-line:** There were many Italian communities on the eastern shore of the Adriatic, and thus the Italian irredentist movement held dreams of bringing them into a unified Italy. Gabriele D'Annunzio led a ragtag group of Italians to seize the mostly Italian city of Fiume on the Adriatic Coast in 1919, but the Italian government refused to recognize the seizure, and D'Annunzio established an independent government. See entry 4:11–18.

65:38 **Romulus suckling the Tiber:** Frederic comically mixes up legends of the founding of Rome. The twins Romulus and Remus, whom the evil king Amulus ordered killed, were abandoned to die on the Tiber River, near the site of the modern city of Rome. According to legend, they were suckled by a she-wolf in a cave known as the Lupercal and survived to found the city of Rome.

66:3 **Roma is feminine:** The Italian language, like French and unlike English, assigns gender to all nouns. Thus, Rinaldi argues that Rome, as a feminine noun, cannot be the father of nations.

66:9–10 **the Crystal Palace:** This is an obscure reference. Neither the 1909 nor 1928 edition of Baedeker's *Italy: From the Alps to Naples* mentions a Crystal Palace in Milan or anywhere else in Italy. The King Vittorio Emanuele II Galleria (see entry 66:10) possessed an impressive steel and glass cupola over its arcade, but it is separately mentioned here as something to see in Milan, so the reference seems to be to a different structure. The world's most famous Crystal Palace was a huge exhibition center made of steel and glass, designed by Joseph Paxton and built in London, England, in 1851 then destroyed by fire in 1936.

66:10 **the Cova:** See entry 10:27–28.

66:10 **Campari's:** A bar and café inside the King Vittorio Emanuele Galleria in Milan, established in 1862 by Gaspare Campari, the inventor of the bitter cocktail ingredient Campari. In Hemingway's short story "Get a Seeing-Eyed Dog," set in Torcello, an island near Venice, the wife remembers Campari and Gordon's gin as their favorite drink whenever she and her husband (clearly based on Hemingway and his fourth wife, Mary) stay at the inn on the island (*CSS* 488). Campari's café is listed in Baedeker's *Italy: From the Alps to Naples* 1928 and is still in the Galleria today (25).

66:10 **Biffi's:** A fine restaurant inside the King Vittorio Emanuele II Galleria in Milan, still there today (Baedeker, *Italy* 1928 25).

66:10 **the galleria:** The Galleria King Vittorio Emanuele II is the world's oldest indoor shopping mall. It was designed by architect Giuseppe Mengoni and built between 1865 and 1871 in the heart of Milan. Built in the form of a cross, it stands between and connects the plaza of the Duomo (cathedral) to its south and the plaza of the famous La Scala opera house to its north. It has a beautiful cupola of glass and steel covering the intersecting arms of the cross.

66:11 **the Gran Italia:** This is probably a reference to the Caffé-Concerto Grande Italia, located near the Galleria and the Piazza della Scala, listed in Baedeker's *Italy: From the Alps to Naples* 1928 (25).

66:12 **the Scala:** *Teatro alla Scala* (its full name in Italian) is Milan's world-famous opera house, which hosted premieres of works of Giuseppe Verdi and other great opera composers. It was also no more than a five-minute walk from the Red Cross hospital where Hemingway was treated, the Galleria, the cathedral, and important art museums in the heart of Milan. The magnificent building was completed in 1778. Rinaldi, as we have already seen, is a great fan of opera.

66:15 **sight draft:** Defined as a "check or other draft that is payable to the payee when the payee presents the draft to the appropriate party. It contrasts with a time draft, which is not payable until a stated date in the future" ("Sight Draft"). Essentially, Frederic is drawing money from an account owned by his grandfather, on the assumption that his grandfather will immediately honor the drafts.

66:16 **grandfather:** The generous grandfather seems to have had no actual biographical counterpart in Hemingway's life except for his second wife Pauline's very generous Uncle Gus Pfeiffer, to whom *A Farewell to Arms* is dedicated. See entry Dedication.

66:18–19 **patriotic grandson who is dying that Italy may live:** We do not know if it is Rinaldi who makes this sacrilegious jest alluding to Christ's crucifixion, but it is a jest consistent with his character.

66:19 **Garibaldi:** Rinaldi makes reference to the great Italian patriot Giuseppe Garibaldi (1807–1882) who, with Giuseppe Mazzini (1805–1872) and other revolutionaries, fought to liberate and unite Italy into a republic. He twice fled from Italy because of his rebellious campaigning, to South America (1834–48) and to the United States (1850–54) before returning to Italy and further struggles to unify and free the country from papal and foreign control, resulting in Italian unification (the *Risorgimento* in 1871). Thus, Frederic Henry's presence in support of Italy in its current war suggests a parallel, if somewhat strained and exaggerated, with Garibaldi.

66:22 **Federico:** One of six times in the novel that the Italian version of Frederic Henry's first name is used (34:4, 67:1, 151:8, 151:39, 152:10). In comparison, the name *Frederic* appears only once. See entry 74:3. Frederic's friend Ettore uses *Fred* three times on page 107, but no one else uses that name for Frederic. He is also called *Enrico* three times (34:4, 151:17, 153:31).

66:34 **They had not got nurses yet from America:** This is Hemingway's fabricated reason to have a British nurse like Catherine transferred from the front lines to a newly established American hospital in Milan. See entry 65:12.

66:35 **riparto:** Mark Cirino points out that the correct Italian word intended here is *reparto*, which means *military detachment or department*, not *riparto*, which means *allotment* ("You Don't Know" 59).

67:2 **Many things:** Here and again at 67:4, Rinaldi is using the Italian phrase *tante cose*, literally *many things*, but which Mark Cirino points out is "roughly equivalent to 'all the best'" ("You Don't Know" 52).

67:2 **Ciaou. Ciaou. Ciaou:** See entry 10:11.

67:3 **lysol:** As a trademark the common disinfectant, *Lysol* should be capitalized.

67:6 **The next day in the morning:** Most previous editions of the novel have an extra space before the beginning of this paragraph, indicating a gap in the narration. In this case, it is only one night of drunken, presumably dreamless sleep. In the original holograph manuscript, however, there is not even a paragraph break here (JFK item 64). The typescript has no paragraph break, but there is a handwritten correction adding a paragraph symbol and two horizontal lines to indicate the need for extra space before the paragraph (JFK item 65).

67:6–7 **left for Milan and arrived forty-eight hours later:** Frederic's train journey is approximately 250 miles from Udine to Milan. For it to have taken forty-eight hours, it must indeed have been a "bad trip." The train would head west across the Tagliamento River just beyond Codroipo, where in book 3, Frederic will nearly be executed before narrowly escaping during the Caporetto Retreat. Then the train would likely have stops in Treviso, Mestre, Padua, Vicenza, Verona, Brescia, Bergamo, and Monza before arriving in Milan. Today such a train trip would take just under four hours.

67:10 **grappa:** See entry 15:15.

67:19 **The soldier would not take the penny:** Frederic's penny tip may seem cheap to us, but we must understand the context. Italian soldiers were paid only fifty centimes (pennies) a day during most of the war. So Frederic's tip is 2 percent of the soldier's daily wage (Wilcox, *Morale and the Italian Army* 62). Therefore, it is likely the soldier's rejection of the tip is not the result of his feeling insulted but is instead a case of the soldier's honor and personal generosity. Incidentally, a wage of fifty centimes was for most Italian soldiers a likely drop in income. According to historian Vanda Wilcox, manual and farm laborers in Italy could earn up to two lire (200 centimes) per day in 1910 (62).

BOOK TWO

CHAPTER 13

71:2–3 the American hospital: As discussed earlier (see entry 65:12), Hemingway is bending history in placing an American hospital in Milan in 1917. However, he is no doubt relying on his own personal experience at the American Red Cross Hospital in Milan in 1918, so we can assume that the fictional hospital in *A Farewell to Arms* is at the same location as the actual one where Hemingway was treated, at 4 Via Cesare Cantù and the intersection with Via Armorari. There is a plaque on the building on the Via Amorari side commemorating it with an inscription in Italian, which translated means "In the summer of 1918, in this building, converted to the American Red Cross Hospital, Ernest Hemingway, wounded on the Piave Front, was admitted and treated. Thus, the true story of 'A Farewell to Arms' was born here." The cathedral, the Galleria, and La Scala are all just five-minute walks away. The location, in other words, both for young Ernest Hemingway and for Frederic Henry, could hardly be better to enjoy Milan's finest amenities. Today the former hospital building houses financial services.

72:28 "You are the first patient": Hemingway was also the first patient in the new American Red Cross Hospital in Milan when he arrived there in July 1918.

73:3 five lire: This would equal about 67 cents at the 1917 exchange rate, or $12.80 in 2017 dollars, for a total of $38.40 in 2017 dollars for the two stretcher bearers and the porter (Williamson). In other words, Frederic is tipping generously.

73:6 "And many thanks": As Mark Cirino has pointed out, Frederic here uses the Italian expression *tante grazie*, literally *many thanks* ("You Don't Know" 51).

73:12 She commenced to cry: The behavior of the elderly nurse later identified as Mrs. Walker (73:22) in comparison to the behavior of Frederic is another instance of the conflict of the rational versus the irrational in the novel. Frederic represents the calm voice of reason, whereas Mrs. Walker cannot see through her emotions in order to function rationally in response to a situation for which she is unprepared. Michael Reynolds identifies Miss Anna Scanlan, a fifty-four-year-old nurse at the

Red Cross Hospital in Milan in 1918, as the probable source for the character of Mrs. Walker (*First War* 173–74).

73:37 Lake Como: A large and lovely lake about thirty miles north of Milan. Shaped like an inverted *Y*, the lake is the third largest in Italy, after Lake Maggiore and Lake Garda, and since ancient Roman times has been a favorite resort for the rich and famous of the world. It was recently named one of the world's twenty most beautiful lakes (Heiderstadt).

74:3 Frederic Henry: This is the first and only citing of our protagonist's full name in English, although we get an indication of it elsewhere, when he is referred to as "Federico," an Italian derivation of "Frederic," or "Fred." See entry 34:3–4 for a full discussion of potential sources for Frederic Henry's name.

74:16 Isonze: An apparent inadvertent misspelling of *Isonzo*. The name is spelled correctly at 224:22.

75:10 "sick boy": The nurse whom we will come to know as Miss Gage provides another reminder here that Frederic still has some maturing to do. She will repeat the term at 76:21.

75:16–17 Miss Gage giggled: There seems little question that Frederic en-*gages* Miss Gage in a little mutually flirtatious behavior throughout this scene, behavior that certainly raises questions about the depths of his feelings for Catherine at this point. We are left to wonder what might happen between them if Catherine were not to arrive soon after this.

Charlotte Heilman, one of the nurses who attended to Hemingway when he was a patient at the Red Cross Hospital in Milan in 1918, identified herself as the source for the character of Miss Gage (Reynolds, *First War* 195).

75:39 Miss Van Campen: Charlotte Heilman, one of the nurses at the Red Cross Hospital in Milan in 1918, identified Catherine DeLong, "a small, dignified, capable Johns Hopkins graduate," as the source for the character of Miss Van Campen (Reynolds, *First War* 195).

76:12–13 after she had done something for me very skillfully: Hemingway seems to have enjoyed being coy and vague about intimate contacts, which we assume this to be, although one that is no doubt a routine chore completed by a nurse without necessary feeling for a patient. The coyness adds to the question of sexual contact and enhances the notion of flirtation between Frederic and Miss Gage, his "young and pretty" nurse.

76:23 **Cinzano:** A well-known Italian brand of vermouth or fortified wine. Readers of *The Sun Also Rises* may recall that Jake Barnes walks behind a man in Paris who is "pushing a roller that printed the name CINZANO on the sidewalk" (35).

76:23 **fiasco of chianti:** Chianti is any wine produced in the Chianti region of Tuscany in central Italy. Its traditional container is a short fat bottle wrapped tightly in a straw basket, called a *fiasco,* meaning *flask*. Frederic's use of the Italian word, however, reinforces the notion that the news of the front that he is reading may be a *fiasco,* in the English sense of the term, a failure or breakdown.

77:9–14 **I slept heavily except once . . . went back to sleep again:** This is one of the few instances where Frederic seems to share with us what it means to be afraid of God at night sometimes, as he relates to the priest in chapter 11. See entry 62:23–24. Whatever scares him in his dream stays with him enough to make sleep difficult afterwards. This kind of insomnia, produced apparently by post-traumatic stress, is a reminder of similar struggles of Nick Adams and other Hemingway characters in works like "Now I Lay Me," "Big Two-Hearted River," *The Sun Also Rises,* and "A Clean, Well-Lighted Place." In "Now I Lay Me," Nick, because he is afraid that if he falls asleep his soul will leave his body, uses various methods to prevent himself from sleeping, including prayer and remembering in great detail rivers he has fished and girls he has dated (*CSS* 276–82).

CHAPTER 14

78:6–7 she looked a little older . . . not so pretty: The daylight is the realm of reason, and Frederic, in the light of reason, now sees Miss Gage more clearly than he did in the compromised light of the night. Reason, it seems, subdues whatever attraction he may have had for her. This is important, because he is about to be reunited with Catherine.

79:2 "I don't like her": Miss Gage's initial feelings about Catherine, which do not seem based on any rational motive, would seem to imply a kind of jealousy, indicating her own attraction to Frederic. Hemingway apparently wants us to recognize that Frederic is very appealing to many women, except perhaps to those, like Miss Van Campen, who are averse to those, like Frederic, who are averse to certain rules.

79:24 If he was crazy: The idea of craziness, initially raised early in Frederic's relationship with Catherine (see entry 26:15–19), is an important motif in the novel, part of the irrational side of the conflict between reason and nonreason. In this chapter, it will be repeated at 79:37, 80:26, 80:33, and 81:9, in addition to the use of *mad* at 80:35 and *madness* at 81:10. Here the barber's fear that Frederic is one of the enemy is obviously irrational.

79:27 tipped him half a lira: Frederic tips the barber around seven American cents. In today's terms, the tip would be worth $1.34 (Williamson). This is only 10 percent of the tips he gives the stretcher bearers and the porter on his arrival at the hospital (73:3).

79:39 "he thought I said you were an Austrian officer": In other words, the incident with the barber is one of the several instances in the novel where Frederic's identity is mistaken. See entry 52:2–3.

80:7–8 "How funny if he would cut my throat. Ho ho ho": In a strongly Freudian reading of the novel, Carl Eby sees Frederic's fear in this episode as representative of a general threat of castration, which he believes runs throughout the text (62–63).

80:18 **When I saw her I was in love with her:** Frederic's declaration of love may seem sudden, but it is reasonable to assume he has been thinking deeply about Catherine in the idle days he has spent recuperating after his wounding. Presumably, close to a week has passed, if he has spent five days in the field hospital, as Hemingway did when he was wounded. We also know that the train journey from Udine to Milan took forty-eight hours (67:6–7). While we do not have access to Catherine's thoughts here, given how quickly she gives herself to Frederic sexually in this scene, we can only assume that she is powerfully moved by seeing him wounded and that she will not deny him her physical self in the way she denied her fiancé. In addition, the craziness and madness that are emphasized in their own words underscores how irrational their behavior and feelings are at this point. Certainly, the act of sexual intercourse between a nurse and her patient in the hospital bed seems irrational, but we should recognize the power of the stress of wartime.

80:28 **"You mustn't. . . . You're not well enough":** Note that Catherine says, "*You* mustn't," not "*We* mustn't." She does not seem to have qualms for herself to engage here in sexual activity. In all previous editions of the novel, there was a space before the beginning of this paragraph, indicating an undescribed passage of time between the paragraphs. In this case, the space presumably indicates that they are doing something physically intimate but short of intercourse that could not be described in explicit terms when the novel was published in 1929. The previous paragraph is not part of the original holograph manuscript. It was added in handwriting to the typescript with two horizontal lines and the instruction "(space)" in parentheses added to indicate the need for extra space here (JFK item 65).

80:33 **"I really love you. I'm crazy about you":** Catherine needs to hear this from Frederic, and he satisfies her with an apparently sincere expression of his feelings. With this assurance, she takes the extreme step of having sexual intercourse with him. With the severity of Frederic's leg wounds, the only plausible sexual position is female-superior.

81:5 **Catherine sat in a chair by the bed:** In all previous editions of the novel, there was a space before the beginning of this paragraph, indicating an undescribed passage of time between the paragraphs. We can presume that Frederic and Catherine have had sexual intercourse in the hospital bed during this time. Some readers may find the idea of their sex implausible. It certainly seems a brazen act for Catherine, who, from all other appearances, takes her job as a nurse seriously and professionally. As such, she has far more to risk than Frederic does, both professionally and biologically, since the consequences of a pregnancy would be devastating to her professionally and possibly dangerous to her health (as it, indeed, turns out to be). In the context of the clash between reason and nonreason, their lovemaking is an act of complete irrationality. It is fitting that Frederic describes himself twice in these pages as "crazy" (80:33 and 81:9). Moreover, his behavior, apparently based entirely on wanton desire, is thoughtless and inconsiderate. In short, he still has a long way to go in learning how to love.

What Catherine gives to him here is far greater than what he has given to her. To best understand it, we must realize that she is still acting out of guilt over having refused sexual intimacy to her fiancé. On the one hand, she may still be projecting the dead fiancé onto Frederic, but, on the other hand, if we assume she has genuine feelings for Frederic, she is probably, as Roger Whitlow has pointed out, also protecting herself against further feelings of guilt, should Frederic be killed (20).

In the original holograph manuscript, there is no break, although the paragraph that begins "Catherine sat in a chair . . ." is at the top of a new page, and Hemingway added the two lines "You can't. You shouldn't." "Come on. Don't talk. Please come on" in the top margin (JFK item 64). At this point in the typescript to the novel, there are two handwritten horizontal lines to indicate the need for extra space (JFK item 65).

81:7 **"Now do you believe I love you?"** After their lovemaking, Catherine confirms the madness of it all with an allusion to what is likely a very old cliché of young love, in which the crazier of the pair presses upon the resistant one, who then gives in and, after the presumed copulation, asks in words something like Catherine's.

81:16–17 **"You do love me, don't you?" . . ."You don't know what that does to me."** Catherine's repeated questions, "You do love me?" (80:32), "You really love me?" (80:37), "Now do you believe I love you?" and "You do love me, don't you?" are revealing. She hardly seems convinced by his two declarations of love, both of which are accompanied by the word *crazy* (80:33, 81:9). It should not be surprising that she needs reassurance of Frederic's love, and it may feel odd to us that she does not seem put off by the fact that he does not answer her latest question affirmatively but instead merely insists that she not repeat it again.

81:24–26 **God knows I had not wanted to fall in love. . . . But God knows I had":** Frederic's sharing this thought with us is intended to convince us of his sincerity and obtain our approval of their premarital sex—that we should not see it as another of his temporary flings. Adding "God knows" twice also emphasizes both the truthfulness of the declaration and the religiosity of Frederic's feelings.

CHAPTER 15

82:4–5 **local anæsthetic called something or other "snow":** As Michael Reynolds points out, the anesthetic is probably ethyl or methyl chloride spray, both of which were used during World War I ("Doctors in the House of Love" 116).

82:11 **Ospedale Maggiore:** One of the oldest hospitals in Italy, founded in 1456 by the Duke of Milan. In 1917, it was the leading hospital in the city, so it makes sense that it would have X-ray machines, which the Red Cross Hospital lacks. Hemingway was taken there for physical therapy during his recuperation. In her diary, Agnes von Kurowsky described the Ospedale Maggiore as "pretty up to date for an Italian one" (Villard and Nagel 66). It was located about half a mile southeast of the Red Cross Hospital in Milan. Baedeker's *Italy: From the Alps to Naples* 1928 even recommends the Ospedale Maggiore as a tourist stop, describing it as "an imposing brick structure, with nine courts, begun by Filarete in 1457 in a transitional style of mixed Gothic and Renaissance forms" (36).

82:21 **Cleopatra:** The queen of ancient Egypt (69–30 B.C.), famous for her beauty and legendary love affairs with Julius Caesar and Mark Antony of the Roman Empire. Again, we are reminded of Miss Gage's physical attractiveness. T. S. Eliot's *The Waste Land* also contains an allusion to Cleopatra. See entry 22:36–37.

83:14–15 **I was sick of lying in bed:** Frederic makes an ironic one-liner.

84:1 **"Test the articulation?"** Hemingway makes a metaphoric joke drawing on the dual meaning of *articulation*. The doctors use the word in the physiological sense: to test the movement in Frederic's knee joint, concluding it has "[p]artial articulation" (84:9). As the dialog in the scene continues with Frederic jokingly saying he wants his leg amputated and replaced with a hook (84:31) and then gladly seeing their "foreign bodies" departing, Frederic wins the battle of the words, the other meaning of articulation.

84:12–13 **"That is the left leg, doctor." . . . "You are right":** This scene's Marx brothers style comedy at the expense of the incompetent doctors highlights the pitfalls of putting trust completely in science. Faith can come into play even when scientific facts are concerned. These men of science expect Frederic to have faith in their scientific judgments, which are clearly influenced by their own subjectivity, leading them to support and associate with others of similar limited ability. Hemingway's point seems to be that science, like religion, can also be highly subjective. Frederic, rationally, does not accept the opinion of these clowns regarding his knee and seeks instead the opinion of someone with higher standing in the medical profession, a major from the Ospedale Maggiore, Milan's first-rate hospital.

84:20 **synovial fluid:** This fluid, found in joints, reduces friction between the bones during movement.

84:22 **encysted:** That is, to become enclosed by a thick membrane or shell.

86:9–10 **"Be a good boy":** The doctor patronizes Frederic here. Frederic's judgment in wishing for a second opinion is sound and demonstrates his own superior reasoning.

86:17 **Two hours later:** Previous editions of the novel have a space before the beginning of this paragraph, indicating a gap in the narration. In the original holograph manuscript, Hemingway first indicated the start of new chapter here, then inserted a circled note, "Leave space" (JFK item 64). The later typescript has extra space plus two handwritten horizontal lines to indicate the need for the extra space (JFK item 65).

86:17 **Dr. Valentini:** Hemingway gives the competent surgeon, the major from the Ospedale Maggiore, the name of the patron saint of love, Saint Valentine. According to Herbert Thurston in the *Catholic Encyclopedia,* there were three different saints named Valentine, all of them martyrs, and association of them with romantic, secular, profane love is apparently rooted in a medieval belief that birds mated in mid-February. It is not because any of these saints Valentine were associated with secular love or love of any kind. Little is known of them other than that they were martyred (Thurston). Valentini's demeanor is similar to that of the X-ray physician at the Ospedale Maggiore, described as "excitable, efficient and cheerful," a distinct contrast with the Red Cross Hospital doctor, depicted as a "thin quiet little man who seemed disturbed by the war" (82:11–12, 1–2).

86:21–22 **"Who's the pretty girl?"** Since both Miss Gage and Catherine have been mentioned as being with Frederic at different times in this chapter, and Miss Gage has been compared to Cleopatra, there may be some ambiguity in readers' minds here. However, since Frederic apparently nods assent in response to the question

"Is she your girl?" we can assume Catherine is the nurse in the room with him during Valentini's visit. This is confirmed at 86:36.

86:28 **"She will make you a fine boy"**: Alex Vernon points out the dual meanings of this sentence. As Frederic's nurse, Catherine will restore his health, and as his lover, she will produce a fine son for him (41).

86:30 **"Ask her if she eats supper with me"**: Of course, we are to understand that the doctor's dialogue is entirely in Italian, which Catherine does not speak. The doctor's effusive remarks on Catherine's beauty are a reminder of Rinaldi's earlier attraction to her. Neither Rinaldi nor Valentini, however, chooses to compete with Frederic for her affections.

86:35 **"A drink? Certainly. I will have ten drinks"**: In his positive response, Valentini also contrasts with the Red Cross Hospital doctor, who refused Frederic's earlier offer (86:11–12). In Hemingway's set of values, Valentini's knowledge of cognac is another mark in his favor.

87:7 **a star in a box on his sleeve:** Dr. Valentini's star signifies not only his rank of major but also the esteem Frederic Henry already has for him.

CHAPTER 16

88:1–89:3 That night a bat flew in . . . on the next roof: As he does many of his chapters, Hemingway begins this one with a substantial descriptive paragraph that sets the scene and the tone for what follows. This night is the eve of his surgery. The lovers share the room with a bat, which might be an ominous sign for others, but not for Frederic, whose loving descriptions reflect his comfort with and interest in the natural world. Neither is Catherine or the bat frightened (88:4–5).

The incident is apparently based on an actual event in the Milan Red Cross Hospital on 11 September 1918, which Agnes von Kurowsky recorded in her 13 September 1918 diary entry: "I forgot to mention the bat fight Ernie & I had at 1 A.M. Wed. We finally captured it after chasing it around the room for 3/4 of an hour. It was most exciting" (Villard and Nagel 78). In the novel, Frederic and Catherine calmly watch the bat and allow it to leave on its own. According to Henry Villard, a fellow patient with Hemingway at the Milan Hospital, "it was not unusual for a bat to stray into one of the bedrooms, the windows of which were unscreened. Bats were almost as numerous as pigeons around Milan's famous Duomo nearby" (275n31).

In *A New Slain Knight,* the fragmentary novel Hemingway gave up writing in March 1928 to begin *A Farewell to Arms,* Jimmy Breen and his father also have an encounter with a bat, which they both seem to remember fondly. The passage was posthumously published as part of a separate short story, "A Train Trip" (*CSS* 558).

89:20–21 "You don't know how you'll be": Here as elsewhere in the novel, knowledge of something is tied directly to experience in the material world. Frederic naively believes he will want Catherine sexually the first night after his surgery. Catherine's experience with surgery patients tells her that he will not. She is correct, as it turns out.

89:33 "all our children will have fine temperatures": In case we might have missed it, this should inform us that Frederic and Catherine have been "making babies" in Frederic's hospital bed.

90:13 "we will go somewhere": Catherine's offhand innocent remark foreshadows their flight to Switzerland after Frederic deserts from the army.

90:19 **"people get very blabby under anæsthetic"**: Catherine's superior wisdom and experience again assert themselves here. She knows that patients can be talkative under the influence of an anesthetic, and she is afraid Frederic might reveal something about their sexual relationship that will get her into trouble. In Hemingway's "A Very Short Story," his first and most blatantly autobiographical attempt to tell the tale of his love affair with Agnes von Kurowsky in 1918, there is a similar passage: "He went under the anæsthetic holding tight on to himself so he would not blab about anything during the silly, talky time" (*CSS* 107).

90:24 **"Say your prayers then"**: Although Catherine has no religion, as she states clearly twice (100:17 and 268:20), she is obviously aware by now that Frederic does have some kind of religious belief and that he prays periodically. We must assume that he has shared this fact with her in their moments of intimacy.

90:36 **"you sleep like a little boy"**: Frederic's immaturity is underscored again.

91:6 **"Now you're all clean inside and out"**: We are to understand that, as this conversation has been unfolding, beginning at 89:35, Catherine has not only been bathing the exterior of Frederic's body but also giving him an enema to make certain his bowels are empty before surgery. See Hemingway's "A Very Short Story" for a joke about "friend or enema" (*CSS* 117).

91:13 **"How many have you . . . stayed with?"** The conversation has now turned to a subject with which Frederic has more experience than Catherine—sexuality. She wants to know how many women Frederic has had sex with. Although he has been honest in answering her questions about how many women he has ever loved (none), his answers to the questions regarding his sexual experience are, of course, lies, and Catherine knows it.

91:17 **"Keep right on lying to me"**: This sentence may stir debate among readers as to how much honesty any good relationship can stand. Catherine seems to believe that a certain kind of lying is necessary for a healthy relationship. Her response is a reminder of Shakespeare's Sonnet 138, which Hemingway may well have had in mind as he wrote this section. There the man declares, "When my love swears that she is made of truth, / I do believe her, though I know she lies /. . . . / Therefore I lie with her and she with me, / And in our faults by lies we flattered be."

91:21–36 **"I don't know anything about it." . . ."I knew you wouldn't"**: Frederic's insistence here and again at 91:26 that he does not know the answer to Catherine's questions, besides being lies, highlight the novel's ever-present epistemic theme of what it means to have knowledge, to know something truly. In the subjective whirlwind and intense emotionality of love, knowledge can become an even slipperier and more fragile thing. In this rapid-fire exchange, Catherine shifts from wanting him to lie to wanting him to be truthful. Specifically, she wants to know the truth about declarations of love between people who are engaging in sex: "Does she say she loves him?" (91:27). Frederic answers truthfully: "Yes. If he wants her to" (91:29). Then, when Catherine asks him if the man says that he loves the woman, Frederic knowledgeably says, "He does if he wants to" (91:31). However, when she follows up with a question about Frederic's own behavior, "But you never did? Really?" he lies to her, telling her, "No" twice (91:33, 91:35). Here Catherine's naivete is exposed: "'You wouldn't,' she said. 'I knew you wouldn't. Oh, I love you, darling.'"

Catherine believes without justification (she has faith) that she knows Frederic well enough to be certain he would not have said to any previous sex partner that he loved her, but, as he reveals to us, he most assuredly has said that to women in the past when he did not mean it. Thus, the passage subtly reveals how the question of faith is not limited to religious belief. Human beings, male and female, sometimes must necessarily make decisions based on faith. Is Catherine's faith in Frederic ill-placed? With knowledge of Frederic's past, many readers would probably answer, yes. Yet Catherine's decision here to commit herself to Frederic is also, like the priest's awareness of Frederic's capacity to love, based on an intuition that goes beyond objective reasoning. Although their love will have a tragic ending, it is not because Frederic fails to love her truly. In the end, their love is done in by the randomness of the universe, and few would insist they have made a mistake by falling in love.

91:38–92:1 **Outside the sun was up . . . the points of the cathedral:** It is no coincidence that Hemingway inserts these two prominent symbols, objective correlatives, following this conversation between Frederic and Catherine. Even though Frederic has not been entirely truthful with her and he may be rationalizing silently to himself that his lies have been justified, at this moment he is undoubtedly feeling euphoric and blessed in his love for Catherine. The sunlight on the points of the cathedral are emblematic to him of the sacredness of what they feel for each other. While Frederic's love is still a work in progress, there is every reason for us to believe that what he feels for Catherine is different from anything he has felt for a woman before. So his lie at 91:33, repeated at 91:35, can be regarded as a white one: a lie about previous lies that do not matter now, a lie for the higher purpose of preserving and nurturing their genuine love.

92:6–19 **"I'll say just what you wish. . . . There isn't any me any more":** These several lines plus a few others in the novel make Catherine Barkley a problematic character for many commentators. Edmund Wilson believes she is "not convincing as a human personality" (Baker, *Writer as Artist* 114). Philip Young says she is "idealized past the fondest belief of most people" (91). To Stanley Cooperman, she is "only a love object, in other words, an erotic shadow shaped by passivity" (qtd. in Wexler 111n1). Daniel Schneider suggests that Catherine is "not a distinct character at all but Frederic's bitterness or his desire objectified" (290). Some feminists have been much harsher in their criticism. Millicent Bell describes her as "a sort of inflated rubber woman available at will to the onanistic dreamer" (119). Leslie Fiedler sees Catherine as one of Hemingway's "mindless, soft, subservient [women]; painless devices for extracting seed without human engagement" (318). To Judith Fetterley, one of the most strident of Hemingway's feminist critics, Catherine's pliancy provides Frederic "with the only kind of relationship that he is capable of accepting, one in which he does not have to act, in which he does not have to think about things because she does it for him. . . . , a relationship where there will be no drawbacks, no demands, pressures or responsibilities, only benefits" (210–11). In brief, Fetterley regards Catherine as little more than the embodiment of Frederic's and Hemingway's hostility toward women.

But not all readers agree with these views, and a few of these more positive voices even come from feminists. Roger Whitlow, in *Cassandra's Daughters,* argues that Catherine is "not to be written off as a daydream. She is a very real woman clinging, at the opening of the novel, to the last few shreds of sanity and hoping that Frederick [sic] Henry can help her make the fabric of her mind whole again" (18). Whitlow believes that most critics ignore Catherine's "deeply troubled psychological state" at the beginning of the novel (18). The first important feminist defense of Catherine came from Joyce Wexler, who argues forcefully that Catherine, "[f]ar from being a blind romantic, . . . is a shellshocked victim of the war who chooses love as a method of rechanneling self-destructive feelings of guilt and remorse" (115). Wexler is not at all troubled by Catherine's saying, "There isn't any me any more." "Since Catherine is trying to bury the person she used to be," Wexler says, "her early professions of selflessness reflect the depth of her grief rather than her love for Frederic" (115). And besides, Wexler insists, this pliable wish to satisfy Frederic is only present at the start of their relationship (115). As Wexler sees her, Catherine is the fulfillment of what the priest sees as Frederic's potential to love (120). Sandra Spanier takes Wexler's argument one step further and calls Catherine the "code hero" of the novel, exemplifying, as no other character does, "in the widest range the controls of honor and courage, the 'grace under pressure' that have come to be known as the 'Hemingway code'" (132). In her elegant essay, Spanier insists that Catherine's "willingness to submerge herself in her relationship with Frederic, far from being a sign of female spinelessness, is an act of will," a sign of her determination to "forge a meaningful existence for herself in a world where the traditional structures—morality, religion, patriotism—have proven hollow and empty, even 'obscene'" (134). While Spanier admits that Frederic has superior knowledge of the "physical territory," Catherine is superior in knowledge of the "emotional territory," and she mentors Frederic in "matters of psychological survival" (139).

CHAPTER 17

93:1–8 When I was awake . . ."How is it now?" The original holograph manuscript has much more significant detail regarding Frederic's post-surgery pain. The passage is reprinted in appendix 1 of the Hemingway Library edition (p. 299, item no. 11). In this passage, Frederic expects there to be a limit to the pain, but he finds no such limit. Thus, his experience contradicts what his religious upbringing has taught him: "I thought how our Lord would never send us more than we could bear and I had always believed that meant we became unconscious when it was too bad, hence the success of martyrs, but now it was not so but the pain went way beyond what I could bear" (299:13–17). The pain reduces him to uncontrollable crying and jerking in his diaphragm. When it finally subsides, he tells us he "gave no credit to our Lord" (299:20). The deleted passage is consistent with the general theme in the novel of God's responsibility for the suffering in the world, brought to the fore most prominently in the earlier death of Passini (47:24–48:8), Frederic's later memory of the ants on the campfire (280:7–20) and the suffering and death of Catherine in childbirth (much of chapter 41). It is clear that Frederic has been taught to believe in an interventionist and loving God, and his experience of suffering in the world tells him, contrary to his beliefs, that God does not act to relieve human suffering. His deletion of the passage may indicate Hemingway thought it revealed too much of the iceberg. Miss Gage's question, "How is it now?" shows her awareness of his suffering, though she also, it seems, has been powerless to alleviate it. Frederic experiences it on his own. Catherine is presumably sleeping during this episode of pain, since she will be on night duty, so she does not have firsthand experience of what he has gone through.

The deleted passage also contains an obvious reference to T. S. Eliot's 1925 poem "The Hollow Men." Frederic describes the effects of being under anesthesia as not like dying: "It is not like death's other kingdom nor is it like death, it is just a chemical choking so you do not feel" (299:9–11). Eliot uses the phrase "death's other kingdom" twice in his poem, in sections 1 and 3. Even though Hemingway deleted this passage, it is further evidence of Eliot's influence in the novel. See also entries 22:36–37, 135:19–23, and 274:9–25. Hemingway also alludes to "The Hollow Men" in *Across the River and into the Trees*, as Richard Cantwell contemplates his impending death: "Yes, ecstasy is what you might have had and instead you draw sleep's other brother" (219).

When Frederic says, "I had not been away. You do not go away. They only choke you," he may be comparing the experience of being unconscious under anesthesia to his near death / out-of-body experience when he was wounded and felt himself leave himself (see entry 47:12–17). Passini's death from the same explosion is also described as a choking (47:35). In addition, the reference to choking anticipates the death of the son he conceives with Catherine, who, he learns from a nurse, has died as a result of being choked by the umbilical cord. See entries 279:21–22 and 279:37–38.

The effects described following Frederic's waking from the anesthesia indicate that he was probably anesthetized with ether in one of two methods: either "liquid ether dripped over a nose cone or a gaseous mixture of ether and oxygen administered through a mask" (Reynolds, "Doctors in the House of Love" 118). One of the aftereffects of ether is nausea and vomiting.

Another excision from the beginning of chapter 17 is contained in item number 12 in appendix 1 of the Hemingway Library edition. A piece of it reads:

> Nothing that you learn by sensation remains if you lose the sensation. There is no memory of pain if there is no pain. Sometimes pain goes and you can not remember it from the moment before but only have a dread of it again. When love is gone you can not remember it but only remember things that happen and places. There is no memory of love if there is no love. All these things, however, return in the dark. In the dark love returns when it is gone, pain comes again and danger that has passed returns. Death comes in the dark. (299:31–300:7)

As Mark Cirino suggests, this is essentially an absurd argument, which denies the way that memory works (*Thought in Action,* chap. 3). If what Frederic says here is true, then it would seem impossible for him to write the novel we are reading. In other words, passages like this one underscore the fact that Frederic is writing out of a state of trauma. He does not want to remember, but the memory persists, as memories do, as in the Salvador Dali painting *The Persistence of Memory,* and Frederic can only attempt to cope through dissociation.

93:17 There were three other patients in the hospital now: All previous editions have an extra space before the start of this paragraph, indicating a gap in the narration. The typescript has extra space plus two handwritten horizontal lines to emphasize the need for the extra space (JFK item 65).

Before this sentence, Hemingway cut another long passage from the holograph manuscript, transcribed in appendix 1 of the Hemingway Library edition (299–301, item no. 12). It is a meditation on death, including accounts of executions that Frederic has seen in the daylight by firing squad, hanging, and beheading. Most importantly, the passage reveals that it was about this time that nights began to get bad for Frederic (300:28–29). Hemingway probably made the cut because the passage reveals too much of the iceberg, and besides, we have already figured out that the nights have become difficult for Frederic since he was nearly killed.

93:20–94:3 fuse-cap from a combination shrapnel and high explosive . . . exploded on contact: The structure of the artillery shell may be difficult to imagine, but Hemingway is describing a common type of shrapnel and high-explosive shell that had both a fuse cap and a nose cap, the fuse cap at the tip of the shell to initiate the explosion, followed within seconds by the ignition of the more powerful nose cap.

94:11 Ferguson was a fine girl. I never learned anything about her: As Fern Kory suggests, these lines indicate that there is more depth to the character of Ferguson than the novel can fully present. In a feminist defense of Hemingway's creation of Ferguson, Kory argues that Frederic's awareness that he did not know much about her comes out of his greater maturity in narrating the novel years after the fact (21–22). He is aware of Ferguson's complexity; she is a person whom he can describe as "fine" at times but at others as a person he can get "sick of." See entry 215:3. For one version of Helen Ferguson's backstory, see Miriam Mandel's "Ferguson and Lesbian Love."

Agnes von Kurowsky suggested that the character of Helen Ferguson is based on a combination of two women who served as nurses in the American Red Cross Hospital in Milan when Hemingway was a patient there in 1918. These were forty-year-old Elsie MacDonald (the only Scotch woman on the hospital staff) and thirty-four-year-old Loretta Cavanaugh, described as the "kind and helpful type" (Reynolds, *First War* 174–75).

94:12 Fifty-Second Division: Also known as the "Lowland" Division, the Fifty-second Division of the British army was made up entirely of soldiers from the Scottish Lowlands. In World War I, the division fought at Gallipoli in 1915, in the Middle East in 1917, and on the French front in 1918.

94:13 Mesopotamia: The ancient country in the Middle East between the Tigris and Euphrates Rivers (now Iraq) and the object of Britain's military adventures to protect its interests in the area (mostly oil and prestige among the Muslim population of India).

94:27 "don't get her in trouble": *Getting in trouble* is a common euphemism for *getting pregnant*, particularly out of wedlock. Ferguson is probably aware that Frederic and Catherine are having sexual relations. She is prescient too. In spite of Frederic's optimism, Ferguson's pessimism proves to be more right than wrong.

95:3 "A bump like that could make you crazy": This may seem an offhand diagnosis by Ferguson, but it is clearly part of a general concern in the novel with a "crazy" state of mind, a state of irrationality, an inability to discern what is real and true. The novel includes two other "bumps on the head" as reminders of the importance of maintaining rationality, beginning with Frederic's recommendation to the Italian American soldier in chapter 7 to get a bump on his head that would enable him to get out of fighting on the front. See entry 30:22–23. Later, during his own desertion and escape from the front, Frederic gets another bump when he leaps headfirst into a train car loaded with rifles. See entries 198:14–15 and 256:20–21. Here Ferguson is aware that the effects of brain trauma may not be immediately apparent. Symptoms include fatigue, headaches, visual disturbances, memory loss, poor concentration, sleep disturbances, dizziness, irritability, emotional disturbances, depression, and seizures.

There is a growing consensus among Hemingway scholars that in his final years, Hemingway suffered from what has come to be called chronic traumatic encephalopathy as a result of the numerous concussions and head injuries he suffered over the course of his life. Many now believe the disease was a factor in the mental illness and suicide at the end of Hemingway's life. See Dearborn (583), Farah (26–40), and Kale (138–39). See also entry 51:5–9.

95:8 **"ask her not to do night duty for a while"**: The need for Ferguson to point this out to Frederic highlights the fact that he still remains too self-absorbed. In Hemingway's "A Very Short Story," Luz, the nurse with whom the wounded American falls in love, stays on night duty for three months so that they can pursue their sexual romance (CSS 107).

95:15 **"She would"**: The original manuscript adds, crossed out, "'that bitch'" (JFK item 64).

95:27–96:17 **"I'm a friend of yours . . . you will some day"**: Frederic summons Nurse Gage, with whom he also has a tenuous relationship. She admonishes him for pretending she is unaware of the lovemaking night duty that is tiring Catherine. Like Ferguson, Gage insists on honesty. His request for help is needless. Gage is a friend and thus mildly offended by his duplicity, but she agrees to a friendly drink with Frederic, salutes him with "Here's to you," and explains supervisor Van Camp's annoyance with him. Her final reminder to him of her friendship underscores Frederic's ongoing educative process. In her own way, Miss Gage too plays a role in Frederic's "sentimental education."

CHAPTER 18

97:2 **in the park:** There are two possibilities for the location of this carriage ride in the park. One is the Public Gardens (Giardini Pubblici) about a mile northeast from the cathedral plaza, a common starting point for carriage rides. Baedeker's *Italy: From the Alps to Naples* 1928 describes the Public Gardens as "a beautiful park with ponds, groups of old trees, cages containing various kinds of animals, and an equestrian statue of Napoleon III" (36). The other is what is now called Sempione Park (Parco Sempione) but was just called the Park in 1918, also about a mile away, but northwest of the cathedral plaza. Baedeker's describes it as "once the garden of the Dukes of Milan, afterwards a drill ground, but laid out as a public park in 1893–97" (34). It also contained the Milan Aquarium, an arena for races, built in 1807, and a tall iron tower (which the Stigler Company built for the 1906 International Exposition in Milan, to demonstrate its elevator to the public). Sempione Park is somewhat larger than the Public Gardens, but both were and remain popular places to spend relaxing hours.

97:7 **Biffi's:** See entry 66:10.

97:7 **Gran Italia:** See entry 66:11.

97:8 **the galleria:** See entry 66:10.

97:10 **George:** Frederic has previously mentioned George as someone from whom he can borrow money, in another words, a trusted friend (66:11–12).

97:13 **dry white capri:** See entries 7:39 and 32:17.

97:14 **fresa:** The correct spelling, as Mark Cirino has pointed out, is *Freisa* ("You Don't Know" 59). A product of the Piedmont region of northwest Italy, Freisa wines are produced from red Freisa grapes, known for their bitterness and strong tannins. Consequently, they are commonly sweetened to tone down the bitterness and often feature the fragrance of raspberry, violet, and strawberry (Bredahl).

97:14 **barbera:** Like the other wines on this page, *Barbera* should be capitalized. It is a red wine from the Piedmont region of northwest Italy. Unlike Freisa, it is low in tannins, dark in color, but light in taste. Barbera can also have flavors of cherries, strawberries, and raspberries ("Learn about Barbera Red").

97:21 **margaux:** George's preference, recommended here to Frederic, is a bottle of Margaux (the correct form is capitalized), a red cabernet sauvignon produced in the village of Margaux in the Bordeaux region of southwest France. The best Margaux wines are prized by collectors. One of Hemingway's granddaughters, a daughter of his son Jack, was named Margaux, reputedly because her parents were drinking Margaux wine the night she was conceived.

98:9 **George loaned me a hundred lire:** Frederic's borrowing this substantial sum reveals George's value as a headwaiter and also his regard for Frederic: if he ever gets "short," George always has money. At the 1917 exchange rate of 7.509 Italian lire for one US dollar, 100 lire equaled $13.31, approximately $254 in 2017 value (Williamson). We might wonder how Frederic has become "short" of money, but George does not. He is a sure friend, who also includes Catherine in his generosity. Earlier, Frederic announced his intentions to go to the Gran Italia restaurant and borrow money from George, so this is not his first loan from George (66:11–12).

98:20 **the driver:** Frederic and Catherine take a horse-drawn taxi from the galleria, on the street by the cathedral, to the hospital, even though it would have been no more than a ten-minute walk. However, because of his wounds, Frederic (like Hemingway during his convalescence) was only partially ambulatory at this stage. See entry 71:2–3.

98:24 **swallows:** These small but long-winged birds are known for their swift and graceful flight.

98:32–38 **I loved to take her hair down . . . inside a tent or behind a falls:** Carl Eby has identified hair as one of Hemingway's fetishes. That is, hair was so connected to sex in Hemingway's mind that he could rarely conceive of a "lover or a romantic scene without its active presence" (34). As he says, "Catherine Barkley complains that her long hair is a nuisance in bed, but Frederic loves to have it dangled above him as Catherine makes love to him from on top" (35). Whether we regard Catherine's hair as a fetish for Frederic or not, it is clear in this passage that it signifies a sense of security for the two of them, isolated against the general harshness of the rest of the world. As such, it may remind readers of the homelike good place that Nick Adams creates for himself with his tent in "Big Two-Hearted River" (*CSS* 167).

99:13–16 tried putting thoughts in the other one's head . . . the same thing anyway": This provides another illustration of the way Catherine, in spite of her apparent atheism, is not always a rationalist or materialist in the way she regards the world. She definitely has a mystical side, and it demonstrates how Hemingway is using her character as an exemplar of balance between the extremities of faith and reason. Within limits, Catherine is comfortable in the subjective realm of emotions and the irrational, even though she does not go so far as to believe in an afterlife. For example, earlier she gives Frederic the Saint Anthony medal for good luck, a fact of which he reminds her in this chapter (100:18–19). See entry 37:6–36. Here she happily experiments in the supernatural with Frederic—the transfer of thoughts or mental telepathy—and the results, not surprisingly, are inconclusive, another instance of the novel's unresolved conflict between science and faith. Similarly, as we shall see, it is debatable whether she has clairvoyance (the ability to see the future) or not. See entry 110:1–2.

99:20 they would send her away: The Red Cross rules forbade nurses from marrying (Comley and Scholes 39).

99:32 "You couldn't get to Scotland": This line has created some confusion about Catherine's nationality, causing some to regard her as Scottish rather than English. However, earlier, when we first meet her, she is definitely assumed to be English. See entries 18:12–13 and 18:16. So if that is the case, why does she seem to refer to Scotland as her home here? There are some possible explanations. Given her apparent estrangement from her family (see entry 135:6–13) and her closeness to Ferguson, it is reasonable to think that if she is sent home because of her pregnancy Ferguson will return with her, and perhaps the intention is that Catherine will live with Ferguson in Scotland until she can be reunited with Frederic. Or it is possible that Hemingway intended but forgot to include somewhere else in the novel an explanation for Catherine's living in Scotland, even though she is English. Of course, it is also possible that Hemingway was genuinely confused about which nationality he wanted to give Catherine, so that in one part of the novel he thought of her as English and in another as Scottish. Or it could be an error Hemingway did not catch. Whether she is Scottish or English is not enormously consequential to the meaning of the novel, except that if she and Ferguson are of different nationalities, they are another iteration of the novel's dualities, with Catherine, as English, the more rational and objective of the two, and Ferguson, as Scottish, the more emotional and subjective.

99:36 "There isn't any me. . . . Don't make up a separate me." These sentences are evidence that Hemingway found the first name of Catherine Barkley in the character of Catherine Earnshaw from Emily Brontë's *Wuthering Heights*. Compare them to the strikingly similar words Catherine Earnshaw expresses to Nelly in Brontë's novel:

"Nelly, I *am* Heathcliff—he's always, always in my mind— . . . as my own being—so don't talk of our separation again" (82–83). Hemingway made clear his own high regard for *Wuthering Heights,* including it in his list of books he would "rather read again for the first time . . . than have an assured income of a million dollars a year" (*BL* 161–62), and Lisa Tyler has written persuasively of the influence of Brontë's novel on *A Farewell to Arms,* even calling it a "retelling" of *Wuthering Heights* (79).

Tyler argues that recognizing this allusion in *A Farewell to Arms* helps make Catherine Barkley a "more comprehensible and better realized character, one with whom feminist readers can more comfortably sympathize" (80). Besides the lines under current consideration, Tyler sees parallels in the unconventional religious views of both Catherines, the portentousness of rain in both novels, and the fact that both Catherines die in childbirth (Catherine Earnshaw's child is a daughter named Catherine, who survives, whereas Catherine Barkley's child, called "young Catherine" during pregnancy, is a son who is stillborn). More important, as Tyler suggests, love has become religion for both Catherines. Catherine Earnshaw rejects the conventional idea of heaven, even dreaming that she is thrown out of heaven (80–81). Her soul and Heathcliff's, she says, are the same. Similarly, Catherine tells Frederic, "You're my religion." See entry 100:21.

In "The Butterfly," an essay young Emily Brontë wrote for a French exercise, she made the startling claim that "[a]ll creation is equally insane. . . . Nature is an inexplicable puzzle, life exists on a principle of destruction; every creature must be the relentless instrument of death to the others, or himself cease to live" (qtd. in Miller 163). This prescient vision of Darwin's struggle for existence aside, the words would fit quite well amid some of Frederic Henry's darker ruminations. When Catherine dies at the end of Hemingway's novel, we may ask if Frederic is in the condition of Heathcliff after death of *his* Catherine. If so, it may explain how long it apparently takes Frederic to relate his story to us.

100:4 **"I don't want to hear about it":** Frederic is jealous of Catherine's dead fiancé, and some readers may regard this as evidence of a double standard, as Catherine suggests, reminding him that she is aware of his previous sex partners yet is not jealous of them or threatened by them. While that is true, in defense of Frederic, their positions are not exactly analogous. Catherine genuinely loved her fiancé, whereas Frederic did not love anyone prior to Catherine. It may be immature of him to feel threatened by Catherine's fiancé, but it is not surprising, given how, as we have observed, Catherine's initial feelings for Frederic are simply a projection of her love for her dead fiancé. It is not unreasonable for him to wonder if her present love is still a projection of those feelings. Catherine seems to reassure him, however, by reminding him that he "has everything" and so should not be jealous of a dead person (100:8–9).

100:18–19 **"You gave me. . . ." ". . . gave it to me":** These two lines were added in the margin of the original manuscript, and, oddly, it is "Saint Joseph," not "Saint Anthony" (JFK item 64). See entry 36:6–36.

100:21 **"You're my religion":** This is a full acknowledgement of Catherine's balance between reason and faith. She does not believe in any other world but this, and in this world, love, the realm of emotion, reigns supreme. It is her spirituality. Rinaldi and the priest have represented the opposing sides of reason and faith, and they have been equally close to Frederic in appealing to those sides in him. Catherine shows him that there is a middle way. We have not seen the last of Rinaldi and the priest, but in their final appearances they will both demonstrate their waning influence over Frederic. Catherine's is the most powerful influence from here on.

100:36–37 **"You'll be sick of me I'll be so faithful":** Unwittingly perhaps, Catherine makes explicit the combination of the sacred and the profane in her character.

101:2 **"when I met you perhaps I was nearly crazy":** A final acknowledgement by Catherine that she entered her relationship with Frederic out of the realm of the irrational. But her craziness is in the past. Her love for Frederic is genuine and a part of the subjective realm of feelings, but it is also rational. It is her mechanism for survival in a world gone mad. Frederic is still the student, who must learn what she knows.

CHAPTER 19

In the manuscript, the beginning of this chapter has the following sentences circled and crossed out: "Katherine, 'It's a great advantage to have a wife with religion because it keeps her occupied. But there's a certain advantage in a wife with no religion'" (JFK item 64).

102:2–3 **many victories:** In 1916–17, Italian factories had been working hard to produce, by this time, a huge superiority for the Italians over the Austrians in guns and munitions. By August 1917, which is presumably the timeframe for this chapter, the Italians had 3,750 artillery guns on the Isonzo front, plus another 1,900 mortars. In contrast, the Austrians, whose factories were far less productive, had only 430 heavy artillery and 1,250 field guns (Thompson 279). The Italians had maintained a 10 to 4 superiority in manpower over the Austrians since 1915. In addition, the Italian air force controlled the sky. Consequently, the Eleventh Battle of the Isonzo, after weeks of artillery shelling, began optimistically on 19 August, and although the Austrians were resistant in the southern portion of the front, the Italians captured the Bainsizza plateau and Monte Santo. However, they failed to move up reserves behind the gains and thus were unable to capitalize further. Frederic seems to be narrating this in late August, after these impressive victories but before the battle bogged down in a failed attempt to capture Monte San Gabriele.

102:6 **Ospedale Maggiore:** See entry 82:11.

102:7 **baking in a box of mirrors with violet rays:** As Michael Reynolds has explained, exposing wounds to ultraviolet rays killed bacteria and helped in production of vitamin D. However, the treatment was also later discovered to produce skin cancer ("Doctors in the House of Love" 118).

102:10 **wanted to get home to the hospital from the café:** The original manuscript adds, crossed out, "like a married man" (JFK item 64).

143

102:14 **Anglo-American Club:** An institution near the Red Cross Hospital in central Milan, where English-speaking people could eat, drink, socialize, and read newspapers and magazines published in English.

103:9 **the Carso:** See entry 6:4.

103:9 **Kuk:** This mountain, two thousand feet in elevation, is across the Isonzo River and about 1.2 miles south from Plava. See entries 20:6 and 20:6–20.

103:10 **the Bainsizza plateau:** A karst (limestone) plateau east of Plava, about twenty-three hundred feet in elevation in its central section. It covers about thirty-nine square miles. Mark Thompson explains, "Given the pitch and roll of the gradients, the name 'plateau' is misleading. . . . Mountainous by British standards, the Bainsizza was almost a trackless wilderness—there were no proper roads and very few paths. And it was almost waterless" (250n2).

103:10 **the West front:** The battlefront in France, where the Germans were fighting mostly British and French armies, was, in 1917, the timeframe of the novel, joined by a few American units.

103:11–12 **We were in the war now:** That is, the United States had finally joined the fighting on the French front in the summer of 1917.

103:16 **Monte San Gabriele:** See entry 27:30. The Italians made numerous unsuccessful attempts to capture it but were finally able to achieve the summit on 4 September 1917, only to have the Austrians regain it that afternoon in a counterattack. The Italians then decided to blow the top off the mountain with a heavy artillery bombardment, which not only turned the summit completely to rubble but reduced the height of the mountain by thirty feet. Thompson describes it as looking like a volcano during the bombardment, "spewing fire and rock" (282). However, the Italians were never able to capture and hold the mountain. As Thompson says, the Eleventh Battle of the Isonzo was "a technical victory that felt like defeat" (282), or as Hemingway might have labeled it, "Winner Take Nothing." The Italians suffered 166,000 casualties in the battle, including 40,000 dead, 25,000 of them on San Gabriele (282). It is no wonder that when Frederic returns to the front in October (at the beginning of Book Three), he finds everyone but the priest demoralized. Monte San Gabriele, more than any other specific piece of the Italian front, represents the futility, the absurdity, and the enormous human waste of the Great War.

103:25 **Hundred Years' War:** Frederic refers to the war fought from 1337 to 1453 between England and France. France ultimately prevailed, and England lost all its territory on the European mainland.

103:26–27 **up the Via Manzoni:** The Via Alessandro Manzoni runs from the Piazza della Scala northeast to the Porta Nuova Arch, a gate built during the Napoleonic Era, 1810–13. Presumably the Anglo-American Club (not listed in Baedeker's 1909 or 1928 versions) was also on the Via Manzoni, near the Gran Hotel (see entry 103:27), and Frederic seems to be walking southwest, given that he later comes to the Cova and the Scala, which were southwest from the Gran Hotel.

The street is named for the nineteenth-century Italian novelist Alessandro Manzoni (1785–1873). H. R. Stoneback argues that Manzoni's novel *The Betrothed* may have been a source for *A Farewell to Arms* ("Hemingway's Stresa" 137–39), but the evidence is only circumstantial. Manzoni does not appear on the list of Hemingway's reading compiled by Michael Reynolds, nor does Hemingway mention Manzoni in any of his published letters.

103:27 **the Gran Hotel:** The Grand Hotel & de Milan at 59 Via Manzoni is three blocks northeast of La Scala and the Galleria. In Baedeker's *Italy: From the Alps to Naples* 1928, it is listed as a hotel with 150 beds (24). In the late nineteenth century, it was the only hotel in Milan with postal and telegraph service and so was the preferred choice of accommodation for visiting businessmen and diplomats. The Grand Hotel, still in its original location, celebrated its 150th anniversary in 2013.

Among the hotel's famous clients was the great opera composer Giuseppe Verdi, who, from 1872 until the end of his life, alternated residency during parts of the year between the hotel and his home in the country. His operas *Otello* and *Falstaff* were at least partly composed in his Gran Hotel suite. He died in the hotel on 27 January 1901. Thus, the novel's Gran Hotel, with its Verdi connection, contributes to a pronounced theme of Italian opera in this chapter, which is continued with the characters of Ralph Simmons and Edgar Saunders, and Simmons's singing of Puccini's *Tosca*. See entry 104:30. Today the hotel's clients can stay in the Giuseppe Verdi Suite at the hotel for a little over $1,000 a night ("More Than 150 Years"). Famed tenor Enrico Caruso was a guest at the hotel in April 1902, when he came to Milan to perform Toscanini's *Germania* at La Scala. During his stay, he made the first flat LP recording in the history of music, consisting of ten opera arias, in a room at the hotel.

Hemingway learned something of opera from his mother, Grace Hall Hemingway, who was trained as an operatic singer but was forced to give up her career because her eyes were too sensitive to the bright theater footlights. She taught private voice lessons, however, in the Hemingway family home in Oak Park. For more on Hemingway and opera, see entry 104:22.

103:27 **old Meyers and his wife:** Frederic meets an American couple of dubious status, whom he obviously already knows and who are apparently staying at the Gran Hotel, as they return from an afternoon diversion at the Milan horse races, a "sport" of questionable ethics. Meyers's character is humorously suggested by his reluctance to be friendly, even to his wife, who complains about his secrecy.

104:12 **marsala:** Like vermouth, Marsala (properly capitalized) is a fortified wine, originating from the region surrounding Marsala, Sicily (Greene 270). Fortified with brandy, it comes in both dry and sweet varieties and is most often used today for cooking. In other words, it is not a highly prized wine for drinking. In Hemingway's short story "Out of Season," Marsala is humorously mentioned as what English caricaturist Max Beerbohm drinks (*CSS* 136). According to Carlos Baker, Beerbohm served Marsala when Hemingway visited him in Rapallo in April 1922 (*Life Story* 89).

104:16 **the Cova:** See entry 10:27–28.

104:17 **I bought a box of chocolate:** The Cova was then and remains today noted for its chocolate delights.

104:22 **the Scala:** See entry 66:12. Agnes von Kurowsky's diary entry for Thursday, 19 September 1918, mentions attending an opera that evening at La Scala with Hemingway: "'Ghismonde'—opening night & a ballet—'Le Carillon Magico' also new to Milan, & the most delightful I've ever seen. Mr. Hem—got sick in the middle & had to leave. . . . Dr. Horan went to the opera with us" (Villard and Nagel 80). In a letter home to his family on 28 November 1918, Hemingway mentions that he has been attending operas at the Scala, including Giuseppe Verdi's *Aida*, Eugen d'Albert's *Ghismonda*, Gioachino Rossini's *Mosè in Egitto* (*Moses in Egypt*) and *Il Barbiere di Siviglia* (*The Barber of Seville*), Arrigo Boito's *Mefistofele* (*Mephistopheles*), George Bizet's *Carmen*, and Giacomo Puccini's *La Bohème* (*Letters 1* 160–61). He also attended operas in Chicago and Toronto in 1920 (221, 222, 231, 253, 254–55).

104:22 **vice-consul:** A second level diplomat at the American consulate, which was located at 3 Via Bocchetto, a seven-minute walk to the southwest from La Scala. There may be several vice consuls who assist the consul in charge. Ettore Moretti later calls the vice consul "Mac."

104:23 **Ettore Moretti:** In the manuscript, his name is "Ettore Piani" (JFK item 64). Moretti is almost certainly modeled after Beato Nicola (Nick) Nerone, whom Hemingway met during his convalescence in Milan. Nerone was Italian born, from the Abruzzi region, then, when he was ten years old, emigrated to America and attended high school there. In 1915, he returned to Italy when he was called to service in the Italian army. Like Moretti, Nerone was wounded three times and was awarded multiple decorations for bravery. According to the research of independent Hemingway scholar and Capracotta native Vincenzo Di Nardo, Nerone's first two wounds and the citation for the silver medal (which is what Frederic expects to receive) occurred during his service as part of the Strafexpedition, an Austrian assault on the Asiago plateau in May 1916. His third wound and the citations for the three bronze medals occurred during service on the Isonzo front. After the third wounding, on 8 October 1917, he was hospitalized in Como, where he remained until April 1918, when he was transferred to Milan for physical therapy. For additional information on Nerone, see entry 8:1–2.

104:25 **Ralph Simmons:** Hemingway may have drawn the surname of Simmons from his friend Isabel Simmons Godolphin (1901–1964), a neighbor of the Hemingway family in Oak Park and fellow student at Oak Park High School, although she graduated three years behind Ernest. She visited him and his first wife, Hadley, in Switzerland and Italy in 1923, and she and Ernest were frequent correspondents throughout the 1920s.

104:26 **Enrico DelCredo.** There are two important thematic elements at play here. First, the American opera singer in Italy, Ralph Simmons, extends the motif of identity in the novel, having adopted a stage pseudonym, "Enrico DelCredo." Enrico is Italian for "Henry," Frederic's surname. Second, the name underscores the theme of faith in the novel: "DelCredo" in English would be "of the Creed," a phrase in Italy suggestive of the Roman Catholic denomination of Christianity. Roman Catholics profess their faith during each celebration of the Mass with recitation of the Nicene Creed, which begins, "I believe in one God, the Father almighty, maker of heaven and earth, and of all things visible and invisible" ("Liturgy of the Mass" [12]). In other words, Simmons's pseudonym is an emphatic reminder of the central issue in the novel—the question of Frederic Henry's faith in God. Even though Simmons may seem a minor character, his stage name suggests otherwise, and the importance of his role will be amplified again later in the text, when he lends Frederic Henry his clothes following his desertion from the Italian army. See entry 209:14. In the manuscript, Hemingway added the clause "but he couldn't sing very well" at the end of the sentence but crossed it out (JFK item 64).

104:30 **Piacenza:** A city in northern Italy about forty-three miles southeast of Milan, its population in 1917 was approximately thirty-six thousand (Baedeker, *Italy 1909* 96).

104:30 **Tosca:** The original manuscript has "in Bohem" crossed out (JFK item 64). *Tosca* is a melodramatic and violent opera by Italian composer Giacomo Puccini.

It premiered in Rome in 1900 to lukewarm reviews but was very popular with the public and remains so today. That Hemingway thought first of having Simmons sing in *La bohème* and then changed it to *Tosca,* an opera with a much different storyline and theme, indicates that the content and theme of the opera mattered to him. Aside from the sexuality and violence, the question of religious faith is central to *Tosca* (unlike *La bohème*). The story takes place in Rome in 1800, during Napoleon's invasion of the city. Floria Tosca, the title character, is a beautiful singer who is also devoutly religious. However, she is jealously insecure in her love relationship with Mario Cavaradossi, a cavalier atheistic painter and revolutionary. The evil Scarpia, the Roman chief of police, with connections to the papal authority, exploits Tosca's insecurity. As Scarpia has Cavaradossi tortured and attempts to seduce Tosca, she pleads to God in the opera's most famous aria, "*Vissi d'arte*" ("I Lived for Art"):

> Ever in pure faith,
> I brought flowers to the altars.
> In this hour of pain, why,
> Why, oh Lord, why
> Dost Thou repay me thus? (Illica and Giacosa)

The question is thus the same as that asked by Ivan Karamazov and Frederic Henry: why does a beneficent God allow innocent people to suffer? Tosca never gets an answer. She kills Scarpia, mistakenly believing he has canceled Cavaradossi's execution. When Cavaradossi dies in front of a firing squad and Tosca's murder of Scarpia is discovered, she is left with no choice but to throw herself over the parapet of the Castel Sant'Angelo to her death, without any evidence of divine intervention to save her from suffering. Although, as Miriam Mandel notes, there are two tenor roles in *Tosca*—Cavaradossi and his revolutionary friend Angelotti—we can presume that Simmons, described here as a tenor (105:4), sings the role of Cavaradossi, since the intense audience reaction that Ettore describes would not be expected of a singer in a minor part. Mandel says that *Tosca* was performed eight times in February 1917, with Amedeo Bassi as Cavaradossi (*Reading Hemingway* 158).

104:35 **Modena:** About 110 miles southeast of Milan, in 1917 the city of Modena had a population of approximately twenty-seven thousand (Baedeker, *Italy* 1909 and 1928).

105:6 **Edouardo Giovanni:** Saunders echoes Simmons and the motif of identity as he, too, sings under a pseudonym. Miriam Mandel reports that a singer named Edouardo de Giovanni sang at the Scala on 9 January 1914 and 5 February 1915 (*Reading Hemingway* 154).

105:16 **"Mac"**: Ettore, the Italian native who has lived for years in America, repeatedly calls the vice counsel "Mac." In the next chapter, we learn his name is McAdams, a rhyme with "Nick Adams," the familiar protagonist of many Hemingway short stories (113:37).

105:38 **"three wound stripes"**: Military photos of Nick Nerone, the source for the character of Ettore, show the three wound stripes exactly as described here. We are indebted to Antonio Nerone, Nick Nerone's son, for providing a digital copy of a photo of his father in uniform.

106:14 **"potato mashers"**: Also called *stick grenades* or *stick bombs,* these were hand grenades produced in Germany, called *Stielhandgranate* (stalk hand grenade). The grenade's charge was contained in a steel cylinder mounted at the top of a hollow wooden handle. Unlike British-made grenades, which could only be tossed fifteen yards, the potato mashers could be tossed as far as thirty yards. Potato mashers were also more accurate than other hand grenades because they were less prone to roll when they landed.

106:21 **"a rifle so they can't tell I'm an officer"**: Typically, officers only carried pistols, whereas enlisted men carried rifles. Naturally, officers were prime enemy targets.

106:32 **"Going on three years"**: Frederic's service began in the summer of 1915. It is now 1917, so in truth, he has been a lieutenant two years and is only beginning his third year of service. It is possible that he is self-conscious and embarrassed that he has spent so long at the rank without a promotion.

106:33–34 **"you don't know the Italian language well enough"**: Ettore insists that Frederic cannot be promoted because his knowledge of Italian is not good enough, although we have not seen any particular difficulties in his abilities to communicate with Italians. Each of the speakers in this group is bilingual. For a detailed discussion of Hemingway's problematic usage of Italian in the novel, see Mark Cirino's "You Don't Know the Italian Language Well Enough."

107:1 **"two hundred and fifty dollars"**: Frederic, understandably, lacks precise knowledge of how much a captain in the US Army would be paid. He is a little high in his estimation; a captain with less than five years of service would have been paid $200 a month. He would need to have more than ten years of service to receive $250 a month (Goering). Today, that $200 would be worth $3,820, while $250 would be worth $4,780. American soldiers were reportedly better paid than soldiers in other armies ("How Were Soldiers Paid").

107:4 **"Fred"**: Ettore is the only person in the novel to call Frederic by this nickname, which he uses here and twice more, at 107:28 and 107:31.

107:21 **He touched the stars at his collar:** This is a gesture for luck—one of the ways characters in the novel resort to irrational means to deal with the hard and cruel facts of reality. Ettore and Frederic exchange good luck wishes at 108:1–2. Hemingway was a believer in luck. For example, in *A Moveable Feast*, he describes carrying "a horse chestnut and a rabbit's foot" in his right pocket for luck: "The claws scratched in the lining of your pocket and you knew your luck was still there" (91).

107:27–28 **"Ciaou"**: See entry 10:11.

108:6 **"Don't take any bad nickels"**: More familiarly, "Don't take any wooden nickels," meaning "Don't let yourself get cheated." The phrase was popular in the early to mid-twentieth century, as country folk visiting large cities were frequently the objects of scams designed to take advantage of their naivete. Ettore's warning can serve as a segue into the next chapter, when Frederic and Catherine visit the corrupt world of horse racing and gambling.

108:12 **normal school:** A college specifically established to train teachers.

108:13–15 **Catherine could not stand him. . . . "they're much quieter"**: Catherine dismisses the braggart Ettore as conceited and boring. She responds with her English coolness and understatement.

109:6 **"in the penitentiary at home"**: Mr. and Mrs. Meyers, the American expatriate couple, are also comic characters, and here we learn that Mr. Meyers's shady knowledge of horse racing may have led to imprisonment in the United States.

109:9 **"I don't know how happily"**: There are four expressions of "I don't know" on this page: two by Frederic and two by Catherine, indicating a mutual mood of uncertainty and a movement into the realm of subjectivity, which continues through the end of the chapter. The first usage here regards Mr. Meyers's relative happiness after he was released from prison, certainly something Frederic cannot be sure of, though Catherine believes he must have been happy enough to be out of prison.

109:10 **"jail"**: The original manuscript has "the penitentiary" crossed out and spelled *gaol* (JFK item 64). Hemingway must have briefly considered that *gaol* gave it an appropriate British flavor, since Catherine speaks the line. However, *gaol* and *jail* are pronounced the same.

109:15 **"Listen to it rain"**: Meyers and his maternal wife, with her comic monomania for taking care of "her boys," highlight the very different tragic mode of Frederic and Catherine. Rain falls on all the living and the dead (like the snow with which James Joyce ends his story "The Dead").

109:23 **"I don't know, darling. I've always been afraid of the rain"**: The next "I don't know" is Catherine's response to Frederic's question as to why she is afraid of the rain. Actually she knows (subjectively) why she is afraid of it, but she is not certain that she wants to share her reason with Frederic.

109:29 **"I don't know. I guess I'm sleepy"**: Frederic's drowsiness hinders his ability to think objectively. An objective answer to Catherine's question might be "sleet."

109:34 **"I don't know"**: Catherine again remains reluctant to reveal why she is afraid of the rain.

110:1–2 **"because sometimes I see me dead in it"**: Under Frederic's insistence, Catherine at last reveals why she fears the rain, providing an entirely subjective rationale that she and Frederic ultimately agree is "nonsense" (110:12–13). However, their repetition of *nonsense* only underscores their uncertainty about the meaning of Catherine's vision. In light of what happens in the novel, we have to take seriously whether the subjective truth of her vision turns into an objective truth to be counted as knowledge. In other words, it is unclear whether Hemingway wants us to believe she is clairvoyant.

This dialog between Catherine and Frederic is crucial in the way it elevates rain to what T. S. Eliot defined as an objective correlative, "succinctly an external equivalent for an internal state of mind" (*Sacred Wood* 58). See also C. Hugh Holman and William Harmon, *A Handbook to Literature,* which defines *objective correlative* as "a pattern of objects, actions, or events, or a situation that can serve effectively to awaken in the reader an emotional response without being a direct statement of that subjective emotion. It is a means of communicating feeling" (327).

110:8–10 **"Scotch and crazy"**: Some commentators have used this to support the idea that Catherine is Scottish and not English. But to take what Catherine says literally is to misread the context here. Frederic is the one who first cautions, "I don't want you to get Scotch and crazy tonight," meaning that he does not want her to act in the irrational manner of Ferguson, who, in chapter 17, threatens to kill Frederic if he should get Catherine pregnant. Frederic is saying he does not want her to become something she is not, or at least to become something that he does not think she is. See entries 18:12–13 and 18:16. If we take Frederic's and Catherine's words here as figurative, then "Scotch and crazy" in this context is a unit that denotes irrationality. In that case, when Catherine responds by saying, "but I am Scotch and crazy," she is declaring not her nationality but rather her irrationality at this particular moment. She is simply saying that her rationality is unhinged temporarily, just as it is early in the novel during her initial encounters with Frederic.

In the grand scheme, Catherine's nationality is less important than recognizing this discussion as yet another instance in the context of the war between rationality and irrationality, the objective and the subjective, science and faith, part of the novel's epistemological theme.

CHAPTER 20

This short chapter about a visit to San Siro horse racing track is not nearly as innocuous as it may seem at first glance. F. Scott Fitzgerald thought it contributed nothing to the novel and should be cut, but he misunderstood Hemingway's purposes (JFK item 77). Miriam Mandel rightly sees it as a recapitulation of the novel as a whole, "canvassing such issues as the dishonesty of war, the forgiveness necessary for love, and the psychological underpinnings of retrospective first-person narration" ("Headgear and Horses" 66). Michael Reynolds has asserted, and Mandel agrees, that "[t]he fixed race is Hemingway's metaphor for existence" (*First War* 271; "Headgear and Horses" 66). In the confused atmosphere of crooked racing, the bettors try various means to reason their way objectively to placing winning bets, but these efforts yield very little fruit, so Frederic and Catherine end up relying on purely subjective hunches, and they are much happier as a result, even though their winnings are no greater. The chapter is also integral to the overall subject of the novel—the clash of the subjective and the objective. In addition, it shows another small step in Frederic Henry's growth.

Agnes von Kurowsky writes in her diary of two occasions, 12 and 15 September 1918, on which she attended races at San Siro with Hemingway and others (Villard and Nagel 78–79).

111:9–10 **Old Meyers . . . gave him tips:** Mr. Meyers enlarges on the absurdity of Crowell's "logic" with his own faulty reasoning. Meyers is privy to the "very crooked" racing at San Siro, allowing him to win "on nearly every race." He does not like to give tips, because it means he will win less money, but he helps Crowell because they both have weak eyes. Thus Meyers allows his objective system of betting to be compromised by his subjective feelings for Crowell.

111:11–12 **The racing was very crooked:** See Hemingway's story "My Old Man," where Joe Butler's father is blackballed out of Italy by shady characters, apparently because he has refused to throw the Premio Commercio, a big race at San Siro (*CSS* 153).

111:20 **San Siro:** This horse-racing track is about four miles northwest from the center of Milan. With Capannelle Racecourse in Rome, it is one of the two premier horse tracks in Italy. In "My Old Man," protagonist Joe Butler calls San Siro "the swellest race course I'd ever seen," although his father disparages the quality of racing there compared to that in Paris (*CSS* 152, 153). This reflects Crowell Rodgers's judgment in this chapter. However, as Miriam Mandel has pointed out, due to the war, "many valuable French race horses were sent away [from Paris] for safety," and, consequently, superior horses from the Paris tracks could turn up in Milan, as happens here with Japalac ("Headgear and Horses" 64). In fact, later, in chapter 21, Frederic reads in the newspaper that horse racing has stopped in France (119:5).

Hemingway's own interest in horse racing and betting on it probably began at San Siro. As previously noted, he had attended races there in 1918 with Agnes von Kurowsky and others (Baker, *Life Story* 51) and then again in 1922 during a trip to Italy with his first wife, Hadley (Reynolds, *Paris Years* 54). Hemingway also includes a reminiscence of his time in Milan and at San Siro with Hadley in *A Moveable Feast* (52–54).

111:21 **we drove out through the park:** The four carriage riders (Frederic, Catherine, Ferguson, and Rodgers) take a slightly less direct, but more scenic route through what is today called Parco Sempione (simply the Parco in 1917). See entry 97:2. It is the largest park in central Milan and the only one of significance between the center of Milan and San Siro.

As H. R. Stoneback has written, in Hemingway's work, journeys, even relatively short ones like this, are frequently filled with symbolic significance (see especially *Reading Hemingway's* The Sun Also Rises 188–96). In this case, it is likely that Hemingway carefully selected the route for its relevance to the novel's theme. If we assume their carriage ride begins in the vicinity of the hospital, in order to go through Parco Sempione their carriage would first have driven northwest up the Via Dante, a relatively new avenue at that time, named after the poet of the *Divine Comedy,* Dante Alighieri. Constructed in 1880 over the previous medieval streets, Via Dante runs from the southwest corner of the Piazza del Duomo (plaza of the Milan Cathedral, dedicated to Saint Mary of the Nativity) in a straight line that projects directly through the center of the Castello Sforzesco (Castle Sforza) and Parco Sempione to the Arco della Pace (Arch of Peace). At the end of the Via Dante, Frederic and Catherine's carriage would have had to follow a semicircle along the Foro Buonaparte (named for Napoleon I), around the U-shape of the buildings surrounding the castle, an imposing military fortress built in the fifteenth century by the Duke of Milan, Francesco Sforza.

Over the centuries, the fortress changed hands militarily numerous times. Following the Risorgimento (Italian Unification) in 1871, the castle was demilitarized and turned over to the City of Milan. Today it is a complex of various museums of fine art. The Parco Sempione, whose name comes from the Corso Sempione, a major boulevard dating back to the Napoleonic era and extending the line from the Via Dante to the northwest from the Arch of Peace, was formally a military parade ground for the soldiers stationed in the castle. Thus, the entire arrangement of decommissioned castle, decommissioned parade ground, and Arch of Peace represents a farewell to arms, a movement from war to peace, and a foreshadowing of Frederic's desertion and separate peace. If we include the Dante allusion, we have a passage through hell and purgatory culminating in paradise. Stoneback calls this a "*paysage moralisé,*" a symbolic landscape "informed by literary and historical allusion" (*Reading Hemingway's* The Sun Also Rises 188). The rest of the trip from the park to the race course is unremarkable.

In *A Moveable Feast,* Hemingway's memoir of Paris in the 1920s, as Ernest is strolling through Paris with his wife, Hadley, they look through the Arc du Carrousel up toward the Arc de Triomphe, which stands at the other end of the Champs-Élysées. Ernest asks his wife, "Do you really think that the three arches are in line? These two and the Sermione [sic] in Milano?" There is no Arco Sermione in Milan. He can only mean the Arco della Pace at the Parco Sempione (Simplon Park). Hadley responds, "I don't know, Tatie. They say so and they ought to know" (53). Hadley continues the reminiscence of Milan:

"Do you remember us having fruit cup at Biffi's in the Galleria with Capri and fresh peaches and wild strawberries in a tall glass pitcher with ice?"
"That time was what made me wonder about the three arches."
"I remember the Sermione. It's like this arch." (53–54)

The three arches are not in alignment, but they were designed and constructed at about the same time during the Napoleonic era. The myth that they are aligned no doubt arose from the fact that the road extending northwest from the Parco Sempione, the Corso Sempione, was the original main road connecting Milan and Paris through the Simplon Pass of Switzerland. Hadley is correct that the Arc du Carrousel and the Arco della Pace are similar in that they are close to the same size (both considerably smaller than the Arc de Triomphe) and they both have sculptures of the goddess of Peace driving a team of horses. The Arco della Pace has a team of six horses, whereas the Arc du Carrousel has a team of four horses.

112:23 **one thousand lire:** One thousand lire was worth $141.66 in 1917. In 2017 dollars, the value would be $2,710 (Williamson). These are relatively low-grade horses.

112:26 **one hundred lire:** They are betting about $14.17 on Japalac. In 2017 value, that would be $271 (Williamson). At the odds of thirty-five to one, a Japalac victory would pay them $9,485 in 2017.

112:32 **no elastic barrier at San Siro then:** Miriam Mandel has reported that the elastic starting barrier was not used at San Siro until 1920, when the racecourse completed a major renovation and upgrading of its facilities, including replacing the old wooden grandstands that Frederic mentions two paragraphs earlier (112:10) with stands constructed of reinforced concrete ("Dating the Narration" 55). The word *then* calls attention to the fact that Frederic, as he is telling the story, is aware that San Siro now is not the same as it was in 1917, the time of the action. How much time has passed is the question. This passage enables us to say with certainty that Frederic could not be telling the story earlier than 1920, the year of San Siro's renovations. The Babe Ruth reference in the next chapter provides another kind of time stamp, but that one is more debatable. See entry 118:34–35.

Hemingway had been to San Siro in 1918, before the renovations, and returned in 1922, after the renovations, so he had firsthand knowledge of the track in both its old and new configurations. Some commentators, including James Nagel, believe that Frederic's narration is more or less contemporaneous with Hemingway's writing of it (172). H. R. Stoneback is incredulous that it would have taken as long as ten years for Frederic to recover from his grief to tell us his story. He prefers a timeframe close to five or six years, which would place the telling in 1923 or 1924 ("Lovers' Sonnets Turn'd to Holy Psalms" 35). Miriam Mandel, in line with Stoneback, argues for a period of "five years (or perhaps a bit more)" between the events and the narration ("Dating the Narration" 59). Still others (Gerry Brenner and James Phelan, for example) argue unreasonably for a narration quite soon after the action. Brenner and Phelan's arguments aside, we believe that reasonable though necessarily somewhat subjective arguments can be made for anything between four and ten years, depending upon the length of time we consider necessary for Frederic to put himself together psychologically to tell a coherent tale about his experiences.

113:3–4 **"We'll have over three thousand lire":** At 1917 exchange rates, Catherine is anticipating winning about $425, which would be worth $8,130 in 2017 (Williamson).

113:18–19 **"At the last minute . . . they put a lot of money on him":** "Kempton and the boys" apparently know of the disguised horse Japalac and have bet large amounts of money on him, driving down the pari-mutuel betting odds.

113:22–23 **"I don't like this crooked racing!"** Catherine is the first to express her disapproval of the corruption in the racing, demonstrating her moral superiority at this point over Frederic, who does not seem to be as surprised or bothered by it. Miriam Mandel argues convincingly that this episode reveals Frederic's "lack of self-knowledge and the incompleteness of his growth" in contrast to Catherine's "honest, clear understanding of herself and the war" ("Headgear and Horses" 64). Hemingway also explores crooked racing in his short story "My Old Man" (*CSS* 151–60).

113:24 **"We'll get two hundred lire"**: Presumably this is Frederic's attempt to cheer up Catherine, based on Meyers's information that the odds would be no more than two to one for their 100 lire bet. Two hundred lire was worth about $27 at the 1917 exchange rate, or about $516 in 2017. Of course, this would be split four ways, among Frederic, Catherine, Ferguson, and Rodgers. But even this turns out to be an overestimate.

113:28–29 **"if it hadn't been crooked we'd never have backed him at all"**: This exemplifies what Miriam Mandel calls Catherine's "clear understanding of herself," a trait Frederic still seems to lack ("Headgear and Horses" 64). As such, this is another demonstration that Catherine is no simply drawn playmate for Frederic. She is a complex, intelligent, and mature grown-up woman, who leads Frederic toward self-realization.

113:33 **18.50 after Japalac to win:** The number means a bet on Japalac actually paid 18.50 lire on a 20 lire bet: their pooled bet of 100 lire has earned them 92.50 lire, or $12.32 at the 1917 exchange rate. Dividing it four ways, they each get $3.08, which is worth more than it might seem. In 2017 dollars it would be $58.90, perhaps enough to pay for a meal at a nice restaurant, but not the big win they had anticipated (Williamson).

113:37 **McAdams, the vice-consul:** This is the vice consul of the previous chapter, whom Ettore refers to as "Mac."

114:6 **"Do you mind if we play him too?"** Rodgers and Frederic have not learned anything from their previous attempt to capitalize on the crooked racing. They greedily decide to try again with Meyers's inside knowledge.

114:18–21 **"I don't know. Mr. Meyers' choice."..."You have touching faith"**: Here, Catherine calls Frederic out for his lax ethics and greed. He has not even bothered to remember the horse's name. Once again the payout is minimal, twelve lire for ten. Catherine's reference to faith once more helps place this scene in the context of the conflict between reason and faith and the novel's epistemic theme. In this case, what Frederic would probably defend as good "logic and reasoning," Catherine calls "faith," an unjustified belief. This exchange provides some insight into why she does not place her faith in God.

114:27–28 **"Do you like this?"..."Yes. I guess I do"**: Catherine shows her disappointment in Frederic here, and he reveals how much he still has to learn from her about ethics and integrity, as well as reason and faith.

114:38–39 **"a horse we never heard of and that Mr. Meyers won't be backing"**: Operating out of her disappointment, Catherine now takes full control and leads Frederic away from the corruption. He acquiesces and places himself in her hands.

115:2–3 **a horse named Light For Me . . . fourth in a field of five**: Miriam Mandel has pointed out that Light For Me was a real horse that won important races in Paris between 1923 and 1928 at the Auteuil and Enghien race courses ("Dating the Narration" 55). As a regular follower of the Paris races (see, for example, *A Moveable Feast* 49–65), Hemingway would naturally have been familiar with Light For Me. Mandel believes the name of the horse can help us date the narration in the novel as being no sooner than 1923, or at least five years after Catherine Barkley's death. Most importantly, the name of the horse symbolizes the light that Catherine sheds on Frederic's world, enabling him to grow into a clearer vision of himself, the world, and his place in it. That the horse finishes fourth in a field of five does nothing to diminish that light, although it may foreshadow Frederic's ultimate loss of his loved one.

115:6 **"I feel so much cleaner"**: This is Catherine the teacher, not just speaking of herself but also leading Frederic toward a stronger, more ethical stance.

115:15 **"Don't you like it better when we're alone?"** Catherine continues in her teaching mode, subtly distinguishing the superiority of where they are at this moment in contrast to what they have left behind among the corrupt betting crowd. But she is a gentle taskmaster. Once she is convinced she has made her impression on Frederic, she agrees to rejoin the others.

115:17 **"I felt very lonely when they were all there"**: Catherine's subjective remark is a reminder of the preeminence of emotion and feeling in a love relationship. In essence, she is emphasizing to Frederic that the corrupt world of fixed races is an enemy to love and that they must not allow that world to interfere with and potentially destroy their love.

115:23 **"No. . . . We'll stay here and have our drink"**: Frederic's response to Catherine's offer to rejoin the group is an indication that she has taught him something in this little lesson. In other words, he recognizes the value of what they have and how the corruption of the world can compromise it.

115:25 **"You're awfully good to me," she said**: The original manuscript adds, crossed out, "Afterwards I remembered how she did not want us to lose any of our time with other people" (JFK item 64).

CHAPTER 21

116:1 **September:** It is now September 1917. In his own life, Hemingway, having graduated from high school in June 1917, was beginning work as a cub reporter for *The Kansas City Star*. See the timeline in appendix B at *The Hemingway Blog* (Roos).

116:3–4 **The fighting ... went very badly ... could not take San Gabriele:** The Italian supreme commander, General Luigi Cadorna, called a halt to the Eleventh Battle of the Isonzo on 19 September 1917 (Thompson 282). See entries 27:30 and 103:16.

116:9–10 **riots twice in the town against the war and bad rioting in Turin:** Although Mark Thompson in *The White War* does not mention riots in Milan, he does describe rioting in Turin, "Italy's only proletarian city," over food shortages in August 1917. Soldiers put down the protest, but more than forty people died (271). Italy was divided on the war, the upper class being generally in favor but the peasant classes heavily against, as Frederic Henry's conversations with his drivers indicate. Most of the war's casualties came from the peasant classes, and Marxists were able to exploit the discontent and organize protests in the cities.

116:10 **A British major at the club:** The British major is possibly modeled on G. M. Trevelyan (1876–1962), the head of the British Red Cross in Italy, a distinguished Cambridge historian and author of *Scenes from Italy's War* (upon which Hemingway clearly relied in writing *A Farewell to Arms*; see entry 4:4–7). Trevelyan also authored a three-volume history of England (1937), and three books on Giuseppe Garibaldi, the great Italian general and nationalist (1907, 1909, 1911). Here the British major, whom Frederic chats with in the Anglo-American Club in central Milan, helps advance the plot by providing the perspective of an allied field-grade officer, whose opinions carry the authority of a more experienced observer.

116:11–13 **Italians had lost ... on the Carso besides:** The British major's numbers are similar to those Mark Thompson reported for the Eleventh Battle of the Isonzo in *The White War*, where he gives a total figure of 166,000 casualties for the Italians, a number that includes the Bainsizza plateau (east of Plava), Monte San Gabriele, and the Carso (the plateau southeast of Gorizia). According to Thompson, "[s]ome 400 of the 600 battalions involved in the battle had lost one-half to two-thirds of their strength. [Italian generals] Cadorna's and Capello's actions in the Eleventh Battle were so careless and self-destructive that historians have struggled to account for them" (282).

116:15–16 **the offensive in Flanders was going to the bad:** The major is perhaps excessively pessimistic here in referring to the fighting in the Third Battle of Ypres in Flanders (the northern, Dutch-speaking portion of Belgium). Historian Martin Gilbert reports that although the British, the French, and their allies suffered horrible losses, with a total of 244,897 casualties in the battle, they were fewer than had been suffered in the Battle of the Somme the year before, and the German losses were nearly twice as great (365).

116:17 **the Allies would be cooked:** Through the mouth of the major, Hemingway launches thirteen repetitions of the colloquial term *cooked*, meaning "to be in an inescapably bad situation," ending at 117:16 (*Oxford English Dictionary Online*).

116:18–19 **We were all cooked. The thing was not to recognize it:** Some readers see this as Hemingway's central meaning across all his works. Others object to such a pessimistic view. Frederic does not seem to fully agree with the major, although in these two pages he certainly provides him with a significant soapbox from which to express his "world pessimism" (117:19).

117:6 **The old Hun:** An informal and derogatory term applied to all Germans during the two world wars. In this case, by attaching the informal honorific "old," the major is complimenting Germans for their fighting ability. The term originated in 1900 in a Kaiser Wilhelm II speech to German troops departing for China to suppress the Boxer Rebellion: "Just as a thousand years ago, the Huns under their King Etzel made a name for themselves which shows them as mighty in tradition and myth, so shall you establish the name of Germans in China for 1000 years" (qtd. in de Wit).

117:12–13 **the Trentino:** This province in northern Italy amid the Dolomite Mountains gets its name from its capital city, Trento.

117:13 **cut the railway at Vicenza:** A city in the northeast of Italy, on the rail line about halfway between Milan and the eastern front on the Isonzo River. If the Austrians could capture Vicenza, virtually the entire Italian army would be cut off from its supply line and would have to surrender.

Ernest Hemingway at nineteen, soon after he returned to the United States in 1919, in uniform with the ribbons awarded him following his wounding. (Ernest Hemingway Collection, John F. Kennedy Presidential Library and Museum)

Below: The Isonzo River at Gradisca today, looking north toward Gorizia and the surrounding mountains, as described in chapter 1 of the novel. (Photo by Michael Kim Roos)

Monte San Gabriele today, overlooking Gorizia (*far right*). Italian artillery bombardments blew thirty meters off the top of the mountain in futile attempts to conquer the Austrian trenches and tunnels. Tens of thousands of soldiers on both sides died on its slopes, and the Italians captured it nine times, but each time the Austrians were able to retake it. See entries 5:7–8 and 27:30. (Photo by Michael Kim Roos)

A stone atop Monte Santo, carved by Italian soldiers when they captured the mountain during the Eleventh Battle of the Isonzo in August 1917. In English, the carving reads: "Hurray! Red on top of this mountain. It is the dawn." See entry 55:26–27. (Photo by Michael Kim Roos)

Below: The building, today, that housed the American Red Cross Hospital in Milan, at the intersection of Via Amorari and Via Cesare Cantù, where Hemingway was treated following his wounds and where he fell in love with Agnes von Kurowsky. A plaque commemorates Hemingway's stay there and credits it as the inspiration for *A Farewell to Arms*. (Photo by Michael Kim Roos)

Ospedale Maggiore, where Hemingway and Frederic Henry were X-rayed and received mechanotherapy for their wounds. Today the magnificent building houses parts of the University of Milan. See entry 82:11. (Photo by Michael Kim Roos)

Milan Cathedral (Duomo), the Church of Saint Mary of the Nativity, today. It is the largest cathedral in Italy. Construction began in 1386 but was not fully completed until 1965. The south entrance to the Galleria is to the left of the plaza. See entry 129:5–22. (Photo by Michael Kim Roos)

A recent photo of the interior of the Galleria Vittorio Emanuele II at night. Designed and completed in 1867 by architect Giuseppe Mengoni, it is a four-story cross-shaped arcade topped with glass and steel, sheltering retail stores and restaurants like Biffi's. See entry 66:10. (Photo by Michael Kim Roos)

Hemingway in the sidecar of a motorcycle, in the fall of 1918 in Milan. The driver is unidentified. In the background is the Arco della Pace (Arch of Peace), which stands at the northwest end of the Parco Sempione in Milan. See entry 111:21. (Ernest Hemingway Collection, John F. Kennedy Presidential Library and Museum)

Agnes von Kurowsky (*second from left*) with Hemingway and two other Red Cross nurses during an outing at San Siro racecourse in Milan in September 1918. See entry 111:20. (Ernest Hemingway Collection, John F. Kennedy Presidential Library and Museum)

Hemingway riding as tail man competing in a bobsled race on the slopes above Montreux, Switzerland, in 1923. The other riders and spectators are unidentified. See entry 255:6. (Ernest Hemingway Collection, John F. Kennedy Presidential Library and Museum)

A view of Lake Maggiore today from a third-floor suite in the Grand Hotel des Iles Borromées in Stresa. The view is looking northwestward toward the Borromean Islands, three of which are identified. See entries 124:13–14, 124:19, and 212:2. (Photo by Michael Kim Roos)

Italy, 1915

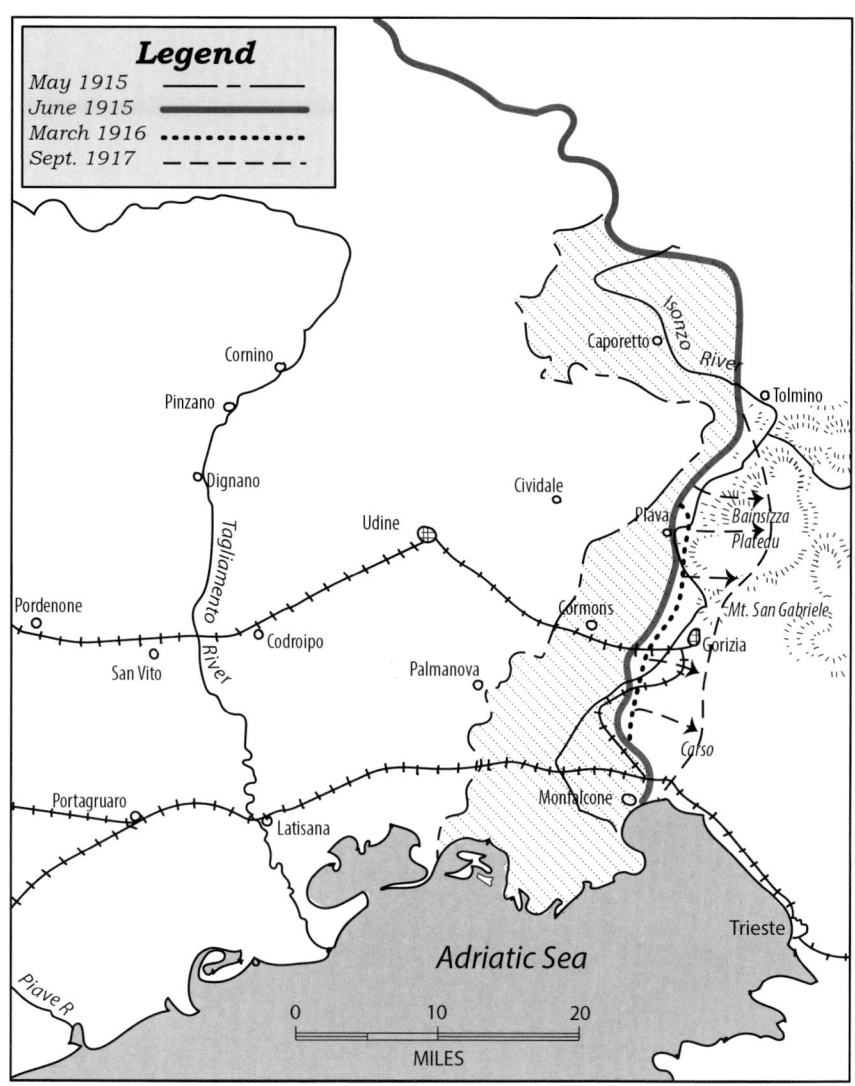

The Isonzo Front

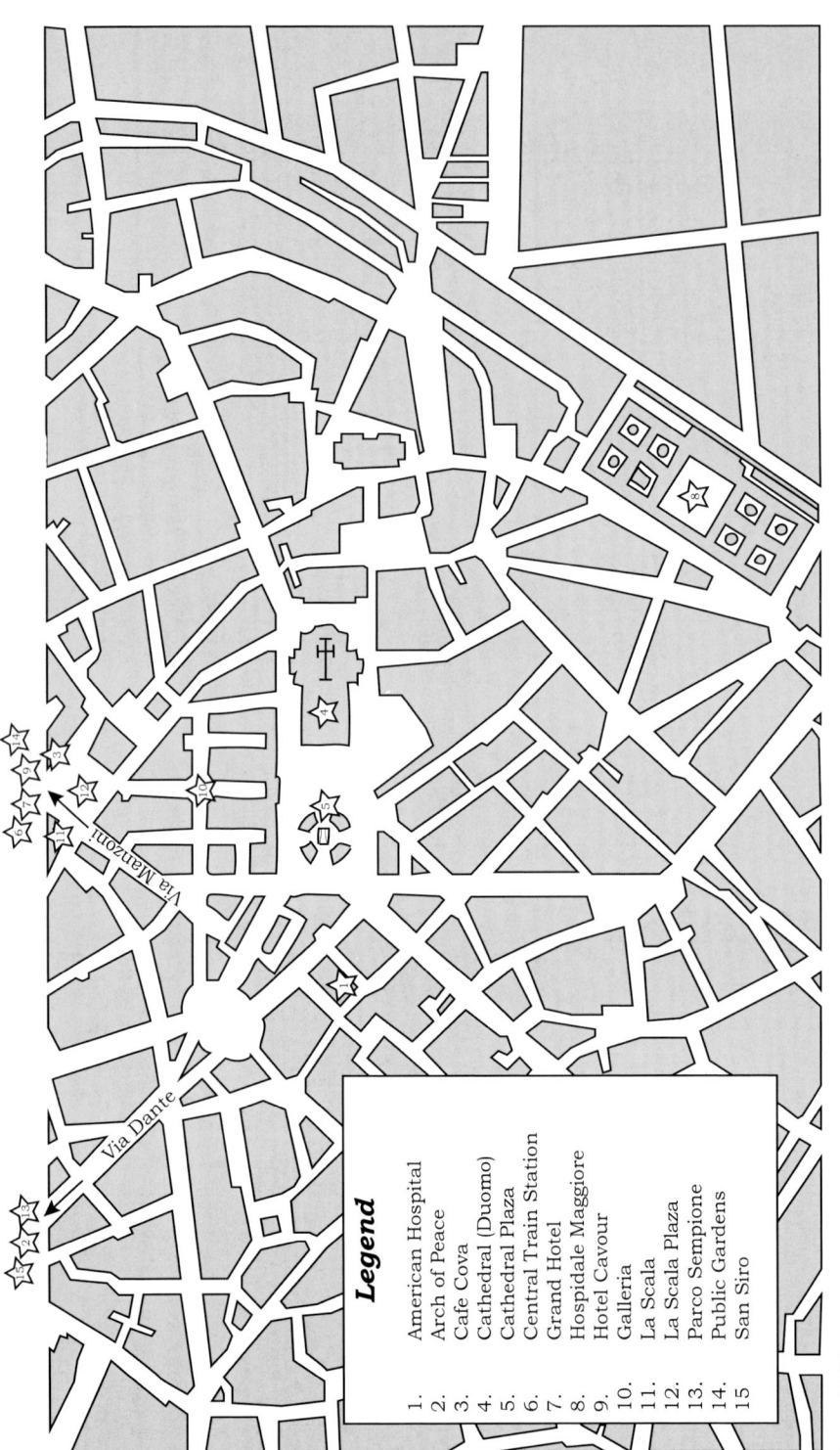

Central Milan

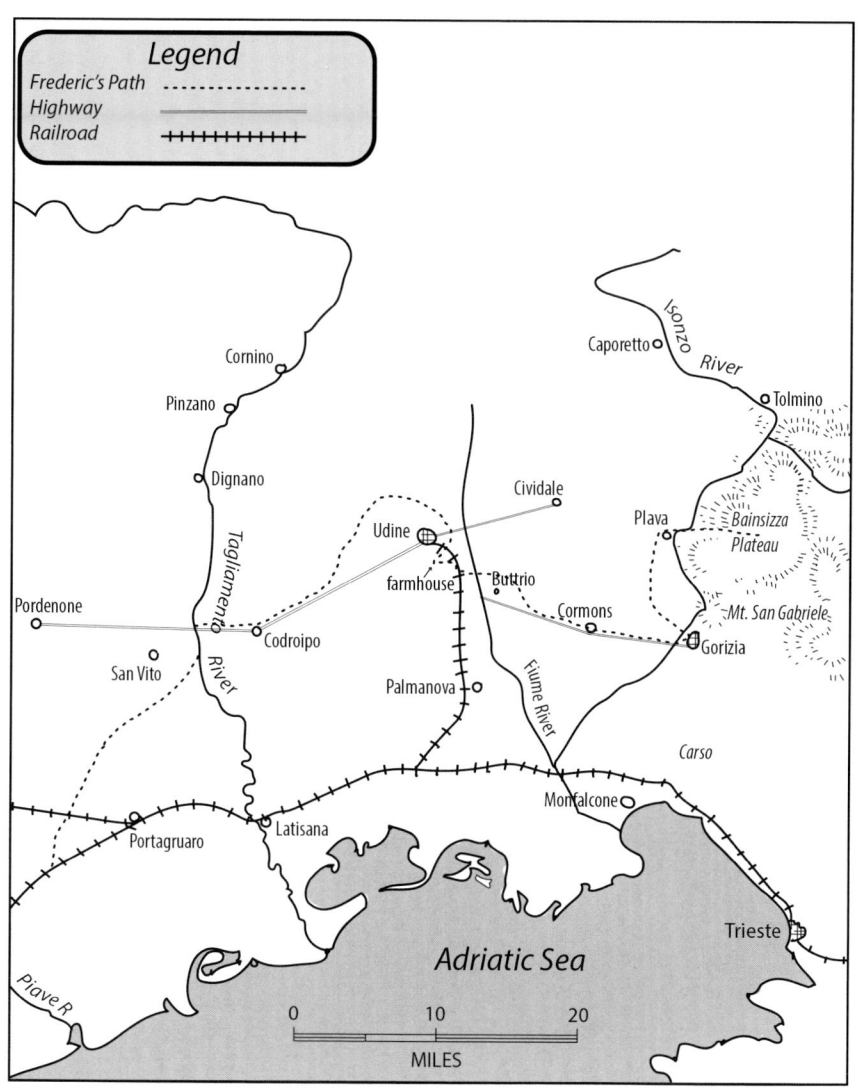

Frederic's Retreat

Lake Maggiore

117:14 **They tried that in 'sixteen, I said:** On 15 May 1916, the Austrians launched a surprise attack, known as the Strafexpedition (Punishment Expedition) on the Asiago Plateau in the Trentino that nearly broke through the Italian lines and threatened Vicenza. However, by mid-June the Italians were able to send reinforcements in time to halt the advance and prevent the capture of Vicenza (Thompson 163–66). As the major points out, the Austrians were not assisted by the Germans in that attack. He is presciently warning of a much different outcome if the Germans join forces with the Austrians against the Italians, as happened in October 1917 in the Battle of Caporetto.

117:20–21 **home to the hospital:** See Carlos Baker's groundbreaking study *Hemingway: The Writer as Artist* on the alternating pattern in the novel between "not-home" and "home" (101–09).

117:23–24 **my course at the Ospedale. Maggiore was finished:** This is an error introduced in the Hemingway Library edition of the novel. Obviously, there should not be a period and paragraph break after "Ospedale." The full sentence should read as it appeared in all previous editions: "There were still some treatments to take before my course at the Ospedale Maggiore was finished and I walked along the side street practicing not limping."

117:25 **silhouettes:** An old man cuts a profile of Frederic on solid black paper pasted on a background of white, an emblem of Frederic's vaguely questionable identity. Note that Frederic insists that the silhouette be done with his military hat on, suggesting that he is more comfortable in his military than his civilian identity.

118:7 **"For pleasure":** Frederic uses the Italian phrase *per piacere*, literally *for pleasure*, meaning *please* (Cirino, "You Don't Know" 51).

118:10 **thee:** We should understand that *thee* would be *la* in Italian and thus an archaic form of the second-person pronoun *you* in English.

118:14–16 **The convalescent leave started October fourth. . . . October twenty-fifth:** These dates help to frame the action over the next few chapters. Frederic still has a few more sessions of physical therapy at the Ospedale Maggiore, which are to end on 4 October. Then he is to begin a three-week convalescent leave, meaning he is scheduled to return to the front on 25 October. As we will see, the convalescent leave gets canceled, so the date of his return gets moved up a few days. Frederic seems to return to the front on 22 October, two days before the Germans and Austrians begin the attack that would lead to the Caporetto Retreat.

118:18 **Corriere Della Sera:** This is the evening newspaper published in Milan. In English, the name means the *Evening Messenger* (or *Courier*) and should properly be italicized. It is still widely considered the major Italian newspaper, comparable in reputation to *The New York Times* in the United States. It played a major role in building support for the Great War in Italy, particularly in publishing most of the inflammatory speeches of Gabriele D'Annunzio, a close friend of its editor, Luigi Albertini (Thompson 42–43). Frederic clearly relies on it for much of his war news.

118:19–20 **my grandfather . . . a draft for two hundred dollars:** This is one of the novel's few references to Frederic Henry's family. His grandfather seems to be the only relative with whom he has any close contact, and their relationship, at least as far as Frederic is concerned, is focused entirely on money. See entry 66:15. Two hundred dollars, equal to $3,820 in 2017, ought to have been plenty of money for Frederic to use for personal expenses for a few months, enough to carry him through the period of desertion from the army and escape to Switzerland (Williamson).

118:21 **a dull letter from the priest at our mess:** This curious reference to the priest would seem to undercut attempts to establish the priest as a superior role model for Frederic. If Frederic is telling this story years later from a state of redemption, after he has theoretically learned what the priest "always knew," would he be likely to present the priest in such pejorative terms? Even identifying his friend as "the priest at our mess" seems pejorative, certainly not a description that gives the priest any special standing.

118:22 **a man I knew who was flying with the French:** There is nothing in the rest of the novel nor in Hemingway's life that would aid us in identifying this man. It remains a curious and mysterious detail.

118:23 **a note from Rinaldi:** Not surprisingly, whenever the priest is mentioned, Rinaldi is likely to be also. Here again, we have parallel letters from these two important characters. While neither letter seems to be of great import, Frederic does provide us with some detail of Rinaldi's—his request for phonograph albums from Milan along with a jest about "skulking in Milano," suggesting at least that Frederic does not find Rinaldi's letter "dull," as he did the priest's. Rinaldi's request for music and longing for Frederic's companionship enlarge our sense of him as a passionate man in love with life and, as such, a positive role model for Frederic.

118:32–34 **The Chicago White Sox . . . and the New York Giants:** These details are accurate. The White Sox and Giants were ahead in the American League and National League standings in September 1917 and went on to play in the 1917 World Series—contested from 6 to 15 October 1917—which the White Sox won, four games to two. Hemingway probably wants us to recall that the White Sox returned to the World Series two years later, in 1919, only to go down in infamy under the "Black Sox" betting scandal, in which eight of the team's players were charged with throwing the World Series to the Cincinnati Reds. In bringing up the White Sox here, so soon in the text after the corrupt gambling at the racetrack, Hemingway is no doubt reminding us of how gambling is emblematic of general corruption in the world. Hemingway bet on the White Sox to win the 1919 World Series (*Letters 1* 244).

118:34–35 **Babe Ruth was a pitcher then playing for Boston:** This is often cited as an indication of how long after the original events Frederic Henry is narrating the story, but there has been disagreement as to how to interpret it. Some background explanation is required: Babe Ruth began his major league career with the Boston Red Sox in 1915 and starred for them as a pitcher. Boston won three World Series championships with him on the team, the last in 1918. Babe Ruth was truly outstanding, winning eighteen games in 1915, twenty-three in 1916, and twenty-four in 1917, the season to which Frederic is referring in this passage. By 1918, Ruth may have been the best left-handed pitcher in baseball. However, since he was also an outstanding hitter, he preferred to play every day as a fielder rather than to pitch every fourth day. Significantly, in preparing to enter the Great War, the United States began military draft conscription in September 1917, the exact time frame of chapter 21, and, because many baseball players were of draft age, team rosters, including that of the Red Sox, soon became depleted. Ruth, who had not yet been called to the draft, used the opportunity to make his case for being a full-time player. Even with his limited plate appearances as a pitcher, Ruth had a batting average consistently above .300 and slugged several very long home runs, during an era when home runs were quite rare. Consequently, during the 1918 season, Ruth played every day, usually as an outfielder, although he still also pitched frequently. The Red Sox won the 1918 World Series by four games to two over the Chicago Cubs, with Ruth pitching a shutout in game 1. In 1919, Ruth pitched even less, but, as an everyday player, he set a major league record, with twenty-nine home runs. He was by now a nationwide phenomenon as part of a nascent Red Sox dynasty.

However, in December 1919, the Red Sox shocked the nation by selling Ruth's contract to the New York Yankees. Red Sox owner Harry Frazee reportedly needed money from the sale to finance theatrical productions. Thus, Ruth went on to his legendary career with New York, from 1920 to 1934, setting single-season and career home-run records in the process. During Ruth's years in New York, the Yankees appeared in the World Series seven times, winning four of them—1923, 1927, 1928, and 1932. In 1928, when the Yankees won their second straight four-game World Series sweep and Hemingway was writing *A Farewell to Arms,* Ruth was at the pinnacle of his career, seemingly invincible. Frederic's feeling the need to remind us that during the time frame of the narrative Ruth was a pitcher for the Red Sox would indicate that significant time has passed since 1917. This lends credence to the views of commentators like James Nagel, who believe that Frederic is writing the story around 1928, when Hemingway was writing, more than ten years after the events in the novel. The implications of this are significant, since the suggestion is that even ten years after Catherine's death Frederic is still grieving and seems to be unmarried.

As an aside, Babe Ruth appeared as himself in the 1942 film *The Pride of the Yankees*, along with Hemingway pal Gary Cooper, who had played the role of Frederic Henry in the 1932 film adaptation of *A Farewell to Arms*. In *Pride of the Yankees*, Cooper had the lead role, as Lou Gehrig. In 1943, Cooper would play Robert Jordan in the film adaptation of Hemingway's 1940 novel *For Whom the Bell Tolls*.

118:36–37 **The American news was all training camps:** That is, the news was all about the military training of American troops preparing for entry into the Great War.

119:2–3 **I wondered . . . if they would close down the major leagues. They probably wouldn't:** This statement reflects Frederic's thinking in 1917. Naturally, writing several years later, he would know that the major leagues were never shut down during World War I.

119:4–5 **There was still racing in Milan . . . stopped racing in France:** Milan would remain largely untouched by the fighting, about 100 miles from the Trentino front and some 250 miles from the Isonzo front. However, the Paris racetracks were within range of big German artillery guns on the French front and were thus shut down by this time.

119:10 **"I'm late, darling":** Catherine's first words in this extended dialogue are a double entendre, perhaps unintended by her, but surely intended by Hemingway. Not only is she late in getting to Frederic's room, but she is also late in terms of her menstrual period, because, as she reveals in the course of this conversation, she is pregnant.

119:17 **"I don't know. But I will":** Catherine does not have objective knowledge of how she will arrange to be with Frederic during his convalescent leave. But she has intuitive, subjective knowledge that she will manage it.

119:19–20 **"nothing to lose":** An odd expression, given Catherine's physical state. Suddenly, she and Frederic have much more to lose than they have had before, now that there is an unborn child in the picture. This could be an example of verbal irony. The word *nothing* becomes a very important part of the next several lines of dialogue. It will be repeated seven times.

119:34 **"Nothing. Nothing's the matter"**: As we have noted before, readers of lines like this in Hemingway's writing cannot avoid being reminded of his short story "A Clean Well-Lighted Place," which is all about *nothing* or *nada*. See entry 28:7. Catherine's predicament may be giving her troubling thoughts on existential questions. The news she is about to drop on Frederic will certainly trigger his own troubling ruminations on existential questions.

119:37 **"You can tell me"**: Frederic speaks this line. The original manuscript adds, crossed out, "'Aren't we the same person?'" (JFK item 64).

120:10–11 **"It's almost three months along"**: The time frame means that the child was probably conceived in late June 1917, and Catherine would be expecting to give birth in late March 1918.

120:16–17 **"I did everything . . . it didn't make any difference"**: Catherine's statement suggests that she has used certain contraceptive methods, probably postcoital, that would either prevent fertilization after sex or induce a miscarriage. In the early twentieth century, Lysol and other disinfectants, astonishingly, were promoted as contraceptive douches (Knowles). Catherine may have also tried one of various natural methods to induce a miscarriage. These include high dosages of Vitamin C, brewer's yeast, bitter lemon, raw cinnamon, black or blue cohosh, pennyroyal, nutmeg, mugwort, papaya, common rue, ergot, saffron, and tansy. Michael Reynolds adds that a large dose of quinine was also thought to terminate pregnancy ("Doctors in the House of Love" 122).

For good reason, feminists complain that contraception seems to be entirely Catherine's responsibility (see Fetterley 205). In spite of the availability of condoms and in spite of Ferguson's previous warnings of the possibility of pregnancy (see entry 94:27), Frederic has apparently done nothing prophylactic, and Catherine is emphatic about not wanting to make trouble for him, another factor in feminist complaints about her character and Frederic's. But we should see in this exchange another example of Catherine's more advanced maturity, which he is not concealing from us. Hemingway wishes us to see Frederic as immature and irresponsible, measures of how much he has to learn from her.

Catherine, more fully than Frederic, recognizes that a child will complicate their lives immensely, especially under the conditions of wartime, and she is accepting the responsibility for it, although she has done what she could do to prevent the pregnancy. As a pregnant woman, she must now face the fact that she will have to leave the Red Cross soon, no later than whenever her pregnancy is discovered by others, and then she will probably have to return to the United Kingdom to have the baby. At three months pregnant in late September, she would be planning on a late March delivery date. If, as she assumes, the war will still be going on in March

1918 and that Frederic will still be in the service, she and Frederic would necessarily have to be separated by an even greater distance than that between Milan and the Isonzo front.

120:37–38 **"Where will you be?" "I don't know yet. But somewhere splendid"**: Again Catherine lacks objective knowledge of how the pregnancy and childbirth will be worked out, but subjectively she is confident that things will be fine. Her brave cheerfulness and confidence that she can manage the childbirth on her own if necessary is admirable.

121:11 **"You always feel trapped biologically"**: Expressed in the indefinite you, encompassing all of us, this line could easily serve as the theme of the novel. The biological trap, which lies at the core of human existence, indeed is the essential problem Frederic is trying to solve throughout the text. Although it is the word *always* that hurts Catherine the most, she apparently misunderstands his use of it here, taking it to mean something like "there is always a sense of entrapment when a man impregnates a woman." But Frederic is probably using the statement universally: it is the human predicament, and Catherine's becoming pregnant with Frederic's child is just another instance that reminds Frederic that we are all "always" biologically trapped. He is searching for evidence that there is an escape from that trap, but the trap has all the evidence of science in its support. Humans, like all living creatures, are impelled biologically to procreate and to die. It is the predicament of every generation, every individual. Religious faith is the only thing that offers any hope of an escape from that trap, and in spite of his words here, Frederic will not give up that hope.

Whether Hemingway remembered it as he wrote this passage, the idea for Frederic's line probably originated in spring 1921, during an exchange between Hemingway and his fiancée, Hadley Richardson. After Ernest suggested that marriage was "something of a trap," Hadley responded in a letter, "Biologically speaking, 'tis a trap—or socially rather—biologically of course just there being two sexes is the trap" (qtd. in Reynolds, *Young Hemingway* 209). As Reynolds remarks, "How like Hemingway to give Hadley's observation to the male protagonist, and how like him to remember a good line" (209).

Frederic's lack of enthusiasm reflects Hemingway's own attitude toward Hadley's pregnancy in 1923, an ambivalence (at best) also reflected by male characters in Hemingway's stories "Cat in the Rain," "Out of Season," "Cross-Country Snow" and "Hills Like White Elephants."

121:19 **"I could cut off my tongue"**: H. R. Stoneback suggests that this line is another reference to Saint Anthony of Padua, whose tongue and jawbone, it is said, are miraculously preserved in the Basilica of Saint Anthony in Padua ("Lovers' Sonnets Turn'd to Holy Psalms" 51). See entry 37:6–36. Saint Anthony of Padua died a natural death in 1231, but when his body was exhumed in 1263, everything was decomposed except for his tongue, emblematic, it is believed, of the saint's remarkable powers as a public speaker and deliverer of sermons.

However, given that Frederic's comment about being biologically trapped arose from the conflict of science and faith within him, it may more likely allude to François-Jean Lefebvre de la Barre (1745–1766), who was executed for the crime of not saluting a Roman Catholic religious procession, among other blasphemous acts. For punishment, de la Barre had his tongue cut out after he was tortured. He was then beheaded and his body burned with Voltaire's *Philosophical Dictionary* nailed to his torso. Voltaire, of course, was well known for his critical views of the Roman Catholic Church and labeled a heretic by some. Hemingway certainly would have been familiar with Lefebvre de la Barre's statue near the Basilica of the Sacré-Cœur in Montmartre, Paris.

121:29–30 "**only us two and in the world there's all the rest of them**": Catherine emphasizes this idea several times in the novel, highlighting the isolation and uniqueness of what she and Frederic share and how they must remain unified against an array of forces that can destroy them.

121:32–34 "**Nothing ever happens to the brave.**" "**They die of course**": The conspicuous use of *nothing* aside, Frederic's naivete in believing the brave are immune to suffering is quickly refuted with Catherine's matter-of-fact rejoinder. Frederic later expresses a much different view, reflecting the degree of change he undergoes in the course of his experience. See entry 216:24–30. *Nothing Ever Happens to the Brave* is the title of Carl Rollyson's 1990 biography of Hemingway's third wife, Martha Gellhorn.

121:36 "**I don't know**": Catherine expresses skepticism regarding Frederic's assertion that the brave only die once, and she is aware that Frederic is making an allusion to a famous text, though neither of them can remember the source.

121:37 "**The coward dies a thousand deaths, the brave but one**": In Shakespeare's *Julius Caesar*, Caesar declares, "Cowards die many times before their deaths; / The valiant never taste of death but once" (2.2.34–35). Frederic, however, cannot provide the objective knowledge for the source of the lines (121:39).

122:1–4 "**He was probably a coward. . . . He simply doesn't mention them**": Catherine once again demonstrates more wisdom and knowledge of cowardice and bravery than Frederic has. Statements such as this one establish her moral authority. She may be thinking of a different quote from a different Shakespeare play. In his 1942 introduction to the *Men at War* anthology, Hemingway cites another Shakespeare quotation, which parallels the one from *Julius Caesar*:

CHAPTER 21 · 167

I was very ignorant at nineteen and had read little and I remember the sudden happiness and the feeling of having a permanent protecting talisman when a young British officer [Eric Edward "Chink" Dorman-Smith] I met when in the hospital first wrote out for me, so that I could remember them, these lines:

"By my troth, I care not: a man can die but once; we owe God a death . . . and let it go which way it will, he that dies this year is quit for the next." (xii)

In any case, this quote, taken from Shakespeare's *Henry IV Part 2*, Act III, Scene ii, closely pertains to Frederic and Catherine's story, and in being the words not of a Caesar but of a common soldier, a recruit of Henry IV, wonderfully named Feeble, it reveals Hemingway's view that the nature of war may be both philosophically and simplistically perceived. White hunter Robert Wilson uses Feeble's lines in Hemingway's short story "The Short Happy Life of Francis Maccomber" (*CSS* 25). Mark Cirino has an extended discussion of this reference in *Thought in Action* (chap. 7n16).

Hemingway also alludes to Feeble's lines in *Across the River and into the Trees*, where Richard Cantwell and the Gran Maestro at the Gritti Palace Hotel remember "the men who decided that they did not wish to die; not thinking that he that dies on Thursday does not have to die on Friday" (59). See Cirino's commentary on this passage in *Reading Hemingway's* Across the River and into the Trees (63–64).

122:5 "I don't know . . . inside the head of the brave": Catherine's assertion forces Frederic to back down and admit that they are speaking of something that is very subjective—inside the head—which can never be verified.

122:12–13 "I'm like a ball-player that bats two hundred and thirty and knows he's no better": Frederic is confident in this bit of self-knowledge, subjective as it is. He knows (possesses a justified belief) that he is not brave. Sport again illustrates his self-knowledge: a baseball player with a .230 batting average is not very good, mediocre at best. It means that, not counting bases on balls, the hitter reaches base safely no more than 23 percent of the time. Good hitters should reach base at least 30 percent of the time. Note that Frederic uses an objective statistic to quantify his subjective awareness of his lack of bravery.

122:14–17 "It's awfully impressive." . . . "But still a hitter": Being British, Catherine does not know baseball and its esoteric statistics. However, she knows enough to understand correctly that the major leagues must have many "mediocre" hitters. Frederic may be correct that he will never be a Babe Ruth or a Hall of Famer, but he can still be in the game. The duel between knowing and not knowing is settled, at least for the time being, with that comic truce followed by lighthearted banter to close out a troubling chapter on a lighter note.

122:32–33 **"For three years . . . the war ending at Christmas"**: There are two important points to make about this line. First, Catherine acknowledges how her view of the war has grown much more realistic than her "childish" fantasies that it would end at Christmas. She has matured into an adult, in other words. The second point is that she associates this childish fantasy with Christmas, one of the most important religious holidays, if not the most important, of the year. For her, at least, the implication is that religious belief is a childish fantasy.

122:34–35 **"our son will be a lieutenant commander"**: Catherine imagines that the child they have conceived will be not only male but an important soldier in this seemingly never-ending war. Frederic too here anticipates a male child. These feelings will change later. See entry 252:22–23.

122:37 **"an hundred"**: a Britishism, spoken by Catherine, of course. Frederic would say, "a hundred." Catherine is referring to the Hundred Years' War. See entry 103:25.

123:7 **"your compatriots"**: Frederic's fellow Americans in the hospital.

123:8 **"read the papers"**: The newspapers, whether regarded as objective or subjective, are a poor substitute for Catherine.

CHAPTER 22

124:1 **the next day it was raining:** The motif of heavy rain, here as elsewhere in the novel, is associated with imminent doom, disaster, failure.

124:11 **the jaundice:** Jaundice is a symptom of liver disease, in this case certainly hepatitis of some kind. The word *jaundice*, from the French *jaune*, for *yellow*, is, as here, diagnosed by the yellow color of the whites of a patient's eyes. In Frederic's condition, the jaundice can be caused either by alcoholic hepatitis or hepatitis A, an infectious viral disease that would no doubt be aggravated by the quantities of alcohol he has been drinking. Alcoholic hepatitis is an inflammation of the liver caused by toxic chemicals released during the consumption of large quantities of alcohol over an extended period of time (Matthis). Given Frederic's relative youth—he is presumably still in his twenties—it seems unlikely that he could have developed alcoholic hepatitis, and even if so, it is certainly not intentionally self-induced. Hepatitis A is typically spread by consuming food or drinking water contaminated by infected feces, certainly possible during unsanitary wartime conditions (Matheny and Kingery). Symptoms for alcoholic hepatitis and hepatitis A both coincide with Frederic's description: nausea, vomiting, diarrhea, jaundice, fever, and abdominal pain. But today a diagnosis of alcoholic hepatitis would lead a doctor to forbid alcohol for the rest of the patient's life. Frederic, of course, quickly resumes drinking when he gets back to the front and thereafter, even if he says to Rinaldi that he "can't get drunk" (147:14). However, after getting inebriated with some regularity earlier in the novel, Frederic drinks only moderately from this point forward.

There is an autobiographical basis for Frederic's illness. In a letter from Italy to his family on 1 November 1918, Hemingway claims to have suffered a case of jaundice at the end of his convalescence from the wounds he had received: "It makes you feel rotten and look like an inhabitant of the flowery kingdom but is nothing to worry about" (*Letters 1* 148–49). Henry Villard, who was a jaundice patient in the Red Cross Hospital in Milan at the same time Hemingway was treated for his wounds there, suspected that his own jaundice was the result of "questionable food (for one thing, we suspected that our 'steaks' were mule meat), perhaps too much black coffee and chocolate bars, cigarettes and peanut butter, or perhaps it was unwashed fruit" (Villard and Nagel 5).

124:13 **Pallanza:** A resort town, on the north shore of Lago Maggiore, farther from Milan than Stresa, where Frederic later finds Catherine after his desertion. Pallanza is therefore less crowded than Stresa (see entry 124:16), even though both were (and remain) popular resorts. The 1928 edition of *Baedeker's Italy: From the Alps to Naples* describes Pallanza as a "town of 5100 . . . opposite the Borromean Islands, with a fine view of these and of the lake. Being sheltered and sunny, it is a favourite resort in spring and autumn" (14). The town also features "a splendid park belonging to the Marchese della Valle di Casanova" (14). See entry 233:12.

124:13–14 **Lago Maggiore:** On the south side of the Alps, spanning the border between Italy and Switzerland, this is the second largest lake in Italy (after Lake Garda) and the largest lake in southern Switzerland. It will become the avenue of escape for Frederic and Catherine.

124:16 **Stresa:** This popular resort is on the south side of Lago Maggiore, which will be featured in Book Four of the novel. Baedeker's 1928 edition of *Italy: From the Alps to Naples* describes it as "a little town of 1800, . . . cooler and airier than most other places on the lake . . . a favourite summer resort" (15).

124:19 **islands where the fishermen live:** The Borromean Islands, which include Isolino di San Giovanni (Little Island of Saint John), the closest to Pallanza; Isola Madre (Mother Island), with an uninhabited palace with pre-twentieth-century Italian art; Isola dei Pescatori (Island of the Fishermen), also known as Isola Superiore, occupied "almost entirely by a fishing village"; and Isola Bella (Beautiful Island), with the Borromeo Palace and terraced gardens, a popular tourist attraction (Baedeker 1928 14). The islands are easily accessible from both Pallanza and Stresa, on opposite sides of Lago Maggiore.

125:4–9 **They were mostly vermouth . . . Miss Van Campen found:** Hemingway here, through his surrogate Frederic Henry, provides us with insight into his wide-ranging taste for alcohol, with a catalog of the various types of wine and liquor Frederic has been drinking, surreptitiously or not, while a patient in the hospital. We can get a general sense of its large quantity from his cache of empty bottles, described as "mostly vermouth bottles, marsala bottles, capri bottles, empty chianti flasks and a few cognac bottles," in other words, multiples of all of these. For vermouth, see entry 60:9. For Marsala, see entry 104:12. For Capri, see entry 32:17. For Chianti, see entry 76:23. For cognac, see entry 55:1.

Frederic has already sent most of the empty bottles out with the porter, leaving the brandy and kümmel. (Frederic seems to be using the terms *brandy* and *cognac* interchangeably here.) Miss Van Campen discovers "eleven empty bottles of brandy and that bear liquid" (the kümmel). Since Frederic has described these as only "a few cognac bottles," it must be that there were quite a few more than twelve bottles of vermouth, Marsala, Capri, and Chianti. He also describes those as "large" bottles, implying they were all larger than the cognac bottles and the bear bottle. In other words, it is reasonable to conclude that Frederic has consumed more than thirty full bottles of alcohol, some of them extra large, during his hospital stay in Milan, which seems to have been four months (June, July, August, and September of 1917). The quantity he has drunk is an issue because Miss Van Campen will accuse him of deliberately bringing on the jaundice to avoid for as long as possible going back to the front.

125:14 **kümmel:** A "sweet liqueur flavored with caraway seeds, fennel, and cumin . . . popular in Germany and the Alps" (Greene 270). The Smirnoff company, of Russia, frequently distributed it in a bear-shaped bottle. According to Carlos Baker, Hemingway brought home from the Italian front a bear-shaped bottle of Kümmel, along with other liqueurs, and shared some with friends and his sister Marcelline (*Life Story* 58). He told her, "Don't be afraid. There's great comfort in that small bottle. . . . Taste everything, Sis. . . . Sometimes I think we only half live over here. The Italians live all the way" (Sanford 184).

125:36 **"producing jaundice with alcoholism":** Miss Van Campen's accusation here is subjective rather than objective. She has never liked Frederic, and she allows her subjective attitude toward the consumption of alcohol to influence her judgment.

126:5 **"Have you ever had jaundice, Miss Van Campen?"** Frederic attempts to counter her with an objective argument in his defense. However, he lets his emotions excessively flavor his response, and his argument fails miserably.

126:10 **"scrotum":** Hemingway's original word choice here and again at 126:18 was *balls* (JFK item 64), but his editor, Maxwell Perkins, refused to allow that word to pass, deeming it too profane for the public in 1929. For the serial publication of the novel in *Scribner's Magazine,* there is a blank in place of *balls* (Reynolds, *First War* 74). For the book, Hemingway reached a compromise with Perkins to substitute *scrotum.*

126:24–25 **"going to suggest that she had never experienced childbirth":** Frederic's original assertion, that few women have ever experienced the pain of a kick to the scrotum, is nothing but a bit of ignorant sexism, which only further damages his case by infuriating Miss Van Campen to the point of making her even more determined to punish him. But then, to Miss Gage, he amplifies his sexism by implying that Miss Van Campen is less of a woman if she has never given birth. The image of childbirth, however, powerfully resonates both in the present and the future for Frederic, who has just learned in the previous chapter that Catherine is pregnant. Even more poignantly, as the first-person narrator and presumed author of this story, Frederic is also fully aware as he writes, in remembrance of things past, that Catherine will die in childbirth at the end of his narration. Here Hemingway's Proustian point of view is devilishly effective on the level of both the present moment and the future denouement. In revealing Frederic's sexism and self-destructive tendencies, Hemingway demonstrates to us how much farther Frederic has to go to reach maturity. Gage is correct in her response: "You're a fool" (126:26).

CHAPTER 23

128:3 **It was made up at Turin:** Literally, this odd phrasing means that various parts of the train have been assembled in Turin before departing for Milan. Turin (Torino, in Italian) is a city eighty-seven miles west-southwest of Milan, about two hours by train. In Baedeker's *Italy: From the Alps to Naples* 1909, it is described as having a population of 360,000, "the seat of a university, of an archbishop, and of a military academy, and head-quarters of the 1st army corps" (43). It was the home of the House of Savoy, the ruling family of Italy, and the seat of government for the Kingdom of Sardinia from 1720 to 1860 and the Kingdom of Italy until 1865. It remains today Italy's second leading industrial city (after Milan), a major manufacturer of automobiles, with the headquarters of Fiat, Lancia, and Alfa Romeo, and during the Great War it was a major source of military arms and equipment.

None of these would seem essential reasons for Hemingway to insert Turin into the novel here. Turin does nothing to advance the plot. It is not essential for us to know that the train originated in Turin, and even if Hemingway wanted to add the superfluous minor detail that the train was assembled in Turin, why did he use the curious phrasing "It was made up at Turin," when it would have been enough to say that the train "originated in Turin"? The reason probably has everything to do with the object for which Turin is most famous—the Shroud of Turin, the alleged burial cloth of Jesus, bearing the imprint of his face and body. Brought to Turin 1578 from Chambery in the Savoy region of France, having been deeded to the Royal Family of Savoy, the shroud, as Baedeker describes, is kept in a special chapel of the Cathedral of Saint John the Baptist in a "coffin-like urn over the altar" (1909 46). No certain historical record of the shroud exists before the fourteenth century, when a French bishop issued a statement that the shroud was a fake. The Roman Catholic Church has officially been noncommittal on the piece's authenticity, neither formally endorsing it nor rejecting it. However, recent scientific radiocarbon tests have dated the cloth to the Middle Ages, thus casting serious doubt on its authenticity, but many believers refuse to accept the results of those tests. Thus, the shroud serves as an apt symbol of the conflict of science and faith, and Hemingway's odd phrasing, "It was made up at Turin," could be his subtle comment on the fakery of the shroud.

Hemingway received an invitation to spend Christmas 1918 in Turin with a Signor Bellia and his family, whom Hemingway met during his convalescent leave in Stresa. See his 29 September 1918 letter to his family, in which he describes Signor Bellia as "one of the richest men in Italy . . . with three beautiful daughters" (*Letters 1* 144–45). The invitation competed with a similar one from Nick Nerone, to spend Christmas in the Abruzzi. See entry 8:1–2. Ultimately Hemingway declined both invitations and decided to go instead to Taormina, Sicily, with James Gamble (Baker, *Life Story* 55–56).

128:8 **platform tickets:** These tickets enable persons not traveling on a train to gain admission to the platform.

128:9 **musettes:** Small leather or canvas bags carried by shoulder straps, used to contain a soldier's personal effects.

128:10 **five o'clock:** Since the train that will return Frederic to the front leaves the Milan station at midnight, he has about seven hours of freedom to enjoy with Catherine Barkley before he leaves.

128:11 **his lodge:** As caretakers, the porter and his wife would live in quarters (a lodge) at a main entrance, where they could supervise comings and goings of workers, patients, and visitors to the hospital.

128:12–13 **His wife called me "Signorino" and cried:** *Signorino* is an Italian address of courtesy for a young man or boy, clearly a term of endearment from the porter's wife, reinforced by the profusion of her tears.

128:19 **grappa:** See entry 15:15.

129:1 **a dark blue cape:** Catherine's blue cape shields her from the ominous rain, at least for now. See entry 110:1–2.

129:5–22 **the cathedral . . . fine in the mist:** A central image in this chapter and a powerful symbol of Roman Catholic faith, the Milan cathedral is certainly one to hold an architecture student's eye. Constructed over a period of six centuries, it is the largest cathedral in Italy outside of Vatican City. Dedicated to Maria Nascenti, the Virgin Mary of the Nativity, it also resonates with Catherine's pregnancy and the childbirth experience that awaits her. When Frederic asks Catherine, "Would you like to go in?" she firmly, directly, and simply replies, "No" (129:10–11). The cathedral offers no comfort to Catherine, who has no religion other than Frederic. When Frederic and

Catherine pass their possible counterparts, "a soldier... with his girl in the shadow of one of the stone buttresses" of the cathedral, Frederic sees the comparison: "They're like us," but Catherine rejects it without happiness in her voice, "Nobody is like us" (129:15–16). Frederic projects his own desire onto the couple, expressing hopefully: "I wish they had some place to go," a reminder of a similar sentiment he expressed early on with Catherine in the garden in Gorizia (26:25). But Catherine is not in a hopeful mood: "It mightn't do them *any* good," probably referring as much to herself as to the couple. "*They* have the cathedral," she says, indicating how different, in her view, the couple are from her and Frederic (129:20, emphasis added). The cathedral can protect the couple, she assumes, but not her and Frederic. As Frederic notes in his narration, he and Catherine "were past it now" (129:20), suggesting that their relationship has moved beyond any influence from the cathedral and what it represents. Yet, as they look back at it, Frederic informs us, "It was fine in the mist" (129:22). His view of the cathedral remains fundamentally different from hers, and he apparently keeps his sentiment to himself. We get the sense that he might be able to find comfort inside the cathedral in a way that she would not.

In Hemingway's "A Very Short Story," in which the wounded American recuperates in a hospital in Padua rather than Milan, the nurse (Luz) and her lover pray together in the cathedral before he goes back to the front (*CSS* 107).

129:29 Mürren: A ski resort in central Switzerland. Baedeker's *Switzerland: Together with Chamonix and the Italian Lakes* 1928 describes it as "superbly situated on a terrace high above the Lauterbrunnen Valley, . . . one of the most frequented spots in the Bernese Oberland both in summer and for winter sports, and is especially popular with English people," which probably explains why the English Catherine would bring it up (207). The reference also suggests that she, at least, has been thinking of the possibility of an escape to Switzerland for her and Frederic.

The novel presents mixed signals as to whether Catherine is an experienced skier. A comment Catherine makes later when they are in Switzerland suggests that she may be an experienced skier, so it could be that she has been to Mürren before. See entry 255:4–5. There is no indication in any of the biographies that Hemingway ever visited Mürren, although he skied often at Les Avants and Gstaad in Switzerland and Schruns in Austria.

129:35 "the way I go to the hospital": Presumably, Frederic is referring to the Ospedale Maggiore, where he has been going for physical therapy. He is apparently heading for the armorer's shop to buy a pistol.

130:4–5 Two women were behind the counter: That the proprietors of the armorer's shop are women is another reflection of the effects of the war on the lives of ordinary people. Almost certainly, in normal times, an armorer's shop would be operated by men, who have been called to service, leaving the women to operate the business in their absence. That is the downside. On the upside, business is no doubt brisk during wartime.

130:22 **"Fifty lire. It is very cheap"**: At the 1917 exchange rate of 7.509 lire for a US dollar, fifty lire would have been approximately $6.66 (Williamson). In 2017 dollars, the price would be $127. Frederic does not tell us the brand or type of gun, but since he buys two clips for it, we know it is not a revolver but a semiautomatic handgun, probably something similar to the Astra 7.65 mm he had before he was wounded. See entry 25:5. A quick survey at Gunbuyer.com indicates that semi-automatic handguns currently (February 2018) range in price from $170 to $4,750. Therefore, by these standards, Frederic seems to be getting a good deal.

Hemingway owned at least three Colt Woodsman .22 caliber semiautomatic pistols over the course of his lifetime (Calabi, Helsey, and Sanger 109–20). These are smaller bore firearms than the 7.65 mm Astra, which is approximately equivalent to a .30 caliber pistol (McAdams). However, in contrast to Frederic's disparagement of the Astra, Hemingway obviously had great affection for and confidence in the Colt Woodsman, writing in 1938:

> Now standing in one corner of a boxing ring with a .22 caliber Colt automatic pistol, shooting a bullet weighing only 40 grains and with a striking energy of only 51 foot pounds at 25 feet from the muzzle, I will guarantee to kill either Gene [Tunney] or Joe Louis before they can get to me from the opposite corner. This is the smallest caliber pistol cartridge made; but it is also one of the most accurate and easy to hit with, since the pistol has no recoil. I have killed many horses with it, cripples and for bear baits, with a single shot, and what will kill a horse will kill a man. (*Hemingway on Hunting* 189)

Hemingway had all three Colt Woodsman pistols with him on Safari in Africa in 1953–54 (Calabi, Helsey, and Sanger 120). Colt discontinued the Woodsman in 1977; vintage Woodsman pistols can cost over $2,000 today on the used gun market.

130:25 **"Have you any need for a sword?"** The woman's futile attempt to sell Frederic a sword recalls Catherine's earlier romantic "silly idea" that her fiancé would come back to her with "something picturesque like a sabre cut," but instead they "blew him all to bits." See entry 17:21–22. Frederic has enough wartime experience to have dispensed entirely with all romantic notions about what might happen to him at the front. Sabers are anachronisms there, and the woman is forced to agree.

131:9–14 **"little mirrors"..."Not especially"**: This exchange foreshadows Catherine's response to the heavily mirrored room she and Frederic take at the hotel across from the railroad station. See entry 133:12–14. The male lark's melodious calls are used to defend their breeding areas and to attract mates. That Italians use the mirrors to attract larks and then kill them is understandably disturbing to Catherine, and she wants to know if Frederic ever hunts larks in America. As an English woman, she, of course, would also be well aware that the term *bird* is commonly used in Britain for a sexually attractive woman. In other words, her question is a subtle indicator that under the present circumstances, with him about to leave for the front, Catherine is very conscious that Frederic is thinking of her as a sex object. It is not that she is unwilling to give herself to him, but she naturally wants assurance that she is more to him than an object for sexual pleasure. His response that he does "[n]ot especially" hunt larks may not entirely reassure her.

131:30–31 **She had pulled my cape around her so it covered both of us:** Frederic and Catherine stand together, wrapped in Frederic's cape for protection against the rain that Catherine fears so much. Even though this clearly stirs Frederic's desire, Catherine seems to gain confidence in his love, perhaps due to the protection of the cape.

132:1 **full of people going home:** A reminder that, even in wartime, many citizens are essentially untouched by the experience. These people and the homes to which they are returning after a normal day's work seem undisturbed, especially in comparison to Frederic and Catherine, whose union is being sundered by Frederic's forced return to the fighting at the front.

132:12–13 **"a hotel . . . where we can go":** Presumably filled with desire, Frederic takes control of the situation, knowing a hotel in Milan where they can get a room as a couple without luggage. His knowledge, we can presume, comes from experience. Milan was one of the cities where he spent his debauched leave the previous year. See entry 10:18–19. In 1917, Milan's central station was located about 1.2 miles from the cathedral, at what is today called the Piazza della Republica. A new, larger central train station was opened a half mile farther out in 1931.

132:22 **Via Manzoni:** Then as now, the Via Manzoni was an important shopping district in Milan, with fine clothing stores. It ran northeast from the Piazza alla Scala to the Archi di Porta Nuova and the Piazza Cavour. See entries 103:26–27 and 134:30.

133:6 **"woodcock":** In continuing the bird motif in this chapter, Frederic's ordering woodcock, a game bird, for dinner to be served in their room may not be the most reassuring item for Catherine, who has been thinking about herself as a "game bird" about to be scored. See entry 131:9–14.

133:12–14 **furnished in red plush . . . satin coverlet:** The room's many mirrors echo the little mirrors used to attract game birds for shooting. See entry 131:9–14. Understandably Catherine is feeling like a game bird herself, attracted for Frederic's consumption. The room's decor leads to her recognition that this hotel caters to unwed couples and men with prostitutes, who do not have luggage with them.

133:22 **She let her cape fall on the bed:** This gesture amplifies Catherine's sense of vulnerability at this moment, letting go of the protection of her cape.

133:24 **"I never felt like a whore before":** The environment designed to promote and facilitate illicit sexuality clearly disturbs Catherine, creating the subjective sensation of feeling like a "whore." Love is all about subjectivity, feelings, and Frederic must learn to be more sensitive to his loved one. Her feeling like a whore is legitimate. Obviously, Frederic has not yet learned to rise above his own selfish desires, visions he has no doubt been developing in his own mind of passionate lovemaking before he must leave for the front. As such, he finds himself in another aspect of the "biological trap," where the man's sexual desire becomes his own worst enemy. Feminist commentators rightly point to this scene as another example of Frederic's insensitivity and selfishness (see Fetterley 209). At the same time, it is important to understand that Frederic has chosen to include this unflattering detail as he tells the story years later, an implicit confession of his own insensitivity and an indicator that he has grown in the time since this scene.

133:36 **"I'm a good girl again":** Feminists complain about this, but Catherine deserves some slack here. Surely she does not want to separate from Frederic on such a sour note. This night is as important to her as it is to him. That is, she wants it to be a confirmation of their love, and she would like to have an hour or so of intimacy as much as he would. She only does not want to feel like a whore.

134:2 **and then after:** This short phrase is a typical Hemingway indicator of lovemaking. After they make love, they feel as if they have made the sleazy hotel room into their home, another haven of domestic love. See, for example, the scene with Jake Barnes and Brett Ashley in chapter 7 of *The Sun Also Rises* (54–55).

134:7–8 **a bottle of Capri and a bottle of St. Estephe:** They consume two bottles of wine. For Capri, see entry 32:17. St. Estephe is a red wine from the Bordeaux region of France. Although Frederic consumes most of the two bottles, he seems unconcerned here about any ill effects from his bout with jaundice.

134:9–11 **For dinner . . . dessert:** Some of the greatest pleasures of reading Hemingway are his gastronomic descriptions. Here as elsewhere the precise details of this room service dinner delight our senses as much as they must have delighted those of Frederic and Catherine. This gourmet meal includes a shared woodcock (typically eight to eleven ounces), probably roasted. Soufflé potatoes (*pommes souflées* in French) are thinly sliced russet potatoes, deep fried at least twice at successively hotter temperatures until they puff up like balloons. They are often served with a hollandaise sauce for dipping. *Purée de marron* is made of chestnuts, a thick sauce that would have added flavor to both the woodcock and the potatoes. A *zabaione* is a popular Italian dessert in the form of a custard or pudding, made from egg yolks, sugar, and white wine. Cognac can also be added. After this tasty meal, their regard for the hotel improves significantly.

134:22 **"something really sinful":** As Debra Moddelmog points out, Catherine's remark underscores how the novel can be seen as a "re-evaluation and re-valuation of . . . desires and behaviors that in the early 20th century, and even now, might be considered immoral and queer" (20). When they are reunited in Book Four, Catherine will continue to push Frederic toward extending the boundaries of their behavior together.

134:30 **Hotel Cavour:** This is the site imagined in chapter 7, in which Frederic indulges in an erotic fantasy about taking Catherine along the Via Manzoni in Milan to a luxurious hotel. See entry 32:6–7. They both agree that the Milan hotel across from the train station, where they are now, is not the equivalent of the Cavour, which Frederic asserts would not have taken them. The Cavour, still in its original location but modernized, is named for Camillo Benso, the Count of Cavour (1810–1861), an Italian statesman who was a leading figure of the Risorgimento (Italian unification).

135:1 **"I thought you were a crazy girl":** Frederic reveals to Catherine what we have already known: that at first he believed that she was truly off-balance mentally. Catherine readily admits to her previously unstable mental state, but she insists it was not "complicated," in other words, nothing from which she could not easily recover. And by this time, she has proven to both Frederic and herself that she has, in fact, recovered nicely.

135:6–13 **"given my father gout"** . . . **"You won't have to meet him."** This brief exchange about fathers is indicative of how little we know of Frederic's and Catherine's families and the degree to which they have cut themselves off from their relatives. Frederic reveals that he has only a stepfather, whom she will never have to meet, just as he will not have to meet her father.

In the context of Hemingway's own life, prior to the writing of *A Farewell to Arms*, his relationship with his parents had descended to a low level, resulting from his perception that they were unhappy with his published writings and then his attempts to conceal from them the disintegration of his marriage and divorce from his first wife, Hadley. In April 1928, as he was in the middle of writing his novel, their relationship serendipitously took a positive turn, as he and his second wife, Pauline, were in Key West, and his parents appeared on the dock as part of a tourist stop, from all indications, completely unaware that Ernest was staying there (see Reynolds, *American Homecoming* 171). The reunion and their first meeting with the pregnant Pauline was warm, though brief, and correspondence between them improved remarkably over the coming months. However, engulfed by health and financial worries, Clarence retreated more and more into a shell of deep depression, and just as Ernest was engrossed in revising his novel, his father committed suicide on 8 December 1928. Thus, by the time he finished *A Farewell to Arms,* Ernest could say, with Frederic, that he had no father.

135:18 **we could hear the rain:** The ominous rain reinserts itself into their consciousnesses and adds a sense of foreboding. The lovers must part.

135:19–23 **a motor car honked . . . A girl who wouldn't live with a man:** The honking car triggers Frederic's recollection of lines from "To His Coy Mistress," a carpe diem poem by the English poet Andrew Marvell (1621–1678). In all previous editions, these lines were indented (as they are in the holograph manuscript, JFK item 64) and separated from the rest of the text before and after with an extra line of space. Also in the manuscript, Hemingway had added and then crossed out two more lines from the poem: "Thy beauty shall no more be found / Nor in thy marble vault shall sound my echoing song" (item 64). The poem is a passionate expression of an essentially rationalist materialist outlook, with no hint of pleasures beyond this world, and as such it represents another indication of Frederic's inability to share the priest's love of God. Frederic's soul seems to reside in this world, a world of secular rather than spiritual love.

Catherine too knows the poem, but her reminder to him that it was about "a girl who wouldn't live with a man" reveals how painfully aware she is of the poem's relevance to her previous fiancé, with whom she refused to make love. Our understanding this helps us appreciate her motives in so freely giving herself sexually to Frederic.

Hemingway also poetically alludes to other lines of Marvell's poem in a 16 June 1931 letter to Ezra Pound, in which he asks about the well-being of T. S. Eliot, whom he calls Major Eliot:

A poop on the Major—
With his quaint pamphlets gone to bust
And into footnotes all his lust—(*Letters 4* 528)

These lines correspond to Marvell's lines

> then worms shall try
> That long-preserved virginity,
> And your quaint honour turn to dust,
> And into ashes all my lust.

Hemingway would return to these lines again in chapter 12 of *Death in the Afternoon*, in the section that became the short story "A Natural History of the Dead," applying the words maliciously to literary humanists: "But regardless of how they [humanists] started I hope to see the finish of a few, and speculate how worms will try that long preserved sterility; with their quaint pamphlets gone to bust and into foot-notes all their lust" (*DIA* 139; *CSS* 338). In *Death in the Afternoon,* he concludes by explaining to his audience, an old lady, that the lines came from Andrew Marvell and that he learned "how to do that by reading T.S. Eliot" (139).

135:24–28 **I wanted to talk facts. . . ."Don't worry, darling"**: In keeping with the materialist and objective tone of Marvell's poem, Frederic wants to be objective about the realities they face as they separate, although Catherine, who more fully understands than he does that the subjective realm must predominate in any love relationship, brushes aside his concern about the place and manner of her impending childbirth. She is comfortable in her intuitive feeling that she will be able to manage it on her own, if necessary.

135:30–136:17 **"It's nearly time to go." . . ."You go first"**: Most of their remaining dialogue in the chapter contains references to time—the present or future—and its control of their lives.

CHAPTER 24

137:2–5 paid for the dinner . . . paid the bill for the room: Just as in *The Sun Also Rises,* where Jake Barnes continually evaluates what it means to get one's money's worth in the world, Frederic Henry similarly faces constant reminders that all experiences must be paid for in one way or another.

137:6–10 remembered me as a friend . . . so many friends in a war: First, this is a reminder that Frederic has used this hotel before his relationship with Catherine, a reminder of the dissolute past he has left behind as he has entered his real love with Catherine. This is also an illustration of the war's impact on human relationships, the deterioration of trust. Frederic's cynical conclusion of this transaction is a sharp insight into his awareness of that impact. Frederic did not have to pay in advance, presumably as other such clients would because of his friendship with the manager based on prior patronage and good credit. Yet, that friendship does not grant him blind privileges. The manager's trust, in wartime at least, will only go so far.

137:15 "How do you feel, Cat?" At this turning point in their relationship, Frederic begins calling Catherine in direct address by the pet name "Cat"; he does so a total of twenty-two times in the rest of the novel. However, as the narrator he continues to refer to her primarily as Catherine. In contrast, Catherine has privately been addressing Frederic as "darling" since the beginning of their relationship, in chapter 5. In fact, she uses it a hundred times over the course of the novel. There is, naturally, considerable irony that in chapter 24, in Frederic's perception of her, Catherine has been transformed from "victim bird" at the beginning of chapter 23 into the bird's enemy, the *cat,* a creature of power. In Thomas Mann's *The Magic Mountain,* a novel Hemingway read in February 1928, just prior to his starting to write what would become *A Farewell to Arms,* the protagonist is in love with Clavdia Chauchat, whose last name in French essentially means *hot cat,* while her first name suggests *claws.* For more on Mann's influence, see the introduction to this volume.

Carl Eby has pointed out Hemingway's "easy alignment of cats with women" (121–22). Hemingway's pet names for his first wife, Hadley, included "Feather Kitty" and "Feather Cat." In a letter to Hadley in 1939, twelve years after their divorce, he addressed her as "Kath. Kat" (*SL* 496), perhaps indicative that he identified Catherine Barkley, at least to some extent, with Hadley. He also commonly called his fourth wife, Mary, "Kitten."

137:17 **"I feel hollow and hungry":** Hollowness, hunger, and loneliness denote both physical and existential states that Hemingway repeats often in this novel—as "lonely and empty" and "lonely and hollow" (41:20 and 41:23)—and elsewhere, as in, for example, his later novel *To Have and Have Not,* where he describes Harry Morgan as feeling "cold and hollow all around his stomach" (169). For an extended discussion, see Kirk Curnutt's *Reading Hemingway's* To Have and Have Not.

137:20 **the carriage:** A reminder of "Time's wingèd chariot" in Marvell's "To His Coy Mistress." See entry 135:19–23.

138:25–26 **"young Catherine."** Here, Frederic begins referring to and thinking of their unborn child as "young Catherine." Whether or not this indicates any feminist notions on the part of the author, it is noteworthy that Hemingway felt frustrated that he never had a daughter. Eventually, he took to referring affectionately to young women in his life as "daughter." See entry ix:2. For further reading on Hemingway's desire for a daughter see Kenneth Lynn (376) and Mary Welsh Hemingway (214–15).

138:28–33 **I stepped out into the rain . . . get in out of the rain:** In this paragraph and elsewhere in this chapter, Hemingway deftly uses prepositions, specifically *out* and *in,* to highlight dualities and human attempts to resolve them. The prepositions blend effortlessly with the money and carriage-as-time motifs into a poetic whole in which opposites or dualisms paint a world of contradictions marching on to absurdity and madness held at least temporarily at bay by love and courage and prepositions that orient and attempt to stabilize people within their chaotic world.

138:36 **The porter:** Before this paragraph in the original manuscript, Hemingway drew two horizontal lines to indicate that he wanted extra space here. Below them, he started a paragraph and then crossed out, "I do not think I will forget that trip back to the front. The Train" (JFK item 64).

139:32 **ten lire:** Frederic pays the porter and the machine gunner the equivalent of $1.33 each at the 1917 exchange rate, which in 2017 would be worth $25.40—a reasonably generous tip, considering the amount of time they have spent in helping him out (Williamson).

139:35 **Brescia:** A city in northern Italy about fifty miles east of Milan, with a 1917 population of approximately eighty thousand. Baedeker's *Italy: From the Alps to Na-*

ples 1928 describes it as "beautifully situated at the foot of the Alps" (39). Frederic is returning to the front by the same train route that brought him to Milan. See entry 67:6–7.

140:5 **Verona:** A city in northern Italy about a hundred miles east of Milan, or another fifty miles east of Brescia on the train route taking Frederic back to the front. At the time of the novel, its population was about eighty-seven thousand. Baedeker's *Italy: From the Alps to Naples* 1928 describes it as "the largest and most beautiful town of the Venetian 'terra ferma'" (74). It is also the setting for Shakespeare's play *Romeo and Juliet*. Hemingway once described *A Farewell to Arms* as his *Romeo and Juliet*. For further discussion of the resonance between Hemingway's novel and Shakespeare's play, see Carlos Baker, *Hemingway: The Writer as Artist* (98–101).

BOOK THREE

CHAPTER 25

The beginning of Book Three makes clear the overall pattern in the book, first discussed in detail by Carlos Baker in *Hemingway: The Writer as Artist*. Book One ends with Frederic's leaving the battlefront after being wounded, his first, temporary, farewell to military arms. Book Two ends with Frederic and Catherine's temporary farewell to each other's loving arms. In Book Three, Frederic is reunited with his military brethren until he escapes almost certain execution at the hands of their military arms and returns to Milan, where he hopes to be again in Catherine's arms. Books Four and Five extend this pattern of motion *toward* and *away* from the war and each other, movement that foreshadows the conclusion and highlights the novel's unresolved antitheses through Frederic's farewells to both the arms of war and the arms of love.

143:1–17 **Now in the fall . . . It did not feel like a homecoming:** As does Book One, the first chapter of Book Three begins with a vivid description of a seasonal change, from summer to the fall of 1917. With the muddy roads, "wet dead" leaves, and the men "tamping stone in the ruts from piles of crushed stone," a sense of despair permeates the scene. In Frederic's absence over the course of the summer, there has been much bitter fighting, alluded to later but without detail in Frederic's conversation with the major. See entries 102:2–3 and 103:16.

By the time Frederic arrives back at the front, the fighting has resolved into another stalemate. An Italian colonel, Angelo Gatti, who served as historian for the Supreme Command in the war, captured the state of mind of the Italian army, as blood flowed freely down Monte San Gabriele: "I feel something collapsing inside me; I shall not be able to endure this war, none of us will; it is too gigantic, truly limitless, it will crush us all" (qtd. in Thompson 282). One profound effect of the Eleventh Battle of the Isonzo was to convince German military leaders that the Austrians would break without German assistance. Seven high-quality German divisions were soon sent to join the three Austrian divisions already in place on the Isonzo (296).

143:2 **I rode to Gorizia from Udine on a camion:** Frederic has traveled the distance from Milan to Udine by train, where passenger services ended due to the fighting at the front about twenty-five miles away. From there, he rides by military truck (a camion) to the headquarters of Italy's Second Army in Gorizia. See entry 4:25.

143:15 **Town Major's house**: The town major is the chief executive officer in command of the garrison in Gorizia. He is not the major to whom Frederic reports on his return.

144:9 **"Did you ever get the decorations?"** These "two ribbons" are the everyday substitutes for medals (he is to receive a silver and a bronze) to be worn or displayed formally, which Frederic has not yet received. An often reproduced photograph of the young Hemingway in uniform shows two ribbons on his left chest pocket. Hemingway received a silver and a bronze medal for his actions in the war.

144:17 **Caporetto:** This village is today the town of Kobarid in Slovenia, about thirty-four miles north from Gorizia, depending on the route taken. With a population of approximately a thousand, it sits in a valley of the Julian Alps near the Italian border at the confluence of the Natisone and Isonzo rivers. Between 1915 and 1917, the town was nearly completely destroyed by the war. Today it has an award-winning museum commemorating the Battle of Caporetto. Since Hemingway had never visited Caporetto, Frederic's description of it as "a little white town with a campanile [a bell tower] in a valley . . . clean . . . [with] a fine fountain in the square" must have been taken from research. The town does not appear in Baedeker's *Italy: From the Alps to Naples* 1928, since it was not a part of Italy in 1928, nor is it today. The major informs Frederic that six of their ambulances are now located at Caporetto. G. M. Trevelyan, who commanded a British Red Cross ambulance unit stationed in Caporetto and provided Hemingway with one of his important historical sources for the novel, describes the town as "a happy valley" and "a health resort"

> where drivers who had had a particularly severe time at Plava or Gorizia could serve a turn under peace conditions. The atmsosphere of the place was idyllic, protected as it was by great Monte Nero, safe in the hands of the Alpini. . . . A shell was the rarest of events, and Caporetto roofs were intact. The statue of a local Austrian poet looked out on the square, where life, civil and military, went on as in the age of gold. There, beside our garage, was the school where some sympathetic Italian officers taught the little Slovene children and kept them happy little mortals, whom it was a joy to see at work or play. (176)

144:25–26 **the Bainsizza:** See entry 103:10. The Bainsizza plateau had been the site of some of the heaviest fighting of the Eleventh Battle of the Isonzo, from 18 August through 12 September 1917, which proved to be an indecisive bloodbath for both the Italians and the Austro-Hungarians. Although Italians captured much of the Bainsizza, the Second Army, to which Frederic is attached, now found itself split in two on separate sides of the Isonzo. Frederic learns from the major that four of their ambulances are still on the Bainsizza, while two more are in the mountains, besides the six that are at Caporetto. Two other ambulance sections are on the Carso. See entry 144:26.

144:26 the Carso: See entry 6:4. The Italian Third Army was responsible for that area of the front. Frederic's unit is part of the Italian Second Army, responsible for the area north of Gorizia. Control of at least part of the Carso enabled the Austrians to prevent the Italians from achieving their important goal of Trieste until nearly the end of the war.

145:8 "I don't believe they will attack": According to Mark Thompson, the Italian Supreme Command had been "aware for at least three weeks that an attack was imminent on the upper Isonzo" (298). But Italian commanders did not take the threat seriously, and Hemingway presents the opinion of the major in charge of the ambulance unit as indicative of the general command, which, led by Supreme Commander General Luigi Cadorna, did not expect an attack until 1918. Hemingway's description of the heavy rain is historically accurate: Cadorna, secure in believing there would not be an attack till spring, in October took a break with his wife to Venice, but the rains there and all over northeastern Italy were so heavy that he cut the trip short and returned to the front on 19 October, still calm in his outlook. As late as 23 October, he took King Victor Emmanuel III to a ridge above Caporetto to observe the lines, and the two were convinced that nothing was imminent, even though Austrian deserters had provided information of the time and place of the attack to come (298–99). Thus, the rain amplified Italian complacency that the fighting was over for the fall, and the meaning of the rain in the novel envelops not only the ominous foreboding of Catherine's fate but also the fate of the Italian army.

145:11 "an army of ten million": Frederic is certainly exaggerating, perhaps joking cynically or else trying to buck up the major's spirits. The United States had declared war on Germany on 16 April 1917 but would not declare war on Austria until 7 December 1917. Initially, however, the US Army consisted of only 108,000 men. The Marine Corps, the best American soldiers, had only 15,000 (Keegan 352). It would take time for the American military to build itself to a size that could make a significant difference in the war. The US military draft was instated on 18 May 1917, calling up 1 million recruits in the first wave, with another million to follow (353). By the end of the war, American ground forces totaled nearly 4 million men, but only half were actually deployed in Europe, far below Frederic's number (372–73). Naturally, Italy had hopes of benefitting from some of those Americans, but, as the major predicts, the vast majority of them served in France. In Hemingway's short story "A

Way You'll Never Be," Nick Adams, one of the few Americans serving on the Italian front and still suffering from severe post-traumatic stress disorder after being badly wounded, is sent prematurely to the Italian front lines in an American uniform with the idea of improving the morale of the soldiers there. But Nick is still quite unstable and suffers a breakdown in front of the soldiers and his friend, the Italian captain Paravicini, who concludes that Nick's presence in such a state of mind is likely to do far more harm to morale than good and sends him back to headquarters.

146:11 **"Is that all the articulation you have?"**: See entry 84:1.

146:25–26 **"Tell me all about everything"**: Rinaldi is probably using the common Italian phrase *dimmi tutto,* meaning *tell me everything.*

147:1 **"I don't think; I operate"**: The war is capable of turning humans into unthinking automatons, yet Rinaldi and Frederic both still have the capacity to "feel like hell" (147:3–4).

147:12 **"get the ashes dragged"**: An expression meaning *to have sex.* Rinaldi's medical prescription is a common one for military psychic disorders: alcohol and sex; getting "the ashes dragged"—or *svuotare la cenere,* in Italian—*emptying the ashes.* But Frederic has already had some of this medicine with Catherine, and alcohol is contraindicated because of his hepatitis. He agrees to a drink but without getting drunk.

147:32–33 **"I think of you trying to clean your conscience with a toothbrush"**: Rinaldi here provides a glimpse of the pre-Catherine Frederic, the man who lived like Rinaldi, in the material world of hangovers and harlotry, although Frederic apparently felt guilt that Rinaldi did not share, then or now. However, as we shall see, Rinaldi is gnawed by the fear of physical consequences of his lifestyle—venereal disease.

148:10–12 **I was glad to see Rinaldi again. . . . We understood each other very well**: In spite of Frederic's changes, he and Rinaldi still connect. We should not discount Rinaldi's importance to Frederic's character. Some readers prefer to believe that Frederic, in the course of his development, moves away from Rinaldi and toward the priest, yet Frederic never rejects either of these exemplars. Instead, he moves to some degree away from both Rinaldi and the priest toward what Catherine represents—a balance between the subjective and the objective—a religion of earthly love. This becomes evident in the immediately following dialogue.

148:22 **"is she good to you practically speaking?"**: Rinaldi, the materialist, only wants to know if Catherine is good to Frederic in bed.

148:24–25 **"Does she——?"** The dash here is also a dash in the manuscript. It is unclear whether Hemingway's intentions are that Rinaldi says something unprintable, referring to Catherine's sexual skills, or that Frederic interrupts Rinaldi before he can say anything profane. James Meriwether argues that such ambiguity is the result of using dashes to replace unprintable words of profanity and thus is another reason to restore Hemingway's original intentions in a revised edition of the text (453–54).

148:34 **"sacred subjects":** Rinaldi is becoming aware that Frederic has developed a religion of love, an idea that is alien to Rinaldi and will separate the two friends from here on. Rinaldi, as he admits, has no sacred subjects. He has no religion in any sense of the term.

149:15 **"I am the snake of reason":** Rinaldi explains that his married friends do not like him because he is the voice of reason, the "snake" that can ruin their Garden of Eden. As we have noted, romantic love depends on subjective rather than objective elements—feeling, trust, faith. Rinaldi's comment thus highlights again the conflict of reason and faith, of objectivity and subjectivity, in the novel. Rinaldi consistently speaks on the side of reason.

149:16 **"The apple was reason":** In the original manuscript, Hemingway wrote, "The apple was knowledge," then crossed it out (JFK item 64). In case we are missing the real issue here, Frederic highlights it for us. The two friends are arguing about the interpretation of Genesis, chapter 2, in which Adam and Eve are forbidden by God to eat the fruit of the tree of knowledge of good and evil (2:17). The serpent, however, tells Eve she "shall not surely die" if she eats the fruit (3:4). Eve accepts the argument, eats the fruit, then shares it with Adam, "And the eyes of both were opened" (3:7).

So, depending on our perspective, Frederic and Rinaldi are both correct. Frederic's interpretation of the biblical text is that eating of the fruit from the tree of the knowledge of good and evil grants the power of reason to Adam and Eve, opening their eyes and granting them the ability to see the true nature of things, the ability to "know" both objective and subjective truths. Such an interpretation implies that knowing the nature of good and evil means knowing and experiencing suffering in the world. In this view, God originally attempted to shield his creations from such knowledge, even though he placed in their midst the means to attain it. In Rinaldi's rationale, Adam and Eve would have remained innocent of such knowledge, would have lacked the power of reason, if not for the intervention of the serpent, the snake. In this novel, Hemingway through Frederic explores the questions of what humans can and cannot know. Thus, Frederic comes to know of the existence of good (Catherine's love) and evil (war, suffering, death) in the world, and he attempts to rationalize evil's existence.

But his attempts will yield little success. In his inability to find reason for the nature of the world, Frederic will elect to cling to the things he can know, which are generally, though not entirely, sensual experiences, and find things that he can value and cherish, things that make life worth living.

149:23–24 **"Even with remorse you will have a better time"**: Rinaldi is wise enough to concede that Frederic, in finding love, is far more likely to find real happiness in this world than he is.

149:29–30 **"one is bad for my work and the other is over in half an hour or fifteen minutes"**: Presumably the only two things that Rinaldi likes besides his work are alcohol (bad for his work) and sex (over in fifteen minutes or less). There is no love in Rinaldi's life.

149:37 **"You should be glad not to be a Latin"**: This statement is another indication of Rinaldi's growing recognition that he and Frederic are now different. Earlier in the novel, he has insisted that Frederic is "really an Italian. All fire and smoke and nothing inside" (see entry 57:20–23). Perhaps trying to cheer Rinaldi up, Frederic denies such a thing as a Latin.

150:6 **"Like Saint Paul"**: Frederic is responding to Rinaldi's phrase "for your liver's sake," with a reference to the Apostle Paul's First Letter to Timothy: "Drink no longer water, but use a little wine for thy stomach's sake and thine often infirmities" (5:23). Rinaldi corrects him, illustrating that, in spite of his atheism, Rinaldi knows his Christian teachings. His familiarity with the writings of Paul will come up again soon in conversation with the priest. In *The Sun Also Rises,* Bill Gorton may be having fun with this passage from Paul when he encourages Jake Barnes to "utilize the product of the vine" (122).

150:17 **"A tall girl for a sister," he quoted**: If Rinaldi is indeed quoting a text here, the text remains unidentified. The phrase in Italian is *una ragazza alta per una sorella*. Presumably Rinaldi means he would rather have a tall girl for a sister than for a lover.

150:20 **"Rinaldo Purissimo"**: Rinaldo the Purest. This suggests that Rinaldi's full name is Rinaldo Rinaldi, identical to the name of the friendly mechanic in Hugh Dalton's *With British Guns in Italy,* a likely source for Hemingway's use of the name (118). See entry 10:1.

150:21 **"Rinaldo Sporchissimo"**: Rinaldo the Dirtiest.

150:35–36 **"Self-destruction day by day ... Just the thing for a surgeon":** In spite of the good-natured banter, Rinaldi is now drunk on the cognac and drinking more. We can see his mood darken considerably as a result.

151:36–38 **"That Saint Paul ... for us who are still hot":** Rinaldi again shows some familiarity with Christian doctrine, although there is no evidence that Saint Paul was a "rounder and a chaser" before his conversion to Christianity. He was a devout Jew who persecuted Christians, until he was blinded on the road to Damascus and converted to Christianity. Saint Paul, or Paul the Apostle, was the first chief interpreter of Christian doctrine, whose preaching helped establish the essential Christian doctrine that Jesus Christ was the Son of God, sent in expiation and propitiation to die for the original sin of humans and open the gate of heaven to the salvation of believers in this truth.

151:39 **"Federico":** Here and again at 152:10, in the original manuscript, Hemingway wrote "Enrico," crossed it out, and replaced it with "Federico" (JFK item 64).

152:2 **"I never discuss a Saint after dark":** Frederic is presumably trying to make a joke, but his reference to the dark recalls his earlier statement to the priest that, although he does not love God, he is "afraid of Him in the night sometimes." See entry 62:23–24. Here the priest smiles, perhaps remembering the previous exchange.

152:5–6 **Cavalcanti ... Brundi ... Cesare:** It is unclear whether these are names of officers who previously participated in the baiting of the priest or allusions to important figures in Italian literature and philosophy. If the latter, Cavalcanti may be a reference to Guido Cavalcanti (circa 1255–1300), thirteenth-century Italian poet and friend of Dante Alighieri, who, unlike Dante, was reportedly an atheist. Brundi is unidentified, but Hemingway may have been thinking of Giordano Bruno (1548–1600), a Dominican friar, mathematician, and cosmological theorist, who promoted a Copernican view of the solar system, pantheism, and reincarnation, beliefs of which the Inquisition found him guilty and burned him at the stake. Cesare may be a reference to Cesare Bonesana-Beccaria (1738–1794), an Italian philosopher of the Age of Enlightenment, who lived in Milan. Another possibility is Cesare Borgia (1475–1507), an Italian nobleman and illegitimate son of Pope Alexander VI, who became a Roman Catholic cardinal but, after his father's death in 1503, was the first man in history to resign a cardinalcy. Regardless, Rinaldi is trying unsuccessfully to drag Frederic fully to his side of materialism and objectivity.

152:25–27 **"You're dry ... I know, when I stop working":** Rinaldi is drunk and clearly suffering a kind of breakdown, but this passage encapsulates his materialist position. His assertion that he *knows* there is nothing beyond the material world is subjective knowledge, of course. It cannot be proven or disproven.

152:34 **"The white meat is from officers":** Frederic's joke helps relieve some of the tension as Rinaldi laughs and admits he is "a little crazy" (152:37). See entry 26:15–19. He drinks even more, however, which does little to improve his rationality.

152:39 **The major shook his head at him:** The major is discouraging the priest, who, out of his genuinely compassionate nature, has just said that Rinaldi should take a leave of absence to recover from the obvious effects of the strain he has been under. The major's motives are unclear. He may be afraid that the priest's comment will only increase Rinaldi's evident mental instability or he may simply be unable to do without Rinaldi's services as a surgeon.

153:6–10 **"What if I have it.... We put our faith in mercury":** "It" is syphilis. Rinaldi is describing the symptoms of the sexually transmitted disease, which begin with genital ulcers. After these heal and for several weeks following, there is a generalized rash, often accompanied by fevers, aches and nocturnal bone pain. There could then be a long latent period, lasting months or years, with few symptoms. In the final phase, more abscesses and ulcers can appear, often ending with severe debility, madness, or death (Frith 51).

There was no certain cure in 1917, but mercury, which had been in use, in various forms, as a treatment for infectious diseases since the fourteenth century, was a common treatment. By 1894, there were injections of mercurial compounds used for treatment, although, as might be expected, there were terrible side effects, and many patients died of mercury poisoning rather than of the disease. In 1905, German scientists discovered that the bacterium *Spirochaeta pallida* was the cause of syphilis. Another German scientist, Paul Erhlich, began experimenting with arsenic compounds in treating syphilis in rabbits and by 1909 had found success with the compound dioxy-diamino-arsenobenzol-dihydrochloride, which in 1910 began to be manufactured under the trade name Salvarsan, popularly called the "magic bullet." Erhlich won the 1908 Nobel Prize in Medicine (Frith 53).

Rinaldi, the novel's representative man of science, seems behind the times. He insists, "We put our *faith* in mercury" (emphasis added). Science, in other words, does not have a reliable answer for syphilis at the time of the novel. Reason fails, and faith steps in, with no more effectiveness in the long run, though there may be short-term palliative effects. However, Hemingway later admitted that "arsenic" should be substituted for "mercury" in Rinaldi's line (Meriwether 450). See Michael Reynolds, "Doctors in the House of Love" (114).

153:11–12 **"Or salvarsan" ... "A mercurial product":** Salvarsan is not a mercurial product, as Rinaldi insists, but one derived from arsenic. Hemingway later admitted that Rinaldi's line should be "An arsenical product" and asked his French translator, Maurice Coindreau to correct it for the French edition (*Letters 4* 382). See entry 153:6–10. Throughout this scene, Rinaldi behaves with increasing irrationality. The point seems to be that the chaos and stress of war is breaking down human capacity for reason. Rinaldi's later description of syphilis as an "industrial accident" drives this point home. Industry and war are both products of scientific progress, yet the powers of science and reason are unable to control "accidents" such as this. The major's tolerance for Rinaldi's bad manners, interrupting him "quietly," indicates that they all know he is suffering from physical and mental exhaustion.

153:14 **"You'll never get it. Baby will get it":** Rinaldi knows the priest's vow of chastity will prevent him from ever getting syphilis. However, he predicts that Frederic will get it, since Rinaldi assumes Frederic has been engaging in promiscuous sex. Frederic later reveals to Catherine that he has had gonorrhea in the past but was cured. See entry 257:12.

153:17 **with hard sauce:** This is not in the original manuscript (JFK item 64). Hard sauce is made with sugar, butter, and some kind of liquor, typically brandy or rum.

153:26 **"Fredi":** This is only time in the novel this name is used for Frederic. Ettore Moretti calls him "Fred" three times in chapter 19. See entry 107:4.

153:33 **Peduzzi:** Hemingway also previously used this name for the gardener/fishing guide in his early short story "Out of Season," which is set in Cortina d'Ampezzo, a resort town in the Dolomite Mountains of Italy (*CSS* 135–41). In his memoir *A Moveable Feast,* Hemingway claims that in writing "Out of Season" he was using his newly discovered theory "that you could omit anything if you knew that you omitted and the omitted part would strengthen the story and make people feel something more than they understood" (75). What he left out, he says, was the "real end of it," the fact that Peduzzi hanged himself (75). This theory, which came to be known as the iceberg theory, is described in *Death in the Afternoon* (172). See entry 3:1–5.

153:36–37 **"They talk about an Austrian offensive ... it won't be here":** The chapter ends with the major's reaffirmation of Italian refusal to take seriously the threat of an Austrian attack, a blindness or irrationality that led to the ensuing chaos of the Caporetto Retreat.

CHAPTER 26

155:7 Rinaldi's bed: That Frederic chooses to lie down on Rinaldi's bed for his conversation with the priest is not an innocuous detail. In the exchange that follows, Frederic speaks primarily from the position of reason and objectivity, in opposition to the priest, whose views come out of his subjective knowledge and faith.

155:13 "I think it will be over soon": The priest's belief (his thought) that the war will be over soon is intuitive, not based, of course, on any objective knowledge. But he understands this, as his words "I don't know why, but I feel it" express. His two sentences demonstrate how thought and consciousness can have their foundation in either objectivity or subjectivity. In other words, thinking is not the opposite of feeling. Thinking can have its foundation in objective reasoning or in feeling, as in this case. As events will reveal, the priest's intuition is not correct. The Italians will soon experience their worst defeat of the war, an event that can only prolong the war considerably. Thus, the priest's belief is unjustified and does not count as knowledge. Later, in the midst of that event, Frederic will need to root his thinking in objective reasoning and suppress his feelings in order to survive the chaos of the Caporetto Retreat.

155:17 "I feel that way myself": Frederic is referring to the gentleness the priest has observed in people, an observation that gives the priest the feeling that the war will end soon. Frederic's own gentleness, however, has not come so much from his war experience as from the softening effects of his growing love for Catherine, and, perhaps for that reason, his gentleness does not seem to have produced a similar thought in himself that the war will be ending soon.

155:18–19 He was surer of himself now than when I had gone away: This is Frederic's judgment of the priest, but it does not indicate that Frederic agrees with him. He will press the priest with questions that come out of his skeptical objectivity.

156:3–8 "What will happen?" . . . "Both sides": Frederic's firm questions, with "What will happen?" repeated and amplified by the image of Frederic stroking the blanket, touching an object of the real world, clearly convey his skepticism about the priest's subjective feelings. Frederic is trying to draw a clearer sense of logic out of the priest, who at first replies weakly that he does not know what will happen, but when pressed again, expresses his belief that both sides will stop fighting.

156:11 **"I don't believe both sides will stop fighting at once":** We know this is a firmly held belief on Frederic's part, something he has reasoned out objectively, because he has expressed it before, in Book One, in conversation with his ambulance drivers just before he is wounded. See entry 43:18. Frederic may feel more gentle now that he is in love with Catherine, but his experiences in love and war have not changed his opinion that, however bad it is, war must be fought until it is won, and winning armies do not stop fighting until they have achieved the victory they seek.

156:16–17 **"The Austrians won. . . . They kept them from taking San Gabriele":** In his view of the Eleventh Battle of the Isonzo, Frederic disagrees with most historians, who saw it as an Italian victory for having captured the Bainsizza plateau. Mark Thompson, however, calls it a "technical victory that felt like defeat" (282), and John Macdonald agrees with Frederic that it was an "unequivocal victory for the Austro-Hungarians" (148). Macdonald provides three reasons in support of his view: first, the Italians failed to capitalize on opportunities for a breakthrough and total victory; second, the capture of the Bainsizza convinced the Italian leadership that they were one step from victory and this conviction clouded their thinking; and third, the high casualty rate the Italians suffered had a devastating effect on morale of the soldiers.

Frederic is surprisingly forthright and confident in this scene, and it can only be that his love with Catherine has given him a sense of superiority over the priest, who lacks Frederic's worldly experience, both in war and in love. Thus, the tables are turned: Frederic has now become the teacher and the priest the student. Frederic asks, "Who won the fighting this summer?" as a test, to see if the priest knows the correct answer. The priest believes no one won, but Frederic immediately corrects his student by pointing out that the Austrians did because they achieved their objective in preventing a breakthrough and the capture of Monte San Gabriele. The failure to capture the mountain militarily can be seen, in the context of this novel, as an emblem of the failure of the priest to convert Frederic to a full life of faith. Frederic's continued skepticism is conveyed in the rest of the conversation. See entries 27:30, 103:16, and 143:1–17.

156:24 **"I don't know":** Frederic's statement here regarding how long the war will last is realistic. He knows what he does not know. It is not an indication of doubt in his thinking.

156:25 "It is in defeat that we become Christian": In the manuscript, Hemingway was apparently hesitant about Frederic's statement here. He wrote and crossed out "Christian" twice and then added it back (JFK item 64).

156:27 "I don't mean technically Christian. I mean like Our Lord": This recalls a statement by Jake Barnes in *The Sun Also Rises* that has stirred some controversy. When Bill Gorton asks Jake in the pivotal chapter 12 if he is "really a Catholic," Jake responds, "Technically." Bill follows up, "What does that mean?" and Jake replies, sounding a bit like Frederic Henry, "I don't know" (124). Frederic is here distinguishing between those who are nominally (technically) Christian, attend services, and fulfill church requirements and those who practice Christianity by imitating the life of Christ, presumably by extending love and compassion to others. This is what Frederic means when he says that it is only in defeat that we become Christian. His attitude, in other words, is that to make war is to set true Christianity aside. Just as Frederic's "technically" recalls Jake's "technically," Jake's "I don't know" anticipates Frederic's many such usages and the epistemic theme of *A Farewell to Arms*. This dialogue between Frederic and the priest includes one "I don't know" by Frederic (156:24) plus two others by the priest (156:4, 157:15). As we have said before, these many iterations of the phrase expressly highlight limitations to human knowledge, both objectively and subjectively.

156:29–30 "How would Our Lord have been . . . in the Garden?" This question represents Frederic's most direct challenge to the priest's Christianity. When the priest asserts that Jesus would have been the same if he had been rescued from crucifixion, Frederic firmly disagrees and in the process discourages the priest, possibly shaking his faith. All the priest can fall back on are his subjective feelings: "I believe and I pray. . . . I have felt it very close" (156:33–34). Frederic's opinion, that Jesus would have been different if he had been rescued, is subjective, something purely hypothetical that we can never know. But he is basing his opinion on inductive reasoning, having observed the behavior of winners and losers, leading to his conclusion that they behave differently. Inductive reasoning is never certain, of course, but here Frederic's reasoning has more foundation in logic than does the priest's subjectivity.

157:1–4 "They were beaten to start with . . . see how wise he is": Frederic now applies his reasoning to the peasant soldiers, a logic that anticipates the soldiers' behavior during the Caporetto Retreat, during which many of them will surrender to the Austrians or throw down their weapons and desert. The priest is unable to respond, seemingly defeated by the power and confidence of Frederic's argument.

157:6–8 "Now I am depressed myself . . . without thinking": Frederic acknowledges the danger of too much thinking to the point where it affects feeling. Since there is a natural feedback loop between thinking and feeling, the implication here is that there needs to be a balance of thinking and feeling, of subjectivity and objectivity.

157:12 **"It may be worse"**: Fatigue and depression are setting in, and Frederic may be sorry that he has so clearly discouraged the priest. Here he backs away somewhat from a hardline emphasis on the necessity of victory, which can bring its own complications.

157:16 **"It has to be one or the other"**: That is, the outcome of war has to be either victory or defeat. Frederic maintains his certainty on this point. War is a zero sum game.

157:19–20 **"What do you believe in?" "In sleep"**: The priest, shaken now and unconfident, asks this question as a student might ask a teacher. Frederic's response has elicited much commentary among those arguing over the state of his soul. It challenges those who wish to see the novel as demonstrating his movement toward the faith of the priest and redemption. What must be admitted is that throughout this short chapter, Frederic shows little inclination toward a wholesale acceptance of a Christian faith, even making what many would consider the blasphemous suggestion that Christ would have been different if he had been rescued from crucifixion. Now, at the end of the conversation, he gives the priest no more reason to think that a Christian awakening is imminent.

157:23–24 **"I said that about sleeping, meaning nothing"**: The two friends part on good terms. The priest, in spite of how his thinking has become less hopeful in conversation with Frederic, still says he enjoys talking with Frederic. Frederic's response is polite; he has no wish to hurt the priest, so he explains his remark with a phrase that some critics have taken to indicate atheism: that is, that he believes in "nothing." We cannot easily dismiss the phrase, given how careful Hemingway was with his words, but in context here there is no reason to believe Frederic is using a double entendre. He likes the priest, and he does seem to be genuinely trying to ease the priest's mind, even if he is also obviously unwilling to make an expression of Christian faith.

157:34–35 **"Ciaou"**: See entry 10:11.

CHAPTER 27

158:4 **Bainsizza:** See entry 103:10.

158:10 **screened by matting:** See entry 40:1–3.

158:16 **Ravne:** This is probably a reference to Grgarska Ravne, a small village on the southern edge of the Bainsizza plateau.

158:19–20 **The Austrians . . . he did not believe it:** Gino reflects the mistaken beliefs of the Italian Supreme Command.

159:3 **dolce:** Italian for a sweet dessert, which in this case is a bread pudding, made from stale bread, milk or cream, eggs, sugar, and cinnamon, plus other optional ingredients like raisins and nuts.

159:7 **Caporetto:** See entry 144:17. In spite of its idyllic setting, Caporetto is where the main breakthrough of the Austrians and Germans will occur, which will lead to the Italian army's disastrous retreat. The battle would thereafter be known as the Battle of Caporetto, the Caporetto Retreat, or the Caporetto Disaster. As Charles Bakewell, one of Hemingway's sources for the novel, recounts, Napoleon was the first military leader to recognize the strategic importance of Caporetto, in defending Italy against an Austrian invasion. Napoleon told his commander in Italy that if the Austrians broke through at Caporetto, the next line of defense would have to be the Piave River (Bakewell 19; Thompson 296). In the fall of 1917, Napoleon's words proved true.

159:10 **San Gabriele:** See entries 27:30, 103:16, and 143:1–17.

159:11 **Lom:** This tiny village stands atop a strategic hill about twenty miles northeast of Plava. Hemingway seems to have picked up this detail, as he did others, from G. M. Trevelyan, who describes how, during the Eleventh Battle of the Isonzo in August 1917, "the Austrians could not be dislodged from their fastness round Lom protected by the steep banks of the Vogercek torrent. By this failure the strategic way was left open for the disaster of Caporetto" (142). Trevelyan seems to be referring to the small present day Slovenian village of Tolminski Lom. The Vogercek Torrent (*Vogrscek* in Slovenian) is a small tributary to the Isonzo River running in a steep gorge to the south of Tolminski Lom.

159:12 **Ternova ridge:** Another detail from G. M. Trevelyan, though correctly it is *Ternovo* (144–48). This refers to a ridge above what is today the Slovenian town of Trnovo ob Soci on the Isonzo River about four miles north of Caporetto.

159:19 **babbitting metal:** Any of several alloy metals used for bearings.

159:24 **Croats:** A mostly Roman Catholic ethnic group that was part of the large Austro-Hungarian Empire until its demise at the end of World War I. Their region, Croatia, became part of Yugoslavia on 4 December 1918 and achieved its status as an independent country on 25 June 1991. Croats make up 90 percent of the population of Croatia today but are also a significant minority in Bosnia and Herzegovina. They speak Croatian, a Slavic language.

159:25 **Magyars:** Ethnic Hungarians, then part of the Austro-Hungarian Empire. They speak Hungarian, a Uralic language related to Finnish and Estonian. The borders of present-day Hungary were not firmly established until the Treaty of Trianon was completed in 1920.

159:31 **I had expected it to be flatter, more like a plateau:** Again Hemingway undoubtedly relied upon G. M. Trevelyan's description of the Bainsizza plateau: "As in the case of the equally famous 'Asiago plateau,' only a small part of it was flat. It chiefly consists of mountains. . . . Although it is not so flat as the Carso, it has the same limestone surface and same queer *doline* or cup-shaped hollows. . . . The whole land wore a severe beauty" (150).

159:33 **"Alto piano . . . but no piano":** The Italian word for *plateau* is correctly one word, *altopiano*. Here, probably deliberately, Hemingway breaks it into two words, *alto* and *piano,* which individually mean *high* and *plain,* to emphasize Gino's mild joke and word play, meaning *It's high but not a plain.*

160:4–5 **"it was a fortress rather than a mountain":** Frederic is referring to the fact that the Austrians had spent the previous two years fortifying Monte San Gabriele with a network of mountain trenches and caverns that added greatly to the Italians' difficulty in capturing the mountain.

160:9–10 **people always over-shoot downhill:** Frederic is correct that shooting downhill at the same aim angle as the ground will cause the shot to go high. The same rule applies to uphill shooting. In both cases, the shooter needs to compensate by aiming lower than for level ground shooting (Plaster).

160:19 **Verona:** See entry 140:5.

160:21–23 **"you can work out military problems . . . somebody else's country":** Gino is pointing out how much easier it is to be logical, scientific, and objective if the army is not fighting in its home territory, where emotional attachments and subjectivity are more likely to cloud judgments. This is another instance where the clash of the objective and subjective comes to the fore. Frederic agrees with Gino.

160:26 **"The Russians did, to trap Napoleon":** Gino refers to the strategy the Russian army employed in 1812 against Napoleon's invading French army. Instead of directly engaging the French army in battle, the Russians retreated, while fighting small skirmishes, eventually even abandoning Moscow. Stretched to the limit, with dwindling supplies, Napoleon finally had to turn his army around and return to France, defeated. For extended fictional treatment of Napoleon's defeat in Russia, see Count Leo Tolstoy's classic novel of the war and events surrounding it, *War and Peace,* one of Hemingway's significant influences in writing *A Farewell to Arms.*

160:28–32 **Brindisi . . . Taranto:** These are both port cities in the extreme south of Italy, in the heel of the boot, Brindisi on the Adriatic Sea and Taranto on the opposite side, fifty miles west on the coast of the Ionian Sea. Frederic's point is that there is not enough room in Italy to trap Napoleon the way the Russians did, with the vast expanse of Russia at their disposal. Although Frederic implies that he has passed through Brindisi, there is no evidence that Hemingway ever visited either of these cities.

160:35–36 **"we found fields of potatoes the Austrians had planted":** This is another minor detail Hemingway obtained from G. M. Trevelyan's *Scenes from Italy's War.* In describing the Bainsizza plateau, Trevelyan says, "Here and there were patches of wood and scrapings of peasant cultivation, and in some districts the Austrian army had planted potatoes over a wide acreage" (150).

161:3 **"The dogfish are selling it somewhere else":** Hemingway is literally translating the Italian speech of Gino and Frederic. The Italian word translated as *dogfish* is *pescecani,* which is literally *fish dog* but is the Italian word for *shark.* However, the Italian word is also used figuratively to mean *war profiteer* or *black marketer.* Even if readers do not know the Italian source, *dogfish* nevertheless "serves to suggest not only Frederic's fluency but his awareness of the metaphoric basis of language and of the difference between what seems to be and what actually is" (Lewis, *War of the Words* 147). For Hemingway's attitude on war profiteering, see his introduction to the 1948 edition of *A Farewell to Arms,* included in the Hemingway Library edition, where he declares, "I believe that all the people who stand to profit by war and who help provoke it should be shot on the first day it starts by accredited representatives of the loyal citizens of their country who will fight it" (ix:34–37). In Hemingway's later Italian novel, *Across the River and into the Trees,* the protagonist, Colonel Richard Cantwell and his friend the headwaiter at the Gritti Palace Hotel in Venice are part of a secret order with only five members, the Order of the Brusadelli, bound together with "true, good hatred of all those who profited by war" (59). For more on *pescecani,* see Cirino, *Reading Hemingway's* Across the River and into the Trees (43).

161:10 "It can't win a war but it can lose one": Frederic is offering his own twist on the common aphorism that "an army marches on its stomach," which has been inconclusively attributed to Frederick the Great of Prussia (1712–1786) and Napoleon Bonaparte (1769–1821), though most often credited to Napoleon ("An Army Marches"; *Familiar Quotations* 421).

161:13–27 I was always embarrassed . . . regiments and the dates: This is one of Hemingway's most famous passages. The critique of abstract rhetoric that exhorts young men to die heroically and honorably for their country recalls the speeches of the young Hemingway's hero Gabriele D'Annunzio, who is, in fact, the likely specific speaker to whom Frederic Henry refers in this passage.

We have already discussed Henry James as a potential source for this passage. See entry Epigraphs (Unused). But D'Annunzio is even more likely and compelling. One clue is a passage from Hemingway's later novel *Across the River and into the Trees,* where the protagonist, Richard Cantwell, recalls being forced to listen to one of D'Annunzio's speeches in the rain, with the orator shouting, "Morire non è basta," an inexact translation of "to die is not enough" (50). Cantwell later applies a series of epithets to D'Annunzio: "writer, poet, national hero, phraser of the dialectic of Fascism, macabre egotist, aviator, commander, or rider, in the first of the fast torpedo attack boats, Lieutenant Colonel of Infantry without knowing how to command a company, nor a platoon properly, the great, lovely writer of *Notturno* whom we respect, and jerk" (51–52). Cantwell's thoughts reveal Hemingway's complicated feelings about D'Annunzio as he wrote *Across the River and into the Trees* in 1948, but these feelings were probably already formed by 1928 as he wrote *A Farewell to Arms.*

Either while he was in Italy in 1918 or soon thereafter, the young Hemingway read D'Annunzio's lush and self-aggrandizing novel *The Flame.* See entry 4:11–18. We might guess that, with this level of enthusiasm, Hemingway must have heard D'Annunzio speak in public, but Mark Cirino doubts it, since Hemingway never mentioned in any surviving letters from 1918 that he had heard the great orator speak in person (*Reading* 55). According to biographer Lucy Hughes-Hallet, D'Annunzio "was called upon to speak to the troops lined up along the Piave [where Hemingway served and was wounded] again and again" in 1918 (374).

If Hemingway did not hear D'Annunzio in person, he surely read of his speeches in the newspaper accounts at the time or had contact with people who had heard the great orator speak. From the outset of Italy's involvement in the war, D'Annunzio spent significant time at the front lines, and the commanders called on him to inspire their troops. General Armando Diaz, for example, believed, "If d'Annunzio could speak to the soldiers before every battle, . . . that battle would be three-quarters won" (qtd. in Hughes-Hallet 363). To further build enthusiasm among the Italian public, D'Annunzio's speeches were commonly published verbatim in Italian newspapers. As Hughes-Hallet describes them, these speeches "were incantatory, designed to work, not on their hearers' intellect, but on their emotions. . . . Words toll through them like leitmotifs—words like blood, dead, glory, love, pain, sacred, victory, Italy, fire" (328). Another D'Annunzio biographer, Alfredo Bonadeo, quotes from a famous D'Annunzio exhortation to war that patterned itself on the Sermon on the Mount:

> O blessed be those who have more, for they will be able to give more, to be more ardent . . . Blessed be those who, waiting and trusting, have not wasted their strength, but preserved it by means of a warrior's discipline. . . . Blessed be the youths who hunger and thirst for glory, for they will be sated. . . . Blessed be the pure of the heart, blessed be those who will return victorious, for they will see Rome's new visage, Dante's forehead crowned anew, Italy's triumphant beauty. (73)

It is easy to imagine how a young, adventurous, and highly romantic Hemingway would have fallen under the spell of D'Annunzio's incantations. But in the writing of the novel in 1928, Hemingway was no longer that young man, and his protagonist is certainly not that young man. Frederic fully recognizes the stark brutality, the obscenity of manipulating the emotions of young men to turn them into sacrificial lambs for the cause of national glory. In consequence, George Peele's "evergreen" abstraction of "duty" (in the poem that provided *A Farewell to Arms* with its title) is or soon will be tossed onto the ash heap of history. See entry The Title.

Hemingway's passage profoundly and eloquently speaks in favor of objectivity as opposed to subjectivity, of reason as opposed to the kind of faith that D'Annunzio tried to stir in his audiences. Frederic recognizes the wickedness in using empty abstractions to motivate young men to die in battle. Here, just as in Wilfred Owen's classic war poem, "Dulce Et Decorum Est," Hemingway, through Frederic, insists there is no beauty or dignity or honor or glory in dying in modern warfare, no more than in taking the meat from the Chicago stockyards and burying it.

Hemingway may have also been inspired by Turgenev's nihilist, Yevgeny Bazarov, who declares, "Aristocracy, Liberalism, progress, principles . . . if you think of it, what a lot of foreign . . . and useless words! To a Russian they're good for nothing. . . . What's the object of these abstractions to us?" (*Fathers and Sons* 58). However, Frederic's tone is not entirely bleak. The abstractions are contrasted with the concreteness of villages, roads, rivers, and regiments. There remain acts and objects and moments to hold onto and treasure. Such an attitude is the essence of Hemingway.

Other modernist takes on this opposition of the concrete and the abstract in language can be found in the 1926 E. E. Cummings poem "next to of course god america i" and "The Body of an American," by John Dos Passos, the last chapter in his novel *1919*, published in 1932.

161:26 **were obscene:** In the original manuscript, Hemingway wrote "a little obscene" and crossed it out (JFK item 64).

163:1–2 **that night but we heard that they had broken through to the north:** The breakthrough in the north at Caporetto occurred during the afternoon of Wednesday, 24 October 1917, so "that night" must refer to the night of 24 October and early morning hours of 25 October (Thompson 305; Cavallaro 32; Edmonds 52).

163:8 **the twenty-seventh army corps:** The Twenty-seventh Corps of the Italian army, under the command of Lieutenant General Pietro Badoglio, was charged with holding the area around Caporetto to the north along the Isonzo River (Gooch 234–40). The combined Austrian and German forces, using a mixture of phosgene and chlorine gas against the ineffective Italian masks and then employing Hutier tactics (a precursor of blitzkrieg warfare) with infiltration by small infantry units led by Lieutenant Erwin Rommel—a tactic General Oskar von Hutier perfected on the Russian front at the siege of Riga—overwhelmed the unprepared Italians (Macdonald 162–70). Rommel would become famous as a German field marshal in World War II, known as the "Desert Fox" for his successful tactics in the North African desert.

163:11 **"we are cooked":** The captain's phrase, which would have been expressed in Italian as *siamo cotti*, recalls the language of the British major with whom Frederic Henry chats in chapter 21 at the Anglo-American Club in Milan. There the major concludes, in English, of course, that "we are all cooked. The thing was not to recognize it." See entries 116:17 and 116:18–19. Later in the manuscript, Hemingway apparently toyed with the idea of using *cooked* instead of *fucked* in certain instances. See entries 165:12 and 178:24.

163:13 **The word Germans was something to be frightened of:** Until this point in the war, the Germans had not sent large numbers of troops to the Italian front, and so long as the Germans did not interfere, the Italians generally held the upper hand against the Austrians, if only slightly. However, the collapse of the Russian army and its withdrawal from the war in the midst of the Bolshevik Revolution freed German troops, at least for the time being, to help the Austrians against the Italians. The Italian near breakthrough on the Bainsizza in the Eleventh Battle of the Isonzo, which ended in September 1917, was another factor that convinced German chief of general command, Field Marshal Paul von Hindenburg, to move six to eight divisions to the Italian front (Thompson 295). The German army had already demonstrated its superior military capabilities in the war. See entry 117:14.

163:19 **Monte Maggiore:** A fifty-three-hundred-foot mountain ten miles west of Caporetto. The plan described was indeed that of Supreme Commander General Luigi Cadorna, but Monte Maggiore fell too quickly to implement it (Falls 40–43).

163:22 **"The word ... to retreat came from the Division":** Contradictory messages here underscore the reality that poor communication was a significant contributing factor in the Caporetto disaster. In actuality, there had been orders for some units to pull back but not yet an order of general retreat.

163:35 **The next night the retreat started:** The next night is the night of Thursday, 25 October. Hemingway's history is again accurate. The definitive message from the Supreme Command ordering the Italian Second Army to retreat was sent out at 3:00 P.M. on 25 October 1917 (Thompson 309).

163:37 **Cividale:** This town in northeast Italy is about ten miles southwest of Caporetto and ten miles east of Udine. The Germans captured the town on 27 October (Rommel 228).

163:37 **Udine:** See entry 4:25. On 27 October the King and the general's Supreme Command moved from Udine about seventy miles west to Treviso (Thompson 318), indicating they did not expect the retreat to hold at the Tagliamento River, an anticipation that turned out to be correct.

163:37–38 **The retreat was orderly, wet and sullen:** In the original manuscript, Hemingway added the sentence: "No one yet had any idea that they were out of the Army" (JFK item 64).

164:3 **That night:** This is still the night of Thursday, 25 October.

164:5 the next day: This is Friday, 26 October. Frederic and his crew haul "all day in the rain to evacuate the hospitals and clearing station at Plava" (164:5–6). For Plava, see entries 20:6 and 20:6–20.

164:9–10 We came into Gorizia in the middle of the next day: Since Frederic has told us they spent all of the previous day (26 October) evacuating the hospitals at Plava, he and his crew must arrive in Gorizia around noon on 27 October. Michael Reynolds incorrectly identifies this as 26 October (*First War* 120). He seems to miscount the two days Frederic and his men have spent helping to evacuate wounded men and emptying the hospitals. Hemingway's timeline is accurate according to Thompson, Trevelyan, Cavallaro and other historical sources.

164:12 the girls from the soldiers' whorehouse: It would seem that the last to be evacuated, aside from the ambulance drivers, are the prostitutes who serve the common soldiers.

164:17–18 The girls from the officers' house: The prostitutes from the Villa Rossa, who served the officers, have received higher priority than the prostitutes for the enlisted men. Frederic apparently wanted to confirm this with the matron. See entry 27:31.

164:19 Conegliano: This town is about fifty miles west of Udine and about thirty miles beyond the Tagliamento River, which at this point is where the Italians hope to stop the Austrian-German advance. G. M. Trevelyan mentions that the plan was for a hospital to be set up in Conegliano following the retreat (179–80). Trevelyan and his British ambulance crew evacuated their posts on the night of 27 October 1917, with much the same timing as Frederic and his group. Neither the hospital nor the bawdy houses would be established in Conegliano, because the retreat would have to continue further to the Piave River.

164:33 "Mother Superior": The term is used here ironically for the madam of the bawdy house, since it usually applies to the nun in charge of a convent.

164:38–39 "The government gyps us": *Gyp* is a slur for gypsies, the Romani people, and Bonello uses it here as slang for *cheat*. This is a reminder that the Italian government provided the prostitutes for the soldiers.

165:8 Pordenone: This town is about twenty-five miles west of Udine and about ten miles beyond the Tagliamento River—a reasonable place for the ambulances to rendezvous, assuming the retreat stops at the Tagliamento. In Hemingway's "A Very Short Story," the nurse, Luz, is sent to establish a hospital in Pordenone after the conclusion of the war. There she falls in love with an Italian major and ends her relationship with the American protagonist of the story, to his bitter disappointment.

165:12 **"I'm so—sleepy"**: In the manuscript, oddly, Hemingway wrote and scratched out the word *cooking* and replaced it with the long dash before "sleepy" (JFK item 64). The intended word is apparently *fucking*, but Hemingway seems to have considered using *cook* and its derivatives in places where the word *fuck* was realistically intended. Eventually he decided to use dashes for *fuck*, a word that he wrote only twice and then scratched out in the manuscript, apparently because he knew that it had no chance to be printed. See entries 179:36 and 179:39. For more on censorship in the novel, see entry 29:2. The drivers are naturally sleepy because they have been working around the clock evacuating the wounded.

165:35 **"where the old man corks off"**: *To cork off* is slang for *to sleep*. Mark Cirino has pointed out that in this section of the novel Hemingway's use of dialogue in Italian translated to English is inconsistent with what has elsewhere generally been a very disciplined control of language to convey a realistic sense of translated Italian ("You Don't Know" 52–53). Here, Bonello, while speaking Italian, uses a very American sounding phrase "corks off," which has no Italian equivalent. Other examples of Americanisms are Frederic's use of "monkey suit" for a mechanic's overalls (165:22) and Piani calling the major "fish-face" (165:39).

166:15 **Bartolomeo:** Aymo's first name. Mark Cirino has reported that Frederic's driver was named for a well-known world-class Italian competitive cyclist, Bartolomeo Aymo (1889–1970). In the mid-1920s, Aymo was among the elite cyclists in Europe, finishing fourth in the Tour de France in 1924 and third in 1925 and 1926. Thus, he was noted for coming close but not winning the big races and was admired for his toughness and tenacity as well as his willingness to sacrifice himself for the sake of other riders on his team. Bicycle racing appears prominently in *The Sun Also Rises* (235–37) and *A Moveable Feast* (59–65).

Here, Frederic's Aymo demonstrates his selflessness by cooking pasta for Frederic and the other drivers. A. E. Hotchner claimed that Hemingway made a connection between bike racing and *A Farewell to Arms* after a suffering a serious injury from pulling a skylight down on his head: "The next day I went to the bike races," Hemingway told him, "and feeling wonderful from all that loss of blood, I finally began to write *A Farewell to Arms*" (50). For a more detailed discussion of the real Bartolomeo Aymo and Hemingway's love of cycling, see Cirino, "A Bicycle Is a Splendid Thing."

166:19 **"monkey meat"**: Military slang for meat in a can.

166:37 **Rinaldi's bed:** Frederic sleeps in Rinaldi's bed because there had been only a cot set up for him since his return to the front. See entry 155:7. However, the image emphasizes the importance of Rinaldi's traits of reason and objectivity, which will be all the more valuable now for survival in the midst of a retreat.

167:5–6 **"On a retreat we drink barbera":** See entry 97:14. Bonello is suggesting that ordinarily the wine the drivers get is of a quality inferior to that of Barbera.

167:9–10 **"To-morrow we'll be in Udine . . . where the slackers live":** Bonello is perhaps anticipating getting access to the king's or Supreme Commander Cadorna's wine stocks where they have been headquartered in Udine. The "slackers" are those who direct the war but do not fight in it. See entry 163:37.

167:17 **"We may drink——before Udine":** In the manuscript, the missing word is *shit* (JFK item 64).

167:23 **"the king's bed":** See notes 4:19, 4:25, and 163:37.

167:25 **"To-morrow maybe we'll sleep in——":** In the manuscript, the missing word is *shit* (JFK item 64).

167:26 **"I'll sleep with the queen":** Bonello is joking, of course, perhaps out of ignorance that the Queen of Italy, Queen Elena (1871–1952), the wife of King Victor Emmanuel III, worked as a nurse during the war, setting up hospitals and tending to the wounded. Therefore, it would have been highly unlikely to find her with the king in Udine. And even if she were with him, they would already be evacuated well before Frederic and his crew would arrive. The comment, however, reflects Bonello's anarchism and disrespect for the aristocracy in general.

167:28 **"You'll sleep with——"** In the manuscript, the missing word is *shit* (JFK item 64).

167:29 **"That's treason":** Bonello continues to joke, accusing Piani of committing treason by equating the queen with shit.

167:32 **"It's time to roll":** Another jarring Americanism, this is a line Frederic would necessarily have to speak in Italian to his drivers but for which there is no Italian literal equivalent (Cirino, "You Don't Know" 53).

167:35 **Cormons:** This small town is about nine miles west of Gorizia on the way to Udine. Their intended route is to take them through Cormons, Udine, and Codroipo across the Tagliamento to Pordenone, a distance of only fifty-seven miles, which under normal conditions should take no more than two hours. However, Frederic and his three drivers encounter anything but normal conditions.

168:8 **"Aldo"**: This is Bonello's first name; no historical source for Aldo Bonello's name has been identified.

168:17 **"It's not much of a place"**: Lying in a watery lowland plain, Pordenone is not a resort town as Gorizia is and lacks its picturesqueness. Although today it has a population of approximately fifty thousand and is the administrative center of the province of Pordenone, it gets no mention in Baedeker's *Italy: From the Alps to Naples* 1928.

CHAPTER 28

169:1–2 As we moved out through the town . . . the rain and the dark: Frederic and his mini-convoy of three ambulances are leaving the town of Gorizia as part of the general retreat in the late night of Saturday, 27 October 1917. Simultaneously, units of the Italian army, along with civilians, were also retreating from the north and the south of Gorizia. The northern sector was the most chaotic. Hugh Dalton, in *With British Guns in Italy,* describes in detail the retreat of the Italian Third Army in the south, which was more orderly than that from the north, although it too suffered from a logjam of traffic trying to cross the bridge over the Tagliamento at Latisana (103–29). Hemingway relied heavily on Dalton's and G. M. Trevelyan's separate accounts of the retreat.

169:11–19 I got out . . . as far as Udine: Hugh Dalton describes taking similar action, although he walked ahead as the retreat column was nearing Latisana on 30 October (124–25). For both Dalton and Frederic, the walk ahead makes no difference in their movement. It merely provides a sense of how long the column of stuck traffic is. Trevelyan, whose unit joined the column just west of Cormons, describes the traffic as stretching "all the way on to Udine, and beyond, through Codroipo to the Tagliamento" (181).

170:26–27 a dialect I could not understand: The two teenage sisters, whom Aymo has picked up, probably speak Friulian, the Romance language spoken in Friuli, the extreme northeastern region of Italy, in which this portion of the novel takes place. The language dates back a thousand years, its roots in Latin. Today approximately six hundred thousand people speak Friulian.

170:29 "Sorella?" Frederic uses the Italian word for *sister,* which the girl obviously understands. The Friulian word is *sûr.*

170:37 like two wild birds: Frederic's use of this metaphor reminds us of Catherine's feeling like a game bird about to be shot when she and Frederic take the cheap mirrored hotel room near the train station. See entry 133:12–14. The sisters here are terrified of what the men might do to them. Aymo's awkward attempts to reassure them that he and Frederic are good men only seem to make matters worse.

171:1–5 "No danger of ——." . . . "No place for ——": In the holograph manuscript, in place of each of the four dashes among these five lines, Hemingway oddly wrote and scratched out the word *cooking* and drew a long dash above each (JFK item 64). See entry 165:12. In the typescript, there are simply dashes, but in the copy of the novel he gave to James Joyce, housed in the University of Buffalo Library, Buffalo, New York, Hemingway wrote the word *fucking* above each dash, although it is hard to imagine that Joyce, of all people, would have missed the intended meaning of the dashes. JFK reference librarian Stacy Chandler and Hemingway scholar John Beall contributed to this note.

171:18 An idea came to him: This is a brief, minor departure from a strict first-person point of view, since Frederic, as narrator, has no way of reading Aymo's mind.

171:18 "Virgin?" Since Aymo no doubt uses the Italian word *vergine* and the Friulian word is *virgin,* the girl has no difficulty understanding him.

171:28–29 More likely they were from horses or men going to sleep: This is another detail likely drawn from G. M. Trevelyan's *Scenes from Italy's War,* in which Trevelyan, describing the retreat on the same road from Cormons to Udine on which Frederic's group is traveling, says, "We found there was a tacit understanding on the retreat that no one moved at all for half the night, because all the horses and most of the drivers went to sleep" (181).

171:32–172:4 A retreat was no place. . . . Blow her again to me: In the original manuscript, Hemingway marked this passage for deletion but then decided to keep it (JFK item 64).

171:33 Real virgins. Probably very religious: Frederic's tired and sleepy mind drifts into reverie that ultimately leads his thoughts back to Catherine, but it is noteworthy that religious faith is not far from his mind. He knows, however, that survival under the current circumstances is going to require a high degree of rationality.

171:34–35 In bed I lay me down my head: Frederic's sleepy stream of consciousness continues with an allusion to the familiar children's bedtime prayer:

> Now I lay me down to sleep.
> I pray the Lord my soul to keep.

If I should die before I wake,
I pray to God my soul to take. Amen.

The questions of faith and God's protection are never far away in the novel. Hemingway also alludes to the prayer in his wartime short story "Now I Lay Me," in which Nick Adams suffers from a fear that his soul will leave his body if he falls asleep. Thus, he resorts to a variety of strategies to keep himself awake, one of which is prayer (*CSS* 277).

171:38–172:5 Blow, blow, ye western wind . . . the small rain would not quiet it: Frederic recalls a classic poem-song from English folk literature, often entitled "Western Wind," with some variations, but essentially what Frederic paraphrases over these seven lines. The original lines appear thus in the *Oxford Book of English Verse*, which we know Hemingway resorted to in his search for titles to the novel:

The Lover in Winter Plaineth for the Spring
Western wind, when wilt thou blow,
That small rain down can rain?
Christ, if my love were in my arms
And I in my bed again! (Quiller-Couch 53)

Invoking Christ is part of the tradition of courtly love that blends religious with secular imagery and meaning, and it connects us again to the opposition of reason and the material world with the realm of faith and religion. In the poem, the rain is welcomed as it is brought by the western wind, which will move the speaker closer to his love. Frederic similarly wishes for some impetus to bring him closer to his love, although in his case, the rain is a hindrance, and his movement throughout the retreat (from east to west) is against a westerly wind.

As David Wyatt has pointed out, Hemingway also quoted these four lines in a lengthy letter to Ernest Walsh written in January 1926, citing it as his "idea of Poetry" (70; *Letters 3* 14). In the same letter, Hemingway also praises another poem that Frederic Henry quotes in the novel, Andrew Marvell's "To His Coy Mistress." See 135:19–23. A third poem Hemingway cites in the letter is a medieval one known as "Twa Corbies," which includes the line "I wot there lies a new-slain knight," from which Hemingway took the tentative title, *New Slain Knight*, for the novel he was writing and never finished, before he began writing *A Farewell to Arms* in March 1928 (*Letters 3* 14). In the same letter, Hemingway argues strenuously for the quality and eminent status in American literature of Mark Twain's *Huckleberry Finn*, anticipating his pronouncement in *Green Hills of Africa*: "All modern American literature comes from one book by Mark Twain called *Huckleberry Finn*" (*GHA-HL* 17).

172:4–5 **we were in it. Every one was caught in it:** The vagueness of the pronoun *it* is one of Hemingway's effective tools to build tension around the unknowable qualities of this world. These two sentences are also a reminder of the "biological trap," which catches everyone. See entry 121:11. Here, the rain, the stopped traffic, and the onrushing Germans and Austrians only exacerbate the sense of entrapment in horror.

172:8–9 **I'm sorry he makes you so uncomfortable:** "He" here refers to Catherine's unborn child that Frederic assumes (correctly) is a male, a switch from the assumption he holds in chapter 24 when he and Catherine part in Milan, that the fetus is female. See 138:25–26.

172:10–18 **I was asleep all the time . . . whenever you want me:** Frederic dreams a vision of Catherine and this exchange of dialogue.

172:19 **"——," Piani said:** In the manuscript, the missing word is *shit* (JFK item 64).

172:20–21 **three o'clock in the morning:** Another of the novel's frequent reminders of the passage of time. It is now the wee hours of the morning of Sunday, 28 October. The specific time is likely an acknowledgement of his source G. M. Trevelyan, who led his group of British ambulances into the column of the retreat at three o'clock on the morning of 28 October (180).

172:22 **barbera:** See entries 97:14 and 167:5–6.

172:30 **have to get off that main road:** Probably not coincidentally, Frederic's conclusion is the same one reached by G. M. Trevelyan, who was leading a group of British Red Cross ambulances during the retreat on the same road from Cormons to Udine. In *Scenes from Italy's War*, Trevelyan wrote, "Under these conditions the only thing to be done was to get off the main road and let the cars work round singly or in small convoys by the by-roads and strike in again near Codroipo to cross the Tagliamento bridge" (182).

172:32–173:1 **In the night many peasants . . . as they moved along:** These are more details consistent with G. M. Trevelyan's *Scenes from Italy's War*, which describes "thousands of farm carts, bearing the fugitive peasantry and their household goods," joining the column (182).

173:10–12 **I was certain . . . it would be all over:** Frederic's observation about the column's vulnerability to an attack from the air mirrors G. M. Trevelyan's: "The rain fell steadily . . . impeding the pursuit and preventing the full use of aeroplanes. The Italians had no sufficient means at hand to combat aircraft, and a vigorous attack might have rendered impossible the passage of the crowded and narrow bridge" (184–85).

173:17 **small road that led off to the north:** Frederic and his crew leave the main road between Cormons and Udine with a right turn to the north.

173:26 **"They'll be good to push":** A bit of ironic foreshadowing. When Aymo's ambulance gets stuck in the mud and it comes time for the sergeants to help push, they will not be of any use at all. See entries 176:18 and 177:3.

173:36 **Bersaglieri:** See entry 38:10.

174:3 **"How's your leg, Tenente?"** Aymo provides another example of his unselfish concern for others, which helps to explain Frederic's high regard for him.

174:20 **came out with a clock in his hand:** The sergeants' selfishness contrasts with Aymo's unselfishness. Their behavior will culminate in their desertion from Frederic's band of refugees. Frederic's order to put the clock back foreshadows his later, more serious, altercation with them.

175:12 **"An army travels on its stomach":** Here Frederic more directly quotes the famous dictum attributed to either Frederick the Great of Prussia or Napoleon Bonaparte that food is essential to an army's success. See entry 161:10.

CHAPTER 29

176:1–2 At noon we were stuck . . . ten kilometres from Udine: As the chapter begins, it is midday, Sunday, 28 October. In a little over twelve hours since they left Gorizia, they only have traveled approximately twenty-five kilometers or about fifteen and a half miles. Ten kilometers from Udine would place them, as Michael Reynolds suggests, near the village of Buttrio and the Torre River, which they will have to cross (*First War* 123).

176:4–5 to the left . . . bombing on the main highroad: Frederic and his crew are to the north of the main road between Cormons and Udine, heading west. Thus, as Frederic says here, the main road is to their left, south.

176:18 "We have to go": The two engineering sergeants whom Bonello picked up have selfishly decided it is in their own best interests to take off on their own rather than stay and help extricate Aymo's car from the mud.

177:3 "You can't order us. You're not our officer": The sergeants are probably correct that Frederic has no real authority over them. Frederic, as a lieutenant in charge of an ambulance unit, is a medical officer. Medical officers do not typically have command authority outside of the medical department. Thus, Frederic would only have command authority over his drivers.

177:9 I missed: We have been prepared for Frederic's poor shooting since he revealed to us early on how difficult it was for him to hit anything with his previous pistol. See entry 25:5. In addition, he has had no opportunity to test this pistol bought from a gun shop in Milan just before returning to the front. See entry 130:22.

178:14 It was my fault: Frederic recognizes his responsibility for the suffering of others who are with him on this retreat. His acceptance here prepares him to accept responsibility later for the fate of Catherine and their baby.

178:24 **"It's ——ed," I said:** In the manuscript, Hemingway first wrote "finished," struck through it, and then wrote "cooked," which he also heavily struck through, with a long dash above it to replace it (JFK item 64). The novel's typescript has "It's F——ed" (JFK item 65), with the clear intended meaning of *fucked*. By the time Hemingway had the manuscript typed he had obviously decided to go with the most profane alternative. Scribner's decided to delete the *f* prior to publication. If Hemingway had left it as "It's finished," there would have been an allusion to the last words of Christ on the cross: "When Jesus therefore had received the vinegar, he said, It is finished: and he bowed his head and gave up the ghost" (John 19:30). If Hemingway had used "It's cooked," the meaning would have resonated with previous usages of *cooked*, meaning *finished*. See entries 116:17, 163:11, 165:12, and 171:1–5.

178:38 **If we could get across, there was a road:** In this instance, Frederic's reasoning powers fail him, and he makes perhaps his worst decision during the retreat, aside from the questionable shooting of the sergeant. He should understand that there is only a slim chance that the ambulances will be able to cross a muddy field to get to the road on the other side. When, predictably, they get hopelessly bogged down, the fault lies entirely with Frederic.

179:7 **ten-lira note:** Frederic gives the two sisters the equivalent of about $25 each in 2017 dollars (Williamson).

179:18 **"Give me two hundred lire":** Bonello offers to turn himself into the Austrians for the equivalent of $509 in 2017 terms (Williamson).

179:29–30 **"A bicycle is a splendid thing":** Hemingway gives this line to Bartolomeo Aymo, the man named for the famous Italian cyclist of the 1920s. See entry 166:15.

179:36 **"the cavalry":** In the manuscript, Hemingway initially wrote "the fucking cavalry" but then crossed out *fucking* (JFK item 64). This instance and 179:39 are the only places in the holograph manuscript where Hemingway actually wrote the word *fucking*.

179:37 **"I don't think they've got any cavalry":** Frederic is essentially correct. Trench warfare and mountain fighting made the use of horseback soldiers problematic.

179:39 **any —— cavalry:** The manuscript has the word *fucking* scratched out and replaced with a long dash (JFK item 64). It is a rare instance in which Hemingway actually wrote the word intended. Striking it out would indicate that he had no illusions about the possibility that the word could be printed. The typescript has "F———ing" (JFK item 65).

180:8 **that —— of a sergeant:** The manuscript has *son of a bitch* crossed out and replaced with a long dash (JFK item 64). Since *son of a bitch* is printed several times in other contexts in the novel, this apparent bit of self-censorship would seem to indicate that Hemingway ultimately intended this word to be *fuck* or an Italian equivalent, which he knew could not be printed in the finished novel. The typescript has a long dash (JFK item 65).

180:9 **"What will you say in confession?"** Aymo's question to Bonello suggests that Aymo is religious, a Roman Catholic, and that he has moral concerns about Bonello's killing of the sergeant. Thus, the exchange contrasting Aymo's faith with the atheism of Bonello and Piani reinforces the essential theme of the novel—the conflict between reason and faith.

180:10 **"I'll say, 'Bless me, father, I killed a sergeant'":** Bonello's joke refers to the opening line of the Catholic penitent, who, speaking to a priest in the confessional, begins, "Bless me, father, for I have sinned."

180:11 **"He's an anarchist. . . . He doesn't go to church":** Italian anarchism developed in the nineteenth century under the heavy influence of the radical Russian anarchist and atheist Mikhail Bakunin (1814–1876). Bakunin believed people should obey the laws of nature rather than any human or divine authority. He also denied class privileges, declaring that capitalism, the state, and religious authority are not compatible with the freedom of the peasantry. In *God and the State,* he reversed Voltaire's famous statement "If God did not exist, it would be necessary to invent him" by declaring that "if God really existed, it would be necessary to abolish Him" (18).

180:14 **"We're socialists":** Bonello and Piani are making a fine distinction, since many forms of anarchism are collectivist in nature, as is socialism. Socialism, however, is generally regarded as less radical than anarchism, with the latter more likely to emphasize individual liberty. In that sense, one irony of this particular situation is that the sergeants' self-centered behavior might be viewed as more anarchistic than the behavior of Frederic and his drivers, whose conduct better demonstrates the socialistic concern for the common good of all. In an interview with George Plimpton late in his life, Hemingway declared, "A writer without a sense of justice and of injustice would be better off editing the Year Book of a school for exceptional children than writing novels" (Bruccoli, *Conversations* 128).

180:14 **Imola:** This Italian city-commune about thirty miles southeast of Bologna has a population today of around seventy thousand. It has some historical and architectural distinction, including a museum and library of two hundred thousand volumes. Baedeker's *Italy: From the Alps to Naples* 1928 does not mention it.

180:29–30 **going fast against time:** The last sentence of the chapter reemphasizes the important theme of time, which, under the circumstances, with enemy soldiers and death following them, becomes even more precious.

CHAPTER 30

181:1 **Later we were on a road that led to a river:** It is still the afternoon of Sunday, 28 October. Although Frederic does not name it, the river must be the Fiume Torre (Tower River), a tributary of the Isonzo running between Udine and Cormons. During much of the year, the riverbed is dry, as Frederic notes later (181:13), but during the rainy season, as here, the waters can be torrential. Although the river is taken from the actual geography of northeastern Italy, it is important to note that Hemingway begins fictionalizing the topography here, for purposes that will become clear later. The road leading to the river and the bridge that crosses it in actuality could only be what is today SR56 (Strada Regionale or Regional Highway 56), the main road from Gorizia to Udine. This is the only road south of the Via Cividale with a bridge crossing the Fiume Torre and a railway bridge paralleling it. But, of course, that road, in reality, was also the main route of the retreat out of Cormons and jammed with traffic. Since the traffic would have interfered with Hemingway's intentions here, he eliminates it as well as the bridge (which has been destroyed by the retreating Italians).

At about the same time that Frederic and his men reach it downstream, Lieutenant Erwin Rommel and his squad of German soldiers reached the Fiume Torre, which he described in his memoir as a "vicious stream six hundred yards wide," about eight miles upriver, near Primulacco (229). However, the Italian rear guard stopped Rommel's outfit from crossing the river. The Germans built a makeshift bridge out of vehicles in the night and crossed the river on the morning of 29 October after the Italian rear guard retreated. Rommel would receive the Pour le Mérite for his actions on the Italian front and achieve fame in World War II. See entry 163:8. In *Across the River and into the Trees*, Richard Cantwell speaks admiringly of Rommel, having fought against him during the Battle of Caporetto, "half way from Cortina to the Grappa, where we held" (122). Cantwell says that after the war they met and skied together (see Cirino, *Reading* 111).

181:17 **"It's probably mined.... You cross first, Tenente":** Bonello, the funniest man in Frederic's crew, is joking here. Frederic has the authority to determine who will be the first to cross the bridge, and Bonello would surely obey if ordered to do so. A little later, after they see a German staff car crossing a bridge, Frederic has to say to Bonello, "Don't be funny" (182:34).

181:19 **"I'll go. . . . It won't be mined to blow up with one man":** Frederic takes no offense at Bonello's joke and chooses to go first on the bridge, reasoning that if the railroad bridge is mined, it will be set to blow under the weight of a train or a much larger group of men. This is one of many examples during the retreat where Frederic demonstrates the necessity of reason for survival. As Piani acknowledges, "That is brains" (181:20).

182:1 **"If I had brains I wouldn't be here":** Bonello continues to provide comic relief, while underscoring the irrationality of modern warfare.

182:10 **Udine in the rain:** Udine is about five miles away from the railroad bridge across the Fiume Torre, so it seems implausible that Frederic would be able to see it under the rainy conditions, when visibility would be low.

182:22 **"A German staff car crossed on the upper bridge":** Michael Reynolds has correctly pointed out that Hemingway took this accurate detail from historical reports, although Reynolds gets the date wrong (*Hemingway's First War* 121). Around midday on Sunday, 28 October, German general Albert von Berrer received a false report that Udine had been taken from the Italians, so he ordered the driver of his staff car to go straight into the town from Cividale. In the process, the car got well ahead of advancing German troops, and not long after crossing the bridge over the Fiume Torre on the Via Cividale in San Gottardo, a suburb of Udine, the general ran into a group of Italian Bersagliari bicycle troops in the rear guard who promptly shot and killed him and the other Germans in the car (Caviglia 193–95; "Udine"; Cavallaro 128–29, 135n2; Möller 73–75). Reynolds mistakenly has the date as 27 October (*First War* 121), apparently relying on Cyril Falls's erroneous *The Battle of Caporetto* as his source (51) and missing in his timeline the day Frederic spends evacuating the field hospital at Plava. See entry 164:9–10. However, all other authoritative sources we have found give 28 October as the date of von Berrer's death.

Hemingway's timeline thus is accurate, although he takes some liberties with the geographic details. The map between Cormons and Udine shows that the bridge described as blown up here could only be the bridge on what is today Regional Highway 56 near the village of Lovaria. See entry 181:1. It is the only highway bridge over the Torre that has a railway bridge a short distance to its north, in this case approximately three hundred yards and clearly visible from the highway bridge. However, the bridge of the Via Cividale, which General von Berrer's auto crossed by all accounts, is over four miles away and beyond several bends in the river. Realistically, it would not be visible to Frederic and his men as they crossed the railway bridge. However, Hemingway obviously wanted to include the von Berrer reference as an illustration of the random chaos of war, so he fictionalized and distorted the geography to enable Frederic to report it.

Hemingway later paid tribute to von Berrer in his short story "A Natural History of the Dead," first published as part of *Death in the Afternoon* in 1932 and then again in *Winner Take Nothing* in 1933: "[A]nd so was General von Behr [sic] [a fine general] who commanded the Bavarian Alpenkorps troops at the battle of Caporetto and was killed in his staff car by the Italian rear guard as he drove into Udine ahead of his troops, and the titles of all such books should be *Generals Usually Die in Bed*, if we are to have any sort of accuracy in such things" (*DIA* 140; *CSS* 339). Hemingway was alluding to the 1930 novella *Generals Die in Bed*, by Canadian Charles Yale Harrison, but he also calls to mind Siegfried Sassoon's 1918 poem "Base Details":

If I were fierce, and bald, and short of breath,
I'd live with scarlet Majors at the Base,
And speed glum heroes up the line to death....
And when the war is done and youth stone dead,
I'd toddle safely home and die—in bed.

Sassoon also authored *Memoirs of an Infantry Officer* (1930), one of the important books on the Great War published around the same time as *A Farewell to Arms*.

182:39–183:1 **They ... moved smoothly, almost supernaturally:** The image of the German bicycle troops, only their heads visible over the stone rail of the bridge, is an eerie demonstration of how the material world can sometimes trick the mind into seeing more than what it is actually seeing—another instance of subjectivity clashing with objectivity.

183:1–2 **They were bicycle troops:** This objective sentence corrects the previous subjective one. For rapid movement, German infantry battalions in World War I typically had one company of bicycle troops. They could be effective when using the tactics of infiltrating small units of men behind enemy lines, as they did successfully in the Battle of Caporetto. The Italians had bicycle troops as well, and ironically, General von Berrer was reportedly killed by Bersagliari bicycle troops. See entry 182:22. Bicycle troops did not fight as cavalry do, that is, mounted; they dismounted their bicycles before engaging in combat.

183:4 **carbines:** These rifles had shorter barrels than standard rifles, essential for a soldier to be able to clip the gun to a bicycle frame.

183:5 **Stick bombs:** The German version of hand grenades. See entry 106:14. See also Cirino, *Reading Hemingway's* Across the River and into the Trees (37–38).

183:18 **"The whole bloody thing is crazy":** Frederic expresses his frustration at the retreat's irrationality. He does not see any logic to the Italian conduct of it. In using the term *crazy*, he connects the retreat with other instances of irrational behavior in the novel. See entries 26:15–19 and 79:24, for example.

183:34 **We walked along the railroad track:** Frederic and his three drivers are walking northwest toward Udine on a railroad track that is laid on a raised embankment above the lowland plain on both sides.

183:36–37 **the castle on the hill . . . the campanile and the clock-tower:** The entry for Udine in Baedeker's *Italy: From the Alps to Naples* 1928 describes the Castello (castle) that "rises" above the Piazza Vittorio Emanuele (named for the king of Italy), a cathedral with a "hexagonal campanile" (bell tower) and a clock tower that resembles the one at Venice (87).

183:37–38 **many mulberry trees in the fields:** In the original manuscript, Hemingway wrote and crossed out, "I remembered what they did with the silk worms in winter. They were in their cocoons [sic] of course but they made silk of their cocoons" (JFK item 64). In "Now I Lay Me," one of several Hemingway short stories set during the war in Italy, Nick Adams lies awake at night listening to "the silk-worms eating. The silk-worms fed in racks of mulberry leaves and all night you could hear them eating and a dropping sound in the leaves" (*CSS* 276).

184:2–3 **another group of bicyclists passing along the road:** The German bicycle troops are on the road to the north of the tracks. Thus, Frederic and his men take cover on the south side of the railroad embankment.

184:9 **"We'll walk along the tracks":** Frederic and his men now choose to walk shielded by the railroad embankment to their right, so as not to be seen by German troops on the other side.

184:16 **The railway moved south away from the highway:** Hemingway is obviously fictionalizing the landscape here. There is no such place on the map where the railway moves away from a highway. However, in continuing to follow the tracks, Frederic and his men are now certainly moving in a more southerly direction. Udine still lies to their north.

184:24–25 **I thought we had better cut to the south and work around the town that way:** Frederic's plan at this point is to go south of Udine yet apparently north of the main line of the retreat column, which they will necessarily join at Campoformido. This is confusing, since earlier Frederic describes the main line of the retreat column as going "as far as Udine" (169:19). Thus, if Hemingway had been strictly adhering to reality, Frederic and his men would necessarily have met the main line of the retreat again, yet they do not. See entry 169:11–19.

184:26 **Campoformio:** The town, a village about five miles southwest of Udine, is known today as Campoformido. The Treaty of Campo Formio, between Napoleon's France and Austria, was signed here in 1797.

184:31 **We all started down the embankment:** Frederic and his men descend on the south side of the railroad embankment to head toward the small "branch road" Frederic has spied to their south (184:23–24).

184:36–37 **Two more shots came from the thick brush:** The shots come toward them from the brush surrounding the small branch road to the south.

185:8 **"The ——," he said:** In the original manuscript, Hemingway wrote "cocksuckers," then crossed it out (JFK item 64). He put the word back in the typescript (JFK item 65). Hemingway apparently still had hopes that his publishers would allow his use of this realistic bit of profanity.

185:9–10 **"There can't be any Germans over there":** Frederic is correct in his reasoning that the Germans would have all been to their north as the Germans and Austrians came down to Udine from the mountains and Cividale to the northeast. Thus, Aymo has been mistakenly killed by his own army, another instance of the irrationality of war.

185:18 **"No. . . . It was because we started across the field":** Frederic continues to use his powers of logic to understand what is happening. He recognizes that they were fired upon because they were coming from the direction of the Germans toward soldiers in the Italian rear guard, who no doubt had orders to shoot at any men who came from that direction.

185:27 **"You reason it out, Tenente":** In his anger over Aymo's death, Bonello mocks Frederic's attempts to reason through what has happened and use what he has learned to help plot their movements thence forward. Bonello has crossed over into the realm of irrationality, as will be confirmed when he chooses to give himself up to the Germans (188:3).

185:32 **"I'm not going to try them"**: Bonello signals his intent not to go in the Italians' direction.

185:33–34 **"lie up as near to Udine as we can get and then go through when it's dark"**: Frederic's statement seems to imply a movement westward on the south side of Udine and an attempt to go through the town or south of it under the cover of darkness. However, later text indicates that they travel around the north of the town. See entries 188:31 and 188:35–37.

185:35–36 **down the north side of the embankment:** They will now use the cover of the railroad embankment on their left to conceal them from the Italians, even though they risk being seen by Germans on their right. But Frederic correctly assumes that the Germans are more intent on capturing the center of Udine, and so their primary attention will not be to the south. However, the reality is that Frederic, Bonello, and Piani are facing danger on all sides as they proceed west.

186:10 **I walked toward it, seeing it very clearly:** Frederic's reasoning powers are necessarily sharp as he approaches the farmhouse, absorbing all the sensory data to ensure that he and his men are not exposing themselves to danger from either Germans or Italians.

186:21 **"We ought to lie up in the barn":** Frederic logically recognizes that their safety will be much more ensured if they take refuge in the barn's hayloft.

186:25–187:2 **I found a stone stairway. . . . It seemed like a good place:** This highly detailed paragraph conveys all of Frederic's sensory impressions, as he gathers data that will enable him to make the most effective and logical decisions for their safety. Referring to it as "a good place" recalls Hemingway's description of Nick Adams's camp in "Big Two-Hearted River": "He had made his camp. He was settled. Nothing could touch him. It was a good place to camp. He was there, in the good place. He was in his home where he had made it" (*CSS* 167).

187:7–9 **we had heard . . . I did not believe it:** Frederic's thoughts turn to possible disguises of the enemy, part of the novel's motif of reality versus sham, truth versus lies, wisdom versus ignorance, rationality versus irrationality, as well as the fluidity of nationality and identity. Using his rational mind, Frederic discounts the rumor on the basis that there was no need for the Germans to do it. The landscape and the lack of communication and orders made the task of breaking through the Italian army at Caporetto easy for the Germans, without resorting to disguise. He might have added that the use of tactics like poison gas and infiltration also paralyzed the Italians in the battle.

Hemingway's source for this passage may have been Charles M. Bakewell's *The Story of the American Red Cross in Italy,* which contains the following description of the Caporetto Retreat: "Here were others, wolves in sheep's clothing, Austrians and Germans disguised in Italian uniforms, giving contrary orders. Great was the confusion. How was one to know whom to believe?" (22). Frederic's skepticism may reflect Hemingway's own skepticism regarding Bakewell's details.

187:17–23 The hay smelled good. . . . You could not go back: After Frederic has worked his logical mind hard to be certain that the barn and its hayloft will be a safe refuge, he relaxes, and fatigue naturally sets in, sending his mind into a reverie about the past. The image of the destruction of both the barn and the woods mirror the destruction of the environment in which the war is being waged.

This passage is an anomaly in the text because it is the only instance in which Frederic remembers his past. As David Wyatt points out, the passage recalls the single memory Jake Barnes has of his own past in *The Sun Also Rises,* the recollection of returning home after a football game (*SAR* 192–93). Wyatt notes the déjà vu quality of both passages. That is, both Jake and Frederic are reexperiencing the past triggered by elements of the present (72).

In contrast to what we know of Jake, however, Hemingway never specifies in *A Farewell to Arms* where in the United States Frederic Henry is from. We understand the memory to come from some kind of rural environment, where a hemlock woods once stood along with the barn. Hemlocks are fir trees that grow in temperate regions that get a healthy amount of rainfall, like Michigan, and there are numerous references to hemlock trees and hemlock wood in his stories. There are hemlock planks in the dock in "Up In Michigan" (*CSS* 62); the Adams family Michigan cottage is surrounded by hemlock woods in "The Doctor and the Doctor's Wife" (75), "Ten Indians" (257), "Fathers and Sons" (372), and "The Last Good Country" (509); and Nick and Kate make love under a hemlock tree in "Summer People" (501). Thus, we might infer that Frederic Henry has a background similar to that of Nick Adams, who has spent at least part of his childhood in the Michigan woods.

187:20 the wall of the barn: In the original manuscript, Hemingway added after this a long passage that extended the memory of Frederic's youth but then crossed it out:

> It was a hot day and after a while we would go to the lake to swim. The path to the lake was hot on your bare feet until it went in the woods where it was cool in the shade from the hemlocks. The path crossed a cedar swamp and the foot log was rotted so the wood was soft and powdery with hard stretches in it at the sides. The sand beach at the cove was smooth and the water was clear over the sand. The birches grew close to the edge of the water where they had been peeled the bark

was brown. You leaned your air rifle against a [birch?] tree and there was an old log half sunk in the sand that you put your clothes on. (JFK item 64)

187:25–26 I listened to the firing to the north toward Udine: This important detail further establishes their location. They seem to be due south of Udine at this point.

188:3 "He went away, Tenente. . . . He wanted to be a prisoner": Bonello has allowed his fears to get the best of him. Because of Aymo's death, he illogically thinks it is wiser to go in the direction of the Germans than toward the Italians, and so he has departed, presumably heading northeast away from Frederic and Piani.

188:7 "You see we don't believe in the war anyway": As anarchists/socialists, Piani and Bonello would not have supported Italy's war against Austria. They were drafted into the army. The Italian Socialist Party, led by Filippo Turati, opposed Italy's decision to enter the war (Thompson 35).

188:9 "I did not want to leave you": The decision to proceed toward the Italians may be logical, but Piani's statement here stresses that he also has subjective reasons not to go with Bonello toward the Germans—that is, caring for the well-being of a comrade, Frederic. Piani understands that objectivity and subjectivity need to be balanced.

188:14 "I cut it while we were talking": That Frederic has not noticed that Piani has already cut the sausage indicates how much Bonello's desertion has shaken him.

188:17 "Luigi": Piani's first name. Unlike Bartolomeo Aymo's name, there appears to be no historical source for the name Luigi Piani.

188:31 That was a very strange night: A very strange night indeed, one that illustrates the illogic of the entire atmosphere of the retreat, although Hemingway provides few details of Frederic and Piani's path to the Tagliamento River. After leaving the barn, they walk together for about nine hours, which may seem an implausible amount of time to cover a distance of more than thirty miles in the heavy rain and the dark circling around the north side of Udine to the western side of the bridge over the Tagliamento. But plausibility seems not to have been Hemingway's concern. See entry 188:35–37.

188:35–37 we crossed the road and went on to the north. . . . We got past the town to the north: As illogical as it may seem, Hemingway certainly has Frederic and Piani circle Udine on its north side, choosing a route that is not only roughly four or five miles longer than a direct route west skirting the south side of Udine but that requires them to follow Bonello and head straight into the onrushing Germans and then, in the starless darkness, negotiate at least two major changes of direction in terrain completely unfamiliar to them. It is certainly an irrational decision on Frederic's part, but irrationality seems to have been Hemingway's point. It is just one more instance of illogic in a series of illogical events—including the deaths of General von Berrer and Aymo—that illustrate the madness of modern warfare. The madness, of course, culminates in Frederic's completely irrational arrest and likely execution if not for his escape at the Tagliamento bridge. See entry 191:27–29.

189:10 **"How do you feel, Tenente?"** After Aymo's death, Piani has assumed the caring role of Aymo for the rest of the retreat to the Tagliamento, exemplifying the kind of love the priest exemplifies, the wish to "do things for . . . to sacrifice for." See entry 62:27–29.

189:18–20 **"I don't know. . . . I don't know"**: Frederic is undecided on what to report about Bonello's desertion, understanding that subjective emotions complicate objective facts.

189:21–22 **"if the war went on . . . bad trouble for his family"**: As Piani points out to Frederic here, one of the complicating subjective factors in what to do about Bonello is that Bonello's family, in light of his desertion, would likely be persecuted.

189:28–29 **"A basso gli ufficiali! Down with the officers!"** The phrase should correctly be "*Abbasso gli ufficiali!*" (Cirino, "You Don't Know" 59). In the chaos of the retreat, officers are being unfairly held responsible for the defeat. Irrationality is rising to the fore. Hemingway had also previously used the phrase (also incorrectly spelled) in his 1927 short story of the war in Italy, "In Another Country": "The people hated us because we were officers, and from a wine-shop some one would call out, 'A basso gli ufficiali!' as we passed" (*CSS* 207).

189:33 **"I won't make . . . make trouble for his family"**: Recognizing the negative emotions running through the retreating mob, Frederic decides he will not judge Bonello harshly for his desertion. His decision helps foreshadow his own desertion a short time later.

190:1 **"Viva la Pace!"** The phrase means *Long live the peace!*

190:6–7 **"Andiamo a casa!" . . . "They throw away their rifles"**: The Italian phrase means *Let's go home!* Hemingway probably drew these details from *Scenes from Italy's War*, in which G. M. Trevelyan describes Italians crying "Andiamo a casa" during the retreat and throwing away their rifles so that "no fool of an officer can turn us back to fight when it is no use" (174). Another possible source is Charles M. Bakewell's *The Story of the American Red Cross in Italy*, who writes, "Some of the soldiers threw away their guns as they ran, and sang and shouted 'Peace! We are going home. The war is over. One man can't fight alone'" (22).

190:27 **"The Germans have stopped outside Udine":** The Germans captured Udine on 29 October (Trevelyan 183). Hemingway also added and then crossed out, "They're waiting for more troops. They'll take the town in the morning" (JFK item 64). This is a supposition on Frederic's part, not a fact he could know.

190:36 **"Are you married, Luigi?"** Frederic's question to Piani comes no doubt from his own thoughts of Catherine in this struggle to make it through this chaotic retreat alive and see her again.

191:1 **"No":** Frederic, of course, is not technically married to Catherine, though he and she certainly regard themselves as essentially married. It seems Frederic does not wish to share with Piani the details of his relationship to Catherine, which would likely distract him from the concentration he needs for survival during the retreat.

191:9 **Before daylight we reached the bank of the Tagliamento:** Frederic and Piani reach the east bank of the Tagliamento River in the predawn hours of 29 October. From later events, we can surmise the time to be approximately four o'clock, or roughly nine hours after they left the farmhouse outside of Udine.

191:14 **The wooden bridge was nearly three-quarters of a mile across:** Hemingway's estimate is probably a slight exaggeration. The bridge that crosses the Tagliamento today—not the same one, of course, but in almost the exact same location—is about two-thirds of a mile long. The width of the river bed at that point is about a half mile.

191:19–20 **the box of an artillery caisson:** An artillery caisson is a two-wheeled carriage with a box for artillery ammunition that is pulled by horse or tractor.

191:22–23 **I wondered what it would be like if a plane bombed it in the daytime:** G. M. Trevelyan describes having much the same thought as he crossed the bridge over the Tagliamento (185).

191:27–29 **At the far end of the bridge . . . flashing lights:** G. M. Trevelyan arrived by ambulance at the far end of the bridge over the Tagliamento the evening prior to Frederic's arrival there, and he describes a "hopeful and active world, where officers and Carabinieri were sorting out the men as they arrived over the bridge, and orders were being given and obeyed" (185–86). But Trevelyan apparently did not linger, as he and his crew drove on to arrive at Pordenone later that night. What he saw as hopeful activity might well have been the summary executions that Frederic encounters.

On 27 October, Supreme Commander General Luigi Cadorna issued an order that the "harshest means would be used to maintain discipline. 'Whoever does not feel that he wins or falls with honour on the line of resistance, is not fit to live'" (Thompson 316). During the retreat, particularly at the Codroipo bridge, where things seem to have been most chaotic, Carabinieri, battle police, may have taken justice into their own hands and conducted summary executions (see entry 21:12). Here the Carabinieri are screening the retreating forces for soldiers who have discarded their weapons or officers separated from their units (identified as cowards, deserters, or enemy agents disguised as Italian soldiers). Frederic's accent may be cause enough for his arrest and drumhead trial and execution as an enemy in disguise, a speaker of a non-native tongue. The whole scene is a brutal illustration of the irrationality of war. See the long section on the retreat in Mark Thompson's *The White War,* with a chilling depiction of the growing anger and rebelliousness of many of the soldiers (294–327).

Part of the mass confusion at the Codroipo bridge was the result of Cadorna's ordered allotment of the bridges over the Tagliamento for the retreat. The Italian Third Army, under the Duke of Aosta's command, had not given ground to the Austrians on the Carso and maintained order during the retreat, so they were rewarded by being assigned the two southernmost bridges, at Latisana and Codroipo, for crossing the Tagliamento. The Second Army, in which Frederic and his men serve and which Cadorna blamed entirely for the German and Austrian breakthrough at Caporetto, were given the more problematic and vulnerable northern bridges at Pinzano, twelve miles north of Codroipo, and Cornino, another five miles north, which only had a railway bridge (Falls 65). However, it is likely in all the confusion that very few retreating soldiers of the Second Army actually received Cadorna's command, and thus many converged on the centrally located bridge at Codroipo.

While Hemingway was not present to witness any summary executions during the Caporetto Retreat, he may have heard such accounts from Italian soldiers with whom he came into contact during his time in Italy in 1918 and/or have read newspaper accounts of them. Michael Reynolds quotes one such story, from *The London Times:* "Discipline has been restored to the Italian army by ruthless execution of deserters and the situation is improving. . . . The retreat is now methodical" (*First War* 133). This was apparently the only account Reynolds could find of the executions. He is probably correct that Hemingway's best source for this scene was likely Charles M. Bakewell's *The Story of the American Red Cross in Italy,* which includes the following account:

> There were other tragedies of the retreat besides those affecting the civilian population. Some of the soldiers had thrown away their guns in the flight before the enemy, an unpardonable offense in a soldier. These were caught at the bridge cross-

ings. And more than once, in the early dawn, regiments were drawn up on three sides of a hollow square as these unfortunates were led out before them to face the firing squad. (23)

192:15 "Shoot him if he resists": See entry 191:27–29.

192:29 "So do you, you ——": In the typescript of the novel, the deleted word is *cocksucker,* deemed too profane for Hemingway's editor, Maxwell Perkins, so it was replaced with the dashes for publication, with Hemingway's reluctant agreement (Bruccoli, *Only Thing* 110).

193:19 "Have you ever been in a retreat?" The lieutenant colonel is the voice of reason in this argument, but the voices of irrationality are in control. The supremely irrational response, "Italy should never retreat" carries the day, and the lieutenant colonel is summarily executed.

193:25–26 "The questioning is stupid." He made the sign of the cross: Although the lieutenant colonel is shown as the voice of reason in the face of extreme unreason, Hemingway also carefully presents him to us as a man of faith, that is, a combination of reason and faith and one who dies with courage and dignity. Others die with less dignity, and Frederic chooses to attempt to escape rather than to die an absurd death. See Hemingway's essay "Dying, Well or Badly," reprinted in *Hemingway on War.*

The lieutenant colonel's faith and death with dignity recalls Hemingway's short story/drama "Today Is Friday," written in 1926 and published in the collection *Men Without Women* in 1927. The subject is the crucifixion of Jesus Christ, but presented through the responses of three Roman soldiers as they share drinks in a bar afterward. The first soldier seems to have been inspired by Christ's courage and dignity in death, repeating several times, "He was good in there today." He also had shown mercy in putting his spear into Christ to relieve him of his suffering. The second soldier, however, is the hardened and worldly skeptic, who asks, "Why didn't he come down off the cross? . . . Show me the guy that doesn't want to come down off the cross." The third soldier seems the most disturbed by the events of the day: "I feel like hell," he repeats (*CSS* 271–73). The three soldiers could also represent three different responses to the lieutenant colonel's execution. Frederic is the one who chooses to come down off the cross.

194:1–2 obviously a German in Italian uniform. I saw how their minds worked: While the minds of the battle police are working irrationally, Frederic's own mind is working rationally, enabling him to reason clearly enough to see that he is also sure to be executed. So he makes a rational decision to avoid certain death and plunges into the river.

CHAPTER 30 · 233

In *Three Soldiers,* the 1921 war novel by John Dos Passos, protagonist John Andrews also deserts by diving into a river, in his case, the Seine in France, although he is not in danger of imminent execution (*Novels* 417). Like Frederic Henry, Andrews tries to get back to a woman he loves, Geneviève Rod, but their love has gone cold, and in the end, Andrews is arrested for desertion.

194:19 **ran for the river:** Having crossed the bridge, Frederic clearly leaps into the river from the west bank, contrary to Reynolds's claim that he goes in near the east bank (*First War* 126). Many commentators interpret Frederic's plunge into the river as a kind of baptism. Whether we wish to see it in religious or secular terms will depend upon our frame of reference, but it is apparent that Hemingway wishes us to recognize the act as a cleansing for Frederic, part of his "good-bye to all that," a "farewell to arms" or a "farewell to absurdity." In plunging himself into the river, Frederic is severing his ties to the military and the war.

194:26–27 **I kept my head behind it. . . . I did not want to see the bank:** As Frederic floats southward downstream in the Tagliamento, he conceals himself from any Italians who may be searching for him from the west bank of the river. Thus, at this stage he is on the eastern side of the log, floating southward. This fact is important later to help us understand onto which bank he emerges. See entry 195:17–18.

194:32 **We:** Frederic/Hemingway briefly shifts here from first-person singular to first-person plural as Frederic personifies his piece of timber as a companion in desertion, aiding his getaway.

CHAPTER 31

195:1–3 You do not know how long . . . it may be very short: The chapter begins with a comment on two important themes of the novel: subjectivity and time. Note also the shift to second person, a technique Hemingway commonly uses when he wishes to draw the reader into sharing in an experience and to universalize it.

195:4–5 lucky to have a heavy timber to hold on to: Another subject of the novel is luck, the randomness of existence. Frederic recognizes here that his survival owes something to the good fortune of having a log to hold on to.

195:7–8 I hoped we would move toward the shore: Frederic continues the personification of the log as his companion with the first person plural pronoun, begun at the end of the previous chapter. See entry 194:32. The companions, Frederic and the log, continue following the current downstream for approximately five miles as daylight develops. He uses the first-person plural pronoun five more times before he leaves the log for the shore (196:3).

195:14 Mestre: See entry 60:20.

195:17–18 The timber swung slowly so that the bank was behind me: This describes an important maneuver for us to understand toward which bank of the river Frederic swims. Frederic was first on the eastern side of the log as it floats southward downstream, so that it helped to protect him from being seen by Italians on the western bank of the stream. Now after the log swings around in the current, he is on the western side of the log, with his back to the western shore. Therefore, when he kicks away from the log, he is propelling himself toward the western bank (196:2–3). This contradicts the interpretation of Michael Reynolds, who has him climbing out of the river on the eastern bank (*First War* 126).

196:18–20 I knew. . . . I thought. . . . I began to think: Frederic continues to maintain the kind of rationality that will enable him to survive now on his own as a fugitive from justice. His life is in every bit as much danger as it was the day before during the retreat. Thus, rationality is essential to his survival.

196:20 opposite San Vito: A detail that apparently threw Michael Reynolds off the track so that he incorrectly put Frederic on the east bank of the Tagliamento (*First War* 126). As H. R. Stoneback accurately points out, Reynolds's misinterpretation rests on a misunderstanding of the way Hemingway is using the word *opposite,* here meaning something like *in line with* in the same way he uses the word at 191:33, 191:36, and 191:39, as Frederic nears the Carabinieri on the far side of the bridge over the Tagliamento, again at 197:32 in reference to the train passing Frederic, and at 198:3 as the train crosses the bridge ("Lovers' Sonnets Turn'd to Holy Psalms" 55). It is also certainly a mistake to interpret the usage as meaning Frederic is opposed to what San Vito (Saint Vitus) represents.

On the purely literal and realistic level, the town of San Vito al Tagliamento is a mostly nondescript Italian community, with a population today of about fifteen thousand, in the province of Pordenone, approximately four miles southwest of the bridge where Frederic plunged into the Tagliamento. It is named for Saint Vitus (San Vito in Italian). The name has its root in the Latin word for life—*vita*. Thus, San Vito confirms to Frederic that he has survived this close brush with sudden death, and it represents a lovely combination of the novel's religious and secular sides.

196:27 I slapped and rubbed myself: While removing his clothes to wring them out and then slapping and rubbing himself to stimulate his blood flow in the chilly weather would all be perfectly natural and understandable actions for anyone in Frederic's situation, his nakedness and slapping also help reinforce the symbolic rebirth Frederic has just experienced.

196:27–28 I had lost my cap: For a discussion of the symbolism of hats in the novel, see Mandel, "Headgear and Horses."

196:29 I cut the cloth stars off my sleeves: As a tenente (lieutenant), Frederic has two stars on each of his sleeves, designating his rank. Since officers separated from their units are being arrested and possibly summarily shot, he needs to remove any signs of his rank.

196:31–32 three thousand and some lire: At the 1917 exchange rate of 7.509 lire to a dollar, this would have been worth $400, which would amount to $7,650 in 2017 terms (Williamson). In other words, Frederic is carrying a substantial amount of money.

196:38–39 a campanile rising out of the plain: A campanile is a bell tower, a symbol of time. With Frederic moving in a southwesterly direction, the campanile he sees may be of the church of Sant'Andrea in Cordovado, which would be approximately four miles away.

197:1 I limped along the side of the road: In this bit of dissemblance on Frederic's part, the limping is another sign of shrewd thinking to disguise his identity.

197:4 That day I crossed the Venetian plain: The day is 29 October 1917. The retreat is still going on as Frederic makes his way southwest.

197:8–18 I was working across the country . . . a train might come from Portogruaro: Unlike the previous day, where Hemingway needed to change geographic details enough to place Frederic in a spot where he could witness General von Berrer's German staff car heading dangerously into Udine, on this day there is no need to distort the map, and Hemingway's descriptions are quite accurate. Frederic continues for about fifteen miles in a southwesterly direction, crossing two railroad tracks (easily identifiable on a map), until he comes to the main train line from Venice to Trieste. He is about five miles southwest of the town of Portogruaro, near the railroad bridge over the Loncon River, which is the unnamed stream that flows into the marsh (197:14–15). Frederic is looking for a train that will be coming from Portogruaro and heading southwest toward Mestre (the mainland borough of Venice). All of these details demonstrate how badly off target Michael Reynolds was in placing Frederic on the east side of the Tagliamento River and meeting the train line near Latisana, which is east of Portogruaro. Had Reynolds been correct, why would Frederic want to catch a train coming from Portogruaro to Latisana? It would be heading back toward the east, away from where he needs to go. And of course, under the conditions of the retreat, it would be highly unlikely for any trains to be running in that direction anyway. Another important consideration is that if Frederic had followed the eastern bank of the Tagliamento down to Latisana, he would have had to join the heavy traffic of the retreat there, crossing the Latisana bridge over the Tagliamento, as described by Hugh Dalton (124–25). On 29 October, the Italians still had hopes of holding the Germans and Austrians at the Tagliamento, so there would not have been retreat traffic west of Latisana, and if there had been, it would have been south of the railroad, so Frederic would not have had to cross it. By the time he reaches the tracks near the Loncon, Frederic has walked, since the afternoon of 28 October, when he and his men were about six miles southeast of Udine, a total of close to forty-seven miles, not counting the four to five miles he rode the log down the Tagliamento. He (implausibly) covers approximately thirty-two miles during the day and night of 28–29 October and another fifteen miles during the day of 29 October.

197:38–198:2 caught the rear hand-rods . . . my feet on the coupling: Frederic's knowledge of riding freight trains is probably based on Hemingway's catching train rides during his youth in northern Michigan. See his 1925 short story "The Battler" (*CSS* 97–103), in which Nick Adams is punched off a freight train by a deceitful brakeman and encounters a seriously demented boxer named Ad Francis and his companion, Bugs.

198:3–7 **We were almost opposite . . . as we passed. . . . We were past:** After Frederic hops the train, he bonds with it into another "we," as he had done with the log on the Tagliamento. See entry 194:32. For the meaning of "opposite," see entry 196:20.

198:14 **a violent bump:** A reminder of other bumps in the novel and in Hemingway's life: the soldier who wishes to get out of going to the front and whom Frederic encourages to "get a bump" on his head (see entry 30:22–23); the severe head injury and possible skull fracture Frederic experiences in his wounding, which Ferguson says can make him "crazy" (see entry 95:3); and the actual serious bump Hemingway received in pulling down a skylight on his head in his Paris apartment in March 1928, which apparently inspired him to begin writing *A Farewell to Arms* (Reynolds, *American Homecoming* 166–67; Hotchner 50). Ferguson's line resonates most profoundly in this instance, as Frederic must maintain his rationality and clear thinking if he is to survive. Thus, the bump continues the emphasis throughout Book Three on the necessity of reason in the face of a world that continually presents obstacles and ways to undercut the faculty of reason.

198:25–26 **washed away . . . with rainwater:** In this ironic detail, Frederic washes his injured forehead with the ubiquitous rainwater—elsewhere in the novel a symbol of doom, but here an aid to conceal him from authorities, who will be looking for deserters from the front. A visible wound would mark Frederic as a soldier from the front.

CHAPTER 32

199:2 very hungry: Frederic has not eaten anything that we know of since before nightfall on 28 October, when he and Piani had sausage, "a jar of something," and wine in the barn of the farmhouse south of Udine (187:29–30).

199:4 Valentini: The doctor who performed surgery to repair Frederic's knee. See entry 86:17.

199:9–11 The head was mine . . . and not too much remember: Frederic reminds himself and us of the importance of properly using his mind, which contains his ability to recognize both objective and subjective truth. Remembering would take him too much into the subjective realm at a time when he needs to remain objective.

199:12–14 I could remember Catherine . . . only about her a little: As Mark Cirino explains, this is "a rant against consciousness told in a lush, stream-of-consciousness mode" (*Thought in Action,* chap. 3). This should be read ironically, not as a real rejection of thought or memory. After being in objective mode throughout the entire retreat, Frederic allows his mind to go into subjective mode in remembering and thinking about Catherine.

199:17 not thinking only feeling: That is, being in the subjective mode.

200:1 You: Frederic shifts into the second person through most of the rest of this paragraph.

200:5–6 seeing now very clearly and coldly—not so coldly as clearly and emptily: Frederic recognizes that he must not allow his subjective feelings to overwhelm him, at least not just yet. He still has a good journey ahead of him before he can be reunited with Catherine, and even then he and she will have to face the problem of how to evade the authorities and get out of Italy. Thus, objectivity (seeing very clearly) will remain essential. He retracts the word *coldly* because he also understands that the warmth of his feelings for Catherine are the whole point of his survival now. So he changes the word to *emptily,* suggesting that for the time being, he needs to set aside (set outside himself) his feelings, so that they do not interfere with what he must do in order to get back to Catherine alive.

200:24–25 **not my show any more . . . bloody train:** *Show,* like *theatre of war,* is probably a British figure of speech from World War I, where Hemingway met British military personnel—a "stiff-upper-lip" understatement associating a severe military engagement with a mere entertainment. See entry 26:37–27:10. *Bloody* is, of course, another well-known Britishism—an expletive intensifier considered very obscene in the nineteenth century and through the Great War, similar to the way *fucking* is used today, although *bloody* has become much milder in usage since then. The bankrupt British alcoholic Mike Campbell uses the word excessively in *The Sun Also Rises.*

200:25 **Mestre:** See entry 60:20. Frederic will ride the train for about 30 miles before arriving in Mestre. From there, he will need to catch another train and travel an additional 160 miles to Milan.

200:27 **Piani would tell them they had shot me:** That is, Frederic assumes that when Piani rejoins the ambulance unit, he will tell the authorities Carabinieri shot Frederic at the Tagliamento bridge. However, since the Carabinieri would not have Frederic's papers to record that he was executed, they may report him as drowned or missing.

200:29–30 **I wondered what they would hear in the States:** Another third-person plural pronoun, *they,* has a different antecedent here—in this case Frederic's family in America. It is one of the few instances in the novel where he gives them a passing thought and the second time he has referred to them coldly as "the States."

200:31–37 **what had become of the priest . . . Anyone would worry:** This passage is reminds us of the importance of the priest and Rinaldi to Frederic and his growth and development as a person. Neither of them receives more importance than the other in his thoughts, though Rinaldi receives a bit more attention here, specifically as to Frederic's belief that he does not have syphilis.

200:38 **I was not made to think:** This only shows how unsuccessful are Frederic's attempts to keep himself from thinking. The whole of this short chapter consists of his thoughts.

201:4 **It was getting dark:** The night of 29–30 October 1917 approaches as chapter 32 and Book Three come to an end.

BOOK FOUR

CHAPTER 33

205:1 I dropped off the train in Milan: Book Four, like Book Two, begins with Frederic arriving by train in Milan. Books One, Three, and Five, in contrast, all begin ominously, with somber descriptions of the fall of the year. This difference between the odd- and even-numbered books highlights the dichotomy the novel presents between the brutalities of the world, which dominate the odd-numbered books, and the idyllic nature of Frederic and Catherine's love, which dominates the even-numbered ones. It would now seem to be Tuesday 30 October 1917. However, later references imply that the date is Wednesday 31 October, which could only be explained if Frederic has spent an extra day in Mestre that Hemingway has chosen not to relate to us (see entry 217:4–5). At any rate, from this point forth, there is less necessity that the story consistently match the historical chronology.

205:4 I went in for some coffee: In the original manuscript, Hemingway wrote and crossed out, "I had gotten one train in Mestre and ridden it as far as Verona all the way. I had very good luck" (JFK item 64). This would seem to indicate that Frederic has taken more than one train from Mestre to Milan, a fact that may also help to explain the unaccounted-for extra day in the chronology.

205:7–8 drank a glass of coffee and ate a piece of bread: The first food Frederic has had in about thirty-six hours, since he and Piani had sausages and wine in the farmhouse south of Udine.

205:11 grappa: See entry 15:15.

205:13 "On me": Mark Cirino points out that this is another instance where Hemingway falters in translating the Italian that Frederic and the bartender are speaking here ("You Don't Know" 54). There is no literal Italian equivalent for the English phrase *on me*, which, of course, means that the bartender is offering to pay for the drink or give it to Frederic for free. In the Italian translation of *A Farewell to Arms*, by Fernanda Pivano, the Italian phrase used to mean *on me* is *offro io,* which translates literally to *I offer* (211).

243

206:12 **"You are a South American?"** Once again Frederic is mistaken for something other than what he is, part of the recurrent motif of his questionable identity. In this instance, he is still wearing the uniform of the Italian army, with which he no longer identifies, and is fleeing from the Carabinieri, who took him for a German disguised as an Italian. He knows he needs to get out of the uniform into civilian clothes and establish a new identity. The bar proprietor does not know Frederic personally, but, although he mistakes his nationality, he clearly recognizes that Frederic is a deserter, and he sympathizes with him. His offers to Frederic are extraordinarily generous.

206:14–15 **"Speak Spanish?" "A little":** This exchange provides us a small rare fact about Frederic's backstory: he can speak a little Spanish. Earlier, we were told that he would like to go to Spain if there were no war. See entry 32:2.

206:25 **"I value the address of a friend":** Frederic's use of "I value" mimics and connotes the Italian phrase *Io voglio,* meaning *I want.* Mark Cirino contributed to this note.

206:26 **ten-lira note . . . to pay for the coffee:** Frederic is paying $1.33 at the 1917 exchange rate, but that's $25.40 in 2017 (Williamson). So he is either expecting to receive a large amount of change or including in the ten lira his offer of buying a grappa for the proprietor of the bar, still a large overpayment. See entry 206:27.

206:27 **"Have a grappa with me":** As elsewhere in Hemingway, drinking together is a bonding experience, in this case an offer of friendship and token of appreciation for all that the proprietor of the bar is offering him. See, for example, Jake Barnes and Bill Gordon sharing wine with Basques on the bus ride to Burguete in chapter 11 of *The Sun Also Rises* (104–05).

207:4 **"I can give you papers":** The proprietor has obviously performed similar services for other deserters. He is offering Frederic fraudulent leave papers that would help him explain to the Carabinieri what he is doing away from the front.

207:7 **"I have papers":** In the original manuscript, Hemingway wrote and then crossed out a long exchange in which Frederic requests leave papers and a *tessera* (identity papers) from the barman (JFK item 64). Apparently, Hemingway decided that this would have unnecessarily complicated the plot, so he removed the complication.

207:25 **"Have you had breakfast?"** In spite of his hunger and having eaten only a "piece of bread" (205:8), Frederic turns down the opportunity to eat a real breakfast for free with the porter and his wife, presumably because he is in a rush to change his clothes and find Catherine.

207:33 **"The English lady nurse"**: This may be confirmation that Catherine is English rather than Scottish, although it is also possible that Frederic would use the term *English* to refer to anyone from Great Britain. See entries 99:32 and 110:8–10.

207:38 **Stresa**: See entry 124:16.

208:5 **ten-lira note**: Frederic is offering to the hospital porter the equivalent of $25.40 in today's terms to pay for the porter's silence and protection from the police, but the porter refuses it (Williamson).

208:11 **"We are dumb"**: The porter is promising Frederic that he and his wife will tell no one that they have seen him.

208:17–18 **Porta Magenta**: This district, a half mile west of Milan's city center, was named for one of the city gates that were part of the city's Roman walls. The gate itself was demolished in the nineteenth century, but the district retained the name.

208:31 **"They intern you"**: Simmons explains that the Swiss will place certain restrictions on aliens seeking refuge in their neutral country during wartime.

208:37 **a great flop at Piacenza**: See entry 104:30. In chapter 19, Simmons is mentioned as having returned to Milan after singing in Piacenza, where he had sung *Tosca* and described it as "wonderful." Here he is either more honest and retracts that statement or is referring to a later singing engagement that did not go so well.

209:2 **Lyrico**: The Teatro Lirico was Milan's second opera house, designed and built by Giuseppe Piermarini, who also designed and built the Scala at the same time. The Lirico opened 21 August 1779, just over a year later than the Scala. The two theaters were less than half a mile apart in central Milan, the Scala lying to the north of the Duomo and Galleria and the Lirico to the south. The Lirico closed in 1998, but an often delayed and expensive renovation project began in 2009. As of late 2018, the theater remains closed.

209:5 **"I don't know"**: Of course Frederic knows he is in a bad mess. He is being reticent with everyone he meets, for fear that they might reveal his whereabouts to the authorities.

209:6 **if you don't want:** In the original manuscript, Hemingway added then crossed out, "Have you killed some Dago?" (JFK item 64). For *Dago,* see entry 57:32.

209:7 **"bloody front":** In this meeting, Simmons uses a variety of expressions that give us the sense that he is British. Besides *bloody,* other seeming Britishisms include *Not a bit of it* (209:12) and *My dear fellow,* repeated six times. In chapter 19, nothing in any of Simmons's remarks sounds British. When he calls Ettore Moretti "just a wop from Frisco" he sounds very American (104:39).

209:14 **"You're about my size":** This is another confusing detail regarding Simmons. In chapter 19, the singer is described as "fat" and "shopworn around the nose and mouth as though he had hayfever" (104:28–29). Although Frederic never describes himself in any physical detail, given the degree of his strenuous physical activities, we can assume that he is fit and trim, certainly not fat. Thus, given Simmons's new British manner of speaking and description here as about the same size as Frederic, we wonder if Hemingway simply forgot his earlier characterization of Simmons.

However, if we recall that Simmons has been singing in Italy under the stage name Enrico DelCredo (Henry of the Creed), Hemingway seems not to have forgotten that he wished to link Frederic with Simmons in a significant way involving the question of faith. Why else would he have him dress in Simmons's clothes? Later, the disguise does little to fool the authorities, who recognize him as a deserter in Stresa. In sum, the details associated with Simmons seem more likely to add up to bad faith rather than good faith—certainly little reason for us to declare that Simmons reinforces an image of Frederic as a man of Christian faith.

209:15 **"I've clothes but they're all at Rome":** Frederic's clothes are in Rome because he was studying architecture there before the war.

209:16 **"It's a filthy place":** Among Italian cities, Hemingway seems not to have held Rome in the same high esteem as Milan and Venice. Earlier, Frederic says he does not like Rome because it is "hot and full of fleas" (65:36–37).

209:18 **"I wanted to be an architect":** We are three-quarters through the book before we learn why Frederic was in Italy when the war started: he was studying architecture in Rome. While Frederic's studying architecture does not play a significant thematic role, it may be a nod to Hemingway's friend and fellow writer John Dos Passos, who studied architecture in Spain in 1916 before volunteering as an ambulance driver in World War I. It is worth noting that in a review of *A Farewell to Arms,* Dos Passos used a little architectural terminology to describe Hemingway's novel as "the best written book that has seen the light in America for many a long day.... The book is a firstrate piece of craftsmanship by a man who knows his job. It gives you the sort of pleasure line by line that you get from handling a piece of wellfinished carpenter's work" (qtd. in *Letters 4* xxix). In "A Way You'll Never Be," one of Hemingway's war stories set in Italy, the Italian army captain Paravicini is an architect (*CSS* 308). In his book-length study of Hemingway's work, Mark Cirino argues that Frederic's passion for architecture is only truly revealed by the way he carefully structures his story (*Thought in Action* chap. 3). In *Death in the Afternoon,* Hemingway argues that "Prose is architecture, not interior decoration, and the Baroque is over" (191).

209:28 **Helvetia:** Another name for Switzerland, derived from the Helvetii, the tribe that inhabited the Alpine region in Roman times.

209:38 **"Africana":** As Miriam Mandel has stated, *Africana* or *L'Africaine* (*The African Woman*) is an opera by Giacomo Meyerbeer with a libretto by Augustin Eugène Scribe dealing with fictional events in the life of Portuguese explorer Vasco da Gama (*Facts in the Fictions,* 115). It is most likely that Simmons sings here part of the most famous aria from the opera, "*Pays merveilleux . . . O, paradis*" (Wonderful country, Oh paradise), sung in the play by da Gama (a part for a tenor like Simmons). The opera explores the clash between European Christian culture and Africa's pagan culture, and da Gama is clearly torn between the two, embodied in his love for the two beautiful women in the story—the European Inès and the African Sélika. In the end, although spellbound by the wonders of the new land, da Gama chooses Inès and leaves Sélika heartbroken and suicidal. In short, Hemingway alludes once more to an opera, as he did earlier to *Tosca,* that dramatizes the conflict between Christian faith and the non-Christian material world. See entry 104:30.

CHAPTER 34

211:1 **I felt a masquerader:** In a sense, Frederic has been a masquerader through much of the novel, if by *masquerader* we mean a person who does not have a clear identity. He has been borrowing the identity of an ambulance driver for the Italian army, but now, having cast that aside, he must come to terms with his true self. It is understandable that the transition is not easy, especially if he is still unsure to what he is transitioning. But Catherine will complete his identity once they are reunited.

211:3–4 **ticket at Milan for Stresa:** Today, the fifty-five-mile train ride from Milan's Central Station to Stresa takes about an hour and costs about $10 for a second-class ticket.

211:4–5 **I could not wear Sim's hat, but his clothes were fine:** We are not told if Sim's hat is too large or too small for Frederic, but we are still left puzzled how Frederic could fit in the clothes of man described earlier as "fat" (104:28).

211:7–8 **Lombard country:** Lombardy, the northcentral region of Italy, of which Milan is the capital.

211:9 **did not think much of me:** In the original manuscript, Hemingway wrote and crossed out "looked at me scornfully. I felt they were right" (JFK item 64).

211:11–12 **In the old days I would have . . . picked a fight:** This statement provides a measure of Frederic's growth in character, from the immaturity of his earlier days to his relative maturity now.

211:12 **Gallarate:** A northwestern suburb of Milan about halfway between Milan and Stresa.

211:13–14 **I had the paper . . . did not want to read about the war:** Frederic's disinterest suggests he may have the paper as part of his disguise and his new persona as a civilian.

211:14–15 **I had made a separate peace:** Frederic anticipates by about six weeks the popular use of the term *separate peace*, although Hemingway, writing in 1928, would have been very familiar with the term. It comes naturally out of the treaty that the allies of Great Britain, France, Italy, Japan, and Russia, signed on 30 November 1915, declaring that none of the allies were "to conclude peace separately during the present war" (Grey et al.). Frederic, as an inveterate reader of newspapers, would have been familiar with the treaty. The term *separate peace* became widely used, when, after the Bolshevik Revolution in November 1917, Russia reneged on its obligations and dropped out of the war by making a separate peace with the Central Powers of Germany, Austria-Hungary, Bulgaria, and Turkey on 15 December 1917. As Frederic rides the train to Stresa on 30 or 31 October 1917, the Bolshevik Revolution is still in progress, and Russia's "separate peace" has not yet been negotiated. Nevertheless, we do not have to think of this as an anachronism, since Frederic is certainly writing his story well after December 1917, possibly as late as 1928, so he can comfortably assume that his readers understand the irony in his use of the term.

Hemingway had already used the term *a separate peace* in the chapter 6 vignette of *In Our Time*, originally written in 1923. In the vignette, Nick Adams lies wounded during a battle between the Italian and Austrian units, and he attempts a joke shared with a fellow wounded soldier named Rinaldi: "Senta *Rinaldi. Senta. You and me we've made a separate peace*" (*CSS* 106). The vignette is also not anachronistic because the battle in which Nick and Rinaldi have been engaged almost certainly occurs in 1918, long enough after the Russian "separate peace" for the term to be in common usage.

John Knowles used the term for his 1959 novel *A Separate Peace*, which takes place during World War II.

211:18 **The season had been over a long time:** Stresa is most popular in the summer, and its tourist hotels are now diminished at the beginning of the fall and its rains. In fact, Baedeker's *Italy: From the Alps to Naples* 1928 states that the Grand Hôtel & des Isles Borromées was closed from November to 15 March (15).

212:2 **The Grand-Hôtel & des Isles Borromées:** Hemingway spells the name precisely as it is spelled in Baedeker's *Italy: From the Alps to Naples* 1928. Today the hotel website gives the name as "Grand Hotel des Iles Borromées." The premier luxury hotel on the south shore of Lake Maggiore in Stresa, established by the Omarini brothers, opened with 120 rooms on 21 March 1863. The building was enlarged in 1868 and again in 1912 to accommodate 300 beds, according to Baedeker's. The hotel remained open throughout the Great War and continues today, trumpeting its connection to Hemingway's novel. The website declares, "In September 1918, the American writer Ernest Hemingway arrived in Stresa for the first time at the age of 19, recovering from a war wound. Reminiscing about the beauty of the place, Hemingway, set part of his novel 'Farewell to arms' in the hotel" ("150 Years of History").

The Borromean Isles (Isles Borromées), which lend their name to the Grand Hotel in Stresa, are famously beautiful islands in Lake Maggiore opposite Stresa. See entry 124:19. The Boromeo family owned them since the twelfth century, and they are associated with San Carlo Borromeo (Saint Charles Borromeo) (1538–1584), the Roman Catholic Archbishop of Milan from 1564 to 1584, who led the Counter-Reformation in the Catholic Church to eliminate corruption and restore discipline and morals (Stoneback, "Hemingway's Stresa" 134). A 112-foot high statue of Saint Charles Borromeo, the *Sancarlone,* constructed in 1697, stands at the southern end of Lake Maggiore near the town of Arona.

212:8 **I took a good room:** Frederic does not share with us what he pays for his "good room," but during the offseason in wartime, he undoubtedly got a good deal. In Baedeker's *Italy: From the Alps to Naples* 1909, rooms at the Grand Hotel are said to range from 5 to 15 lire, or just $1–3 at the 1913 exchange rate (the earliest available data at Samuel Williamson's *MeasuringWorth.com*). In 2017 terms, that would be a range of $25.50 to $76.50, an incredible bargain for a luxury hotel. Prices have since inflated considerably. A check of prices for a night in November 2017 revealed rooms starting at $250 and going up to $3,600 for a single night in the ultra-luxurious Hemingway Suite. Although Hemingway stayed at the hotel and signed the guestbook in 1948 as "an old client," there is no evidence that he stayed there when he went to Stresa on convalescent leave in 1918. In all likelihood, as H. R. Stoneback suggests, he stayed at the small hotel near the station where the barman tells him Catherine and Helen are staying ("Hemingway's Stresa" 133–34). See entry 213:4.

212:11 ***letto matrimoniale:*** Italian for a double bed, literally "matrimonial bed."

212:14 **salted almonds and potato chips:** Frederic's diet for the time being remains something less than fully nutritional, in spite of his certain hunger. He has not mentioned having taken any other meal during the day he has spent in Milan visiting the porter and his wife and then Simmons before taking the train to Stresa since the piece of bread and coffee and two grappas at breakfast time.

212:16 ***borghese:*** Short for *borghese vestiti,* literally *bourgeois clothes* but here meaning *civilian clothes* or *out of uniform.* The barman, whose name we later learn is Emilio (228:13), knows Frederic from the past and has seen him previously in his military uniform.

212:22–23 **"Trolling this time of year you catch some beautiful pieces":** The barman's statement is another instance of Hemingway's bilingualism and humor. The barman presumably uses the Italian phrase *bei pezzi* to mean *beautiful pieces,* with perhaps a pun on *pesce* for *fish* but also, as one male to another, adding some sexual innuendo, referring to attractive women. The barman knows Frederic in his previous identity as a playboy.

212:27–28 **my relatives had stopped sending it:** Frederic provides another possible indication of estrangement between him and his family.

212:29–30 **two English girls:** See entries 99:32 and 110:8–10. In using the word *English* here, Frederic is assuming that the English language is a more common indicator of nationality in this context, where some Italians might not distinguish among English, Irish, Welsh, and Scotch British.

212:35 **"One of them is my wife":** Although this is not technically true, Frederic is in the process of establishing his new identity—Catherine's husband. He is not just stating this in order to present an acceptable public image that will allow him and Catherine to cohabitate at the hotel. He is putting on a figurative new set of clothes and getting used to its fit.

212:37 **"The other is my wife":** The barman makes a "stupid joke," assuming Frederic, as the playboy the barman used to know, is lying about having a wife but redeems himself with his apology and assistance in finding Catherine.

213:4 **a little hotel near the station:** H. R. Stoneback has identified two small hotels that existed near the Stresa station in 1917–18: the Hotel Continental and the Hotel Croce Bianca ("Hemingway's Stresa" 134). Stoneback argues in favor of the Croce Bianca (White Cross) as the likely choice for the one in the novel, the name being associated with the Knights of Malta, the Roman Catholic religious order of Hospitallers, whose banner is a white cross on a red background (134). Whichever hotel it is, Stoneback plausibly suggests it was the one at which Hemingway stayed when he visited Stresa while on convalescent leave in 1918. Unlike the Grand Hôtel and des Isles Borromées, neither the Continental nor the Croce Bianca remains in operation today.

213:5 **"How about some sandwiches?"** After salted almonds, potato chips, and two martinis, Frederic finally decides to eat something closer to real food.

213:10–11 **I ate three and drank a couple more martinis . . . so cool and clean:** We might wonder what kind of sandwiches he eats, but he is clearly more impressed with the four martinis he imbibes. Although there are, of course, variations, the standard recipe today for a dry martini is gin with a splash of vermouth. A wet martini may have three parts gin and one part vermouth. However, early twentieth-century recipes generally called for much more vermouth in the martini, as much as one half

(Barnes). The coolness and cleanness of the martinis, which Frederic twice emphasizes (212:15 and 213:11), underscores the continuation of the ritual cleansing away of the war. The martinis make Frederic feel "civilized" and are contrasted with the baseness of the red wine, grappa, bad coffee, bread and cheese he had been consuming in the army.

213:14 **did not think at all:** After all the objective reasoning he has had to do in order to survive the retreat and his desertion to this point, Frederic needs a respite, if only temporary, until he will require more reasoning skills to get himself and Catherine to Switzerland.

213:19–21 **the feeling of a boy who . . . has played truant:** Frederic remains clearly ambivalent about his desertion (as he is about so many things), and this comment may make us wonder if he believes he has matured very much, comparing himself, as he does, to a truant schoolboy. However, this is almost certainly a transitional feeling, subjective as it is, since he has left his old assumed identity in the war and is seeking something truer, which he believes he will find in his relationship to Catherine, as her husband-lover. Without Catherine's presence, he may still feel like a masquerader in this new identity.

213:22 **Catherine and Helen Ferguson:** All previous editions have an extra space before this paragraph, indicating a gap in the narration of unspecified duration, in this case presumably long enough for Frederic to finish his sandwiches and martinis and walk to the "little hotel near the station" (213:4). Both the holograph manuscript and typescript at the JFK Library show that Hemingway clearly intended the extra space (JFK items 64 and 65).

213:30–31 **I sat down at the table:** In the manuscript, the page ends here, with the quote from Henry James and the reference to "the survivor of a great calamity," which we discuss in the entry on Rejected Epigraphs at the beginning of this volume, on the back of the page. In addition, Hemingway listed some potential titles—"The World's Room," "A Separate Piece [sic]," and "Hill of Heaven." For discussion of alternate titles to *A Farewell to Arms*, see Roos, "Appendix A: Alternate Titles."

213:32–33 **"You're a fine mess. . . . Have you eaten?"** This is some wordplay and humor. Ferguson's calling Frederic a "fine mess" unintentionally puns on the fact that she and Catherine are at *mess*, the military term for *dinner*. Her displeasure at seeing Frederic is immediately counterbalanced with her humorous yet mannerly attention to his well-being—concern that he has eaten.

213:37 **mufti:** A Britishism for civilian as opposed to military clothing. The word originates from the Arabic word *mufti,* an Islamic scholar. It came into common British usage in the early nineteenth century, perhaps because off-duty British officers frequently wore Eastern-style gowns and tasseled caps. Frederic, of course, is dressed in the European American–style suit of Ralph Simmons, with his own new hat.

213:38 **"I'm in the Cabinet":** Frederic's flippant reply—that is, I'm a high-ranking government official, usually a civilian—draws no laughter from Ferguson, who extends her *mess* motif.

214:6 **"I get in my own messes":** Here Catherine assumes full responsibility for her actions, for better or worse—a statement that supports Sandra Spanier's feminist reading of her as the novel's "code hero"—an exemplar of strength, integrity, and grace under pressure.

214:13–14 **"A snake with an Italian uniform: with a cape around your neck":** Labeling Frederic a "snake" recalls Rinaldi's labeling himself "the snake of reason." See entry 149:15. Ferguson, in this scene, unwittingly highlights the conflict of reason and faith or objectivity and subjectivity, taking the side of subjectivity (her legitimate concern for Catherine's well-being) against what she senses as Frederic's calculating and self-centered objectivity, his Italianate serpenthood. Catherine's cape, which has been mentioned repeatedly (see, for example, entries 129:1–2 and 133:22) is here treated not as a protective device but as part of the novel's disguise motif. In Ferguson's view, Frederic has destroyed Catherine's innocence and led to her being cast out of Paradise.

214:27–28 **"you're God knows how many months gone with child":** Ferguson reminds us of the powerful image appearing in chapter 1, where soldiers march as though "six months gone with child." Hemingway reuses the phrase here fully aware of the implications, which are much the same as they are in chapter 1. See entry 4:11–18. In other words, we are reminded of the foreshadowing of the death of the child Catherine is carrying, of the conjoined images of birth and death, and of the biblical Annunciation by the Angel Gabriel. Just as in chapter 1 there is supreme irony with the image of the soldiers, whose leather boxes of ammunition underneath their capes make them appear to be "with child," there is irony here in the way Ferguson plays the role of Elizabeth to the Virgin Mother, yet there is none of the joy of the Gospel of Luke, none of the "Blessed art thou among women and blessed is the fruit of thy womb." Instead Ferguson thinks the situation is "dreadful."

214:37–39 **"I hate you. . . . You dirty sneaking American Italian":** Ferguson spits this venom at Frederic, and by labeling him an Italian, she echoes Rinaldi's line. See entry 57:20–23. Frederic is silent throughout this exchange, probably seething with resentment at Ferguson's negativity, yet perhaps recognizing there is some legitimacy in what she is saying.

215:3 **"You're unreasonable, Fergy"**: Catherine, the novel's holder of the middle ground between reason and faith, tries to bring her friend back to that middle ground. In Ferguson's defense, the rest of the novel reveals to us that, even though her reaction to Frederic here is highly emotional, as she admits, Ferguson is not entirely unreasonable. She correctly senses that the outcome will not be a good one for Frederic and Catherine. Frederic (with Catherine's complicity) has put Catherine in jeopardy and should be held accountable for what happens to her.

215:31 **sick:** In the original manuscript, Hemingway wrote and crossed out "a little tired" (JFK item 64).

215:32–34 **"you want to leave me . . . and this is how it is"**: Ferguson's displeasure results from more than her dislike of Frederic and the damage she fears he will do to Catherine. As she explains here, this is supposed to be a pleasure trip to the Italian lakes for her and Catherine, and she rightly understands that the trip has been blown apart and that Catherine will leave her by herself, flying into Frederic's arms. For a discussion of the lesbian implications of Ferguson's feelings for Catherine, see Miriam Mandel's "Ferguson and Lesbian Love." See also Debra Moddelmog's "We Live in a Country Where Nothing Makes Any Difference."

216:4 **That night at the hotel:** All previous editions of the novel have an extra space before the beginning of this paragraph. Both the holograph manuscript and the typescript have indications that Hemingway desired extra space here (JFK items 64 and 65). The space helps signal the narrative change to Frederic's "separate peace." Eliminating it makes that change less evident.

216:5 **our shoes outside the door:** Leaving shoes outside the door is a custom in good hotels, like the Grand Hotel in Stresa, so that the staff will clean and polish the shoes during the night and return them for the next day's use. Hemingway's 1925 short story "Mr. and Mrs. Elliot" includes such a reference. On his wedding night, Hubert Elliot seems to find the shoes outside the Boston hotel room doors sexually exciting, but when he returns to his room, he finds his new bride asleep, and he is afraid to wake her (*CSS* 124).

216:15–16 **It has only happened to me like that once:** Frederic again reminds us of the novel's retrospective narration, indicating that an undefined amount of time has passed since the events described. He may be suggesting that he has had other relationships since Catherine but that no other relationship has provided him with the same kind of sensation, that they could "feel alone when we were together, alone against the others" (216:14–15). In the next sentence, he explains, "I have been alone while I was with many girls and that is the way you can be most lonely," with no time indication as to whether this was before or after his relationship with Catherine.

216:19–24 I know that the night is not the same as the day . . . an even better time: While the passage immediately following this one has received more attention from commentators, these two sentences are at least as important thematically, if not more so. As in other parts of the novel, Frederic is speaking years after the events take place, as the narrator rather than as the protagonist. Enough time has passed to broaden and deepen his perspective on the things that have happened to him.

Significantly, Frederic begins with the declaration "I know." There is no lack of certainty here, even though he means this in subjective, not objective terms. What he is about to tell us he is sure of. What he knows is the subjective difference between the night and the day. He has tried to explain this difference before, unsuccessfully, with the priest. See entry 12:15–17. Even here, he says that "the things of the night cannot be explained in the day, because they do not then exist." This does not mean that the things of the night are not true. There *is* such a thing as subjective truth.

Frederic here establishes that now, at the time of writing the novel, as opposed to the time of the events, he clearly understands the distinction between these two realms, that they are different, perhaps irreconcilably different, but during his relationship with Catherine he found a way to unite the two, so that "there was *almost* no difference in the night except that it was an even better time" (emphasis added). Frederic *knows* all this now; he has learned it through his relationship with Catherine. However, as he speaks to us now as narrator, he also understands that the unification of the night and the day is an extraordinarily rare experience that has only happened once to him, in the love he shared with Catherine.

216:23 almost no difference: In the original manuscript, Hemingway wrote and then crossed out, "almost no terror in the night and no danger and" (JFK item 64).

216:24–30 If people bring so much courage. . . . no special hurry: This passage, one of the two most frequently cited in the novel (along with the "abstract words" piece at 161:13–27), is deservedly memorable and prepares us for the conclusion, where Catherine is both broken and killed. A key to understanding what Frederic and Hemingway are getting at here is the way God (for whom "all things are possible") is depersonalized in the phrase *the world* and the pronoun *it*. A major part of what has concerned Frederic in the novel is whether or not it is subjectively true that God is in control of all events that happen in this world. Certain elements of this passage have the ring of objective truth ("the world breaks everyone"), even if we may wish to argue with them. Frederic distinguishes between breaking and killing in a way that suggests that *breaking* has to do with a person's psychological health and *killing* has to do with physical death. In that light, he is saying that those who do not break down psychologically will be killed more quickly than those who do. This, of course, ascribes a very malevolent willfulness to the world that, by extension, must apply to a divine omnipotence that seems to have little compassion for the conscious beings it has created and for whom it bears responsibility.

Many readers of this passage have selectively pulled out the sentence "The world breaks every one and afterward many are strong at the broken places" and used it as an inspiration for strength in adversity—putting it on bumper stickers, posters, coffee cups, mobile phone cases. However, taking that sentence out of its bitter context distorts its meaning. "Those that will not break it kills," Frederic tells us, clearly implying Divine displeasure at human resistance to Godly power. Refusing to break seems to be taken as an act of defiance of God's will, and the omnipotent God enacts His vengeance on those we normally assume to be the finest humans in His creation: "the very good and the very gentle and the very brave." With those descriptors, Frederic is certainly thinking of Catherine. At the same time, psychologically breaking and healing may contribute to longevity in life, which may be Frederic's predicament as the survivor of this tragedy. He knows that he will be killed also eventually, but "there will be no special hurry." Ultimately, there is little if any indication here that Frederic has learned to love God the way that the priest does.

Readers of F. Scott Fitzgerald may be reminded of a place in *The Beautiful and Damned,* in which Anthony Patch attempts to console his mistress, Dorothy Raycroft, telling her that life "just hurts people and hurts people until finally it hurts them so that they can't be hurt ever any more. That's the last and worst thing it does" (215). Fitzgerald's words sound like a rough early draft of Hemingway's, and it is small wonder that, when Hemingway finally and reluctantly allowed Fitzgerald to read the typescript for his new novel, Fitzgerald, although critical of many other aspects of the book, highlighted this passage, calling it "one of the most beautiful pages in all English literature" (JFK item 77).

Fitzgerald had many flaws, but he had a brilliantly fine-tuned ear for good writing. However, he mistakenly believed the passage would be better at the end of the novel. Hemingway did attempt to follow his advice (see alternate endings nos. 34 and 35 in appendix 2 of the Hemingway Library edition, 317–18). Finally, though, he chose not to put the passage at the end but to leave it where he originally intended it, here in chapter 34. It was a wise choice. Putting it at the end would have stamped the novel with a bitter and sardonic tone that would have deprived it of much of its lovely ambiguity. It works far better in this tender moment at the conclusion of this paragraph describing the depth and value of their love in the midst of Frederic and Catherine's first night together following his desertion.

216:31 **I remember waking:** Both the holograph manuscript and the typescript have indications that Hemingway wanted extra space before the beginning of this paragraph (JFK items 64 and 65). The first Scribner's edition, the Modern Library edition, the 1948 illustrated edition, and the Everyman's Library edition of *A Farewell to Arms* have such an additional space. However, the 1969 Scribner's edition begins the paragraph at the top of page 250, with no asterisks to indicate extra space between paragraphs.

The word *remember* is another reminder that this is a Proustian retrospective narration, told to us after an undefined but no doubt considerable passage of time. As James Nagel has emphasized, instances like this one give us reason not to see the novel as a realistic presentation of people and events, but as a tale filtered through the memories and consciousness of a possibly flawed narrator, Frederic Henry (171).

216:32–33 **sunlight . . . The rain had stopped:** Appropriately, for this brief spell of love and tranquility, the ominous rain has subsided, to be replaced by a welcoming sunlight. On this day, at least, all is well.

216:39–217:3 **"How are you, darling?" . . . "Do you want breakfast?"** The genuineness of their love is evident in their first words the next morning, which express the concern each has for the other. Catherine begins by asking him how he is and rather than answering that question, Frederic asks her how *she* feels and then if she wants breakfast—indications that he is learning how to love according to the priest's definition. See entry 62:27–29.

217:4–5 **November sunlight:** By a strict accounting of the days reported in the novel, this ought to be the morning of 31 October. If Hemingway intends this to be the first day of November, either he has lost track of his days or there has been an extra unreported day during the retreat and Frederic's escape. The only point in the narrative where an extra day could occur would be in Mestre, where Frederic tells us only that he "fixed the dates" on "an old order of movement." See entry 217:22–23. It is possible he had to wait a day to catch a train that would carry him back to Milan. At the same time, perhaps Hemingway was well aware of the discrepancy in dates, so Frederic's "fixing" of them is his own private joke on us all. The discrepancy recalls the confusion of the calendar in *The Sun Also Rises*.

217:9 **"I don't want the paper now":** Frederic is still avoiding reading about the war. See entry 211:13–14. He will resume reading about it later, but for now he prefers to bask in the warmth of their love.

217:13 **"if I ever get it straight in my head":** Frederic understands that it will take time for him to get strong enough in his "broken places" in order to relate this tale, either to Catherine or to us. That he is now telling it indicates that he has gotten at least enough of it straight so that he can share the story with the world.

217:19 **"how did you come from Mestre to Milan?"** Catherine's question implies that in the night Frederic told her the story of his retreat experiences and desertion up to the point of his arrival in Mestre, where he would need to catch another train to Milan. From there he apparently purchased a ticket and rode as a normal passenger.

217:22–23 **"I fixed the dates on it in Mestre":** This is another reminder of the relevance of time, which is not always absolute or fixed (see entry 217:4–5). Hemingway perhaps "fixes" this date as 1 November because he wants to suggest a new month and a new beginning for Frederic and Catherine.

217:35 **"Switzerland is down the lake":** The border of Switzerland is northward from Stresa. Most people would probably describe that as "up the lake."

217:37 **It was clouding over outside and the lake was darkening:** These ominous signs perhaps produce Frederic's dark thoughts in the next line, about living "like criminals" (217:38).

218:8 **A little while later:** Although the holograph manuscript has no extra space before this paragraph, the typescript has a hand-drawn horizontal line to indicate the need for extra space (JFK item 65). All previous editions have followed Hemingway's wishes and have an extra space before this paragraph. The gap would imply a passage of time during which Frederic and Catherine again make love.

218:8–9 **"You don't feel like a criminal do you?"** After their apparent lovemaking, Catherine continues their conversation, revealing that she, at least, is still aware that as an unmarried couple their sharing a *letto matrimoniale* (double bed) would not meet the approval of respectable society in 1917. Frederic only feels like a criminal in that he is wanted for desertion from the army.

218:19 **"Let's not think about anything":** The chapter ends with Frederic's exhortation to continue to bask in the subjectivity of their love. He probably recognizes that this can only be a temporary break from objectivity.

CHAPTER 35

219:4–5 The army had not stood at the Tagliamento . . . falling back to the Piave: In the original manuscript, Hemingway introduced this with "I could not keep away from the papers" then crossed it out (JFK item 64). This is where the novel gives up strict adherence to the historical timeline. The latest possible date for this moment in the novel is 1 November 1917, if we grant Frederic an extra day in Mestre. See entry 217:4–5. Here he reads in the newspaper that the army is "falling back to the Piave." However, Germans and Austrians crossed the Tagliamento at the northern bridge at Cornino only on 2 November, and a general order to retreat to the Piave was not issued until 4 November (Schindler 260; Thompson 320). So Hemingway is clearly telescoping events, and exact dates become difficult to determine from here until near the end of the novel.

The Piave River is about thirty miles west of the Tagliamento River, flowing across the Venetian Plain southward into the Adriatic Sea. The place names in this paragraph can be traced to Hemingway's wartime and post-wartime Italian experiences. Hemingway was seriously wounded at the Piave River near the town of Fossalta on 8 July 1918.

In a 19 November 1929 letter to Maxwell Perkins, Hemingway expressed his belief that the Austrians had not been ambitious enough in their objectives: "At the time of Caporetto the Austrian objective was The Tagliamento. If it had been Milan they would have reached there. [French General Ferdinand] Foch said their objective should have been Lyons. As it was they tried for the Tagliamento and reached the Piave and lost the war there" (*Letters 4* 156).

219:6–8 San Dona . . . lovely villas: San Donà is a town less than three miles southeast and across the Piave River from Fossalta, where Hemingway was wounded. Frederic remembers the river and the town from trains he has taken to and from the Isonzo battlefront. In this case, Frederic's memory coincides with Hemingway's. Being on the east side of the Piave, San Donà fell into Austrian hands, and during the next year, until the conclusion of the war, the city suffered near total destruction of the lovely architecture that Frederic here remembers.

219:9 **Cortina D'Ampezzo:** This popular and fashionable ski resort lies in the Dolomite Mountains. Before the war, it was and had been for centuries part of Austria, and at this point in the novel, November 1917, it remained securely in Austrian hands. Therefore, when Frederic visited it before the war, as he tells us, he was leaving Italy and traveling into Austrian territory, but until 1915, Italy and Austria were essentially allies, so there would have been little to hinder him crossing the border between the two countries. Hemingway set his early short story "Out of Season" in Cortina D'Ampezzo, basing it on a visit he and his first wife, Hadley, had made there in the spring of 1923. See entry 153:33.

219:12 **Cadore:** Hemingway probably means the commune of Pieve di Cadore, near where the road departs from the Piave River after having followed it closely for many miles. It is the birthplace of Italian painter Tiziano Vecelli (c. 1488–1576), known in English as Titian. Cadore is the name of the northernmost region of the Italian province of Belluno in northeastern Italy today, near the Austrian border.

219:13 **how the army that was up there would come down:** In the original manuscript, Hemingway followed this with "There was only the one road" then crossed it out (JFK item 64). Frederic is thinking of the logistics of transporting the large force the Italians had in the Dolomite Mountains to the north, especially the Italian Fourth Army, made up largely of Alpini troops, elite specialists in mountain fighting. Although, like the Third Army on the Carso, the Fourth Army's positions were not in danger of being overtaken by the Austrians, the army was forced to retreat to avoid being cut off by the German and Austrian advance to their south.

219:15 **Count Greffi:** As Michael Reynolds has explained, the character of Count Greffi is based on Count Giuseppi Greppi (1819–1921), a chance acquaintance Hemingway made when he visited Stresa during a convalescent leave in September 1918 (*First War* 166–69). In a 29 September 1918 letter to his family, Hemingway wrote:

> The second night I was here the Old Count Grecco [sic] who will be 100 years old in March took charge of me and introduced me to about 150 people. He is perfectly preserved, has never married, goes to bed at midnight and smokes and drinks champagne. He told me all about his dining with Maria Theresa the wife of Napoleon the 1st. He has had love affairs with all the historical women of the last century it seems and yarned at length about all of them.
>
> He took me under his wing and gave me a great send off. (*Letters 1* 145)

An extraordinary individual, Count Greppi had been a diplomat in the service of both Austria and Italy as recently as 1915. In the holograph manuscript and typescript of the novel, Hemingway used the Count's real name, "Greppi" and only changed it slightly to "Greffi" in the galley stage before publication in *Scribner's Magazine* (JFK items 64 and 65). The count's character in the novel closely follows the descriptions we get in the *Times* obituary and Hemingway's 1918 letter.

Marcelline Hemingway Sanford's memoir includes a photo of young Hemingway outdoors at Stresa with two gentlemen and a young woman. Sanford writes that on the back, Hemingway identified them as "Conte Greppie, his daughter Bianca, and the 'kid brother'" (170). However, neither of the two gentlemen in the photo resembles the photo of Count Greppi that Michael Reynolds published, nor do they appear at all close to the age of ninety-nine that Count Greppi was in 1918 (*First War* 167). It seems likely that Marcelline misunderstood Ernest's caption and that the count was not in the photo but that his brother and his brother's daughter (therefore the count's niece) were the ones pictured.

220:4 **champagne cocktails:** Philip Greene provides the following recipe for a champagne cocktail: "Place a sugar cube at the bottom of a champagne flute. Saturate the cube with Angostura bitters. Slowly fill flute with champagne" (55).

220:9 **Count Greffi was ninety-four years old:** A minor discrepancy: the real Count Greppi was ninety-eight in 1917. When Hemingway met him in 1918, he was ninety-nine. As his letter to his family correctly states, the Count would turn one hundred in March 1919. See entry 219:15.

220:10 **Metternich:** Klemens von Metternich (1773–1859) was chancellor of Austria from 1821 to 1848 and one of the country's most important historical figures of the past two hundred years. He was a particularly skilled diplomat in settling disputes and avoiding wars. According to Count Greppi's *New York Times* obituary, the count began his diplomatic career under Metternich (qtd. in Reynolds, *First War* 168). In the original manuscript, Hemingway added then crossed out, "his niece was old enough to be my mother. He was a lovely fragile" (JFK item 64).

220:11 **mustache and:** In the original manuscript, Hemingway wrote then crossed out, "many suits of clothes that he changed several times a day" (JFK item 64).

220:30 **a spinner and a heavy sinker:** According to H. R. Stoneback, Lake Maggiore fishermen prefer minnows or worms as bait for lake trout, rather than the spinner Frederic and the barman use ("Hemingway's Stresa" 135).

221:19 **"Next year they'll call my class. But I won't go":** See entry 52:8. As the war progressed, armies were forced to draft older men to replace the younger men lost in battle. The barman's opposition to the war prepares us for his later offer of his boat for Frederic and Catherine to leave Italy for Switzerland (229:18).

221:21–22 I was at the war once in Abyssinia. Nix: Abyssinia is another name for Ethiopia. Italy went to war with Ethiopia in 1894–95 over a disputed treaty, which Italy claimed made Ethiopia an Italian territory. Ironically, in that war, Germany and Austria supported Italy, Great Britain and Russia supported Ethiopia. Ethiopia defeated Italy and maintained its independence. It is no coincidence that the Ethiopian defeat enters the conversation at this moment, as Italy is in the midst of suffering another humiliating defeat. He saw no reason for the Ethiopian War, and he sees no reason for the current war. In *The Sun Also Rises,* Count Mippipopolous has two scars from arrow wounds he received in Abyssinia (60).

221:23 "I don't know. I was a fool": Once more, Frederic is unsure of why he joined the Italian army, but here, at least, is an indication that he has learned something since he was first asked this question. See entry 19:11–13. He is no longer completely at a loss to explain his enlistment. He now admits it was a foolish decision, an admission that we can regard as evidence of growth. The line reminds us of Catherine's response when Frederic asked her, during their first meeting, why she did not marry her fiancé. See entry 16:19–20.

222:3–4 "eleven o'clock. L'heure du cocktail": The bartender is expected to be on the job from 11:00 A.M., when those in the leisure class may want a drink before or with lunch. As we have seen, Frederic drinks alcohol at almost any hour of the day, but here he demurs. It is not that Frederic is averse to drinking before noon. He and the barman each had two vermouths earlier on Fishermen's Island.

222:13–14 I lay on the bed and tried to keep from thinking: In the original manuscript, Hemingway wrote and crossed out, "I realized that my life was completely empty and that outside the weather looked blacker" (JFK item 64). Even without the deleted sentence, clearly something is bothering Frederic. When he is alone, disturbing thoughts enter his mind that he must fight off, as here, perhaps still feeling like a truant schoolboy or worse, a criminal.

222:19–20 "What's the matter, darling?" "I don't know": Frederic may have made a separate peace, but he has not yet made peace with himself regarding his desertion. In a state of transition, whenever he is without Catherine he seems not to know who he is. He is struggling to understand what is going on in his own psyche.

222:36 "Othello with his occupation gone," she teased: Catherine alludes to words by the protagonist in Shakespeare's *Othello,* who is a general in the Venetian army, a great and heroic warrior. He is also a dark-skinned Moor, whose ethnicity, as he is surrounded by people of fair skin—including his employers, his wife, and his underlings—is a continual source of tension, perhaps contributing to his insecurity and the ease with which his ensign, Iago, is able to stir jealousy within him over his wife's innocent contacts with Cassio. One of Othello's most powerful speeches comes soon after Iago convinces him that his wife has been unfaithful, and the speech resonates strongly with Hemingway's novel, particularly at this moment:

O, now, for ever
Farewell the tranquil mind! farewell content!
Farewell the plumed troop, and the big wars,
That make ambition virtue! O, farewell!
Farewell the neighing steed, and the shrill trump,
The spirit-stirring drum, the ear-piercing fife,
The royal banner, and all quality,
Pride, pomp and circumstance of glorious war!
And, O you mortal engines, whose rude throats
The immortal Jove's dead clamours counterfeit,
Farewell! Othello's occupation's gone! (3.3.348–57)

Ultimately, Othello strangles his innocent wife in a jealous rage. Bickford Sylvester makes a case for the influence of Shakespeare's play on Hemingway's novel, arguing that the price of Frederic's "separate peace" is the "sacrifice of his male need to do as well as to be," and Catherine is sensitive to this, recognizing more fully perhaps than Frederic does how much he has given up in making Catherine the center of his life (178). In Sylvester's view, Othello's "Farewell content" is a more important source for the novel's title than is the poem by George Peele. This is not necessarily an antifeminist interpretation, but it is one that insists on differences between what men and women need to make them content. For perspectives similar to Sylvester's, see also Robert Solotaroff's "Sexual Identity in *A Farewell to Arms*" and John Beversluis's "Dispelling the Romantic Myth."

For a much different reading, one that views Frederic as a blissfully ignorant Othello, see Ernest Lockridge's "*Othello* as a Key to Hemingway." For yet another variant reading, one that contrasts Frederic favorably with *Othello,* see Andrew J. Wilson's "Bidding Goodbye to the Plumed Troop." While Frederic cannot be accused of murdering his lover as Othello does, he can be held indirectly accountable for Catherine's death in that he impregnated her and her pregnancy directly causes her death. Guilt over that fact is probably one motivating factor driving him to tell his story.

Hemingway also alludes to Othello's "Farewell" speech in his early unpublished story "The Passing of Pickles McCarty," or "The Woppian Way," where the narrator describes Italian poet Gabriele D'Annunzio as a "hero with his occupation gone" (JFK item 843). For more on D'Annunzio, see entry 4:11–18.

222:37 "Othello was a nigger," I said: Modern readers may cringe at this line, but we should understand that the words are Frederic's, not Hemingway's, at a point where Frederic still has much growing to do. Shakespeare merely identifies Othello as a Moor, a dark-skinned Arab-Berber of North Africa. Frederic declines Catherine's teasing comparison on racial grounds, an obvious difference but with little merit. For one thing, Frederic's occupation has primarily been healer rather than militant combatant, even though he has now killed a man. Additionally, as he states, he is not clouded by the jealousy that brings down Othello.

222:39 "be a good boy and be nice to Ferguson": Frederic's reference to Othello's jealousy perhaps brings Ferguson back to Catherine's mind, and the line reveals again her awareness of Frederic's relative immaturity. She needs him to be "a good boy."

223:4–5 "I don't think . . ." "You don't know much . . . for such a wise boy": This exchange also reveals how little awareness and sensitivity Frederic has at this point in comparison to Catherine, who knows Ferguson well and is very sensitive to her needs, as Ferguson has been to hers. Miriam Mandel takes this line as an indication that Catherine is fully aware of Ferguson's lesbian love for her, even while lacking reciprocal feelings ("Ferguson and Lesbian Love" 22).

223:12–13 She was very impressed by the hotel and the splendor of the dining room: Ferguson seems more prey to the influences of money and class than Catherine is. Frederic has conspicuously not mentioned any reaction from Catherine to the "splendor" of the hotel he has chosen.

223:14 white capri: Catherine and Frederic's beverage of choice when they are together. See entry 32:17.

223:15–16 His niece, who looked a little like my grandmother: A rare if oblique reference to Frederic, this suggests he has not completely forgotten his family, whether this thought occurs at this moment in the narrative or years later as he is writing the story.

223:17 Ferguson was very impressed: Implicit in this statement is that Catherine is not so impressed by Count Greffi. As Frederic implies, Catherine does not need the luxurious settings of the hotel or the impressive aristocratic manners of Count Greffi to be content. The wine makes them "all feel very well," but Catherine has "no need to feel any better" (223:19–20).

223:34–35 I looked strange to myself in the civilian clothes: Frederic has still not adjusted to his new civilian identity.

224:17 **walked toward me:** In the original manuscript, Hemingway added then crossed out "trembling like an electric bulb filament" (JFK item 64).

224:30 **"We could talk Italian":** Unlike most of the dialogue that Frederic has with Italians in the novel, which Hemingway renders in English translated from Italian, Frederic and the multilingual Count Greffi have begun their conversation not in Italian but in English.

224:37–38 **especially one's countrywomen:** We are to understand that the count is very experienced in matters of love. On the real Count Greppi, see entry 219:15.

225:12–13 **play for a franc a point:** Since we later learn that Count Greffi has been reading novels in French, he probably means French francs here rather than Swiss francs. A French franc at the exchange rate of 5.764 francs to a dollar was worth seventeen cents in 1917. In 2017 that would be $3.25. Frederic ends up losing by six points (225:23–24), so he will owe the Count six francs, or about one dollar, which would be worth $19.10 in 2017 (Williamson).

225:19–20 **"Should we talk Italian? . . . It is my weakness now":** From this point, we should assume that Frederic's dialogue with the count is in Italian translated into English.

225:27 **"About anything else":** Frederic is still trying to distance himself from the war and thus is unwilling to talk about it with the count.

225:33 **"'Le Feu' by a Frenchman, Barbusse":** *Le Feu: journal d'une escouade* (in English, *Under Fire: Journal of a Squad*) is a war novel by Henri Barbusse (1873–1935), published in French in December 1916 and in English in June 1917. Thus, when Frederic reads it during his stay in the hospital, the book would have been freshly published in translation. One of the earliest novels about the Great War, it realistically depicts in sometimes brutal detail French soldiers' life in the trenches. In the introduction to *Men at War*, Hemingway calls *Under Fire* the "only good war book to come out during the last war": "Its greatest quality was his courage in writing it when he did. But the writers who came after him wrote better and truer than he did. They had learned to tell the truth without screaming. Screaming, necessary though it may be to attract attention at the time, reads badly in later years" (xv).

225:33–35 **"'Mr. Britling Sees Through It.'" "No, he doesn't":** Count Greffi comically inverts the title of H. G. Wells's 1916 novel *Mr. Britling Sees It Through*, and the mistake is laden with meaning. First it gives Frederic the opportunity to reply, "No, he doesn't," meaning "No, he does not see through it." In other words, Frederic is insisting that H. G. Wells does not have insight into the meaning of things. We should forgive the count his error, because he has drunk so much champagne and because he has probably read the French translation of the novel, which was titled *Mr. Britling commence à voir clair,* which, if translated back into English literally, means "Mr. Britling begins to see clearly." The French translation was published in 1917, in time for the count to have read it, indicating, as does his reading Barbusse, that he is a man who keeps up with the most current literature. While the French title is not necessarily inaccurate based on the content of the novel, Wells's original title was intended to convey the sense that Mr. Britling, his protagonist, finds the strength and the rationale to persevere through the war, in spite of the fact that his son and others close to him have been killed in it. Specifically, *Mr. Britling Sees It Through* was published in the midst of the war with the sturdy patriotic intent of bucking up British spirit in the face of the horrors being experienced. And the book was enormously popular, not only in Britain, where it was the best-selling novel of 1916, but also in America, where it was the best-selling novel of 1917. Russian novelist Maxim Gorky called it "the finest, most courageous, truthful, and humane book written in Europe in the course of this accursed war" (qtd. in Smith 224).

So what is Frederic's problem with *Mr. Britling Sees It Through?* The book moves from Britling's naive optimism about the war to his bleak despair over the senseless waste of lives to a final affirmation of the existence of a loving God, not one who controls events of the world, but a "God of love and righteousness" (407). And so he sets himself a task of writing a treatise that will convey his positive message to the world. Earlier in the novel, Mr. Britling cries, "if I thought there was an omnipotent God who looked down on battles and deaths and all the waste and horror of this war—able to prevent these things—doing them to amuse Himself—I would spit in his empty face" (406). Mr. Britling, however, does not believe in such a God. Frederic, though, seems to, and thus he cannot come to terms with such a God. That would explain why he says Mr. Britling does not see through it. He can find no reason to see an optimistic outcome to this war. For a fuller discussion of Wells's impact on Hemingway's novel, see Roos "What If You Are Not Built That Way?"

Wells made a tour of the Italian front in 1916 and included a mostly propagandistic account of the state of things there in his 1917 collection of essays, *War and the Future.* He also included a chapter on how the war had revived religious feeling in Britain and France, though Wells, typically, was none too kind to established churches. At the end of the chapter he quotes an "eminent Anglican": "There are four stages between belief and utter unbelief. There are those who believe in God, those who doubt like Huxley the Agnostic, those who deny him like the Atheists but who do at least keep his place vacant, and lastly those who have set up a Church in his place. That is the last outrage of unbelief" ("How People Think About the War," section 3). Given how closely Hemingway seems to have followed Wells, it is hard to imagine he did not also read *War and the Future*, and if so, it would have stirred further thoughts on the clash of reason and faith.

226:1–3 "a very good study of the English middle-class soul." "I don't know about the soul": Many readers of Wells's novel agree with Count Greffi's assessment. The count is one of the novel's exemplars as guideposts for Frederic. But Frederic's reply expresses his bleak outlook, and there is no reason to deny his honesty at this point. In spite of all he has been through, including his out-of-body experience when he is wounded, epistemologically he has progressed no further than where he was when Catherine Barkley said, during their first meeting, that death is the end of things. He still does not know. See entry 17:1.

226:4 "Poor boy. We none of us know about the soul": The Count recognizes Frederic's relative immaturity and lack of wisdom, calling him, as Catherine does, "boy." He has surely grown some since his days of being called "Baby" by Rinaldi, but Frederic, as we have seen, still has growing to do. The count, in contrast, is mature enough to know what cannot be known.

226:4–6 "Are you Croyant?" "At night": *Croyant* is French for *a believer*, that is a believer in God. Frederic's response echoes his earlier words to the priest: "I'm afraid of Him in the night sometimes." See entry 62:23–24. Frederic's religious feeling may have even deteriorated some since that early conversation, soon after he was wounded. If we take his statement here at face value (and why should we not?), he is saying that he is only a believer "at night," which, as we have said, is the realm of the subjective. In the day, when the rational mind takes over, belief, it would seem, disappears.

226:10–13 "Would you like to live after death?" . . . "It would depend on the life . . . live forever": The count clearly prefers to live in this world. A life after death, in other words, would have to contain the pleasures he receives in this world. We should note, however, that the count has clearly been untouched by the suffering of the war. Most people would like to live forever in a world immune to suffering.

226:26–27 "What do you value the most?" "Someone I love": Frederic's unhesitant declaration of what he values the most is a certain sign of his growth since the beginning of the novel. See also entry 206:25.

227:19–20 "if you ever become devout pray for me if I am dead": Though the count does not seem to have religious faith, he has not completely given up on the existence of God and an afterlife. The Roman Catholic Church teaches that prayers for the dead can gain them indulgences that may ease their way into heaven.

227:25 **"I might become very devout"**: Frederic too does not rule out the possibility that he will get religious faith, even though he still insists that it "comes only at night" (227:32).

227:33–34 **"you are in love . . . that is a religious feeling"**: The count endorses the notion—which Catherine set forth—that love is a religion (see entry 100:21), reinforcing the idea that Frederic is seeking, through Catherine, a balance between reason and faith. He follows the count's statement with the query "You believe so?" and the count assures him, "Of course" (227:35–36).

227:39 **"We will walk up stairs together"**: The final image of this important chapter is a lovely piece of symbolism that affirms the count's importance to the novel's theme.

CHAPTER 36

228:1 **the rain:** Of course, this is a bad omen.

228:16 **"They are going to arrest you in the morning":** The pronoun *they* is vague, but apparently the local police have noticed Frederic, recognizing him as someone who has been to Stresa before in uniform and now is out of uniform. The disguise of wearing Ralph Simmons's clothes seems not to have worked.

229:7 **I thought a minute.** With Catherine in the night, Frederic has been in subjective mode, but now he must return again to objective mode to reason his way to some form of escape from his predicament.

229:9 **"I don't know the time":** The barman's inability to provide a specific time for Frederic's arrest heightens the sense of urgency, the sense that time is limited, consistent with the novel's general theme of the preciousness of time as well as the theme of epistemology.

229:32 **"It's all right, Cat":** In the manuscript, Hemingway wrote, "It's all right, baby" but changed it to "Cat" in the typescript (JFK items 64 and 65). As Hemingway must have recognized, Rinaldi uses *baby* for Frederic, and thus the term is less appropriate for the more mature Catherine. See entry 137:15.

229:32–33 **"Would you like to get dressed . . . and go in a boat to Switzerland?"** Frederic's question must seem like a joke to Catherine, which explains her response, "Would you?" Her finely developed sense of humor is evident throughout their escape, demonstrating her grace under pressure.

229:38 **"Is the barman crazy?"** Catherine provides another reference to the extreme irrationality of craziness, but, as Frederic assures her, the barman is not crazy, and the situation is serious, requiring the utmost in rationality.

230:13–14 **"Darling, I'm awfully stupid, but why is the barman in the bathroom?"** Hemingway does not miss the inherent comedy in this nonetheless dramatic and tense scene. Catherine's sense of irony is also sensitive to the absurdities of the moment.

230:15 **"Sh—"**: This is probably intended to suggest the interjection for *Be quiet,* but it seems odd in context. Neither Hemingway nor any editor altered or questioned it in the final revisions. It is doubtful that it was intended as a genteel abbreviation of *shit* or Frederic's interrupted "second thought." In other instances, 172:19 for example, when *shit* is the intended meaning, only a blank is used, with none of the letters.

230:29 **"It's a lovely night for a walk"**: Catherine is being sarcastic, but this provides another example of her tough-minded ability to roll with the punches.

231:3 **a ten-lira note**: Frederic's tip to the "second porter" for bringing him a big umbrella is generous, as usual, when he genuinely likes the person helping him. Ten lire would be worth $25.40 today (Williamson).

231:11–12 **The wind was blowing offshore now**: This is fortuitous, since it means that it is blowing northward up the lake, so that Frederic and Catherine will have it at their back, helping them as they row. According to H. R. Stoneback, Stresa locals agree that in November the winds would indeed be blowing offshore, to the north ("Hemingway's Stresa" 132).

231:25 **"If you get through send me five hundred francs"**: If we assume the barman means Swiss francs, since they are going to Switzerland, five hundred Swiss francs at the 1917 exchange rate of 4.7687 francs to a dollar would have been equal to $104.85—$2,000 in 2017 (Williamson). The price is not cheap, but the barman recognizes that the boat is Frederic's ticket to safety. Frederic's flat "All right" seems an acknowledgement of the steep price, but he has little choice. The barman is a friend, but, in addition to losing his boat, he is taking a very big risk on Frederic's behalf. If he is discovered aiding and abetting a deserter, he will certainly be arrested, and the punishment is likely to be severe. The barman deserves to be well compensated for the risk and the loss of the boat. And we should note that he is not asking for the money until and unless Frederic makes it safely to Switzerland.

231:31 **"give me fifty lire"**: The barman asks for the equivalent of $6.66 for the brandy and wine, or about $127 in 2017, again no small amount (Williamson). See entry 231:25. Once more, Frederic is in no position to complain and pays it without question, although "I gave it to him" does not indicate that he took any pleasure in paying it. If the circumstances were different, Frederic might protest. All of this exchange of money recalls Jake Barnes's thoughts in *The Sun Also Rises,* where he says, "Enjoying living was learning to get your money's worth and knowing when you had it. You could get your money's worth. The world was a good place to buy in" (148).

231:38–232:2 **"You know how far?"..."You have to pass Monte Tamara"**: Luino is only the first of four Italian towns on the shores of the lake that Frederic needs to get beyond—first Luino on the east side, then Cannero and Cannobio on the west, and then finally Tronzano (misspelled in the text) on the east side. Hemingway also misspells Monte Tamaro, a 6,437-foot mountain just beyond the Swiss border on the east side of the lake.

232:4–8 **"eleven o'clock"..."seven o'clock"...."thirty-five kilometres"**: The barman anticipates an eight-hour trip to row thirty-five kilometers, just short of twenty-two miles, up the lake. Stresa boatmen agree that such a trip with the aid of November wind should take about eight hours (Stoneback, "Hemingway's Stresa" 133).

232:10 **Isola Bella**: See entry 124:19.

232:10 **Isola Madre**: See entry 124:19. Frederic will need to row a little over a mile past Isola Bella to reach Isola Madre, heading northeasterly up the lake.

232:11 **Pallanza**: See entry 124:13. Once they get past Pallanza, Frederic will have rowed about two and a half miles total.

232:14 **"This wind will blow like this for three days"**: Hemingway's 1924 short story "The Three-Day Blow" is set during such an autumn storm in northern Michigan.

232:15 **the Mattarone**: The Mottarone (the name is misspelled in the text) is a 4,895-foot mountain to the west behind Stresa overlooking Lake Maggiore.

232:21 **"I don't think you'll get drowned"**: Emilio the barman provides another epistemological moment. He can offer no guarantee. He does not *know* that Frederic will not be drowned in the process of rowing up the lake, but he *believes* that he will not. Emilio's expression is probably rendered with some irony, which Frederic appreciates, responding, "That's good."

232:25 **"Did you leave the money for the hotel?"** Emilio is still the dutiful employee of the hotel, making certain Frederic has paid for his room. Frederic has left the money in an envelope in the room, but if he had not, Emilio may be worrying that he would be held accountable.

232:30 **"What does he say?"** Emilio's statement, "You won't thank me if you get drowned," is spoken in Italian, so Catherine does not understand. But the line is no doubt rendered sardonically, and Catherine is aware of his tone, prompting her question to Frederic, who chooses not to translate Emilio's dark words literally.

232:36 **deprecatingly:** A rare use of an adverb by Hemingway and a curious one. The intention is probably self-deprecation, the barman implying that he has not done much to help them, although, of course, he has done a great deal.

CHAPTER 37

233:1 **keeping the wind in my face:** Frederic has his back to the direction he is moving in the boat, rowing north on the north-south lake, and thus he is facing south, toward Catherine, who is sitting in the stern, and the helping wind is in his face.

233:5 **no leathers:** An oar can be wrapped with a strip of leather to protect it from chafing by the metal oarlock. A leather wrap would also cushion the oar and make the rowing experience smoother. Since these oars have no leather wraps, Frederic has to work a little harder to manage them as he rows.

233:7 **I did not feather the oars:** Feathering the oar means turning the blade to be parallel to the water during the portion of the stroke when the blade is out of the water. Frederic does not want to feather the oar because he wants to take full advantage of the wind by having it push against his perpendicular blades when they are out of the water.

233:12 **We never saw Pallanza:** As Frederic explains in the next line, the town of Pallanza sits behind a point (Cape Castagnola) that extends out into the lake and would at least partially obscure the lights of the town as they row past. In addition, the small island, Isola San Giovanni, would also partially hide the town. And because Frederic is facing south, behind their direction of travel, he would need to take his eyes off his task in order to see the lights of Pallanza.

233:15 **Intra:** This town is another mile and a half up the lake past Pallanza on the western shore, which would be on Frederic's right as he rows.

233:21–234:1 **I pulled hard on the right oar and backed water with the other:** This maneuver would steer Frederic from west to east to move the boat back out toward the center of the lake.

234:3 **"We're across the lake":** At Stresa, Lake Maggiore runs from the southeast to the northwest, then divides into two fingers at the point of Pallanza (see entry

273

233:12), with one finger continuing to the northwest and another going northeast toward Switzerland. Frederic and Catherine have crossed over to the finger that heads toward Switzerland.

234:10–11 **"Poor Ferguson . . . we're gone"**: Catherine's concern for the well-being of others is evident here as she thinks of Ferguson's feelings when she discovers that she has been left alone in Stresa. In contrast, Frederic's thoughts are strictly about survival and avoiding arrest.

234:16 **"some thirty kilometres from here"**: Frederic is gauging that they have come 5 kilometers, about 3.1 miles thus far, or about one-seventh of their journey. They still have about 19 miles to go.

234:17 **I rowed all night:** All previous editions of the novel have an extra space prior to the beginning of this paragraph, indicating a gap in the narration. The manuscript has two horizontal lines indicating that extra space should be added (JFK item 64). In the typescript, there is extra space plus two hand-drawn horizontal lines indicating the need for the space (JFK item 65).

234:24 **the long dark point of Castagnola:** Frederic sees behind them the point at Pallanza that helped to obscure their view of the town's lights as they passed.

234:34–36 **The lake widened . . . lights that should be Luino:** Lake Maggiore does indeed widen where Luino, on the eastern shore, sits across from Cannero, on the western shore. They have now gone another nine miles up the lake since they passed the point of Castagnola and have only about nine miles more to go until they reach Brissago in Switzerland.

235:7–8 **"You take this oar . . . and I'll hold the umbrella"**: Frederic releases the oars and pulls them into the boat, giving one to Catherine, which she will hold in the water behind them to use as a rudder for steering, while Frederic will turn around and hold the big open umbrella to catch the wind for a sail.

235:23–28 **She was laughing. . . . "Don't be cross, darling"**: Catherine's lovely equanimity in the face of their troubles is once again evident. Frederic, however, is in no mood for jokes during their journey.

236:3–4 **another point going out a long way ahead into the lake:** Just north of Cannero on the western shore, the land extends into the lake and the lake narrows, as Frederic says at 236:25–26.

236:5 **"Are you warm enough, Cat?"** Frederic's concern for Catherine's well-being becomes more apparent here and elsewhere during their journey and for the rest of the novel.

236:26 **guardia di finanza:** The Guardia di Finanza (properly capitalized) is an Italian law enforcement agency with the responsibility of investigating financial crime and smuggling. As such, it operates boats in Italian territorial waters on the lookout for smugglers.

236:30 **"about eight miles more":** Frederic is actually overestimating the distance they have left. From the point at which the lake narrows above Cannero, Brissago in Switzerland is about six miles away.

236:34 **the right bank:** The bank to Frederic's right is the western shore, since he is facing south as he rows.

236:35 **Cannobio:** The last town of any size in Italy before the Swiss border, which is only two and a half miles to the north. On the western shore of the lake, Cannobio is four miles from the Swiss town of Brissago.

236:37 **a high dome-capped mountain:** This is probably Monte Tamaro, which Emilio the barman has told them they must pass before they get into Switzerland.

237:1 **up the lake at least five miles further:** Again Frederic is overestimating. From Cannobio he is only about four miles from Brissago. When Monte Tamaro is directly to his east, he will be at the Swiss border and only about a mile and a half from Brissago.

237:14 **gunwales:** These are the top edges of the sides of the boat. The term originally applied to wooden sailing warships, on which the sides needed to be reinforced to accommodate cannons.

237:20–23 **"Watch out" . . . "life might be much simpler":** Frederic expresses more concern for the well-being of the child they have conceived than does Catherine, who seems to think it might be better if this pregnancy were terminated. In the context of the novel, however, it is probably intended to reflect her general premonition of a disastrous end to the love she shares with Frederic. Indeed, this passage was editorially challenged in the penultimate version of the novel, the printer's setting copy, because of the implied wish for an abortion. The passage, if not the baby, survived, however.

237:34 **to catch crabs:** A rowing phrase that refers to the inability to pull the oar out of the water.

238:10 **alpini hats:** Members of the Guardia di Finanza wear distinctive headgear, also known as Tyrolean hats, with the brim turned up in the back and a feather in the headband standing up on the left side.

238:11 **carbines:** See entry 183:4.

238:12–13 **yellow on their hats and the yellow marks on their cape collars:** Frederic accurately describes the Guardia di Finanza uniform markings.

238:23 **the Swiss navy:** Catherine makes a joke, since the landlocked Swiss do not have a navy. However, the army has military boats that patrol the lakes like Maggiore, that cross national borders. Frederic is aware of this and remains in no mood for a joke.

238:28 **It was clear daylight now:** All previous editions of the novel have an extra space prior to the beginning of this paragraph, indicating a gap in the narration. The holograph manuscript has two horizontal lines, indicating that there should be extra space here (JFK item 64). In the typescript, there is extra space plus one hand-drawn horizontal line to emphasize the need for the space (JFK item 65).

238:36–37 **a helmet like the Germans:** World War I–era Swiss army helmets resembled German helmets, with sides that came down low over the ears, not the earlier German helmets that exposed the ears and had a spike on the top. Switzerland, however, was a neutral nation.

239:34 **"I've never realized anything before":** After a night of serious focus to bring himself and Catherine to safety, Frederic seems almost giddy now that they have arrived in Switzerland.

239:37–38 **"Isn't the rain fine? . . . It's cheerful rain":** This seems to be more giddiness from Frederic, certainly a subjective observation. The rain will bring doom eventually, even if, for now, it brings no bother.

240:26–29 **A fat gray cat . . . Catherine smiled at me very happily:** This sensuous image underscores Catherine's feline qualities. See entry 137:15.

240:31 **They arrested us after breakfast:** All previous editions of the novel have an extra space prior to the beginning of this paragraph, indicating a gap in the narration—

in this case, merely the time spent eating breakfast. The manuscript has two horizontal lines, indicating there should be extra space here (JFK item 64). The typescript has extra space plus a single hand-drawn horizontal line to emphasize the need for the space (JFK item 65).

241:19–20 **"My cousin has been studying art":** Frederic seems to have developed a storyline to explain his arrival in Switzerland with Catherine. He will pretend she is his British cousin, who has been studying art in Italy. He has created this story apparently without consulting Catherine to learn whether she knows anything about art.

241:29–30 **"Rubens." "Large and fat":** Peter Paul Rubens (1577–1640), Flemish artist, is well known for his fleshy nude or partially nude human figures. Frederic provides simple phrases that Catherine can use to easily demonstrate her knowledge of art, should the authorities question her.

241:31–32 **"Titian" . . . "Titian-haired":** See entry 219:12. Titian's female subjects often have reddish brown hair, and so his name has become a color.

241:32–35 **"Mantegna" . . . "Lots of nail holes":** Andrea Mantegna (1431–1506), Italian artist from the area of Venice and Padua. One of his most famous paintings, which seems to be the referent here for the phrase "lots of nail holes," is *Lamentation for the Dead Christ,* which depicts Jesus's corpse lying on a slab, his head on a pillow, jagged nail holes clearly visible in his hands and feet, as the Virgin Mary, Mary Magdalen, and Saint John weep over him. Because of the low perspective from the feet of the body, Christ appears shortened, diminished in power. There is no attempt to idealize any of the figures in the painting. The stark realism is haunting, or, as Catherine and Frederic agree, "very bitter."
 The use of the image in this novel of faith and reason is ambiguous in that it accentuates Christ's humanity and physical death rather than his divinity. Hemingway would have seen the painting at Milan's Pinacoteca di Brera, the city's main public art museum, where it is still displayed. In Hemingway's story "The Revolutionist," the narrator speaks to the young revolutionist about "the Mantegnas in Milano," but the revolutionist insists that he does not like them (*CSS* 119).

241:36–37 **"I'll be able to talk art with your customers":** Catherine again cheerfully demonstrates that she is anticipating marriage to Frederic, who, she assumes, will be pursuing a career in architecture.

242:1 **Locarno:** A larger Swiss town about five and a half miles northeast of Brissago, near the tip of Lake Maggiore.

242:9–11 **Twenty-five hundred lire . . . twelve hundred lire:** Since Frederic was carrying "three thousand and some lire" soon after his desertion (see entry 196:31–32), this amount, assuming his veracity with the Swiss officials, indicates that Frederic has spent about five hundred lire since he deserted. Thus, he still has the equivalent of $333 at 1917 exchange rates, which would be worth $6,370 in 2017 (Williamson). In addition, Catherine has another twelve hundred lire, or about $3,000 in today's terms. However, keep in mind that Frederic has agreed to pay Emilio the barman the equivalent of $2,000 at 2017 value (see entry 231:25), or almost one-third of what he has, as compensation for Emilio's boat, which they have used for their escape and which has now been confiscated by the authorities. If we subtract what they owe Emilio, the couple has a total of about $7,370 to spend, in 2017 dollars. With this money, they should not have significant financial worries through the next few months. Thus, it is not surprising the officials are happy to welcome them to Switzerland.

242:13 **Wengen:** Baedeker's *Switzerland: Together with Chamonix and the Italian Lakes* 1928 describes it as "next to Interlaken, the most frequented tourist resort in the Bernese Oberland and is also a favourite locality for winter sports" (211).

242:23 **something in a German dialect:** Switzerland is a country with four official languages—German, French, Italian, and Romansh—with Swiss German being the most predominant. The common language in Brissago and Locarno and the surrounding region, however, is Italian. The soldier here must come from a German-speaking region of Switzerland, so the lieutenant speaks to him in his native dialect.

242:34–36 **You did not want something reasonable . . . without explanations:** Frederic's explanation is another case study of reason versus nonreason. Human society sometimes prefers to function irrationally, perhaps to satisfy rationally based bureaucratic rules, which sometimes require irrational actions in order to follow them.

243:3 **Montreux:** A city on the northeastern shore of Lake Geneva in Switzerland. Baedeker's *Switzerland: Together with Chamonix and the Italian Lakes* 1928, which we presume Hemingway owned, given the frequency of his travels to the country, describes it as having "a remarkably mild climate, attracting thousands of visitors (many English) all the year round, especially however in spring and autumn" (319). Montreux's popularity among the English probably explains why Catherine so quickly identifies it as the place she wants to go. One of the most well-known sites in Montreux is the Castle of Chillon "the ancient stronghold of the Counts and Dukes of Savoy" (322), also the inspiration for Lord Byron's famous poem "The Prisoner of Chillon," a narrative about François Bonivard, a Genevan patriot, whom the Duke of Savoy imprisoned in the castle from 1532 to 1536 for revolutionary activities.

243:6 **Lacarno:** This misspelling did not appear in previous editions of the novel. Elsewhere, as in the next two sentences, Locarno is spelled correctly.

243:12–13 **winter sport on the Montreux Oberland Bernois railway:** The Montreux Oberland Bernois railway (also known as the MOB; see entry 254:15–16) was one of the first electric railways in Switzerland and connected Montreux, on the shore of Lake Geneva, with winter sports resorts higher in the mountains, including Les Avants and Gstaad. It also stops in Chamby, where Frederic and Catherine will stay at a pension owned by Mr. and Mrs. Guttingen. Thus, the official is simply asserting that if Frederic and Catherine stay in Montreux, they will have easy access to the winter sports at higher elevations. From having stayed at Chamby on at least three different occasions and passing through Montreux many other times, Hemingway would have been very familiar with the transportation options around Montreux.

243:19–20 **"*luge-ed* into the streets of Montreux":** The official comically makes *luged* into a two-syllable verb. Unlike a toboggan, a luge has metal runners, to slide on the snow or ice. The luge rider lies on his or her back, feet first. As the official says, luging is certainly a winter sport, although Frederic has never heard of it (243:28). It has been part of the Winter Olympics since 1964, with single and double events for men and a single event for women. The disagreements between the officials regarding winter sports are mostly matters of subjective opinions rather than objective facts and serve as an interlude of comedy in this tragic novel.

243:32 **tobogganing:** Unlike a luge, a toboggan has no runners; the bottom rests directly on the snow or ice. As implied here, toboggans originated as a form of transport for native peoples of northern Canada. In objective terms, luging is not tobogganing.

244:1 **Ochs Brothers:** This is a minor misspelling of Och Brothers, Swiss siblings who began manufacturing skis in Geneva in 1907 and opened the first Swiss sports shop in Montreux in 1912 ("Vintage Swiss Och Sport Skis"). Hemingway would have been familiar with the shop from his early visits to Montreux, beginning in 1922.

244:4 **special piste:** A marked path for tobogganing, luging, or skiing.

244:12 **the Engadine:** An Alpine region in the eastern part of Switzerland, the opposite direction from Montreux. In Hemingway's story "Cross-Country Snow," Nick Adams and his friend George wish they could go together "all through the Engadine" (*CSS* 145).

244:12 **Mürren:** See entry 129:29.

244:14 **Les Avants:** A village 2.2 miles northeast of Montreux.

244:32 **"You've forgotten the army":** Catherine reminds Frederic to tip the soldier who has escorted them from Brissago to Locarno, and Frederic gives him 10 lire ($25.40 in 2017), apologizing for not having any Swiss money yet (Williamson). The soldier seems appreciative of Frederic's generosity.

245:15–18 **"Let me see your hands. . . . Don't be sacrilegious":** When Catherine asks to look at Frederic's hands, blistered from rowing all night, he makes a joke about the stigmata of Christ, that is, wounds corresponding to the nail holes of Jesus's crucifixion. According to the New Testament, one of the Roman soldiers thrust a spear into the side of Jesus to make certain he was dead (John 19:34). Thus, Frederic implies that he does not fully bear the wounds of Jesus.

Ironically, Catherine, the one who does not believe in God, cautions him not to be sacrilegious. As noted before, however, in spite of Catherine's lack of religious faith, she has a well-defined sense of what is sacred in this world. Frederic's comment should be linked with his earlier reference to Mantegna, whose painting is described as having "lots of nail holes." See entry 241:32–35. While there is no denying that Frederic's remark here is a reference to Jesus Christ, it is nevertheless an ambiguous one. For another instance where Frederic compares himself to Christ, see entry 25:37.

245:24 **Hotel Metropole:** This Locarno hotel is listed in Baedeker's *Switzerland: Together with Chamonix and the Italian Lakes* 1928 as having sixty-five rooms, with inexpensive prices—starting at four Swiss francs ($11 in 2017) for room only and twelve Swiss francs ($33 in 2017) for room and full board (Williamson).

245:28 **"I get pretty groggy":** The chapter and Book Four close with Frederic still in an unsettled state of mind, while Catherine does her best to comfort him with common sense.

245:32 **We were down on the pavement:** In the original manuscript, above this Hemingway wrote and circled, "August 9," indicating that he had written this far in the original draft by 9 August 1928.

BOOK FIVE

CHAPTER 38

249:1–21 That fall the snow . . . stream in the rocks: In contrast to Books One and Three, which begin with bleak descriptions of the fall, Book Five does not open so ominously, other than the lateness of the snow, which delays the winter sport that Frederic and Catherine have been anticipating. Otherwise, the imagery is quite pleasant, with no hint of the tragic events to come.

249:4 Mrs. Guttingen: The chalet where Frederic and Catherine stay is clearly based on the Gangwisch pension, owned and operated by Gustav and Marie-Therese Gangwisch, a German-Swiss couple, in the village of Chamby, a mile and a quarter up the mountainside above Montreux, overlooking Lake Geneva (*Letters 1* 325). Ernest and his first wife, Hadley, spent two weeks at the Gangwisch chalet in January 1922, then returned for another stay in May 1922 with Chink Dorman-Smith. In a letter to Kate Smith, Ernest claimed that room and board cost them just two dollars a day, equivalent to about $29 in 2017 (*Letters 1* 323; Williamson). In *A Moveable Feast,* Hadley recalls life at the chalet in May:

> Do you remember how Mrs. Gangeswisch [sic] cooked the trout *au bleu* when we got back to the chalet? They were such wonderful trout, Tatie [Hadley's nickname for Ernest], and we drank the Sion wine and ate out on the porch with the mountainside dropping off below and we could look across the lake and see the Dent du Midi with the snow half down it and the trees at the mouth of the Rhône where it flowed into the lake. (55)

249:10 Sitting up in bed eating breakfast: In a letter to Kate Smith written at the Gangwisch chalet in Chamby on 27 January 1922, Hemingway describes getting breakfast served in bed (*Letters 1* 323). This and other details indicate the extent to which Hemingway based this portion of the novel on idyllic times he had with his first wife, Hadley, in Switzerland. We can only wonder the extent to which his second wife, Pauline, was aware of how romantically reminiscent these passages were for him.

249:19–20 a stream at the bottom that flowed down into the lake: The identity of the stream depends on which side of the mountain they are on, since the road described goes around both sides. In the valley on the western side of the mountain, the Baye de Clarens empties into Lake Geneva in the village of Clarens, a mile and half west of Montreux. In the steeper valley on the eastern side of the mountain, the Baye de Montreux empties into the lake in the heart of Montreux.

250:4–5 nails in the soles and heels of our boots: Frederic and Catherine both have hobnailed boots, which are studded with nails to give them good traction on a frozen surface. The rugged and frozen mountainous terrain recalls the priest's pastoral Abruzzi region. Thus, although Frederic sidestepped the Abruzzi during his carousing leave earlier in the novel, here, through Catherine, he achieves the same heaven-on-earth effect in their Alpine idyll. However, whereas the Abruzzi is portrayed as a sexless place, where it is "forbidden to play the flute at night" (see entries 8:1–2, 11:25–26, and 63:25–26), Frederic and Catherine no doubt have a full and satisfying physical relationship. Hemingway provides a darker, ironic view of this environment in his 1927 short story "An Alpine Idyll" (*CSS* 262–66).

250:14–16 island of two trees on the lake . . . like the double sails of a fishing boat: The detailed description of their idyllic home includes this curiously specific close-up detail of an unidentified island on Lake Geneva (Lac Leman). The image evokes Frederic and Catherine's recent heroic water passage.

250:17–18 the plain of the Rhone Valley: The view Frederic describes corresponds to the view from the Gangwisch chalet in Chamby. See entry 249:4. The Rhône River's source is the Rhône Glacier at the far eastern end of the Swiss canton of Valais. From the leading edge of the glacier, the river runs east to west through southern Switzerland, turns sharply north at the Dents du Midi (see entry 250:19), and flows into Lake Geneva (Lac Leman). At the west end of the lake, it becomes a river again and crosses the border into France, where it turns south at Lyon and empties into the Mediterranean just below Arles. From their mountain perch in Chamby, on the north side of Lake Geneva, Frederic is looking southeast up the Rhône valley, where the river flows from south to north into the lake. The steep slopes on the north side of the Rhône valley produce more wine than any other part of Switzerland. In his memoir *A Moveable Feast,* Hemingway remembers the time in May 1922 when he, Hadley, and Chink Dorman-Smith traveled through Switzerland together and stopped in the town of Aigle, just seven miles up the Rhône River from Lake Geneva (Baker, *Life Story* 91–92). Ernest recalls bringing wine from Aigle back to their chalet in Chamby, and he declares that the Sion wine, from further up the Rhône valley, was even better than the wine from Aigle (*MF* 55).

Also during that trip, as recounted in *A Moveable Feast,* Ernest went trout fishing while Hadley and Chink stayed in Aigle reading in the garden at their hotel. In the memoir, Ernest recalls the river as "narrow and grey and full of snow water and the two trout streams on either side, the Stockalper and the Rhône canal. The Stockalper was really clear that day and the Rhône canal was still murky" (54). In a previous instance, Ernest used the same experience to write a lovely piece for the *Toronto Star,* "Fishing the Rhône Canal," published in June 1922, describing the canal as a stream no more than a yard wide, where trout have been caught previously, he muses, by Roman legions and soldiers in the army of Napoleon (*DLT* 170–71). Thus, in writing this section of *A Farewell to Arms,* unlike the scenes on the Isonzo front, Hemingway was relying heavily on his own vivid memories of a landscape with which he was intimately familiar and for which he obviously had great affection.

250:19 **the Dent du Midi**: Frederic seems to be referring to the tallest of the seven peaks known in plural form as the Dents du Midi, translated into English as "the teeth of noon." La Haute Cime (high summit), the westernmost peak and, at 10,685 feet, the highest of the seven, was at one time known as the singular Dent du Midi. As Frederic correctly describes the mountains here, from his vantage point, the Rhône River valley turns sharply to the east at their base, climbing up toward the Rhône Glacier.

250:25 **"Hoyle"**: A rulebook for card games, originally published by Englishman Edmond Hoyle (1672–1769). Although most modern card games were invented after his death, *Hoyle* continues to be used as the name for many different card game rulebooks. The idea of playing by the rules has ironic meaning for Frederic and Catherine, who are living outside of the rules of conventional human conduct. Frederic is a deserter, and they are in an illicit relationship that makes even the war seem like a game "as far away as the football games of some one else's college" (251:8–9). However, in the context of the novel's subjective/objective faith/reason dualities, the rulebook can be seen as emblematic of reason, and as a means of binding them together, it helps to demonstrate the balance Frederic and Catherine are attempting between the subjective and the objective, between reason and faith.

250:34 **Zurich:** The largest city in Switzerland, located in the northcentral part of the country.

251:4–5 **if I woke in the night I knew it was from only one cause:** Frederic does not specify what this one cause is and leaves us to guess. Since he has just described leaving the window open to the freezing temperatures of the night air and he claims that they slept well, it is probably the cold that wakes him, supported by the fact that he says he "would shift the feather bed over, very softly" so as not to awaken Catherine. Most important, he wants us to know that he is no longer suffering from the fears in the night that have previously haunted him.

251:9–10 still fighting in the mountains because the snow would not come: After the Caporetto Retreat, in which the Italian army fled from the Isonzo front and by 9 November reestablished a line of defense on the plane of Northern Italy at the Piave River, the only mountain fighting would have been in the vicinity of Mount Grappa and the Asiago plateau, twenty to thirty miles northwest of Venice (Thompson 322). At this stage of the war, the front stretched from the Swiss border to the Asiago plateau and east to Mount Grappa, where it ran southeast along the plain of the Piave River to the Adriatic Sea (328). This was still the front when Hemingway arrived there as an ambulance driver for the American Red Cross in June 1918.

251:11 Sometimes we walked down the mountain into Montreux: All previous editions of the novel have an extra space prior to the beginning of this paragraph, indicating a gap in the narration and perhaps the passage of days or weeks. The next precise indication of a date occurs at 254:36, "three days before Christmas." Therefore, five to six weeks pass from their arrival in Switzerland to that point in the narrative. The manuscript has two horizontal lines and indication of a new chapter before this paragraph (JFK item 64). In the typescript, there is extra space plus a single hand-drawn horizontal line, but no chapter break (JFK item 65).

251:16–17 three villages; Chernex, Fontanivent, and the other I forget: These are small villages near Montreux. Chamby is about twelve hundred feet above Montreux in elevation, so the walk is probably a zigzag to reduce the steepness. Chernex is about two miles from the heart of Montreux, and Fontanivent is an additional three-quarters of a mile away. Although Frederic cannot remember the name of the third, possibilities include Belmont-sur-Montreux and Vuarennes. Hemingway could have looked at a map to provide the name but chose instead to highlight Frederic's forgetfulness, humanizing him as a narrator as well as demonstrating the fallibility of human reason, which is always influenced by the subjectivity of our experiences. A walking route from Chamby through Fontanivent, Chernex, and Vuarennes to downtown Montreux would be about three and a half miles long and would take about an hour and a half, although with the steep incline involved, the trek would no doubt take less time on the way down than on the way back up.

251:24 We did not know any one in Montreux: This is not quite precise. Frederic later tells us the woman who does Catherine's hair is the "only person we knew in Montreux" (251:34). He also says, the people in the shops "were very glad to see us" (251:31–32).

251:25–27 **swans . . . gulls . . . terns . . . grebes:** Frederic and Catherine may not know many people in Montreux, but Frederic, like Hemingway, the amateur natural historian, certainly knows his birds, as demonstrated in this brief ornithological paragraph. Swans are familiar to everyone. Gulls and terns are related species and are both charadriiformes—that is, bird species that can drink either fresh or salt water and so are common around Lake Geneva. Grebes are freshwater diving birds with sharp beaks, unrelated evolutionarily to ducks.

Hemingway had a lifelong interest in natural history, ingrained by his father, Clarence, "Ed," the medical doctor who established the Agassiz Club in his hometown of Oak Park to teach natural history to young boys (see Roos, "Agassiz or Darwin"). Besides the Saturday Agassiz Club field trips, Ed Hemingway also took his children on frequent explorations of the Field Museum of Natural History in Chicago. In a letter to Kate Smith from Chamby, written in late January 1922, Hemingway enthused about the strange variety of unfamiliar birds in Switzerland: "All new birds to me except great big ravens that teeter on the top of the pines and watch everything you do. Funny little brown and grey birds too. All the swiss [sic] birds seem sort of mumpbacked" (*Letters 1* 324).

251:35 **dark Munich beer:** Munich is a major beer-producing city in southern Germany. In his 10 June 1922, *Toronto Star* article, "Fishing the Rhône Canal," Hemingway mentions drinking a "seventeen percent dark beer" in the Swiss village of Aigle, not far from Montreux (*DLT* 170). Since Hemingway does not mention alcohol content here, Frederic's dark Munich beer is probably a dunkel, a traditional dark, malty beer brewed in Munich with 4–6 percent alcohol content ("Munich Dunkel Lager").

251:36 **the Corriere della Sera:** See entry 118:18.

251:39–252:1 **Everything was going very badly everywhere:** Besides the Italian disaster of Caporetto, on the French front, British and German armies were battling for the town of Cambrai. The battle marked the first use of tanks, by the British, which were initially successful, but then the tanks began to break down. The Germans got fresh reinforcements from the now defunct Russian front, and after great bloodshed, they reestablished the stalemate of trench warfare (Gilbert 378–83).

252:3–4 **read about disaster:** Disaster always goes down better with dark beer and salted pretzels. The disasters Frederic is reading about no doubt begin (but do not end) with the Caporetto Retreat, the statistics of which still stagger the imagination. According to historian Mark Thompson, the Italians suffered 12,000 dead in the fighting during the retreat, another 30,000 wounded, and 294,000 lost as prisoners. But this was only half the story. There were also 350,000 deserters, "roaming around or making for home" (324). Only half of the army's sixty-five divisions remained, and half the artillery, more than 3,000 guns, had also been lost, along with 300,000 rifles, 1,700 mortars, 3,000 machine guns, 1,600 motor vehicles, and untold horses. In territory, the Italians lost 5,400 square miles, with a population of over a million people (324). Over 400,000 civilians became refugees as a result of the battle. (See also Macdonald 172.)

Although the Italians were able to hold on at the Piave River, at the time that Frederic is reading in this passage, presumably in late November or early December 1917, only a month after the retreat, the mood in Italy was still very grim, with little certainty that the Austrians and Germans would not break through and force a total surrender.

252:10–11 **my voice was a little thick from being excited:** Frederic's sexual excitement watching Catherine's hairdressing, with its effect on his voice, connects via the mirror imagery to the pistol-buying episode in chapter 23 and the ensuing stay in the mirrored hotel room. See entries 131:9–14 and 133:12–14. Psychodynamically, Catherine's hair excites him, and again the mirror framing of Catherine as an aesthetic object intensifies his feeling for her. Curiously, this passage was marked for deletion in the typescript of the novel but then retained (JFK item 65).

Carl Eby identifies fetishism in the imagery here as elsewhere in the novel. See entry 98:32–38. Hair style and hair color are also sexually charged in Hemingway's posthumous novel *The Garden of Eden,* which marked a sea change in Hemingway criticism in the way it revealed a far more complex psychology in Hemingway than most readers previously imagined. In both *A Farewell to Arms* and *The Garden of Eden,* the lovers use hair as a means of twinning themselves and merging their identities.

252:11 **The tongs made a pleasant clicking sound:** Catherine is having her hair waved, and the tongs, Carl Eby suggests, indicate she is getting "marcel waves" rather than a permanent (130). Marcel waves, introduced by hair designer Marcel Grateau (1852–1936), were temporary and were produced by an electric curling iron with tongs, as described here. Eby then psychoanalytically suggests that the "marcel waves" may allude to Ernest's sister Marcelline, with whom Ernest was "twinned" as a child by their mother (see Lynn 37–45). Marcel waves were at the height of their popularity in the 1920s. Thus, Catherine is ahead of the "wave" in getting her hair "marcelled" in 1917.

Eby also suggests that "marcel waves" could allude to Marcel Proust, whom we have noted before in this retrospective narration in the manner of Proust's *In Search of Lost Time* (known as *Remembrance of Things Past* in Hemingway's time). See entries 34:3–4 and 37:35. Eby notes that Proust is "an almost serpentine presence" in Hemingway's posthumous novel *The Garden of Eden* (130).

252:22–23 "It's very good for young Catherine": This is the first time that Catherine Barkley refers to the fetus within her as female. Frederic was the first to make such a suggestion. See entry 138:25–26. The idea of Catherine giving birth to a daughter named Catherine is one of the details that connect this novel to Emily Brontë's *Wuthering Heights,* in which Catherine Earnshaw gives birth to a daughter also named Catherine. See entry 99:36.

252:26 "The doctor says beer will be good for me and keep her small": Catherine has obviously had at least one visit with a doctor, probably in Lausanne, a thirty-minute train ride west from Montreux, where there would be better medical facilities and where Frederic and Catherine eventually go for the delivery of the baby. Many readers, understandably, find this passage disturbing, given the doctor's advice and what we know of the effects of alcohol on developing fetuses. All evidence indicates that no amount of alcohol is safe at any time during a woman's pregnancy (Dotinga). And Catherine, Frederic, and her doctor cannot plead ignorance of this either, since the doctor obviously believes that alcohol will negatively impact the size of the infant.

Although Frederic makes a weak joke that if the baby is small enough and a boy, maybe he could be a jockey for horse racing, the unspoken implication of this exchange is, as we shall learn later, that Catherine is too small in the hips to deliver a normal-sized child and she will be at risk in the delivery. Even so, it would seem that a competent doctor, instead of suggesting the intake of alcohol to reduce the size of the child, would make plans for a caesarian section. We should presume that Hemingway, the son of the head of obstetrics at the Oak Park Hospital, who frequently read his father's medical journals and attended at least one birth that we know of, would have known how a competent doctor would have dealt with a patient in Catherine's condition. Hemingway's familiarity with caesarian sections had already been demonstrated in his 1923 short story "Indian Camp" (*CSS* 67–69). Thus, this is yet another example in the novel of incompetence among doctors and, by extension, the fallibility of those who spend the majority of their time in the realm of reason and science.

252:29 "I suppose if we really have this child we ought to get married": Catherine's statement indicates her awareness of societal pressures on unwed parents, though she seems less than fully enthusiastic. Frederic seems ready at any time, but Catherine finds the prospect of marriage in her current condition as "too embarrassing" (252:34).

252:39 "I don't know": This is Frederic's line. The phrase *I don't know* is used fifty-two times in the novel, twenty-three of them by Frederic, far more than any other character. Catherine is next, using it just six times. In response to his direct and simple "I don't know," she replies, "I know one thing," including a specific answer to Frederic's question. In contrast, *I know* is used seventy-four times, twenty by Frederic, but Catherine also uses the phrase twenty times, and Rinaldi uses it thirteen times. Considering that Frederic is the narrator, with a far greater share of the content of the novel in his words, the effect is that, Frederic appears far less certain than the other two characters of what he knows. As we have said before, whenever Frederic says he knows something, we should take him seriously.

253:9 **"And you're not worried?"** Frederic here is the worrier, the one who is more controlled by feeling rather than thinking. In fact, throughout this dialogue, Catherine seems the more rational.

253:14 **"You're a lovely wife":** Frederic and Catherine's discussion of marriage here recalls Hemingway's treatment of the subject in "A Very Short Story," where the couple "wanted to get married, but there was not enough time for the banns.... They felt as though they were married, but they wanted every one to know about it, and to make it so they could not lose it" (*CSS* 107). However, Luz, the woman in the story, is not pregnant, and she ends their relationship after she falls in love with an Italian major.

253:27 **"too late to start if I'd never done it before":** Aside from being another emphasis on the passage of time, this line would seem to imply that Catherine, like Frederic, has not skied before. However, at other times, she speaks as though she has some experience with skiing. See entries 129:29 and 255:4–5.

253:36 **the New York World Almanac:** Founded by the *New York World* newspaper in 1868 and published annually until 1875 and then every year since 1886, the *New York World Almanac* is a compendium of information from around the world. In 1923, the name was changed to the *World Almanac.*

254:3 **"The stockyards":** Apparently these are the Chicago stockyards, which Frederic previously referred to in the passage on abstract words. See entry 161:13–27. Especially given that gruesome reference, it is certainly odd that Frederic should suggest the stockyards as a place in America Catherine might want to see. The reference might be taken as an ominous foreshadowing of the novel's tragic ending.

254:5 **"The Woolworth building":** This is one of the few indications in the novel of Frederic's interest in architecture. The building was constructed at 233 Broadway in New York City, designed by architect Cass Gilbert in a neo-Gothic style for the F. W. Woolworth Company, which had introduced the first successful five-and-dime stores in the United States. From its completion in 1913 until 1930, at 792 feet it remained the world's tallest building. With its gilded lobby, it is registered as a national historic landmark and remains a top tourist attraction in New York.

254:10 **"The Golden Gate! That's what I want to see":** In the original manuscript, Hemingway added then crossed out, "I'm afraid I have it all mixed up with heaven though" (JFK item 64). Catherine is referring to the Golden Gate bridge in San Francisco and confusing it with the "pearly gates" of heaven.

254:16 **M.O.B.:** The Montreux Oberland Bernois Railway. See entry 243:12–13.

254:25–27 **There was a dial. . . . It was five minutes after:** The clock dial is another of the novel's ubiquitous references to the brevity of time. In this case, Frederic notes that the train will leave in five minutes.

254:35 **feel fine:** In the original manuscript, Hemingway wrote and circled "Aug 11" here, indicating he had written this far by 11 August 1928 (JFK item 64).

254:36 **Snow did not come until three days before Christmas:** All previous editions of the novel have an extra space prior to the beginning of this paragraph, indicating a gap in the narration. The manuscript has two horizontal lines indicating there should be extra space here (JFK item 64). Hemingway also wrote and circled "Aug 12" here. In the typescript, there is extra space, plus a single hand-drawn horizontal line to emphasize the need for the extra space (JFK item 65).

Given the novel's emphasis on the conflict between religious faith and reason, it would be interesting to know how Frederic and Catherine spend the day on which the birth of Christ is celebrated. The events of Christmas Day, however, seem conspicuous by their absence from the novel.

255:4–5 **"I wish I could ski . . . rotten not to be able to ski":** This line suggests that Catherine has some experience skiing.

255:6 **bobsled:** In letters to his sister Marcelline and Kate Smith, written from Chamby in January 1922, Hemingway described wild seven-kilometer rides down the mountain from Les Avants to Montreux with Hadley in a two-person bobsled. See also Hemingway's article "Try Bobsledding If You Want Thrills," which appeared in *The Toronto Star* on 4 March 1922 (*DLT* 101–02). Given Hemingway's thrilling descriptions of bobsledding, traveling fifty to sixty miles an hour down steep and rutted mountain roads through heavy forests, skirting the edge of steep drops, it would seem bobsledding is hardly less risky to Catherine's pregnancy than skiing would be.

255:28 **filberts:** Catherine prefers a chocolate bar with filberts, a species of hazelnut, which takes its name, according to common belief, from Saint Philibert, whose feast day, 20 August, comes at peak harvest time for hazelnuts. Philibert was a French abbot who lived from 606 until 684 A.D. and was important to the foundation of French monasticism.

255:30 **"I'll have another vermouth":** Hemingway wrote and circled "Aug 13" at this point in the manuscript (JFK item 64).

255:35–37 **"Do you ski, Mr. Henry?" . . . "No. But I want to learn":** Hemingway and Hadley stayed in Chamby three times (15 January–2 February 1922; 24 May–circa 10 June 1922; and 11 December 1922–circa 6 February 1923), but his letters are unclear as to exactly when he first skied. Although a letter to his family written during their first visit to Chamby, says, "There is skiing too" (*Letters 1* 319), the rest of the letter and additional ones written about the same time to his sister Marcelline and to Kate Smith focus heavily on the thrill of bobsledding and do not mention skiing (321–25). Hemingway also tells Marcelline during the first trip to Chamby that he broke his hand in "a couple places," and that would certainly have restricted any attempts at skiing (321). There would not have been skiing there in May 1922.

However, there is no question that by the third and final visit to Chamby, over Christmas 1922, Hemingway was skiing. He spends a long paragraph in a 1 December 1922 letter to Isabelle Simmons explaining the proper attire for skiing when she would be joining him and Hadley in Chamby (*Letters 1* 375). By April 1924, Hemingway had written his short story "Cross-Country Snow," with its thrilling description of downhill skiing, so he was well-acquainted by then with the experience (Reynolds, *Annotated Chronology* 34). Ernest and Hadley also spent the Christmases of 1924 and 1925 at the ski resort in Schruns, Austria, and he spent New Year's 1926–27 and 1927–28 at a similar resort in Gstaad, Switzerland. In other words, by the time he wrote *A Farewell to Arms,* he was an experienced and proficient Alpine skier.

256:5–6 **"Wouldn't you like to . . . be with men and ski?"** Catherine continues to be concerned that Frederic has needs she cannot satisfy, that they have excluded others from their life together, and that he might need time away from her. Frederic, however, denies needing anyone else in his life besides Catherine.

256:13–14 **"I'm having a child and that makes me contented not to do anything":** Catherine recognizes gender differences that originate in biological realities. Bickford Sylvester sees this theme as the heart of the novel.

256:20–21 **"bump on your head":** Catherine is probably checking out the fresh bump that Frederic received when he jumped onto the train car carrying rifles away from the front during his escape. See entry 198:14–15. It also reminds us of the head injury he received in his wounding and of Ferguson's comment that "[a] bump like that could make you crazy." See entry 95:3.

256:21-22 "would you like to grow a beard?" This would seem another example of Catherine's exploring gender differences between her and Frederic, although she later seems more interested in erasing any differences between them. See entry 257:27–28.

256:37 "I don't think about anything much": This is another indication that Frederic's life with Catherine is based more on feeling than thinking, in the subjective as opposed to objective realm, as a true love relationship ought to be. Throughout this dialogue, Catherine expresses her worries that Frederic will become bored with her, but he gives no indication that he feels boredom is likely.

256:39 "Rinaldi and the priest": Frederic's admitting that he thinks about these two important figures, highlighted among all the people he knows, strongly implies that the conflict between science and faith, reason and unreason, the objective and the subjective remains a central issue in his mind.

257:3-4 "What are you thinking about now?" "Nothing": Once again, in this context the word *nothing* could have different meanings. Frederic might indeed mean simply that he is not thinking about anything, even though we learn quickly that such a statement would be a lie. He is thinking about Rinaldi. In light of that, it is not unreasonable to interpret his meaning as "I'm thinking about nothingness." Support for this interpretation can be found in a later reference to Rinaldi's syphilis, which is clearly about nothingness or the meaninglessness of human suffering. See also entry 280:1–6.

257:6 "I was wondering whether Rinaldi had the syphilis": Frederic's present focus may be on the potential consequences of Rinaldi's thoroughly materialistic lifestyle, or it may be on the meaning of Rinaldi's suffering. See entry 153:6–10.

257:12 "I had gonorrhea": Frederic's admission that he has had a sexually transmitted disease is a reminder of his earlier profligate lifestyle. In the days before antibiotic treatments, unavailable until the 1930s, gonorrhea was typically treated with silver proteinate, first introduced for therapeutic use in 1897. A common symptom of gonorrhea is burning during urination and pain in the testicles. In Hemingway's "A Very Short Story," after the wounded American soldier returns from Italy to Chicago and Luz jilts him, he "contract[s] gonorrhea from a sales girl in a loop department store while riding in a taxicab through Lincoln Park" (*CSS* 108).

257:15–17 "I wish I'd had it . . . to be like you": As Debra Moddelmog points out, this is one of Catherine's oddest statements, given the pain and questionable prognosis of a case of gonorrhea in those days before antibiotics (17–18). For a discussion of this and other "queer" aspects of the novel, see Moddelmog's "We Live in a Country Where Nothing Makes Any Difference."

257:27–28 "we'd be just alike": This kind of twinning of male and female lovers is also found most notoriously in Hemingway's posthumous novel *The Garden of Eden*, wherein David Bourne and his wife, also named Catherine, get identical hairstyles and hair colorings so they look as much the same as possible. Carl Eby sees potentially sinister implications in Catherine Barkley's desire to twin herself with Frederic (206). Debra Moddelmog also finds something "queer," that is, transgressive, in Catherine's desires here (18). Frederic may be agreeable to allowing his own hair to grow but is resistant to the idea of Catherine's cutting her hair. The psychoanalytically inclined might conclude he is willing to explore his own femininity but is less comfortable with Catherine giving up hers.

257:37 "We're the same one": Frederic has now come to see the two of them as unified, a frame of mind he has had to grow into over the course of the novel. However, Catherine seems more enthusiastic in this discussion than he does, with few clues, at least here, as to his inner feelings. His bits of dialogue tend to be short and rather flat in comparison to Catherine's.

258:3–5 "I don't live at all" . . . "any life at all any more": These echoing statements by first Catherine and then Frederic highlight how completely dependent they have become on each other. Whether they can sustainably construct a relationship this way will have to remain an open question, since Catherine dies at the end, but many readers doubt that such a mutually exclusive relationship can endure.

258:12 "Now do you want to play chess?" This reference to a chess game reminds us of how far Frederic has come since the beginning of their relationship, when he regarded Catherine as nothing more than a sexual conquest, seeing it all ahead of him "like the moves in a chess game" See entry 22:36–37. The figurative chess game becomes a literal one, where the partners both play by the rules.

258:15 "And afterward we'll play?" This second usage of *play* illustrates the balance between the objective and the subjective—reason and faith—in Catherine and Frederic's relationship. Playing chess requires logic and reasoning. After the chess, they enter the realm of the subjective and engage in love play. The point is that neither realm should be neglected.

258:20 **One time in the night I woke up:** All previous editions of the novel have an extra space prior to the beginning of this paragraph, indicating a gap in the narration. The holograph manuscript has two horizontal lines indicating there should be extra space here (JFK item 64). In the typescript, there is extra space plus a single hand-drawn horizontal line to emphasize the need for the extra space (JFK item 65). In this instance, it is difficult to say exactly how much time has passed. It might only be a few hours, or it might be days or weeks. We can only say with certainty that the date can be any time from 22 December (the day of the previous conversation) to the middle of January, which is the start of chapter 39.

258:33–38 **"Go on to sleep". . . . Then I went to sleep too:** In the typescript, the chapter originally ended with "'Go on to sleep,' I said." However, as a significant afterthought, Hemingway added the remaining five lines in handwriting to the typescript (JFK item 65). The addition is meaningful because it contains Catherine's expressed wish that they fall asleep simultaneously, to which Frederic agrees. However, as Frederic informs us, they do not fall asleep at the same time, perhaps an indication that they are not as unified as they like to think they are. Or perhaps it is simply a recognition that rarely does love in the real world measure up to the romantic fantasies we want it to be. Such a recognition does not necessarily diminish Frederic and Catherine's love. In fact, it may simply reflect his concern for her well-being.

CHAPTER 39

259:1 **By the middle of January:** We have reached January 1918.

259:1 **I had a beard:** Frederic has been growing his beard since 22 December, when Catherine asked him to grow one, and he agreed to start one immediately. See entry 256:21–22.

259:8 **the Bains de l'Alliaz:** This health spa with mineral baths was established in 1811, from sulphur springs about three miles north of Chamby. A walk there would take about one hour and twenty minutes. In an 11 June 1922 letter to Gertrude Stein, Hemingway describes how he and first wife, Hadley, met their British friend Chink Dorman-Smith at the spa, "and we drank 11 bottles of beer apiece with Mrs. H. sleeping on the grass and walked home in the cool of the evening with our feet feeling very far off and unrelated and yet moving at terrific speed" (*Letters 1* 345–46).

259:9 **hobnailed boots:** See entry 250:4–5.

259:16 **glühwein:** A mulled wine popular in German speaking countries, served hot, with spices and citrus, frequently also with cinnamon and sugar.

260:9–12 **"man with the tiny gold earrings?" . . . "makes them hear better":** This exchange is another that illustrates the conflict between science and faith. The chamois is a species of mountain goat native to European mountains. Frederic says chamois hunters wear gold earrings because they think it will help them hear better. However, there is no scientific evidence to support the idea that gold earrings improve hearing. Catherine, as skeptic and nonbeliever, thinks it much more likely the chamois hunters wear the earrings as a way to distinguish themselves from nonchamois hunters.

260:15 **Dent de Jaman:** A roughly six-thousand-foot mountain about three miles east of Chamby. The name means literally "Tooth of Age."

260:24 "We live in a country where nothing makes any difference": Catherine's assertion here, as Debra Moddelmog suggests, is a "recognition that their retreat to Switzerland is a (temporary) escape from conventional rules and identities" (18). They are free to do and to be whoever and whatever they wish.

260:31 "She won't come between us, will she? The little brat": Catherine again expresses resentment toward their expected child, once more identified as female. Catherine continues to see their relationship as exclusionary of everyone and everything, even the child they have conceived together.

260:33–34 "How are we for money?" ". . . the last sight draft": This exchange informs us that the money with which Frederic and Catherine arrived in Switzerland has been supplemented by a sight draft of an unspecified amount, presumably, like the ones before it, from Frederic's beneficent grandfather. Thus, money will not be a concern.

261:1 "Thank God I'm not your family": Catherine's observation is ironic, considering she wishes to be Frederic's exclusive family.

261:3–4 "Don't you care . . ." ". . . it wore itself out": This exchange fairly accurately conveys the state of Hemingway's relationship with his parents as he was writing the novel. Beginning with his eviction from the family's Michigan cottage in 1920 through their negative responses to his early published writings in the mid-1920s to his divorce from Hadley in 1927, Hemingway's feeling for his family had deteriorated almost to nothing before it was somewhat revived by their chance reunion in Key West in April 1928. But the damage was too deep to be fully repaired. After his father's suicide in December 1928, Hemingway never returned to Oak Park, although he set up a trust fund to support his mother financially for the rest of her life.

261:17–22 "I'm going to cut it". . . . "it would be exciting": The hair motif returns, with Catherine's insistence that she will cut her hair short after their child (presumed female here) is born. Frederic's reticence is interesting but difficult to interpret with certainty. Usually, when a Hemingway character is described as not saying anything, it implies that the character disagrees with or feels some opposition to what the other person has expressed—perhaps that the character wants to say something but chooses not to. Could it be that Frederic would prefer that Catherine not cut her hair but acquiesces to her desires and allows her to be the leader in their relationship? Or is he honest when he says that he would find her exciting with a shorter hair cut?

261:28–29 **"Yes, I want to ruin you." "Good . . . that's what I want too":** We could take this as a positive or a negative for Frederic. Bickford Sylvester sees it as a negative, another instance where Catherine's power over Frederic damages his identity as a male, and it leads to Frederic's feeling powerless, "no good," when he is not with Catherine. However, a positive "ruin" would destroy Frederic's old self-centered but unfocused and unguided identity, one that would facilitate his rebirth as a new person—one who is strong, mature, and fully capable of love.

At the bottom of this manuscript page (numbered 585), Hemingway wrote and circled "Aug 14" (JFK item 64).

CHAPTER 40

262:1 **We had a fine life:** At the top of this manuscript page, numbered 586, Hemingway wrote and circled "Aug 16" (JFK item 64). The novel's penultimate chapter is perhaps more interesting for what Hemingway originally wrote and deleted than for what he retained in it. Hemingway's original intent seems to have been to combine this and chapter 41 into one longer final chapter. The break for chapter 41 was later indicated with a bold line before the sentence that begins "One morning I awoke about three o'clock" (267:1), with "chapter 41" added in the margin. In other words, he originally regarded the combined content of these final two chapters as comprising the novel's conclusion.

In addition, Hemingway's original holograph draft and the typescript contain a long, 622-word cry of pain that was later deleted only just prior to publication. For many years available only to researchers at the JFK Library, it has now been reproduced in its entirety for everyone in appendix 1 of the Hemingway Library edition (item 14, pp. 301–02). Although the decision to delete it was appropriate for a number of reasons, the passage nevertheless provides a fascinating window into the state of Frederic Henry's mind, not only at the conclusion of the novel's events, but also as he is composing the story some five to ten years after the fact.

The passage is one of several in the novel in which Frederic speaks to us from the time of the composition of the novel, as a narrator rather than as a protagonist. Others include the "He had always known what I did not know" passage about the priest (12:19–22), the "abstract words" passage (161:13–27), and the "world breaks everyone passage" (216:24–30). These are all crucial to the theme of the novel, helping us understand how Frederic's experience of the war, his romance with Catherine, and her death and that of their child have affected him. Properly understood, none of the passages conveys a definitive sense that Frederic has achieved any kind of redemption or sense of peace after the fact. Indeed, the bit in question here can only be described as an extremely bitter diatribe on suffering and death and Frederic's continued inability to love God.

It is also a profound rejection of faith and a raw comment on the novel's epistemological theme. For example, at no less than three points in the passage, listed in order below, Frederic reflects on epistemology:

301:37–38 **The only thing I know is that if you love anything enough they take it away from you.**

302:7–8 **The only thing I know is that I do not know anything about it.**

302:18–20 **All that we can be sure of is that we are born and that we will die and that every thing we love that has life will die too.**

These are not the words of a man at peace. In fact, Frederic seems dangerously close to the position of philosophical skepticism, the belief that true knowledge of anything is an impossibility (Dew and Foreman 147–51; Jennifer Nagel 12–29).

At the very least, the passage makes it more difficult to argue that Frederic has moved very far in a positive direction as a result of his love with Catherine. When we look at the places where Frederic is stepping outside his role as protagonist and speaking to us as a narrator, he has still not come to accept his loss and has not overcome his bitterness. As he admits in this deleted passage, he is not "built" the same as the priest is; he cannot find happiness through the kingdom of heaven. He is still, he says, "afraid of God at night" (302:1) and still does not "admire" him.

In short, anyone who wishes to argue that Frederic has gained a profound faith and redemption by the time he tells us his story has to reckon with this deleted piece. That it was cut and shoved beneath the surface of the iceberg does not diminish its importance to our understanding of Frederic's character. Hemingway seems to have only reluctantly cut it, on the advice of F. Scott Fitzgerald just as the novel was set to be published. The decision was proper, not least because the passage, revealing as it does Catherine's death, makes the rest of the novel anticlimactic. Furthermore, its bitter tone is suggested indirectly in plenty of other places anyway, even if it is never so blunt and raw.

For a detailed discussion of F. Scott Fitzgerald's recommendations and Hemingway's reactions to them, see Scott Donaldson's *Hemingway vs. Fitzgerald*. Hemingway was clearly angered by Fitzgerald's notes, writing at the end of them, "Kiss my ass" (JFK item 65), but he took the notes seriously enough to make this recommended deletion, and he tried out one of Fitzgerald's suggested endings before rejecting it. See entries 216:24–30 and 284:3–5.

262:6 **In the night it started raining:** Rain as objective correlative emerges again. Frederic and Catherine's alpine idyll has effectively ended.

262:17 **"young Catherine":** See entry 99:36.

262:20–21 **"go to Lausanne?" . . . "too big a town":** Lausanne lies about nineteen miles west of Montreux on the shore of Lake Geneva. Its 1917 population, around seventy thousand, was about four times that of Montreux. Hemingway stayed in the city from 21 November to 11 December 1922, as he covered the Lausanne Peace Conference, convened to settle territorial disputes between Greece and Turkey in the aftermath of the Greco-Turkish War of 1922 (*Letters 1* 368–69; Reynolds, *Annotated Chronology* 30).

263:32 Vevey: A town about seven miles west of Montreux, slightly smaller in population. Vevey is prominently mentioned in Hemingway's 1927 short story "A Canary for One," in which an American couple are traveling by train from the south of France back to Paris, where they will set up "separate residences," a detail withheld from the reader until the last sentence of the story (*CSS* 261). The two share a train compartment with an American woman who is bringing a canary back to her daughter as a gift to assuage the daughter's grief over her mother's breaking up the daughter's love affair with a European man in Vevey. The wife of the couple remarks, "I know Vevey. . . . We were there on our honeymoon" (260). The mother justifies breaking up her daughter's romance by insisting that American men make the best husbands. The ironic implication is that the American husband is responsible for the failure of the couple's marriage.

263:35 a medium-sized hotel: Frederic provides no more specific details to help us identify the hotel where he and Catherine stay in Lausanne. However, Hemingway may have been thinking of the Hotel Beau-Séjour, where he stayed during his coverage of the Lausanne Peace Conference in late 1922. The hotel was in the heart of the city, a short walk from the train station, with 150 beds, starting at the very affordable price of seven francs a night for a room and sixteen francs for full board, the equivalent of $19.30 and $44.10 in 2017 terms (Baedeker, *Switzerland* 1928 310; Williamson). Other Lausanne hotels listed in Baedeker range from 17 to 320 beds, so the Beau-Séjour would seem to fit the description of "medium sized." The hotel is no longer in business.

264:8–9 March, 1918, and the German offensive had started in France: On 9 March 1918, the German army began its largest offensive of the war on the French front in an effort to achieve a major breakthrough and win the war before large numbers of American troops could be deployed (Gilbert 404–05). The offensive would ultimately fail and would weaken German forces enough to contribute to their defeat in the fall of 1918.

264:26 "Like our home": Throughout the novel, Catherine and Frederic have endeavored to establish a home wherever they are. Although they have, of course, lived a temporary existence during the ten months or so of their romance, Catherine's attitude, that home can be any place in which there is love, contrasts with the attitude of female characters in Hemingway's short stories "Cat in the Rain" and "Hills Like

White Elephants," where the women vividly complain about their itinerant lives with their mates (*CSS* 129, 211).

265:9 **"And play":** Frederic, of course, means subjective sex play as opposed to the rational play of games like chess.

265:11 **"our old white capri":** See note 32:17. Frederic and Catherine have apparently not been able to get their favorite beverage during their nearly four-month stay in Chamby-sur-Montreux.

265:25–26 **not to put ice in the whiskey:** Hemingway rarely misses an opportunity to inform us of his idea of the proper way to prepare and consume an alcoholic beverage. As an aside, Philip Greene believes that when Hemingway's characters drink whiskey it is typically Scotch, since the brands he occasionally names are usually Scotches: White Horse, Haig & Haig Pinch, Old Parr, and Grand Macnish (248).

265:36 **We stayed at that hotel three weeks:** All previous editions of the novel except the Everyman's Library edition have an extra space prior to the beginning of this paragraph, indicating a gap in the narration. The holograph manuscript has two horizontal lines indicating there should be extra space here. Before the lines, Hemingway wrote and circled "Aug 16." After the lines, he wrote and circled "Aug 17" (JFK item 64). In the typescript, there is triple extra space (JFK item 65). Hemingway's intent was to remind us that time is being telescoped as we approach the climax of the narrative. The date at the end of their hotel stay would be around 30 March 1918 (three weeks after 9 March). See entry 264:8–9.

265:38 **cogwheel railway:** Such a train has cogwheels (like gears) that run on a toothed rack rail. This seems a minor historical inaccuracy on Hemingway's part. The original Lausanne-Ouchy line, established in 1877, was a funicular train, in which the cars are attached to a cable that pulls them up and down an incline. The Lausanne-Ouchy was converted to a cogwheel railway in 1959, long after any of Hemingway's visits to the area.

265:39 **Ouchy:** Pronounced *OO-shee*, this is the southern district of the city of Lausanne, which is a port on Lake Geneva. The 1922 Lausanne Peace Conference was held at the Château d'Ouchy hotel on the waterfront. As a journalist covering the conference, Hemingway would walk down the hill daily from his hotel, the Beau-Séjour, to the Château d'Ouchy (Baker, *Life Story* 102; Reynolds, *Paris Years* 84).

266:5 **a gymnasium in the arcade to box:** The Lausanne arcade on the Rue Caroline would have been a short walk up the hill from the Rue Beau-Séjour. Hemingway had begun boxing as a teenager in Oak Park and continued to spar regularly during his years in Paris.

266:18–19 strange to see a man with a beard boxing: The image provides another instance of the novel's theme of identity. Once again, Frederic does not seem to identify himself as the man in the mirror with the beard, although it appears he eventually comes to terms with it and just regards his image as "funny" (266:20). A well-known 1944 photograph of Hemingway depicts him heavily bearded and shirtless, wearing boxing gloves and posing in front of a mirror.

266:22–29 rides . . . in a carriage . . . we could not lose any time together: The carriage rides reintroduce the motif of "Time's wingèd chariot" from Andrew Marvell's "To His Coy Mistress." See entry 135:19–23.

CHAPTER 40 · 303

CHAPTER 41

267:1 three o'clock: Hemingway begins the final ordeal with a specific reference to time, extending the novel's motif of time and its preciousness. This time becomes somewhat problematic later. See entry 271:14.

267:8–9 A little while later I woke again: An unspecified amount of time has passed. How much depends on our definition of "a little while." However, we know it is still before sunrise, which at the end of March in Lausanne would be around 6:15 A.M.

267:15 "every quarter of an hour": By modern standards, this is probably too soon for Catherine to go to the hospital. For a first-time labor in which everything is considered normal, modern doctors recommend waiting until contractions are around five minutes apart before going to the hospital, particularly since first labors, as the nurse in the novel indicates, are usually protracted (Dahlen). Hemingway's second wife, Pauline, had an eighteen-hour labor during her first childbirth experience, which ended with a caesarian delivery of Hemingway's second son, Patrick, on 28 June 1928, during the period in which Hemingway was writing *A Farewell to Arms* (*Letters 3* 405). (See Hawkins 95–96). There is no question that Patrick's birth influenced Hemingway's depiction of Catherine's experience.

267:18 called the garage near the station: This is evidence to support the idea that Hemingway places Frederic and Catherine at the Beau-Séjour Hotel, which was on Rue Beau-Séjour just three blocks from the train station, where there would be taxis waiting.

268:3–4 I brought the elevator up myself: This image recalls a similar moment in the last chapter of *The Sun Also Rises,* when Jake Barnes arrives at the Hotel Montana in Madrid to extricate Bret Ashley from the jam in which she has found herself, following the end of her romance with the young matador Pedro Romero. Whereas Frederic finds no one to operate the elevator and thus operates it himself, Jake cannot "make the elevator work," and so he is forced to walk up to Bret's room (240). If we view the nonfunctioning elevator in *The Sun Also Rises* as an emblem of Jake's own sexual impairment, here the implication, as well indicated throughout the novel, is that Frederic Henry has no difficulty getting his elevator to work.

268:17 started up the hill: The Lausanne Cantonal Hospital was located on Rue du Bugnon, a six-minute taxi ride to the north of Frederic and Catherine's hotel near the train station. Most of Lausanne is built on the side of a steep incline, so any movement north, away from the lake, must travel up the hill. The hospital was established in 1883, with a special maternity clinic built in 1916 ("Les Hospices Cantonaux"). Today, the fully modern Lausanne University Hospital stands on the site. It is unclear the extent to which Hemingway would have researched the Lausanne Hospital to write his novel. As far as we know, he had had no direct experience with it. Much of the description of Catherine's labor and delivery may, in fact, be based on Pauline's difficult labor and caesarian at the Kansas City Research Hospital (Baker, *Life Story* 195).

268:20 She said she had no religion: Just as Brett Ashley does in *The Sun Also Rises*, Catherine Barkley remains consistently irreligious throughout this novel. We can contrast this attitude with Frederic's repeated prayers at different points in this final chapter.

268:39 "He's lying down sleeping": It may be that the doctor is resting up for the time when he is needed, but this initial image does not create a favorable impression. If this is the same doctor who has noted that Catherine is small in the hips and should know that the fetus within her is not small, then he ought to be preparing for a difficult labor and the likelihood of a caesarian section delivery. At the very least, it seems he should be there to greet Catherine on her arrival and make his own initial exam to provide himself with a good sense of where things stand.

269:5 prayed for Catherine: Frederic's own religiousness should be contrasted with Catherine's lack thereof. Frederic's thoughts and actions in the final chapter indicate that he retains faith in an interventionist God, who answers prayers. It is also noteworthy that Frederic apparently does not include the child in his prayers.

269:22–23 When they started to fall off she was disappointed and ashamed: Lines like this tend to stir the anger of feminist critics like Judith Fetterley, who see only hatred of women in the portrayal of Catherine and her ultimate suffering and death: Catherine's role, in this view, is to remain subservient and not to make trouble for her man (205). Other feminist critics, like Sandra Spanier, disagree, seeing Catherine's "subordination of the individual ego to a personal relationship as a mark of maturity" (140). See entry 92:6–19.

269:35 **Outside it was getting light:** Sunrise in Lausanne on 30 March 1918 was approximately 6:15 A.M. Thus, Catherine has been experiencing three and a half hours of labor so far. Switzerland did not begin using Daylight Saving Time until 1941 ("Daylight Saving Time").

269:37 **zinc bar:** The bar has a countertop made out of zinc sheet metal, which has antibacterial properties and is easy to clean with soap and water. Over time, the metal reacts with fingerprints and food stains so that it develops a distinctive patina that lends it character.

270:12 **"There isn't anything, dog":** This line has stirred some controversy between those who wish to make the most out of the novel's so-called *nada* theme and those who are inclined to more positively religious interpretations. If we regard Hemingway as a careful craftsman in his writing, then this detail is surely not meaningless. It adds nothing substantial to the plot. To some readers, Frederic's statement amounts to an acknowledgement of the nothingness, the meaninglessness of existence, and it is consistent with other details in the novel. See, for example, entries 28:7 and 119:34. H. R. Stoneback colorfully calls such interpretation "*nadarasty*": "A hungry dog is a hungry dog," he insists ("Lovers' Sonnets" 48). Maybe so, but the question remains: why has Hemingway included this detail of a hungry dog at this point in the novel? Why has he had Frederic remember such a detail years later as he relates the story to us? On one level, the scene simply illustrates Frederic's compassion for the dog; that is, he empathizes with it. It shows he cares about the suffering of another being and is indicative of growth in his character. Thus, Frederic looks into the refuse can to see if there is "anything I could pull out for him," but he finds "nothing on top but coffee-grounds, dust and some dead flowers," details that seem to suggest death—the death he is fearing for Catherine (270:10, 11).

270:24–25 **I could see Catherine lying on a table, covered by a sheet:** The image of death in the refuse can is followed by a scene that could be taken from a morgue. Although Catherine is not dead yet, this image certainly foreshadows the novel's ending.

270:26–27 **some cylinders. The doctor held a rubber mask attached to a tube:** As Michael Reynolds has pointed out, the doctor is administering to Catherine nitrous oxide, sometimes known as "laughing gas," which had come into common usage by 1918 to alleviate pain in childbirth ("Doctors in the House of Love" 122). However, Reynolds points out that it is not recommended to use nitrous oxide for more than six hours. By the time Catherine is finally taken to the operating room for a caesarian at 7:00 P.M., she has been receiving nitrous oxide for at least twelve hours, well past its effectiveness.

271:14 We had gone to the hospital about three o'clock: All previous editions of the novel have an extra space before the beginning of this paragraph, indicating a gap in the narration. The manuscript has two horizontal lines indicating there should be extra space here. Hemingway also wrote and circled above the lines "Aug 17, Aug 18 0, Aug 19 0," indicating he had reached this point in the manuscript on 17 August 1928 and written nothing on 18–19 August. Below the lines, he wrote "Aug 20," showing he had resumed writing (JFK item 64). The typescript has triple extra space to indicate the need for the space (JFK item 65).

In addition, the statement is problematic. Based on Frederic's telling us at 267:1 that he woke at three o'clock, it must have been some time later that they went to the hospital, probably closer to four o'clock. In fact, the Everyman's Library edition, published in the United Kingdom, changes the time provided here to "four o'clock" (303). It is the only edition of the novel to make such a change, so it must have been a decision made by an editor at Everyman's Library. Whoever made the change, four o'clock makes better sense. Three o'clock is plainly inaccurate. See entries 267:1 and 267:8–9.

271:16 she looked very tired: A new notebook of the manuscript, labeled "Book Two," begins here. Hemingway wrote and circled "Aug 21" at the top of the page (JFK item 64).

271:25 "There one comes": In the original manuscript, Hemingway underlined this, indicating his desire to have it italicized (JFK item 64). He continued to use underlining to indicate italics for Catherine's expressions during the rest of her labor.

271:28 "About a minute": With contractions spaced a minute apart, Catherine should be in the delivery stage of childbirth with a fully dilated cervix, but if the baby is too large for her bone structure, there is nothing that can force the child through the birth canal. Her exhaustion is inevitable unless the doctor intervenes with a caesarian.

271:32 "Couldn't my husband give me the gas?": Frederic's and Catherine's roles have reversed from the time when he was the patient and she the caregiver in the Milan hospital.

271:36 "I want it now": This is underlined in the original manuscript, indicating Hemingway's desire to have it italicized (JFK item 64).

272:7–8 he was lying down and smoking a cigarette: This is another less than favorable image of the doctor, resting and indulging in a casual smoke, while Catherine's suffering is at a peak.

272:11–12: **"There it comes. Give it to me":** Hemingway underlined this in the original manuscript, indicating italics (JFK item 64).

272:13 **At two o'clock I went out and had lunch:** Catherine has now been in labor about eleven hours and has been receiving nitrous oxide for at least seven hours.

272:14 **glasses of kirsch or marc:** Both of these are types of brandy. Kirsch, which originated in Germany, is made from cherries and is colorless. Marc, a product of France, is, like the Italian grappa, distilled from pomace, the solid remains of grapes after juice has been pressed out for winemaking. It normally has a golden color. Philip Greene believes Hemingway acquired a taste for kirsch during a ski trip to Schruns, Austria, in 1924, when "the locals referred to him as the 'Black Kirsch-drinking Christ' due to his suntan, long hair and beard, and taste for the local brandy" (93). See also Baker, *Life Story* 139.

272:18 **choucroute:** The French word for sauerkraut.

272:20 **"A demi or a bock?"** Although in Belgium, to order a demi is to order a half-sized glass or bottle of beer, the context here implies that "demi" refers to the color of the beer. A bock is a dark lager with a strong malt flavor. A demi here, as is later clarified (281:11), means a "demi-blonde" beer, which suggests something between a bock and a blonde beer. Blonde beer, with a golden color, is more likely to be an ale, with a smoother, less malty taste than a bock. A demi-blonde is probably close to what is better known today as an amber ale. Frederic is even more specific in asking for a "light demi."

272:30–31 **I wondered . . . what it had been like:** Catherine's suffering in labor has caused Frederic to contemplate the prevalence of such suffering in the world, another indication of his growing awareness of the philosophical ramifications of what he and Catherine are experiencing.

272:37–38 **I . . . saw myself looking like a fake doctor with a beard:** This image provides another instance of the motif of identity in the novel. Frederic is hyperconscious of what he is not. The question is whether he knows by now who he actually is.

273:2 **The nurse was doing something:** Author Hemingway could have chosen to allow narrator Frederic to know what the nurse is doing. But Frederic's not knowing contributes to the general sense in the novel of how little we can know with certainty in the world.

273:8 **"He's wonderful. You're wonderful, doctor":** In the original manuscript, "wonderful" is underlined in both sentences, indicating Hemingway's desire to italicize the words (JFK item 64).

273:11 **"Give it to me. Give it to me":** Hemingway underlined these two sentences in the original manuscript, indicating italics (JFK item 64).

273:16–17 **"I'm past where I was going to die":** All of the nitrous oxide has clearly made Catherine giddy and somewhat delusional. Her saying this probably only makes Frederic even more fearful and aware of the real possibility that she may die. The scene recalls when Catherine cautions Frederic, as he is about to undergo surgery on his knee, not to get "blabby" when he is under the influence of the anesthetic. See entry 90:19.

273:20–21 **"You will not . . . die and leave your husband":** The doctor's statement may seem condescending, but he probably believes, rightly or wrongly, that it is important for Catherine to maintain a positive attitude. This is not to defend the doctor's competence. He certainly makes significant mistakes that probably contribute to Catherine's death, if not the child's.

273:23 **"Give it to me":** Hemingway underlined this in the original manuscript, indicating italics (JFK item 64).

273:33–34 **It was beginning to be dark outside:** Sunset in Lausanne on 30 March 1918 would have been around 7:00 P.M. See entry 269:35.

274:2 **This was the end of the trap:** Frederic's statement is a clear echo of the earlier reference to being "trapped biologically." See entry 121:11.

274:4 **before there were anæsthetics?** Frederic's question is an indication of his growing awareness of the level of suffering in other human beings.

274:4–5 **Once it started they were in the mill-race:** A mill-race is the channel that confines water into a narrow stream that is forced through the paddlewheel of a mill. Thus, it is another image of entrapment. The pronoun *it* can refer to pregnancy, labor, or, more broadly, life.

274:8–9 **You never got away . . . married fifty times:** Frederic at first thinks of Catherine's suffering as punishment for their illicit lovemaking, but then he rejects that idea. Catherine would of course be suffering in the same way no matter how legitimate their lovemaking had been.

274:9–25 And what if she should die? . . . What if she should die? The intense stream of consciousness in the rest of this paragraph is more than Frederic's simply confronting the increasing possibility that Catherine can die. His repeated use of this direct question in these precise words supports the notion that Hemingway had T. S. Eliot's "Portrait of a Lady" in mind. *In Another Country,* one of Hemingway's alternate titles for *A Farewell to Arms* and an allusion to Christopher Marlowe's *Jew of Malta,* may have drawn the phrase from "Portrait of a Lady," which uses the Marlowe quote as its epigraph (*Complete Plays*). Here, however, there can be no question that Hemingway is alluding to Eliot's poem, which concerns the relationship between a young man (the speaker in the poem) and a lonely older woman. The poem concludes:

> Well! and what if she should die some afternoon,
> . . . . Should die and leave me sitting pen in hand
> . . . . Not knowing what to feel or if I understand
> . . . . Would she not have the advantage, after all?
> This music is successful with a "dying fall"
> Now that we talk of dying—
> And should I have the right to smile? (*Complete Poems* 11)

Frederic uses Eliot's exact words "what if she should die" eleven times in the space of sixteen lines of this paragraph, and once more at 274:36. One usage might have been coincidental, but twelve times makes the allusion unquestionable and thus highlights a central issue for both the speaker of Eliot's poem and Frederic Henry. Hemingway considered using as an epigraph for the novel "The position of the survivor of a great calamity is seldom admirable" (JFK item 64). See entry Epigraphs (Unused). Whether to admire Frederic has been one of the central questions puzzling readers of Hemingway's novel almost since its initial publication.

Another line from Eliot's poem that surely resonated with Hemingway is "Not knowing what to feel or if I understand," which fully reflects the epistemological theme of *A Farewell to Arms.* Both Eliot's poem and Hemingway's novel are narrated by young men who have little clue about the meaning of events around them.

274:19 What reason is there for her to die: Frederic's question goes beyond mere biological/materialist causes for Catherine's death. Those can be determined. Frederic is questioning the higher order of things. He wants to know the cosmic reason for death.

274:33–35 "Either a high forceps delivery . . . and a Caesarean": Today we may be shocked that Catherine's doctor has not considered a caesarean section delivery until this point in her labor, after hours of intense suffering and no progress, but in the early twentieth century, death rates remained high enough that C-sections were still generally regarded as a last resort. For example, in the New Orleans Charity Hospital between 1916 and 1918, out of 1,718 childbirths, only 23 were delivered by C-section, and in 7 of those cases, the mother died (Duffy 200). John Harley Young, in his 1944 *Caesarean Section: History and Development,* which Reynolds cites in "Doctors in the House of Love," nevertheless claims that by 1910 the mortality rate for mothers undergoing a C-section had fallen from 30 to 45 percent in the previous century to only 3 to 10 percent, "depending on when [the caesarean] was performed. By 1918 the mortality rate for mothers was less than 2 percent if the operation were performed early in labor" ("Doctors in the House of Love" 123; J. H. Young 158). However, the rate rose to 10 percent if the operation was delayed until late in the labor. Thus, in postponing the decision to perform a C-section, Catherine's doctor has quintupled the risk that she may die.

A high forceps delivery, as the doctor explains, is even more risky. It is used in cases where the child has not yet descended into the birth canal, so the forceps must reach into the uterus to pull the baby out. Naturally, risk of injury or death to mother and child is significant. The uterus may tear, inducing hemorrhage in the mother, and the infant may be permanently damaged as well. Reynolds states that the risk of mortality from a high forceps delivery was at least 25 percent (123). Thus, the caesarean means a better chance of survival for both mother and child, and the doctor makes the appropriate recommendation, although it nevertheless seems that he has been less attentive than he should have to the lack of progress in Catherine's labor and has waited too long to take action.

See also Hemingway's depiction of a caesarian section in his short story "Indian Camp"—successful, except for the fact that the baby's father, lying in the bunk above his wife with a severe ax wound to his leg, commits suicide during the surgery by slitting his throat with a razor (*CSS* 67–69).

274:36 **What if she should die!** In the original manuscript, this ends with a question mark and is underlined, to indicate italics. The manuscript also notes that this should be in "very small type" (JFK item 64). In the typescript, the request for very small type is repeated in typed letters, and the word "italics" is added in handwriting (JFK item 65). However, no edition of the novel has followed these instructions.

275:8 **"What about infection?"** The holograph manuscript has another "What if she should die?" after this sentence, but it is crossed out (JFK item 64). It is not present in the typescript (JFK item 65).

275:22 **"Please give me that":** This is underlined in the original manuscript, to indicate italics (JFK item 64).

275:23 **"Oh, it doesn't work!"** This is underlined in the original manuscript, to indicate italics (JFK item 64).

275:33 **"There it comes. Oh Oh Oh!"** This is underlined in the original manuscript, to indicate italics (JFK item 64).

275:37 **"Can't they give me something?"** This is underlined in the original manuscript, to indicate italics (JFK item 64).

276:8–9 **"I'm all broken. They've broken me. I know it now"**: Catherine echoes the famous passage from earlier in the novel, where Frederic, speaking as narrator rather than as protagonist, declares, "The world breaks every one and afterward many are strong at the broken places." See entry 216:24–30. Unspoken here, but surely implied, is the remainder of the passage: "But those that will not break it kills. It kills the very good and the very gentle and the very brave impartially" (216:27–28). Just as Frederic does, Catherine uses the third-person plural pronoun *they* to identify those who have the power to break people, a charge that can only be placed at the feet of God. Her final statement, "I know it now," connects her words to the novel's epistemological theme. Her experience has provided her with subjective knowledge of the way the world works. It breaks everyone.

276:14 **"I promise you won't"**: As Nick Adams says to his friend George in "Cross-Country Snow," "There isn't any good in promising" (*CSS* 146).

276:20 **"But what if I should?"** Catherine echoes Frederic's thoughts and words, "What if she should die?" See entry 274:9–25.

276:22 **"Give it to me!"** The second sentence uttered by Catherine is underlined in the original manuscript, to indicate italics (JFK item 64).

276:30 **"It's not working!"** This is underlined in the original manuscript, to indicate italics (JFK item 64).

276:33 **Finally a new doctor came in:** All previous editions of the novel have an extra space before the beginning of this paragraph, indicating a gap in the narration. The manuscript has two horizontal lines to indicate there should be extra space here. Above the lines, Hemingway wrote "Aug 20" and below the lines "Aug 21" (JFK item 64). In the typescript, there is triple extra space to emphasize the need for the extra space (JFK item 65).

277:1–2 **"They've got to give me something":** The two iterations of this are both underlined in the original manuscript, to indicate italics (JFK item 64).

277:11–12 **Two nurses were hurrying toward the entrance to the gallery:** Hemingway may have been aware that the Lausanne hospital was part of a medical college and thus was a teaching hospital with an operating room gallery, where others, especially students, could observe and learn. The nurses here are excited about the rare chance to watch a caesarean delivery. However, their excited laughter after Catherine has been going through such intense suffering is another jarring instance of how little real empathy humans can have for the hardships of another person.

277:21 **I could see it was raining:** As the drama intensifies and Catherine's hour of death nears, that Eliot-like objective correlative, rain, reappears with all its ominousness. It magnifies the fact that Frederic is completely helpless in this moment.

277:26 **a freshly skinned rabbit:** Robert M. McIlvaine finds parallels between Hemingway's depiction of Catherine's caesarean and a similar scene in Theodore Dreiser's novel *The "Genius."* Near the end of the novel, its protagonist, Eugene Witla, a struggling painter in New York, is forced to watch helplessly as his wife, Angela, undergoes a horrifyingly painful labor followed by a caesarean to deliver their child:

> He stared as if this were all a dream—a nightmare. It might have been a great picture like Rembrandt's "The Night Watch." One young doctor, the one he did not know, was holding aloft a purple object by the foot. It might have been a skinned rabbit, but Eugene's horrified eyes realized that it was his child—Angela's child—the thing all this horrible struggle and suffering was about . . . and yet the doctor was striking it on the back with his hand, looking at it curiously. (701)

Though we cannot be sure that Hemingway read Dreiser's *The "Genius,"* the similarity of details in the two novels is noteworthy.

Equally interesting, and unnoted by McIlvaine, is how Eugene Witla, like Frederic Henry, is torn between the conflict of faith and science and for a while seriously explores the teachings of Christian Science, with its denial of the reality of the material world, as a means of bringing peace to his turmoil. But neither the faith of Christian Science nor the scientific materialism of the doctors can save the life of Angela, who dies soon after childbirth, just as Catherine Barkley will die. Finally, Eugene Witla rejects Christian Science: "He came to know that he did not know what to believe" (707). Compare this statement to Frederic's "The only thing I know is that I do not know anything about it," from the deleted segment of chapter 40 of *A Farewell to Arms* (302:7–8). Coincidence or not, Dreiser and Hemingway explored similar themes in their novels and preferred a balance of faith and science to a life dominated by one or the other. Hemingway had used Christian Science prominently in his 1924 short story "The Doctor and the Doctor's Wife," in which the wife's Christian Science faith is contrasted with the doctor's rationalism and science.

277:29 **doing things to a new-born child:** In the original manuscript, Hemingway wrote and crossed out, "tying the umbilical cord of a fresh born child and putting drops in its eyes," indicating he was still considering an ending in which the child lives (JFK item 64).

277:39 **"He nearly killed his mother":** Hemingway used these same words in a letter to his parents following the birth of his second son, Patrick, after an eighteen-hour labor and caesarean delivery on 28 June 1928 (*Letters 3* 403).

278:2–3 **The doctor was busy. . . . I did not wait to see it:** The original manuscript does not include these three sentences. In their place, Hemingway wrote, "They looked at each other" (JFK item 64).

278:10–11 **the great long, forcep-spread, thick-edged wound:** With any caesarean section, there are naturally two incisions: first through the abdominal skin of the mother and then through the wall of the uterus. Classic C-sections were done with longitudinal incisions in both stomach and uterus, as seems to be the case here with Catherine. Because longitudinal incisions were found to be more susceptible to rupture during subsequent pregnancies, modern C-sections usually involve transverse incisions in the lower abdominal skin and in the lower part of the uterus. Although doctors performing caesarians as late as the eighteenth century believed it was best not to suture the uterus, due to the contraction that would occur postpartum, by the late nineteenth century surgeons recognized that suturing the uterus, sometimes in a double layer, produced fewer complications and better results for future pregnancies (Babu and Magon 358). Presumably, the surgeon has already sutured Catherine's uterus by the time Frederic begins watching.

278:12 **like a drawing of the Inquisition:** The Roman Catholic Church established the Inquisition in thirteenth-century France to combat heresy within the church, and the institution became especially prominent and powerful in medieval and early Renaissance Spain and Portugal. Tribunals had papal authority to use torture to elicit confessions from the accused. The most common torture method was the rack, in which the accused was placed on a device, his or her limbs fastened to rollers at both ends and stretched, producing excruciating pain. The Inquisition was formally discontinued following the Napoleonic wars in the early nineteenth century. Hemingway's allusion here to a work of art is another detail Robert M. McIlvaine connects to Dreiser's *The "Genius,"* where the scene in the caesarean operating room is compared to Rembrandt's painting *The Night Watch* (446). See entry 277:26. However, Hemingway's choice of the Inquisition as his drawing's subject puts the scene in the context of the faith and reason conflict we have observed throughout the novel. One possible antecedent is Dostoevsky's "The Grand Inquisitor" chapter from *The Brothers Karamazov*, in which Ivan Karamazov elucidates to his religious and saintly brother Alyosha his quarrel with God and contempt for organized religion. There are numerous drawings of Inquisition torture chambers, any of which could have served as Hemingway's inspiration for this simile. The reference also suggests that Frederic's concerns may include not only Catherine's physical well-being but also her spiritual well-being as an atheist. For more on Dostoevsky's influence on the novel, see the introduction to this volume.

279:17 **"Didn't you know?"** In the original manuscript, to the nurse's epistemological question Hemingway added, "He was dead," then crossed it all out (JFK item 64).

279:21–22 **"The cord was caught around his neck or something":** The nurse's vagueness and lack of medical terminology indicates she has had to draw her own conclusions about what has happened to the baby. Presumably, she has only overheard words spoken by the doctor. However, the umbilical cord cannot actually strangle the fetus, since the fetus is not breathing air while it is inside the womb. It is not uncommon for the umbilical cord to become wrapped around a fetus's neck or one of its limbs, but only very rarely does the wrapping result in complications during childbirth. The umbilical cord delivers oxygen to the fetus through its blood vessels. Only by compression of the cord can the fetus's oxygen supply be restricted. In extremely rare cases, if the cord is wrapped tightly, the cord may become compressed, and there have been some reported cases of stillbirth where "cord around the neck syndrome" is the only apparent cause (Peesay).

279:23 **"So he's dead":** The original manuscript has a question mark at the end of this (JFK item 64).

279:33–34 **I had no religion but I knew he ought to have been baptized:** Frederic's religious ambivalence is on full display here, in the first and only time in the novel where he declares that he has no religion. The past-tense *had* may raise the question of whether his religious feelings have changed at all in the time that has passed since the events of the novel. But then he clouds the issue even more as he seems to contradict himself by insisting that "he knew" the stillborn child "ought to have been baptized." In technical terms, the sacrament of baptism, like all Roman Catholic sacraments, is only for the living ("Pastoral Notes"). And Frederic's son was never alive outside of Catherine, as he admits here. Until recently, the Church taught that the souls of unbaptized babies who died would go to Limbo, a place in which the only punishment is not to be allowed into Heaven. Frederic may also be concerned that an unbaptized infant would not be allowed to be buried in the consecrated ground of a Catholic cemetery. Typically in a case of a stillborn baby, a priest will perform a christening ceremony and confer a blessing on the dead child, commending its spirit to the hands of God.

279:37–38 I wished the hell I'd been choked like that. No I didn't: Frederic may be ambivalent about God, but he is also ambivalent about the material world, with its fact of death. Part of him envies the child for avoiding all the suffering of life leading only to death. But having stated that desire, he quickly takes it back. Like Jake Barnes, who knows suffering as much as any Hemingway character yet who nevertheless finds a way to get enjoyment and satisfaction out of life and insists that the world is "a good place to buy in," Frederic finds too much pleasure in the material world to give it up. He is not ready to die.

280:1–6 You died . . . and they would kill you: This passage provides another instance in which Frederic uses the third-person-plural *they* to refer to the higher power that controls life and death: God. The gist of this paragraph is that God kills for no discernible reason.

280:7–20 Once in camp . . . only steamed the ants: In one of the novel's most important and arresting passages, Hemingway/Frederic composes a parable that effectively illustrates his view of God's responsibility for human suffering and death, comparing the plight of humans to that of ants that he recalls on a burning log in a campfire. In the account, he places himself in the position of God watching the ants, who desperately try to avoid the certainty of death in the fire. Like God, he holds the power to end the ants' suffering and deliver them from death by lifting the log out of the fire to safety. However, all he does is empty a cup of water on the log so that he can drink some whiskey from it—a selfish and heartless gesture that probably only increases the ants' suffering. The clear conclusion of this passage is that Frederic, like Ivan Karamazov, holds God responsible for the suffering in the world.

Inspiration for this parable may have come from a passage in one of the most important sources of Hemingway's anxiety of influence—Stendhal's *The Red and the Black*. Near the end, in chapter 74, "The Shadow of the Guillotine," as Julien Sorel awaits execution for attempted murder, he contemplates God and human suffering, much as Frederic Henry does, and relates his own story about ants, speaking to himself:

> "A hunter fires his gun in a forest, his quarry falls, he runs forward to seize it. His boot strikes an anthill two feet high, destroys the habitation of the ants, scatters the ants and their eggs to the four winds. . . . The most philosophical among the

ants will never understand that black, enormous, fearful body—the hunter's boot which all of a sudden has burst into their dwelling with incredible speed, preceded by a terrifying noise, accompanied by a flash of reddish flame. . . .

"So it is with death, life, eternity, things that would be quite simple to anyone who had organs vast enough to conceive them." (2:341)

In both Frederic's and Julien's accounts, the human agent, as far as the ants are concerned, possesses the powers of an unfeeling, cruel, and mysterious God—actively destructive, inadvertently so, or passively aggressive in allowing the ants to continue in their suffering. Julien's thoughts focus on the ants' perspective, their ignorance of the cause of their fate. Frederic, however, is more concerned with the responsibility of God, imagining himself as potential Messiah and clearly recognizing his own culpability in the ants' suffering. The basic point in both analogies is that the ants are in the same predicament as humans are in their world, at least as Julien and Frederic see it—that is, beset by suffering not of their own making, of which they have no understanding, and over which they have no control. Both passages are key to comprehending the protagonists' status at the ends of their novels. For more on Stendhal's influence on *A Farewell to Arms,* see the introduction to this volume.

280:31 **I went down the hall:** In the original manuscript, Hemingway toyed with the live baby ending here. He wrote and then crossed out

> I went down the hall.
> "The baby is alive, you know."
> "What do you mean?"
> "It's alive, that's all. You want to be careful what you tell people."
> "I'm glad."

This is followed by a few more illegible sentences (JFK item 64).

280:37 **plat du jour:** French for "plate of the day," or the day's special.

280:39 **but it is finished:** The phrase highlights the religious questions that permeate the novel, especially this final chapter. The waiter's language echoes words from the Gospel of John 19:30: "When Jesus therefore had received the vinegar, he said, It is finished: and he bowed his head, and gave up the ghost." See entry 178:24.

281:9 **demi-blonde:** See entry 272:20.

281:17–18 **the break through on the British front:** This is a bitter pun, conscious or not, considering what is happening to the British Catherine while Frederic is sitting in the café, eating ham and eggs and drinking beer. The reference also helps us to date this final chapter. The German army, which had mounted a heavy attack on British and French troops in France, "broke through between the British and French armies, capturing Bapaume and Noyon" on 25 March 1918 (Gilbert 409–10). The move seriously threatened to win the war for Germany. Ultimately, a British counterattack on 30 March staved off disaster, and the Germans were held long enough for the American army to join the fighting in the summer and ultimately win the war for the Allies. The same cannot be said for Catherine.

281:28 **pile of saucers:** In European cafés of that time, drinks were typically served on saucers that remained on the table until the customer was finished and paid the bill. A waiter determined the customer's bill by counting the saucers. Clearly, Frederic is trying to numb his pain with alcohol.

281:33 **paid the reckoning:** This phrase is yet another spur to Frederic's apprehensions, since "reckoning" applies to both what he owes the waiter and the ending of life and the payments for it beyond monetary ones.

281:36–37 **Something dropped inside me:** These words convey a most bitter and ironic parallel to Catherine's empty womb.

281:39 **"Mrs. Henry has had a hemorrhage":** Because the pregnant uterus naturally has a high blood content, there will be an average of two cups of blood lost during a vaginal birth and about twice that amount in a typical caesarean section, since the uterus, rich with large blood vessels, is cut open. However, pregnant women have about 50 percent more blood than nonpregnant women, so a healthy female should be able to tolerate four cups of blood loss (Healthline Editorial Team). A hemorrhage is abnormal blood loss, and if it cannot be stopped, death will result. We cannot be sure of the exact cause of Catherine's hemorrhage. The surgeon might have nipped an organ when making his incision, or he might have failed to properly suture the incision to the uterus. Other possibilities beyond anyone's control include a rupture to Catherine's uterus during her severe labor or failure of her blood to clot properly.

282:5 **Everything was gone inside of me:** This sentence recalls Rinaldi's statement that Frederic was really an Italian, just like him, "All fire and smoke and nothing inside." See entry 57:20–23.

282:6 **I did not think. I could not think:** Deeply distressed by the immanence of Catherine's death, Frederic sets rationality aside and plunges into the realm of pure faith, an outpouring of prayer for her survival.

282:6–13 **I knew she was going to die and I prayed … dear God, don't let her die:** As an officer in the ambulance corps, Frederic is very familiar with the danger of hemorrhaging. See entry 52:38–39. Thus, he descends into a desperate frenzy of prayer, seeking God's intervention to save Catherine, promising anything if God will only save her. Of course, the prayer is not answered. Both religious faith and medical science fail Catherine. Neither offers Frederic a path to happiness. Although his concern for Catherine is enormous, Frederic has little or no grief for the loss of his child.

282:10 **Please, please, please:** Hemingway also used this triplicate phrasing with the cowardly soldier during a bombardment in the chapter 7 vignette of *In Our Time,* where the soldier prays desperately to Christ to protect him from the bombing (*CSS* 110). There the soldier survives, leaving readers to wonder if it is the prayer that saves him. Frederic's prayer, in contrast, is certainly not answered, at least not in the way he hopes.

282:11–12 **You took the baby:** In the original manuscript, Hemingway wrote and heavily struck out something illegible before this sentence, presumably words that indicated the baby was still living (JFK item 64).

282:23 **"Don't touch me":** Catherine's negative response to Frederic's taking her hand may arise out of the hatred she has expressed in the previous line for having to die. Perhaps part of her, understandably, holds Frederic responsible for her impending death. However, she quickly overcomes the feeling and reverses herself.

282:28 **"Do you want me to get a priest":** One final time, Frederic offers Catherine a chance to find conventional religion, but once more she denies the opportunity. When she replies, "Just you," she again confirms that her love for Frederic is her religion.

282:34 **"Cat":** In the original manuscript, Hemingway wrote "baby" (JFK item 64).

282:36–283:2 **"You won't do our things with another girl" … "I don't want them":** Will Frederic pursue other relationships after Catherine's death? The alternate endings suggest not. See entry 284:3–5. However, whether he does not, Catherine wants her relationship to him to remain special and unique. As she says, she wants him to have girls, just without saying or doing the same things she and Frederic have (283:1).

We can understand that at this moment Frederic would insist that he does not want other girls, but, naturally, time will tell. Human beings are human beings, and no one would condemn him for eventually finding love with another woman. Then again, he is soon to be in the position of the Italian major in "In Another Country," who concludes following his young wife's unexpected death, "A man must not marry.

. . . If he is to lose everything, he should not place himself in a position to lose that" (*CSS* 209).

283:6 "I'll come and stay with you nights": A final expression of Catherine's mystical side, which, of course, contradicts her early statement that death is the end of things. See entry 16:39. This is probably her attempt to say something to assuage Frederic's grief, rather than an indication of any change in her nonbelief in an afterlife. Nevertheless, throughout the book Catherine has demonstrated that she is not a thorough materialist, giving Frederic a Saint Anthony medal for good luck and experimenting with him in thought transference, for example. See entries 37:6–36 and 99:13–16.

283:11 "just a dirty trick": These are Catherine's last words, providing her final observation, and perhaps Hemingway's too, on the meaning of suffering in this world. Her courage to the end makes her an exemplar of grace under pressure. As Sandra Spanier insists, "Catherine's death is an artistic necessity if *A Farewell to Arms* is to be an articulation of Hemingway's tragic vision that 'the world breaks everyone'" (142). In addition, calling death "just a dirty trick" is yet another aspersion cast against the powers of the universe responsible for all the suffering, whether she would call those powers God or not. As Hemingway wrote in *Death in the Afternoon*, "all stories, if continued far enough, end in death, and he is no true-story teller who would keep that from you. . . . If two people love each other there can be no happy end to it" (122).

283:20–21 it did not take her very long to die: The alternate endings to the novel begin here. See entry 284:3–5.

283:22 Outside the room, in the hall: All previous editions of the novel have an extra space before the beginning of this paragraph, indicating a gap in the narration. In the manuscript, there is a lengthy ending with no indication of a break (JFK item 64). In the typescript, which has the abbreviated ending as published, there is also no indication of a break or extra space (JFK item 65).

283:30–31 "the only thing to do . . . The operation proved——": The doctor is clearly trying to justify his decisions to Frederic, recognizing that his actions may have been responsible for Catherine's death. We cannot be sure what he intends to say "the operation proved," but Frederic does not want to hear any rationalizations and cuts him off. He seems to recognize that death is just part of the biological trap in which we all find ourselves.

284:3–5 it wasn't any good . . . walked back to the hotel in the rain: Some readers find the flatness of the novel's final sentence unsatisfying. However, for Hemingway it was achieved only with much pain and effort, through some forty-seven different alternative endings. Thus, we can be sure this is what he wanted, one with all emotion stripped away—flat.

Initially, Frederic appears to have some hope that by shutting out all others, darkening the room, and being alone with Catherine's corpse he might be able to communicate with her spirit. But clearly nothing happens. As he declares in one of the drafts for this ending, "She wasn't there" (320:6). Nothing of her essence remains. In comparing her to a statue, he echoes the image early in the novel when he remarks on the marble busts in the office of the hospital in Gorizia as he waits for Catherine. See entry 24:4. Thus, the ending gives us no reason to believe that Frederic's attitude toward her death will be any different than Catherine's was toward her previous fiancé's: that is, "That's the end of it." See entry 17:2.

Finally Frederic has failed to find balance between reason and faith, between objective truth and subjective truth. Although together he and Catherine achieve a degree of balance, her death implies the ultimate impossibility of sustaining it. The cold fact of death erases everything and leaves him with the sense that any meaning behind life is impenetrable. Epistemologically, Frederic seems to know less about the meaning of life at the end than he knows at the beginning. Or, to put it another way, at the beginning of the novel he does not know what he does not know. He is living an aimless life without thinking about anything very much. Now he knows what he does not know, and he hungers for answers to questions he would not have thought to ask previously. The problem is that no answers to those questions are forthcoming. As he says in the deleted portion of chapter 40, "The only thing I know is that I do not know anything about it." See entry 262:1.

The forty-seven alternative endings (appendix 2 in the Hemingway Library edition) are mostly slight variations on just a few truly different endings, but they can shed light on Hemingway's intentions. When we examine these drafts, we need to distinguish between those endings that were rejected for content reasons (that is, their information apparently did not fit with the content of the story that Hemingway wished to tell) and those that were rejected for stylistic reasons (that is, their content is consistent with the story, but Hemingway wished to convey the information differently or to leave it beneath the surface of the iceberg). The only ones that seem to have been rejected for content reasons are those in which the baby survives (endings 7, 8, and 9). Nothing of the content in any of the other endings contradicts the content of the published novel. Some of the content supplements the novel, that is, by providing some additional information either about what happened to some of the characters or about Frederic's thoughts and feelings, but none of them changes the novel's essential meaning.

It was surely a wise decision on Hemingway's part to reject the "Live-Baby" endings. While it may be difficult to say what the effect might have been on Frederic, the child's survival would have surely softened the ending's tragic effect, which seems the opposite of Hemingway's intentions. For example, if Hemingway had wished to show that Frederic achieves some kind of spiritual redemption in the years following Catherine's death, as some critics contend, having the child survive and providing some idea of Frederic's care for him would have been an excellent way to demonstrate it. Depriving Frederic of that opportunity makes it far more difficult to provide compelling evidence of a Christian redemption in him. Hemingway needed an ending that would be consistent in the tone with the rest of the novel and that would convey his sense of the tragedy of life. To produce such an effect, the child, sadly, needs to die along with Catherine. In simple terms, Hemingway rejected the "Live-Baby" ending because, as he notes in one iteration, "he does not belong in this story. He starts a new one" (305).

The rest of the endings would all fit fine with the content of the novel as it stands, but almost all of them would pile on verbiage that would detract from the desired flatness. Those that the editors label "The Religious Ending" (endings 4, 5, and 6) are not truly religious endings. In none of these alternatives does Frederic affirm his faith and love of God. To the contrary, they confirm, in the same terms used in the deleted passage from chapter 40, that Frederic is not "built" the same way as the priest; that is, while he recognizes that the priest loves God and is happy in that love, Frederic cannot love God.

The prevalent tone in the alternative conclusions remains one of emptiness, even in the "Morning After" endings (13 through 25), which have Frederic returning to his hotel room, falling asleep, and then waking up to a brilliant sunny spring morning. For a moment, he does not remember what has happened. But the moment is brief, perhaps only a second, before the realization hits him, and he knows he will never have again what he has lost with Catherine. Hemingway tried endings like these perhaps as means to heighten the sense of irony: that the sun also rises and the rain ends, but Frederic's pain and sorrow over the loss of Catherine does not end. Finally, he must have felt that this would have exposed too much of the iceberg.

Several endings declare that his life has gone on for a long time and "seems likely to go on for a long time" (312). These seriously undercut any argument that Frederic Henry tells the story immediately following Catherine's death (see Brenner). There is also no indication that Frederic has found any great sense of purpose in his life following Catherine's death, a strong sense that he learned things from Catherine that have given him guidance. There is nothing about a career in architecture, for example, or any other career, for that matter. The most we have is this: "You get most of your life back like goods recovered from a fire. It all keeps on as long as your life keeps on" (315:23–24). Nor is there any real indication of further relationships with women. Frederic tells us in one ending (27) that he "walked that night in the rain alone, and always from then on alone," but Hemingway struck through the sentence, as if he did not want to preclude the possibility of future relationships for Frederic.

A number of the endings include information about what happened to some of

Frederic's friends: Rinaldi (313:5–7), the priest (313:7–8), Ettore Moretti (313:8–9), Bonello (316:8–9), Piani (316:9–10), and Simmons (315:21). The information is consistent across different alternate endings, so we can assume these are legitimate details Hemingway believed were part of the story but left beneath the surface of the iceberg.

Hemingway did make a good faith effort to follow F. Scott Fitzgerald's advice to use the "world breaks everyone" passage as the conclusion (endings 34 and 35). It is true that such an ending would have provided an existential framework and would have finished the book with a stroke of eloquence, but it would also have distracted from the emotional flatness that Hemingway was clearly striving for. The "world breaks everyone" passage, finally, loses none of its power by remaining in its place in chapter 34, and, as unforgettable as it is, it casts its shadow from there over everything that happens through the remainder of the novel.

Of the endings that served as drafts of the published conclusion, the most striking deletion is the phrase "She was not there," which appears twice struck through in ending 38 (320), with a third contracted instance, "She wasn't there," remaining unstruck. The phrase highlights the fact that Frederic hopes to find Catherine's essence in the hospital room after she has died, as if he is testing the idea that a spirit survives death, an idea he has probably been carrying with him ever since his out-of-body experience when he was wounded. See entry 47:12–17. However, even without a direct statement that "she wasn't there," the ending has all the sense of emptiness we need. Ultimately, in this spare, flat prose, we can see all too clearly that Frederic is left alone with the sense that nothing of Catherine survives the death of her body. He now has only the painful memories of his time with her, which he has eloquently and unforgettably shared with us in *A Farewell to Arms*.

WORKS CITED

Adams, Henry. *The Education of Henry Adams.* Modern Library, 1918.
———. *Esther.* 1884. Penguin Books, 1999.
———. *Mont-Saint-Michel and Chartres.* 1904. Reprint ed., Penguin Classics, 1986.
"An Army Marches on Its Stomach." *Oxford Reference,* 2018, www.oxfordreference.com/view/10.1093/oi/authority.20110803095425331. Accessed 15 November 2018.
Babu, K. M., and Navneet Magon. "Uterine Closure in Cesarean Delivery: A New Technique." *North American Journal of Medical Sciences,* vol. 4, no. 8, December 2012, pp. 358–61.
Baedeker, Karl. *Italy: From the Alps to Naples.* Karl Baedeker, 1909.
———. *Italy: From the Alps to Naples.* Third revised ed., George Allen & Unwin, 1928.
———. *Switzerland: Together with Chamonix and the Italian Lakes.* Karl Baedeker, 1928.
Baker, Carlos. *Ernest Hemingway: A Life Story.* Charles Scribner's Sons, 1969.
———. *Hemingway: The Writer as Artist.* 4th ed., Princeton UP, 1972.
Baker, Sheridan. *Ernest Hemingway: An Introduction and Interpretation.* Barnes & Noble, 1967.
Bakewell, Charles M. *The Story of the American Red Cross in Italy.* Macmillan, 1920.
Bakunin, Mikhail Aleksandrovich. *God and the State.* Translated by Benjamin Tucker, 1883. CreateSpace, 2017.
Barbusse, Henri. *Under Fire: The Story of a Squad.* Translated by Fitzwater Wray, 1917. CreateSpace, 2009.
Barnes, Bingo. "The Classic Martini: A Brief History." *Boise Weekly,* 4 May 2005. www.boiseweekly.com/boise/the-classic-martini/Content?oid=921951. Accessed 30 November 2018.
Beegel, Susan. *Hemingway's Craft of Omission: Four Manuscript Examples.* U of Michigan Research P, 1988.
Bell, Millicent. "Pseudoautobiography and Personal Metaphor." *Ernest Hemingway's* A Farewell to Arms, edited by Harold Bloom, Chelsea House, 1987, pp. 113–29.
Benedictine Monks of St. Augustine's Abbey, Ramsgate. *The Book of Saints.* 6th ed., Morehouse Publishing, 1989.
Berg, A. Scott. *Max Perkins: Editor of Genius.* Berkley Books, 1978.
Berkeley, George. *Principles of Human Knowledge and Three Dialogues.* 1781. Penguin, 1988.
"The Best Science for Better Lives." *The Lancet,* 2018. www.thelancet.com/about-us. Accessed 11 January 2018.
Beversluis, John. "Dispelling the Romantic Myth: A Study of *a Farewell to Arms.*" *The Hemingway Review,* vol. 9, no. 1, 1989, pp. 18–25.
The Bible: Authorized King James Version. Oxford UP, 1997.
Bishop, John Peale. *The Collected Essays of John Peale Bishop,* edited by Edmund Wilson, Octagon Books, 1975.

Blackmore, Susan. *Dying to Live: Science and the Near-Death Experience.* Grafton, 1993.

———. "An Out-of-Body Experience." *dr susan blackmore,* 8 November 1970. www.susan-blackmore.uk/drugs/an-out-of-body-experience. Accessed 18 April 2018.

Blanke, Olaf, and Sebastien Dieguez. "Leaving Body and Life Behind: Out-of-Body and Near-Death Experiences." *The Neurology of Consciousness: Cognitive Neuroscience and Neuropathology,* edited by Steven Laureys and Giulio Tononi, Elsevier, 2009, pp. 303–25.

Bloom, Harold. *The Anxiety of Influence: A Theory of Poetry.* 2nd ed., Oxford UP, 1997.

Blunden, Edmund. *Undertones of War.* U of Chicago P, 2007.

Bonadeo, Alfredo. *D'Annunzio and the Great War.* Fairleigh Dickinson UP, 2004.

Brasch, James D., and Joseph Sigman. *Hemingway's Library: A Composite Record.* Garland, 1981.

Bredahl, Michael. "Freisa Grapes." *World's Best Wines.eu,* 16 October 2016. worldsbestwines.eu/grapes/freisa. Accessed 11 January 2018.

Brenner, Gerry. *Concealments in Hemingway's Works.* Ohio State UP, 1983.

"Brigata 'Basilicata.'" *Fronte del Piave,* 2018. www.frontedelpiave.info/public/modules/Fronte_del_Piave_article/Fronte_del_Piave_view_article.php?id_a=453&app_l2=397&app_l3=453&sito=Fronte-del-Piave&titolo=Brigata-Basilicata. Accessed 12 November 2018.

"British Field Service Postcard, First World War." *Imperial War Museums,* 2018. www.iwm.org.uk/collections/item/object/205131476. Accessed 5 January 2018.

Brontë, Emily. *Five Essays Written in French.* Translated by Lorine White Nagel, Folcroft Library Editions, 1974.

———. *Wuthering Heights.* 1847. Penguin, 2003.

Bruccoli, Matthew J., editor. *Conversations with Ernest Hemingway.* UP of Mississippi, 1986.

———. *The Only Thing That Counts: The Ernest Hemingway/Maxwell Perkins Correspondence, 1925–1947.* U of South Carolina P, 1996.

Burwell, Rose Marie. *Hemingway: The Postwar Years and the Posthumous Novels.* Cambridge UP, 1996.

Butler, Charles. *A Continuation of the Rev. Alban Butler's Lives of the Saints to the Present Time.* Keating & Brown, 1823.

Butler, Samuel. *The Way of All Flesh.* 1903. Dover, 2004.

Byron, Lord [George Gordon]. "The Prisoner of Chillon." 1816. *Poetry Foundation,* 2018. www.poetryfoundation.org/poems/43842/the-prisoner-of-chillon. Accessed 28 November 2018.

Calabi, Silvio, Steve Helsey, and Roger Sanger. *Hemingway's Guns: The Sporting Arms of Ernest Hemingway.* Shooting Sportsman, 2010.

Carruthers, Glenn. "Who Am I in Out of Body Experiences? Implications From OBEs for the Explanandum of a Theory of Self-Consciousness." *Phenomenology and the Cognitive Sciences,* vol. 14, no. 1, 2015, pp. 183–97.

Casillo, Robert, and John Paul Russo. *The Italian in Modernity.* U of Toronto P, 2011.

Cavallaro, Gaetano V. *Futility Ending in Disaster: Diplomatic, Military, Aviation and Social Events in the First World War on the Austro-Italian Front 1917.* Vol. 2. Xlibris, 2009.

Caviglia, Enrico. *La Dodicesima Battaglia (Caporetto).* A. Mondadori, 1933.

Cecchin, Giovanni. *Americani Sul Grappa.* Magnifica Comunità Pedemontana dal Piave al Brenta, 1984.

Cirino, Mark. "A Bicycle Is a Splendid Thing: Hemingway's Source for Bartolomeo Aymo in *A Farewell to Arms.*" *The Hemingway Review,* vol. 26, no. 1, 2006, pp. 106–14.

———. *Ernest Hemingway: Thought in Action.* Kindle ed., U of Wisconsin P, 2012.

———. *Reading Hemingway's* Across the River and into the Trees: *Glossary and Commentary.* Kent State UP, 2016.

———. "'That Supreme Moment of Complete Knowledge': Hemingway's Theory of the Vision of the Dying." *War + Ink: New Perspectives on Ernest Hemingway's Early Life and Writings,* edited by Gail Sinclair, Steve Paul, and Steven Trout, Kent State UP, 2014, pp. 242–59.

———. "'You Don't Know the Italian Language Well Enough': The Bilingual Dialogue of *A Farewell to Arms.*" *The Hemingway Review,* vol. 25, no. 1, 2005, pp. 43–62.

Colbert, Charles. "Winslow Homer, Reluctant Modern." *Winterthur Portfolio,* vol. 38, no. 1, 2003, pp. 37–55.

Comley, Nancy R., and Robert Scholes. *Hemingway's Genders: Rereading the Hemingway Text.* Yale UP, 1994.

Cummings, E. E. "nexttoofcoursegodamericai," 1926. *Genius,* 2018. genius.com/E-e-cummings-next-to-of-course-god-america-i-annotated. Accessed 30 November 2018.

Curnutt, Kirk. *Reading Hemingway's* To Have and Have Not: *Glossary and Commentary.* Kent State UP, 2017.

Dahlen, Hannah. "Help! How Will I Know When It's Time to Go to the Hospital?" *Pregnancy, Birth and Beyond,* 2012, www.pregnancy.com.au/help-how-will-i-know-when-its-time-to-go-to-hospital/. Accessed 13 November 2018.

Dalton, Hugh. *With British Guns in Italy: A Tribute to Italian Achievement.* 1919. Forgotten Books, 2012.

D'Annunzio, Gabriele. *The Flame,* 1900. Translated by Susan Bassnett, Eridanos Library, 1991.

"Daylight Saving Time History in Switzerland." *Timeanddate.com,* 2018. www.timeanddate.com/time/change/switzerland?year=1941. Accessed 11 January 2018.

Dearborn, Mary. *Ernest Hemingway: A Biography.* Knopf, 2017.

de Wit, Rutger. "Why Were the Germans Compared to Huns during World War I?" *Quora,* 12 December 2016, www.quora.com/Why-were-Germans-compared-to-Huns-during-World-War-I. Accessed 13 November 2018.

Dew, James K. Jr., and Mark W. Foreman. *How Do We Know? An Introduction to Epistemology.* IVP Academic, 2014.

Di Nardo, Vincenzo. "Hemingway." Email to Michael Kim Roos. 27 February 2017.

———. "Nick Nerone." Email to Michael Kim Roos. 14 January 2018.

Di Nardo, Vincenzo, and Michael Kim Roos. "*Addio alle Armi:* la figura del Cappellano, Ettore Moretti e Nick Nerone." *Ácoma,* no. 15, new series, Autumn–Winter 2018, pp. 134–41.

Donaldson, Scott. "Censorship and *A Farewell to Arms.*" *Studies in American Fiction,* vol. 19, no. 1, 1991, pp. 85–93.

———. *Hemingway vs. Fitzgerald: The Rise and Fall of a Literary Friendship.* Overlook P, 1999.

Dos Passos, John. *1919:* vol. 2 of the *U.S.A. Trilogy.* Houghton Mifflin, 1932.

———. *Novels, 1920–25: One Man's Initiation: 1917, Three Soldiers, Manhattan Transfer.* Library of America, 2003.

Dostoevsky, Fyodor. *The Brothers Karamazov.* Translated by Constance Garnett, 1912. Dover, 2005.

———. *The Gambler.* Translated by Constance Garnett, 1917. Dover, 1996.

Dotinga, Randy. "Docs: No Amount of Alcohol Safe during Pregnancy." *WebMD,* 2015. www.webmd.com/baby/news/20151019/no-amount-of-alcohol-safe-during-pregnancy-doctors-say#1. Accessed 15 November 2018.

Dreiser, Theodore. *The "Genius."* 1915. New American Library, 1967.
Duffy, John. *From Humors to Medical Science: A History of American Medicine*, 2nd ed., U of Illinois P, 1993.
Duffy, Michael. "Observation Balloons." *firstworldwar.com*, August 22, 2009. www.firstworldwar.com/atoz/balloons.htm. Accessed 15 Nov. 2018.
Eby, Carl P. *Hemingway's Fetishism: Psychoanalysis and the Mirror of Manhood*. SUNY P, 1999.
Edmonds, Sir James E. *Military Operations Italy 1915–1919*. Imperial War Museum, 1949.
Elder, Robert K., Aaron Vetch, and Mark Cirino. *Hidden Hemingway: Inside the Ernest Hemingway Archives of Oak Park*. Kent State UP, 2016.
Eliot, T. S. *The Complete Poems and Plays: 1909–1950*. Harcourt Brace Jovanovich, 1971.
———. *The Sacred Wood and Major Early Essays*. 1920. Dover, 1998.
Euripides. *Medea*. Translated by C. A. E. Luschnig. *Diotima*. www.stoa.org/diotima/anthology/medea.trans.shtml. Accessed 15 October 2017.
Falls, Cyril. *The Battle of Caporetto*. J. B. Lippincott, 1966.
Familiar Quotations, edited by John Bartlett and Emily Morison Bec, 15th and 125th Anniversary ed., Little, Brown, 1980.
Farah, Andrew. *Hemingway's Brain*. U of South Carolina P, 2017.
Fell, Charles. *The Lives of Saints. Collected from Authentick Records of Church History. With a Full Account of the Other Festivals Throughout the Year*, vol. 3 of 4. 2nd ed., Gale ECCO, 2010.
Fetterley, Judith. "*A Farewell to Arms*: Hemingway's 'Resentful Cryptogram.'" *Journal of Popular Culture*, vol. 10, no. 1, 1976, pp. 203–14.
Fiedler, Leslie A. *Love and Death in the American Novel*. Dalkey Archive, 1966.
Fielding, Henry. *The History of Tom Jones, A Foundling*. 1749. Penguin Classics, 2005.
———. "Preface to *Joseph Andrews*." *Prefaces and Prologues to Famous Books*, edited by Charles W. Eliot, Collier, 1937.
Fitzgerald, F. Scott. *The Beautiful and Damned*, 1922. Digireads, 2016.
———. *The Crack-Up*, edited by Edmund Wilson, 1945. Reprint ed., New Directions, 1996.
Flaubert, Gustave. *The First Sentimental Education*. Translated by Douglas Garman, U of California P, 1972.
———. *Madame Bovary*. 1856. Translated by Francis Steegmuller, Modern Library, 1957.
———. *Sentimental Education*. 1869. Translated by Dora Knowlton Ranous, 1922. Dover, 2006.
———. *The Temptation of St. Anthony*. 1874. Translated by Lafcadio Hearn, 1911. Kessinger, 2010.
Flora, Joseph M. *Reading Hemingway's* Men Without Women. Kent State UP, 2008.
"Fountain of 99 Spouts in L'aquila, Abruzzo, Italy." *Enchanting Italy*, 2017. www.enchantingitaly.com/landmarks/abruzzo/laquila/99-cannelle/. Accessed 15 November 2018.
Frank, Joseph. *Dostoevsky: A Writer in His Time*. Princeton UP, 2010.
Frith, John. "Syphilis—Its Early History and Treatment before Penicillin, and the Debate on Its Origins." *Journal of Military and Veterans' Health*, vol. 20, no. 4, 2012, pp. 49–58.
Fussell, Paul. *The Great War and Modern Memory*. Oxford UP, 1975.
Gilbert, Martin. *The First World War: A Complete History*. Henry Holt, 1994.
Gill, John. *Exposition of the Entire Bible*, 1746. Kindle ed., Amazon Digital Services, 2012.
Gooch, John. *The Italian Army and the First World War*. Cambridge UP, 2014.
Goering, Thomas. "1908–1919 Military Pay Chart." *Navy Cyberspace*. www.navycs.com/charts/1908-military-pay-chart.html. Accessed 11 January 2018.
Graves, Robert. *Good-Bye to All That*. 1929. Revised 2nd ed., 1958. Anchor, 1985.

Greene, Philip. *To Have and Have Another: A Hemingway Cocktail Companion.* Perigee, 2012.

Grey, E., Paul Cambon, Imperiall, K. Inouyé, and Benckendorff. *Declaration between the United Kingdom, France, Italy, Japan, and Russia, Engaging Not to Conclude Peace Separately during the Present War.* Harrison & Sons, 1915.

Griffin, Peter. *Along with Youth: Hemingway, the Early Years.* Oxford UP, 1987.

Hawkins, Ruth A. *Unbelievable Happiness and Final Sorrow: The Hemingway-Pfeiffer Marriage.* U of Arkansas P, 2012.

Hays, Peter L. *Fifty Years of Hemingway Criticism.* Scarecrow, 2013.

Hazard, Paul. *Stendhal (Henri Beyle).* Translated by Eleanor Hard. Coward-McCann, 1929.

Healthline Editorial Team. "Caesarean Section Complications." *Healthline,* 2018. www.healthline.com/health/pregnancy/complications-cesarean-section. Accessed 13 November 2018.

Heiderstadt, Donna. "The World's 20 Most Beautiful Lakes." *Fodor's Travel,* 21 October 2013. www.fodors.com/news/outdoors/the-worlds-20-most-beautiful-lakes. Accessed 1 November 2018.

Hemingway, Ernest. *Across the River and into the Trees.* Scribner, 1950.

———. *Addio Alle Armi* [*A Farewell to Arms*]. Translated by Fernanda Pivano. 1965. Oscar Moderni, 2016.

———. *By-Line: Ernest Hemingway.* Bantam, 1968.

———. *Complete Poems.* Revised ed., U of Nebraska P, 1992.

———. *The Complete Short Stories of Ernest Hemingway: The Finca Vigía Edition.* Charles Scribner's Sons, 1987.

———. *The Dangerous Summer.* Reprint ed., Scribner, 1997.

———. *Dateline: Toronto: The Complete Toronto Star Dispatches, 1920–1924.* Scribner's, 1985.

———. *Death in the Afternoon.* Charles Scribner's Sons, 1932.

———. "Dying, Well or Badly." In *Hemingway on War,* edited by Seán Hemingway, Scribner, 2003, pp. 292–94.

———. *Ernest Hemingway: Selected Letters, 1917–1961,* edited by Carlos Baker. Charles Scribner's Sons, 1981.

———. *A Farewell to Arms.* Scribner's, 1929.

———. *A Farewell to Arms.* Modern Library, 1932.

———. *A Farewell to Arms.* Charles Scribner's Sons, 1948.

———. *A Farewell to Arms.* Modern Standard Authors ed., Charles Scribner's Sons, 1949.

———. *A Farewell to Arms.* Everyman's Library, 1993.

———. *A Farewell to Arms.* Scribner Paperback, 1995.

———. *A Farewell to Arms.* Vintage Books, 2005.

———. *A Farewell to Arms: The Hemingway Library Edition.* Scribner, 2012.

———. *A Farewell to Arms* holograph manuscript. Item 64. John F. Kennedy Library.

———. *A Farewell to Arms* typescript. Item 65. John F. Kennedy Library.

———. *A Farewell to Arms* typescript with comments by F. Scott Fitzgerald. Item 77. John F. Kennedy Library.

———. *For Whom the Bell Tolls.* Scribner, 1995.

———. *The Garden of Eden.* Charles Scribner's, 1986.

———. *Green Hills of Africa: The Hemingway Library Edition.* Scribner, 2015.

———. *Hemingway,* Viking Portable Library ed. Viking, 1944.

———. *In Einem Andern Land* [*In Another Country,* German translation of *A Farewell to Arms*]. Translated by Annemarie Horschitz-Horst, 1930. Rowohlt Taschenbuch Verlag, 2004.

———. "Now I Lay Me." Manuscripts. Items 619–22. John F. Kennedy Library.
———. *The Letters of Ernest Hemingway.* Vol. 1, *1907–1922,* edited by Sandra Spanier and Robert W. Trogdon. Cambridge UP, 2011.
———. *The Letters of Ernest Hemingway.* Vol. 2, *1923–25,* edited by Sandra Spanier, Albert J. DeFazio III, and Robert W. Trogdon. Cambridge UP, 2013.
———. *The Letters of Ernest Hemingway.* Vol. 3, *1926–1929,* edited by Rena Sanderson, Sandra Spanier, and Robert W. Trogdon. Cambridge UP, 2015.
———. *The Letters of Ernest Hemingway.* Vol. 4. *1929–1931,* edited by Sandra Spanier and Miriam B. Mandel. Cambridge UP, 2017.
———. "A Lost Book Review: *A Story Teller's Story.*" *Fitzgerald/Hemingway Annual: 1969.* National Cash Register, 1969, pp. 71–75.
———. *A Moveable Feast.* Scribner's, 1964.
———. "My Pal the Gorilla Gargantua." In *Hemingway on Hunting,* edited by Seán Hemingway, Scribner, 2001, pp. 187–91.
———. *The Nick Adams Stories.* Scribner's, 1972.
———. "Review: *Geography and Plays,* By Gertrude Stein." *Chicago Tribune,* Paris edition, 5 March 1923, p. 2.
———. *To Have and Have Not.* Scribner's, 1937.
———. *The Torrents of Spring.* Charles Scribner's Sons, 1926.
———. "Treachery in Aragon." *Ken,* vol. 1, no. 7, 30 June 1938, p. 26.
———. "The Woppian Way or The Passing of Pickles McCarty." Typed manuscript. Item 843. John F. Kennedy Library.
———, ed. *Men at War: The Best War Stories of All Time.* Bramhall House, 1979.
Hemingway, Leicester. *My Brother, Ernest Hemingway.* Crest Book, 1962.
Hemingway, Mary Welsh. *How It Was.* Knopf, 1976.
Henry, Barklie McKee. *Deceit.* Small, Maynard & Company, 1924.
Hewson, Marc. "'The Real Story of Ernest Hemingway': Cixous, Gender, and *A Farewell to Arms.*" *The Hemingway Review,* vol. 22, no. 2, 2003, pp. 51–62.
"History of Excellence," 2018. *Cova.* www.pasticceriacova.com/en/history. Accessed 11 January 2018.
Holbach, Paul Henri Thiry, Baron d'. *Christianity Unveiled.* 1761. CreateSpace, 2017.
Holman, C. Hugh, and William Harmon. *A Handbook to Literature,* 6th ed., Macmillan, 1992.
Hotchner, A. E. *Papa Hemingway: A Personal Memoir.* Random House, 1966.
"How Were Soldiers Paid during WW1 and WW2?" 2015, *City-Data.com.* www.city-data.com/forum/history/2301340-how-were-soldiers-paid-during-ww1.html Accessed 11 January 2018.
Hughes-Hallet, Lucy. *Gabriele D'Annunzio: Poet, Seducer, and Preacher of War.* Anchor, 2014.
Hurwitz, Harold M. "Hemingway's Tutor, Ezra Pound." *Modern Fiction Studies,* vol. 17, no. 4, 1971, pp. 469–82.
Hutchisson, James M. *Ernest Hemingway: A New Life.* Penn State UP, 2016.
Illica, Luigi, and Giuseppe Giacosa. Libretto to *Tosca* by Giacomo Puccini. 1900. *Operas Arias Composers.* www.opera-arias.com/puccini/tosca/libretto/english/. Accessed 2 November 2018.
James, Henry. *Daisy Miller.* Penguin Classics, 2007.
Josephs, Allen. "Hemingway's Out of Body Experience." *The Hemingway Review,* vol. 2, no. 2 1983, pp. 11–17.
Joyce, James. *Dubliners,* 1916. Viking Critical Library ed., Penguin, 1976.

———. *A Portrait of the Artist as a Young Man*, 1916. Viking Critical Library ed., Penguin, 1977.

———. *Ulysses*. Vintage, 1986.

Kale, Verna. *Ernest Hemingway*. Reaction Books, 2016.

Keegan, John. *The First World War*. Vintage, 1998.

Keeler, Clinton. "*A Farewell to Arms:* Hemingway and Peele." *Modern Language Notes*, vol. 76, no. 7, 1961, pp. 622–25.

Knowles, John. "A History of Birth Control Methods." *Planned Parenthood Federation of America*, January 2012. www.plannedparenthood.org/files/2613/9611/6275/History_of_BC_Methods.pdf. Accessed 14 November 2018.

Kory, Fern. "A Second Look at Helen Ferguson in *A Farewell to Arms*." *Hemingway in Italy and Other Essays*, edited by Robert W. Lewis, Praeger, 1990, pp. 21–33.

"L'aquila, Province of L'aquila, Abruzzo, Italy." *ItalyHeritage*, 2017. www.italyheritage.com/regions/abruzzo/laquila/laquila.htm. Accessed 10 November 2018.

"Learn about Barbera Red Wine." *Vinepair*, 2018. vinepair.com/wine-101/learn-barbera-red-wine/. Accessed 10 November 2018.

"Les Hospices Cantonaux." *Centre Hospitalier Universitaire Vaudois*, October 2018. www.chuv.ch/fr/chuv-home/en-bref/historique/1810–1950/. Accessed 15 November 2018.

Lewis, Robert W. *A Farewell to Arms: The War of the Words*. Twayne, 1992.

———. "Hemingway in Italy: Making It Up." *Journal of Modern Literature*, vol. 9, no. 2, 1982, pp. 209–36.

———. *Hemingway on Love*. U of Texas P, 2011.

Lewis, Sinclair. *Arrowsmith*, 1925. Signet Classics, 1961.

———. *Elmer Gantry*, 1926. New Signet Classics, 1967.

"The Liturgy of the Mass." *The Maryknoll Missal*, edited by Maryknoll Fathers, P. J. Kennedy & Sons, 1964, [3]–[40].

Lockridge, Ernest. "*Othello* as a Key to Hemingway." *The Hemingway Review*, vol. 18, no. 1, Fall 1998, pp. 68–77.

Longstaffe, Moya. Introduction to *The Red and the Black: A Chronicle of the Nineteenth Century*, by Stendhal. Wordsworth Classics, 2015, pp. ix–xxix.

Lynn, Kenneth S. *Hemingway*. Simon & Schuster, 1987.

Macdonald, John, with Zeljko Cimpric. *Caporetto and the Isonzo Campaign: The Italian Front 1915–1918*. Pen & Sword, 2015.

Mandel, Miriam B. "Dating the Narration of Hemingway's *A Farewell to Arms*: San Siro." *The Hemingway Review*, vol. 35, no. 1, 2015, pp. 53–62.

———. "Ferguson and Lesbian Love: Unspoken Subplots in *A Farewell to Arms*." *The Hemingway Review*, vol. 14, no. 1, 1994, pp. 18–24.

———. "Headgear and Horses: Authorial Presence in *a Farewell to Arms*." *International Fiction Review*, vol. 22, no. 1995, pp. 61–66.

———. "Reading and Not Reading *The Black Pig* in *A Farewell to Arms*." *Hemingway and Italy: Twenty-First-Century Perspectives*, edited by Mark Cirino and Mark P. Ott, UP of Florida, 2017, pp. 96–107.

———. *Reading Hemingway: The Facts in the Fictions*. Scarecrow, 1995.

Mann, Thomas. *Buddenbrooks: The Decline of a Family*. Translated by Helen Tracy Lowe-Porter, Vintage International, 1924.

———. *Death in Venice and Other Stories*. Translated by Kenneth Burke, Knopf, 1925.

———. *The Magic Mountain*. Translated by Helen Tracy Lowe-Porter, Knopf, 1927.

Manning, Frederic. *The Middle Parts of Fortune*, 1929. Random House UK, 2014.
Manzoni, Alessandro. *The Betrothed*. Translated by Bruce Penman, Penguin, 1972.
Marlowe, Christopher. *The Complete Plays*. Penguin Books, 2003.
Marryat, Frederick. *Peter Simple*. 1834. Kindle ed., Amazon Digital Services, 2012.
Marvell, Andrew. "To His Coy Mistress." 1681. *Poetry Foundation*, 2018. www.poetryfoundation.org/poems/44688/to-his-coy-mistress. Accessed 8 January 2017.
Marx, Leo. *The Machine in the Garden: Technology and the Pastoral Ideal in America*. Oxford UP, 1967.
Matheny, S. C., and J. E. Kingery. "Hepatitis A." *American Family Physician*, vol. 86, no. 11, 2012, pp. 1027–34.
Matthis, Bradley. "Alcoholic Hepatitis." Received by Michael Kim Roos, 27–28 December 2016.
McAdams, John. "How to Convert Caliber to MM (And Vice Versa)." *The Big Game Hunting Blog*, 2015. thebiggamehuntingblog.com/how-to-convert-caliber-to-mm-and-vice-versa/. Accessed 1 November 2018.
McIlvaine, Robert M. "A Literary Source for the Caesarean Section in *A Farewell to Arms*." *American Literature*, vol. 43, 1971, pp. 444–47.
McLaughlin, Robert L. "'The Only Kind Thing Is Silence' Ernest Hemingway vs. Sinclair Lewis." *The Hemingway Review*, vol. 6, no. 2, 1987, pp. 46–53.
Mellow, James R. *Hemingway: A Life without Consequences*. Houghton Mifflin, 1992.
Meriwether, James B. "The Dashes in Hemingway's 'A Farewell to Arms.'" *Papers of the Bibliographic Society of America*, vol. 58, no. 4, 1964, pp. 449–57.
Meyers, Jeffrey. *Hemingway: A Biography*. Perennial Library, 1985.
Miller, J. Hillis. *The Disappearance of God: Five Nineteenth-Century Writers*. Belknap P of Harvard UP, 1963.
Moddelmog, Debra A. "'We Live in a Country Where Nothing Makes Any Difference': The Queer Sensibility of *A Farewell to Arms*." *The Hemingway Review*, vol. 28, no. 2, 2009, pp. 7–24.
Möller, Hans. *Albert Von Berrer. Das Lebensbild Eines im Weltkerig Gefallenen Deutschen Generals*. Bernard & Graefe, 1941.
Monroe, Robert A. *Journeys Out of the Body*. Harmony, 1977.
Monteiro, George. "The Education of Ernest Hemingway." *Journal of American Studies*, vol. 8, no. 1, 1974, pp. 91–99.
Moore, Walter. *A Life of Erwin Schrödinger*. Cambridge UP, 1994.
"More Than 150 Years of History." *Grand Hotel et de Milan*. www.grandhoteletdemilan.it/en/milan/five-star-historic-hotel-milan/. Accessed 25 January 2018.
"Munich Dunkel Lager." *Beer Advocate*, 2017. www.beeradvocate.com/beer/styles/46/. Accessed 17 March 2017.
Nagel, James. "Catherine Barkley and Retrospective Narration in *a Farewell to Arms*." *Ernest Hemingway: Six Decades of Criticism*, edited by Linda W. Wagner. Michigan State UP, 1987, pp. 171–85.
Nagel, Jennifer. *Knowledge: A Very Short Introduction*. Oxford UP, 2014.
Nickel, Matthew C. *Hemingway's Dark Night: Catholic Influences and Intertextualities in the Work of Ernest Hemingway*. New Street Communications, 2013.
Nicolle, David. *The Italian Army of World War I*. Osprey, 2003.
Oldsey, Bernard S. *Hemingway's Hidden Craft: The Writing of* a Farewell to Arms. Pennsylvania State UP, 1979.

"150 Years of Grand Hotel des Ilês Borromées." *Grand Hotel des Iles Borromees and Spa.* www.borromees.com/en/150-years-of-history.html. Accessed 11 January 2018.

Orr, Mary. *Flaubert's* Tentation: *Remapping Nineteenth-Century French Histories of Religion and Science.* Oxford UP, 2008.

Ortner, Christian M. *The Austro-Hungarian Artillery from 1867 to 1918: Technology, Organization, and Tactics.* Verlag Militaria, 2007.

Othen, Christopher. "Cleon: Cover Artist to the Lost Generation." *Christopher Othen.* July 12, 2016, christopherothen.wordpress.com/2016/07/02/cleon-cover-artist-to-the-lost-generation/. Accessed 13 October 2017.

Oxford English Dictionary Online. Oxford UP, 2016. www.oed.com.

"Pastoral Notes on the Celebration of Liturgical Rites for Deceased Infants and Stillborn or Miscarried Infants." *Bostoncatholic.org,* Archdiocese of Boston. www.bostoncatholic.org/Offices-And-Services/Office-Detail.aspx?id=12540&pid=464. Accessed 21 December 2017.

Paul, Steve. *Hemingway at Eighteen: The Pivotal Year That Launched a Legend.* Chicago Review P, 2018.

Peesay, Morarji. "Cord around the Neck Syndrome." *BMC Pregnancy & Childbirth,* vol. 12, supp. 1, *Proceedings of the Stillbirth Summit 2011,* 28 August 2012. bmcpregnancychildbirth.biomedcentral.com/articles/10.1186/1471-2393-12-S1-A6. Accessed 16 December 2017.

Phelan, James. "Distance, Voice, and Temporal Perspective in Frederic Henry's Narration: Successes, Problems, and Paradox." *New Essays on* A Farewell to Arms, edited by Scott Donaldson, Cambridge UP, 1990, pp. 53–73.

Plaster, John L. "Shooting Uphill and Downhill." *Millet Tactical.* www.millettsights.com/downloads/shootinguphillanddownhill.pdf. Accessed 15 November 2018.

Plimpton, George. "The Art of Fiction: Ernest Hemingway." Bruccoli, *Conversations,* pp. 109–29.

Pound, Ezra. *The Cantos of Ezra Pound.* New Directions, 1975.

Proust, Marcel. *In Search of Lost Time: The Complete Masterpiece.* Translated by C. K. Scott Moncrieff, Terence Kilmartin, and Andreas Mayor. 1922, 1924, 1925, 1927, 1929, 1930. Revised by E. J. Enright. Modern Library, 1992.

Quiller-Couch, Arthur, editor. *The Oxford Book of English Verse, 1250–1900.* Oxford UP, 1924.

Remarque, Erich Maria. *All Quiet on the Western Front.* Translated by A. W. Wheen, 1929. Random House, 1996.

Reynolds, Michael. "*A Farewell to Arms:* Doctors in the House of Love." *The Cambridge Companion to Ernest Hemingway,* edited by Scott Donaldson, Cambridge UP, 1996, pp. 109–25.

———. *Hemingway: An Annotated Chronology.* Manly, 1991.

———. *Hemingway: The American Homecoming.* Blackwell, 1992.

———. *Hemingway: The Paris Years.* Blackwell, 1987.

———. *Hemingway's First War: The Making of* A Farewell to Arms. Princeton UP, 1976.

———. *Hemingway's Reading, 1910–1940: An Inventory.* Princeton UP, 1981.

———. "Words Killed, Wounded, Missing in Action." *Hemingway Notes,* vol. 6, no. 2, 1981, pp. 2–9.

———. *The Young Hemingway,* 1986. Norton, 1998.

Richards, I. A. *Poetries and Sciences: A Reissue of Science and Poetry (1926, 1935) with Commentary.* Norton, 1970.

Rollyson, Carl. *Nothing Ever Happens to the Brave: The Story of Martha Gellhorn.* St. Martin's, 1990.

Rommel, Erwin. *Infantry Attacks.* Translated by Gustave A. Kiddé, 1944. Zenith P, 2009.

Roos, Michael Kim. "Agassiz or Darwin: Faith and Science in Hemingway's High School Zoology Class." *The Hemingway Review,* vol. 32, no. 2, 2013, pp. 7–27.

———. "Appendix A: Alternate Titles." *The Hemingway Blog.* 2018. mikeroos.com/the-hemingway-blog/appendix-a-alternate-titles/.

———. "Appendix B: Timeline." *The Hemingway Blog.* 2018. mikeroos.com/the-hemingway-blog/appendix-b-timeline/.

———. "Appendix C: 1948 Illustrations." *The Hemingway Blog.* 2018. mikeroos.com/the-hemingway-blog/appendix-c-1948-illustrations/.

———. "A Darwinian Reading of Hemingway's 'Big Two-Hearted River.'" *Teaching Hemingway and the Natural World,* edited by Kevin Maier. Kent State UP, 2018, pp. 57–71.

———. "Hemingway's Combat Zones: War, Family, Self." *Midwestern Miscellany,* vol. 47, Fall 2019, forthcoming.

———. "'What If You Are Not Built That Way?' H. G. Wells and the Conflict of Science and Faith in *A Farewell to Arms.*" *Hemingway and Italy: Twenty-First-Century Perspectives,* edited by Mark Cirino and Mark P. Ott, UP of Florida, 2017, pp. 108–26.

Ross, Lillian. "How Do You Like It Now, Gentlemen?" *New Yorker,* 13 May 1950, pp. 36–62.

Sanford, Marcelline Hemingway. *At the Hemingways: With Fifty Years of Correspondence between Ernest and Marcelline Hemingway.* U of Idaho P, 1999.

Sassoon, Siegfried. "Base Details." 1918. *All Poetry,* 6 November 2018. allpoetry.com/Base-Details.

———. *Memoirs of an Infantry Officer.* 1930. Faber & Faber, 1965.

"Saint Anthony the Abbot." *Catholic Online,* 2018. www.catholic.org/saints/saint.php?saint_id=23. Accessed 3 March 2018.

Schindler, John R. *Isonzo: The Forgotten Sacrifice of the Great War.* Praeger, 2001.

Schneider, Daniel J. "Hemingway's *A Farewell to Arms:* The Novel as Pure Poetry." *Modern Fiction Studies,* vol. 14, no. 3, 1968, pp. 283–96.

Schneider, Isidor. *The Temptation of Anthony: A Novel in Verse and Other Poems.* Boni & Liveright, 1928.

Shnayerson, Robert. "Judgment at Nuremburg." *Smithsonian,* 1996, pp. 124–41.

"Sight Draft." *The Free Dictionary,* 2018. www.thefreedictionary.com/sight+draft. Accessed 10 January 2018.

Smith, David C. *H. G. Wells: Desperately Mortal.* Yale UP, 1986.

Solotaroff, Robert. "Sexual Identity in *A Farewell to Arms.*" *The Hemingway Review,* vol. 9, no. 1, Fall 1989, pp. 2–17.

Spanier, Sandra. "Catherine Barkley and the Hemingway Code: Ritual and Survival in *A Farewell to Arms.*" *Ernest Hemingway's* A Farewell to Arms, edited by Harold Bloom, Chelsea House, 1987, pp. 131–48.

Speranza, Gino. *The Diary of Gino Speranza: Italy, 1915–1919,* edited by Florence Colgate Speranza I, AMS P, 1966.

St. Athanasius of Alexandria. *Life of St. Anthony of Egypt.* Translated by Philip Schaff and Henry Wace, Pantianos Classics, 1892.

Stefanovics, Glenn W. "Albert Von Berrer." *Solving Problems Through Force: The Leadership in Austria-Hungary during WWI.* Oocities.org. October 2003. www.oocities.org/veldes1/berrer.html. Accessed 15 November 2018.

Stendhal. *The Charterhouse of Parma.* 1839. Translated by C. K. Scott-Moncrieff, Signet Classic, 1962.

———. *The Life of Henry Brulard*. 1890. Translated by Jean Stewart and B. C. J. G. Knight, Penguin, 1973.

———. *The Red and the Black*. 1830. Translated by C. K. Scott Moncrieff, Modern Library, 1926.

Stoneback, H. R. "Hemingway's Stresa—Getting It Right: Actual and Symbolic Landscape, Deep Structure, and the Borromean Subtext." *Hemingway's Italy: New Perspectives,* edited by Rena Sanderson. Louisiana State UP, 2006, pp. 131–39.

———. "'Lovers' Sonnets Turn'd to Holy Psalms': The Soul's Song of Providence, the Scandal of Suffering, and Love in *A Farewell to Arms.*" *The Hemingway Review,* no. 9, vol. 1, Fall 1989, pp. 33–76.

———. *Reading Hemingway's* The Sun Also Rises: *Glossary and Commentary.* Kent State UP, 2007.

Svevo, Italo. *Zeno's Conscience.* Translated by William Weaver. Vintage International, 2003.

Sylvester, Bickford. "The Sexual Impasse to Romantic Order in Hemingway's Fiction: *A Farewell to Arms, Othello,* 'Orpen,' and the Hemingway Canon." *Hemingway: Up in Michigan Perspectives,* edited by Frederic J. Svoboda and Joseph J. Waldmeir. Michigan State UP, 1995, pp. 177–87.

Thompson, Mark. *The White War: Life and Death on the Italian Front, 1915–1919.* Faber & Faber, 2008.

Thurston, Herbert. "St. Valentine." *The Catholic Encyclopedia.* Vol. 15. Robert Appleton Company, 1912. www.newadvent.org/cathen/15254a.htm. Accessed 1 November 2018.

Tolstoy, Leo. *War and Peace.* Translated by Constance Garnett, 1904. Modern Library, 1931.

Trevelyan, G. M. *Scenes from Italy's War.* Houghton Mifflin, 1919.

Trogdon, Robert W. "'I Am Constructing a Legend': Ernest Hemingway in Guy Hickock's *Brooklyn Daily Eagle* Articles." *Resources for American Literary Study,* vol. 37, 2014, pp. 181–207.

Turgenev, Ivan. *Fathers and Sons.* Translated by Constance Garnett, 1899. Könemann, 1998.

———. *A Sportsman's Sketches,* vol. 1. Translated by Constance Garnett, 1898. Bibliobazaar, 2006.

———. *A Sportsman's Sketches.* vol. 2. Translated by Constance Garnett, 1898. IndyPublish, 2003.

Tyler, Lisa. "Passion and Grief in *A Farewell to Arms:* Ernest Hemingway's Reading of *Wuthering Heights.*" *Hemingway Review,* vol. 14, no. 2, 1995, pp. 79–96.

"Udine—Storia di Udine: la prima guerra modiale." *Viaggio in Friuli Venezia Giulia,* 2018. www.viaggioinfriuliveneziagiulia.it/wcms/index.php?id=64,62,0,0,1,0. Accessed 6 February 2018.

Vernon, Alex. "War, Gender, and Ernest Hemingway." *Hemingway Review,* vol. 22, no. 1, 2002, pp. 34–55.

"Vintage Swiss Och Sports Skis (Restored)." *Antique Ski Shop,* 2018. www.antiqueskishop.com/shopping/antique-skis/28-vintage-swiss-och-sport-skis-restored.html. Accessed 29 June 2018.

Villard, Henry S., and James Nagel. *Hemingway in Love and War.* Hyperion, 1989.

Voltaire. *Candide; or, Optimism.* 1759. Translated by Robert M. Adams, Norton, 1966.

Wagner-Martin, Linda. "Hemingway's Search for Heroes, Once Again." *Arizona Quarterly,* vol. 44, no. 2, 1988, pp. 58–68.

Wells, H. G. *Mr. Britling Sees It Through.* Macmillan, 1916.

———. *Mr Britling Commence À Voir Clair.* Payot & Cie, 1917.

———. *War and the Future.* Kindle ed., e-artnow, 2013.

Wexler, Joyce. "E.R.A. For Hemingway: A Feminist Defense of *A Farewell to Arms.*" *Georgia Review,* vol. 35, 1981, pp. 111–23.

Whitlow, Roger. *Cassandra's Daughters: The Women in Hemingway.* Greenwood, 1984.

Wilcox, Vanda. "Morale and Battlefield Performance at Caporetto, 1917." *Journal of Strategic Studies,* vol. 37, no. 6–7, 2014, pp. 829–54.

———. *Morale and the Italian Army during the First World War.* Cambridge UP, 2016.

Wilkinson, Myler. *Hemingway and Turgenev: The Nature of Literary Influence.* University of Michigan Research P, 1986.

Williams, Wirt. *The Tragic Art of Ernest Hemingway.* Louisiana State UP, 1981.

Williamson, Samuel H. *MeasuringWorth,* 2018. measuringworth.com.

Wilson, Andrew J. "Bidding Goodbye to the Plumed Troop and the Big Wars: The Presence of *Othello* in *A Farewell to Arms.*" *Hemingway Review,* vol. 15, no. 2, Spring 1996, pp. 52–66.

Wright, David. "Ernest Hemingway Had Out-of-Body Experience." *National Enquirer,* 18 April 1978, p. 37.

Woodhouse, John. *Gabriele D'Annunzio: Defiant Archangel.* Clarendon, 1998.

Wyatt, David. *Hemingway, Style, and the Art of Emotion.* Cambridge UP, 2015.

Young, J. H. *Caesarean Section: The History and Development of the Operation from Earliest Times.* H. K. Lewis, 1944.

Young, Philip. *Ernest Hemingway: A Reconsideration.* Pennsylvania State UP, 1966.

INDEX

Abruzzi (Italy), 37–39, 42, 48–49, 53, 112, 146, 175, 284; earthquake, 46–47
Across the River and into the Trees (Hemingway, novel), 11, 25; Order of the Brusadelli, 205; Renata, 25; Richard Cantwell, 11, 25, 59, 93, 134, 168, 205, 222
Adams, Henry, 47, 68, 82–83
Africana/L'Africaine (*The African Woman*) (Meyerbeer), 247
Aida (Verdi), 146
Albertini, Luigi, 162
Alexander VI (pope), 195
Alexander the Great, 91
Alighieri, Dante, 154, 155, 195
All Quiet on the Western Front (Remarque), 3, 73
All the Sad Young Men (Fitzgerald), 3
"Alpine Idyll, An" (Hemingway, short story), 87
Alpini, 92
Amalfi, 36–37, 43, 47
Amalfian Laws, 36
American Caravan, The (Schneider), 87
Americani sul Grappa (*Americans on the Grappa*) (Cecchin), 90
American League, 162
American Red Cross Hospital, 42–44, 113, 121–22, 127, 136, 140, 144, 165, 170
Anarchism, 220, 229
Anglo-American Club, 144, 159, 207
Antony, Mark, 127
Apostle Paul, 194
Aquila (Italy), 112
Arc de Triomphe, 155
Arc du Carrousel, 155
Arco della Pace (Arch of Peace), 154, 155
Asti Spumante, 33
Athanasius of Alexandria, 87
Avezzano quake, 46–47
Aymo, Bartolomeo, 210, 219
Aymo, Bartolomeo, in *FTA*, 210, 213, 217, 219–20, 223, 226, 229–30

Bacall, Lauren, 8
Badoglio, Pietro, 207
Baedecker, Karl, 26, 30, 44, 66–67, 79, 115–16, 127, 138, 171, 174, 176, 184–85, 190, 212, 220, 225, 249–50, 278, 280, 301
Bainsizza plateau (Italy), 143, 144, 159, 190, 199, 202–4
Baker, Carlos, 4, 9, 96, 146, 161, 172, 185, 189
Baker, Sheridan, 81, 99
Bakewell, Charles M., 228, 231, 232
Bakunin, Mikhail, 220
Barber, in *FTA*, 124
Barbera, 139, 211
Barbusse, Henri, 83, 265
Barkley, Catherine, in *FTA*, 6, 44, 53, 100, 254; baby, death of, 12, 24, 253, 308, 315–16, 319; birds as a motif for, 177–79, 213; birth control methods used, 165; bravery, 167, 168; caesarian, 310–13, 318; cape, 175, 178, 179, 253; carriage ride, 138, 154, 303; cat comparisons, 183–84, 269, 276; concerns about Frederic's desertion, 257–58; "craziness," 68–69, 126, 151–52, 180, 269; death, 12, 66, 103, 134, 158, 164, 255, 263, 306, 308, 310, 312, 318–19; description of, 55; escape to Switzerland, 9, 262, 270–80; faith/spirituality, 45, 57–58, 85, 96, 125, 131, 140–42, 157, 166, 175–76, 180, 268, 280, 305, 315, 319–20; family, 180; fiancé, 55–59, 64–65, 68, 70, 141, 177, 262; fiancé, guilt regarding, 57, 64–65, 126, 133, 181; first meeting with Frederic, 41, 54–56; hair, 57, 139; home, definition of, 301–2; honesty, 68–70, 131–32; identity, 60, 140, 151–52, 245, 253; illustration of, 6; isolation, feelings of, 167, 176; labor, 304, 306–11; literary criticisms of her, 132–33; love, 15, 50, 69–70, 125–26, 132, 141–42, 158, 231, 243, 268, 319; meeting with Frederic in garden, 61–64, 68–69, 73; plans for the future, 277; pregnancy, 24,

336

86, 125, 140, 141, 151, 164–66, 169, 175, 182, 184, 216, 218, 263, 275; rain, fear of, 151; reunion with Frederic after desertion, 12, 171, 239–40, 253–58; Saint Anthony medal, 85–88, 109, 140, 320; service as VAD, 58; sexual experience prior to Frederic, 55–57, 63; sexual experience with Frederic, 63–64, 68–69, 74, 125, 130–31, 133, 136, 139, 178–79, 192–93, 213, 256–57; source material for, 4, 42–44, 45, 55, 63, 130, 140–41, 184; tending to Frederic in the hospital, 129–33, 136–39, 164; visit to the race track, 150, 153–58; war, changing perceptions of, 58–59, 78, 169
Barton, R. O. "Tubby," 11
Baseball, 162–64, 168
"Base Details" (Sassoon), 224
Basilica of the Sacré-Coeur, 167
Basilicata Brigade, 73
Bassi, Amedeo, 148
Bassi, Fillipo Vincenza, in *FTA*, 81
Battle of Caporetto, 59, 75, 190, 224
Battle of Caporetto, The (Falls), 27, 223
Battle of the Isonzo: Eighth, 31; Eleventh, 143, 159–60, 189–90, 199, 202–3, 208; Fifth, 29; First, 23, 94; Fourth, 27; Ninth, 31; Seventh, 31; Sixth, 29–31; Tenth, 53, 62, 70, 75, 85, 105, 110, 113; Third, 27
Battle of Somme, the, 56, 59, 160
"Battler, The" (Hemingway, short story), 238; Ad Francis, 238; Bugs, 238; Nick Adams, 238
Bawdy house, 32, 33, 69, 71, 108–9, 209
Bazarov, Yevgeny, 207
Beall, John, 95, 214
Beautiful and Damned, The (Fitzgerald), 256
Beegel, Susan, 85
Beerbohm, Max, 136
Being and Time (Heidegger), 10
Benedict XV, 34, 36
Berg, A. Scott, 7
Bergman, Ingrid, 8
Berkeley, George, 45
Bersaglieri, 88–89, 91, 217; Eleventh regiment, 88
Betrothed, The (Manzoni), 145
Beversluis, John, 263
Beyle, Marie Henri. *See* Stendhal
Bianchi, Don Giuseppe, 37
Bicycle troops, 224–25
"Bidding Goodbye to the Plumed Troop" (Wilson), 263
Biffi's, 116
"Big Two-Hearted River" (Hemingway, short story): insomnia in, 123; Nick Adams, 139, 227

Bishop, John Peale, 9
Bizet, George, 146
Black Forest (Germany), 78
Blackmore, Susan, 99
"Black Sox" betting scandal, 163
Black Tuesday, 5
"Body of an American, The" (Dos Passos), 207
Bogart, Humphrey, 8
Boito, Arrigo, 146
Bolshevik Revolution, 208, 249
Bonadeo, Alfredo, 206
Bonaparte, Napoleon, I, 76, 78, 154, 202, 204, 205, 217, 226, 285
Bonaparte, Napoleon, III, 76
Bonello, Aldo, in *FTA*, 209, 210, 211, 219–20, 222–23, 226–27, 229–30
Bonesana di Beccaria, Cesare, 95
Boni & Liveright, 7
Bonivard, François, 278
Book of Genesis, 54
Book of Saints, 85
Borgia, Cesare, 195
Borromeo, San Carlo (Saint Charles Borromeo), 250
Boston Red Sox, 163–64
Boxer Rebellion, 160
Brandy, 172
Brenner, Gerry, 156
Brescia (Italy), 118, 184–85
Brigata Ancona, 107
Brindisi (Italy), 204
British Red Cross, 22, 27, 38, 41, 54, 55, 62, 63, 159, 190, 216
Brontë, Emily, 63, 140–41
Brooklyn Eagle, 98
Brothers Karamazov, The (Dostoevsky), 100, 148, 315–16
Bruccoli, Matthew, 74
Bruno, Giordano, 195
Bryn Mawr College, 11
Burwell, Rose Marie, 74
Butler, Charles, 24
Butler, Samuel, 87
"Butterfly, The" (Brontë), 141
Byron, Lord (George Gordon), 278

Cadorna, Luigi, 23, 26–27, 29, 31, 32, 52, 75–78, 92, 159–60, 191, 208, 232
Caesar, Julius, 127
Caesarian(s), 310–14, 318
Caesarean Section (Young), 311
Caffé-Concerto Grande Italia, 116
Caffè Cova, 43–44, 145

INDEX · 337

Campari, Gaspare, 116
Campoformido (Italy), 226
Camposanto Monumentale (Monumental Cemetery), 66, 67
"Canary for One, A," 301
Candide (Voltaire), 46
Cantos (Pound), 83
Capannelle Racecourse, 153
Capello, Luigi, 160
Caporetto (Kobarid, Slovenia), 190–91, 202–3, 207–8, 227, 232, 259
Caporetto Retreat, 42, 52, 62, 77, 161, 197, 198, 200, 202, 228, 232
Capri bianco, 79–80, 171, 173, 179, 264, 302
Carabinieri, 62, 92, 231–32, 236, 240, 244
Carmen (Bizet), 146
Carso plateau (Italy), 20–21, 30, 32, 53, 78, 93, 144, 159–60, 191, 203, 232, 260
Caruso, Enrico, 40
Casablanca, 8
Casillo, Robert, 94
Castello Sforzesco (Castle Sforza), 154
Castle of Chillon, 278
Catherine's doctor, in *FTA*, 307–14, 320
Catholic Church, 36, 174; Counter-Reformation, 250
Catholic Encyclopedia (Thurston), 128
"Cat in the Rain" (Hemingway, short story), 166, 301
Cavalcanti, Guido, 195
Cavanaugh, Loretta, 136
Cecchin, Giovanni, 90
"Censorship in *A Farewell to Arms*" (Donaldson), 74
Champagne cocktail, 261
Chandler, Stacy, 214
Charge of the Savoia Cavalleria at Izbushensky, 95
Charles Scribner's Sons, 4, 7, 9, 73, 74, 107, 219
Château d'Ouchy, 302
Chianti, 123, 171–72
Chicago Cubs, 163
Chicago White Sox, 162–63
Cholera, 27–28
Christian Science, 313–14
Cimitero monumentale di Staglieno, 66–67
Cincinnati Reds, 163
Cinzano, 123
Cirino, Mark, 11, 39, 61, 81, 95, 99–100, 102, 117, 138, 149, 165, 168, 205, 210, 225, 243–44, 247
"Clean, Well-Lighted Place, A" (Hemingway, short story), 72–73; insomnia in, 123; suicide in, 72–73

Cleon, 3, 6
Cleopatra, 127, 128
Code of Canon Law, 36
Cognac, 104, 110, 129, 171–72, 195
Coindreau, Maurice, 92, 107, 197
Colbert, Charles, 6–7
Connable, Dorothy, 25
Continuation of the Reverend Alban Butler's Lives of the Saints to the Present Time, A (Butler), 24
Cooper, Gary, 164
Cooperman, Stanley, 132–33
Cormons (Italy), 54, 62, 85, 89, 104, 211, 213–14, 216–18, 222–23
Corriere Della Sera (*Evening Messenger/Courier*), 162
Corso Sempione, 154–55
Cortina d'Ampezzo (Italy), 197, 260
Count Greffi, in *FTA*, 260–61, 264–65, 267–68
"Crack Up, The" (Fitzgerald), 59
Crane, Stephen, 82
Crick, Francis, 10
Criminal Slang (Jackson and Hellyer), 108
"Cross-Country Snow" (Hemingway, short story), 78, 166; George, 78, 279, 312; Nick Adams, 78, 279, 312
Crystal Palace, 115
Cummings, E. E., 207
Curnutt, Kirk, 184

da Gama, Vasco, 247
Daiker, Donald, 78, 93, 103, 106
Daisy Miller (James), 81–82
d'Albert, Eugen, 146
Dali, Salvador, 135
Dalton, Hugh, 21, 30, 31, 42, 54, 78, 92, 194, 213, 237
"D'Annunzio" (Hemingway, poem), 25
D'Annunzio, Gabriele, 25, 40, 50, 115, 162, 205–6, 263
Darwin, Charles, 141
de Aquabello, Enricho, 83
Death in the Afternoon (Hemingway, book), 4, 20, 197, 224, 247; Marvell poem in, 182
Deceit (Henry), 44
Decimation, policy of, 52, 77, 92
de Giovanni, Eduardo, 148
De Iorio, Ugo, 39
de la Barre, François-Jean Lefebvre, 167
DeLong, Catherine, 122
de Maupassant, Guy, 7
Deserters, punishment for, 51–52
Diaz, Armando, 206

Dietrich, Marlene, 6, 8
Di Nardo, Vincenzo, 37, 46, 112, 147
di Simone, Giovanni, 66
"Dispelling the Romantic Myth" (Beversluis), 263
Divine Comedy (Dante), 154
"Doctor and the Doctor's Wife, The" (Hemingway, short story), 228, 314
"Doctors in the House of Love" (Reynolds), 196, 311
Dolomite Mountains (Italy), 29, 73, 160, 197, 260
Donaldson, Scott, 74
d'Onofrio, Don Rodolfo, 37–38
Dorman-Smith, Eric Edward "Chink," 168, 284–85
Dos Passos, John, 7, 33–34, 87, 88, 207, 234, 246–47
Dos Passos, Katy (Smith), 7–8
Dostoevsky, Fyodor, 69, 100, 315
Dreiser, Theodore, 313–15
Dubliners (Joyce), 9
"Dulce Et Decorum Est" (Owens), 206
d'Urbino, Federico, 83
"Dying Well or Badly" (Hemingway, essay), 233

Eby, Carl, 57, 124, 139, 183
Education of Henry Adams, The (Adams), 47, 83
Elena (Queen of Italy), 211
Eliot, T. S., 64, 84, 127, 134, 151, 181, 182, 310
Elizabeth I (Queen of England), 14
Emilio the barman, in *FTA*, 243–45, 250–51, 261, 269–70, 272, 275, 278
Emmanuel, Victor, II (King of Italy), 32, 94, 115
Emmanuel, Victor, III (King of Italy), 32, 77, 92, 94, 115, 191, 211
Erhlich, Paul, 196
Esther (Adams), 47
Ethiopian War, 262
Etzel (King of the Huns), 160
Euripides, 12
Exposition of the Entire Bible (Gills), 24

Falls, Cyril, 27, 31, 223
Falstaff (Verdi), 145
Far Away and Long Ago (Hudson), 83
Farewell to Arms, A (Hemingway, novel): alcohol in, 33, 47, 53, 79–80, 104, 110, 123, 129, 139, 146, 171, 172, 179, 192, 195, 211, 251–52, 261, 264, 302, 309; ants in, 316–17; banning of, 74; bat in, 130; birds as a motif in, 177–79, 213; cats as a motif in, 183–84, 269, 276; censorship of, 73–74, 91, 107, 193, 209–10, 211, 214, 219, 220, 226, 233, 275; cover art, 3; dedication, 4, 116; editing notes, 90, 104, 135, 143, 147, 150, 158, 161, 195, 200, 207, 210, 214, 243, 246, 254, 255, 259, 261, 308, 311–12; endings, alternate, 314, 317, 320–23; epigraphs, 12–13, 57, 252; epistemic theme, 55, 97, 111, 131, 157, 200; Everyman's Library edition, 257, 302, 307; extra spaces in, 75, 117–18, 126, 128, 135, 184, 252, 257, 258, 276, 277; food and drink, descriptions of, 52, 95, 179–80, 251–52; foreword, 9–10; hair as a motif in, 57, 139; holograph manuscript, 12, 75, 80, 81, 84, 91, 95, 109, 117, 128, 135, 181, 214, 252, 257, 258, 276, 311; homosexual references in, 107; identity as a motif in, 54–55, 60, 91, 102, 107, 124, 140, 147, 151–52, 161, 244–45, 248, 251–54, 262–64, 303, 318; illustrated edition of, 4, 6; insanity as a motif in, 68–69, 93, 125–26, 136–37, 151–52, 180, 269; inspiration for, 82–83, 145, 159, 183, 206–7, 238, 316–17; introduction (1948), 4–9, 205; introduction by Seán Hemingway, 11; Italian translation of, 243; liberties with history in, 113, 117, 121; Modern Library edition, 257; music as a motif in, 40, 116, 145, 147–48, 245–47; *nada* theme, 306; publication of (1929), 5; rain as a motif in, 22, 141, 151, 170, 175, 184, 191, 213, 215, 216, 223, 269, 276, 313, 320; reviews of, 246; sales figures, 5; Scribner's edition, 257; time as a motif in, 182, 184, 221, 303, 304; title(s), alternate, 13–14, 82, 252, 310; title, meaning of, 13–14; title, source of, 14
Farewell to Arms, A (1932 film), 164
"Farewell to Arms, A" (Peele), 14–15
Farewell to Arms, A: Appendix A, 135; first draft, 5; Hemingway Library edition, 3, 13, 29, 161, 256; introduction, 205
"Fathers and Sons" (Hemingway, short story), 13, 228
Fathers and Sons (Turgenev), 73
Feast of the Annunciation to Mary, 24
Fell, Charles, 24
Fennel, Jonathan, 28
Ferguson, Helen, in *FTA*, 60, 62–63, 136, 140, 151–52, 157, 252, 264, 275; dislike of Frederic, 253–54; feelings for Catherine, 254, 264; source material for, 136
"Ferguson and Lesbian Love" (Mandel), 136, 254
Fetterley, Judith, 133, 305
Fiedler, Leslie, 133
Fielding, Henry, 12, 82, 83
Fifty-second Division of the British Army, 136
Filarete, 127

Filiberto, Emanuele, 77
First Letter to Timothy (Apostle Paul), 194
Fitzgerald, F. Scott, 7, 9, 59, 87, 153, 256
Fitzgerald, Zelda, 3, 8
Flame, The (D'Annunzio), 25, 205
Flanders (Belgium), 160
Flaubert, Gustave, 9, 82, 83, 87, 88
Florence (Italy), 37, 43
Ford, Ford Madox, 11, 80
Foro Buonaparte, 154
Fourth Crusade, 66
For Whom the Bell Tolls (Hemingway, novel), 13; Robert Jordan, 164
For Whom the Bell Tolls (film), 8, 164
Fox Hunt, The (Homer), 6
Frazee, Harry, 163
Frederick the Great of Prussia, 205, 217
Freemasons, 36
Freisa, 139
French Revolution, 82
Fussell, Paul, 70

Gage (Miss), in *FTA*, 122, 124, 128, 134; feelings about Catherine, 124, 137; source of, 122
Gamble, James, 38, 43, 175
Gambler, The (Dostoevsky), 69
Gangwisch, Gustav and Marie-Therese, 283
Garden of Eden, The (Hemingway, novel), 54
Gardner, Ava, 8
Garibaldi, Giuseppe, 117, 159
Garioni, Vincenzo, 28
Gatti, Angelo, 189
Gavuzzi, in *FTA*, 96
Gehrig, Lou, 164
Gellhorn, Martha, 8, 167
Generals Die in Bed (Harrison), 224
"Genius," The (Dreiser), 313–15
Genoa (Italy), 36, 66–67, 87
George, in *FTA*, 138, 139
Germania (Toscanini), 145
"Get a Seeing-Eyed Dog" (Hemingway, short story), 116
Ghismonda (d'Albert), 146
Giardini Pubblici (Public Gardens), 79, 138
Gilbert, Martin, 160
Gill, John, 24
Gino, in *FTA*, 202, 203, 204–5
God and the State (Bakunin), 220
Godolphin, Isabel Simmons, 147
Gogoltha, 66
Gooch, John, 27, 31, 91
Goodbye to All That (Graves), 14
Gorizia (Italy), 10, 20, 22, 29, 32, 41, 53, 61–62, 70, 84, 89, 160, 176, 189–91, 209, 211–13, 218, 222, 321; capture of, 27, 30, 54; climate, 30; description, 51; H. G. Wells's visit, 31; hospital in, 54
Gospel of John, 317
Granatieri di Sardegna, 92
Grand Hotel & de Milan (Gran Hotel), 145–46
Grand Hôtel & des Isles Borromées, 249–50, 251, 254
Grappa, 53
Graves, Robert, 14
Great Gatsby, The (Fitzgerald), 9
Great War and Modern Memory, The (Fussell), 70
Greco-Turkish War, 301
Greene, Philip, 104, 261, 302
Green Hills of Africa (Hemingway, book), 215; foreword, 9
Greppi, Giuseppi, 260–61, 265
Guardia di Finanza, 276
Guiseppe, Franchesco (Emperor Franz Joseph of Austria), 35
Gulf Stream, The (Homer), 6
Gunbuyer.com, 177
Guttingen (Mr. and Mrs.), in *FTA*, 279, 283

Hall, Caroline Hancock, 5
Hancock, Emmett, in *FTA*, 5
Handbook to Literature, A (Harmon), 151
Harmon, William, 151
Harriman, Averell, 8
Harrison, Charles Yale, 224
Harz Mountains (Germany), 78
Hawkins, Ruth A., 10
Hays, Peter, 45
"Headgear and Horses" (Mandel), 236
Heidegger, Martin, 10
Heilman, Charlotte, 122
Hellinger, Mark, 8
Hellyer, C. R., 108
Hemingway, Clarence, 181
Hemingway, Ernest: as an ambulance driver, 5, 98; bicycling, love of, 210, 219; birth, 6, 49; cats, fondness for, 183; Cuba, home in, 8; death, 5, 8; desire for a daughter, 184; faith and superstitions, 7, 150; guns, 177; head trauma, 101–2, 137; hospital stay/wounding, 37–38, 42–43, 44, 55, 96, 98, 101, 105, 114, 121–22, 127, 136, 170–71, 249, 259; hostility toward women, 133, 166; "iceberg theory" of writing, 20, 85, 88, 136, 197, 321; Italian language, use of, 43, 52; in Italy, 5, 43, 261; jaundice, 170; Key West, residence in, 4,

7, 181; Key West library, 7; letter to family from hospital, 38, 105–6, 260–61; mechanotherapy, 114; medals earned for military service, 105, 190; military service, 5, 8; out-of-body-experience, 97–99; parents, relationship with, 180–81; Paris, residence in, 37, 39; skiing, 176, 283; Spain, travels in, 79; suicide and mental illness, 137; Switzerland, visit to, 283–85, 301–3; visits to track, 158; war profiteering, opinion of, 205

Hemingway, Grace Hall, 145

Hemingway, Gregory, 4, 11; birth, 10

Hemingway, Hadley, 4–5, 25, 37, 39, 55, 147, 154, 155, 181, 283–85; pet names, 183–84; pregnancy, 166

Hemingway, Jack, 139

Hemingway, John Hadley Nicanor, 4

Hemingway, Leicester, 99

Hemingway, Margaux, 139

Hemingway, Mary Welsh, 4, 8; pet names, 184; pregnancy, 8

Hemingway, Patrick, 4, 9–10, 82; birth, 9–10, 304, 314; head trauma, 8, 10

Hemingway, Pauline Pfeiffer, 4, 8, 10, 55, 116, 181, 283; pregnancy and labor with Patrick, 9–10, 55, 181, 304, 305, 314

Hemingway, Seán, 11

Hemingway Blog, The, 159

Hemingway in Love and War (Villard and Nagel), 98, 102

Hemingway: The Postwar Years and the Posthumous Novels (Burwell), 74

Hemingway: The Writer as Artist (Baker), 161, 185, 189

Hemingway's Fetishism (Eby), 57

Hemingway's First War (Reynolds), 5, 12–13, 19, 41, 43, 54, 55, 86, 114, 122, 136, 153, 172, 209, 218, 223, 232, 234, 235, 236, 260, 261,

Hemingway's Reading: 1910–1940 (Reynolds), 7, 24, 94, 145

Henry, Alexander, 82

Henry, Barklie McKee "Buzz," 44, 83

Henry, Frederic, in *FTA*, 5; Abruzzi, desire to visit, 38–39, 46–47, 48–49, 53, 112; architecture, passion for, 246–47; carriage ride, 138, 154, 303; changing perspectives and thoughts of Catherine, 85, 106, 125, 183, 216, 218, 231, 239–40, 275; childhood, 228–29; class and, 91, 102; "craziness," 125–26, 136–37; desertion, 14, 52, 137, 171, 222–40, 257–58, 262; designs on Catherine, 64, 66, 68–71, 73, 80; disguise, 236–37, 248, 253, 264, 269; escape to Switzerland with Catherine, 9, 252, 262, 270–80; faith and religious beliefs, 6, 15, 36, 45, 48, 50, 53, 58, 68, 87–88, 96–97, 100, 101, 110–11, 123, 126, 131, 147–48, 193–94, 198–201, 214–15, 246, 255–56, 267–68, 280, 305, 315, 316–19, 323; family, 75–76, 162, 180, 251; fantasies/dreams, 79–80, 180, 216, 306; first meeting with Catherine, 41, 54–56; flirtation with Miss Gage, 122, 124; head injury, 238; hepatitis, 192; hospital stay/wounding, 45, 75, 89, 95, 96–102, 104–29; identity and, 54–55, 91, 102, 107, 124, 147, 161, 244, 248, 251–54, 262–64, 318; immaturity, 47–48, 65, 71, 84, 122, 131, 141, 158, 165, 167, 173, 179, 264; insomnia, 123; Italian language, use of, 34, 39, 43, 60–61, 72, 74, 100, 117, 122, 138, 149, 201, 204–5, 213, 230, 243–44; Italian version of name, use of, 81, 83, 117, 122, 195; jaundice, 170, 172, 179; jokes and stories, 80–81, 114, 115, 195, 196; love, 6, 15, 47, 50, 57, 68, 70–71, 84, 100, 108, 111, 122, 125, 132, 141, 158, 183, 193, 194, 198–99, 243, 252, 255, 257, 258, 268; marital status as narrator, 164, 319; medals earned for military service, 190; meeting with Catherine in garden, 61–64, 68; narrative descriptions, 30, 33–35, 41, 48–50, 52, 55, 66, 68, 73–74, 79, 90–91, 95, 100, 130, 162–64, 183, 255–57, 312; narrative descriptions from the front, 77–78, 91, 117, 144–45, 149, 189–91, 202–34; narrative descriptions on Tagliamento River, 235–38; on leave, 51–52; out-of-body experience (OBE), 96–97, 98–99, 103, 267; pregnancy and labor, thoughts on Catherine's, 166–67, 169, 182, 184, 214, 275, 306–10, 312; redemption, 24, 322; relationship with priest, 45–46, 48, 50, 79–80, 100, 107, 198–201; relationship with Rinaldi, 42–43, 45–46, 65, 100, 108, 192; reunion with Catherine after desertion, 12, 171, 239–40, 253–58; sexism, examples of, 133, 166, 172–73, 179; sexual experience, 39, 40, 43, 44, 51, 52, 55, 58, 65, 68, 74, 125, 130, 136, 139, 178, 192–93, 256–57; source material for, 5, 14, 44, 47, 62–63, 68, 81–84, 147, 205; surgery, 130, 134–35; surgery, recovering from, 139, 161, 164, 176; train to Stresa, 249–50; train trip, freight, 237–38; train trip back to the front, 185, 189–90; train trip to Milan, 118, 125, 174–78; train trips, 180, 184, 189–90, 239–43, 248, 257–59, 289, 291–92; visit to the race track, 150, 153–58; war, changing perceptions of, 59, 67–68, 78, 93, 110, 205, 206, 241

Henry IV (Shakespeare), 168
Hickock, Guy, 97, 98, 100
"Hills Like White Elephants" (Hemingway, short story), 21–22, 166, 301–2
History of Creation, The, 66
"Hollow Men, The" (Eliot), 84, 134
Holman, C. Hugh, 151
"Homage to Hemingway" (Bishop), 9
Homer, Winslow, 6–7
Hospitallers, 251
Hotchner, A. E., 210
Hotel Beau-Séjour, 301, 304
Hotel Cavour, 79, 180
Hotel Continental, 251
Hotel Croce Bianca, 251
Hotel Metropole, 280
House of Savoy, 94, 114–15, 174
Hoyle, Edmond, 285
Huckleberry Finn (Twain), 215
Hudson, William Henry, 82, 83
Hughes-Hallet, Lucy, 206
Hugo's Language Institute, 53
Humbert I, Count of Savoy, 94
Hundred Years' War, 145, 169

Il barbiere di Siviglia (*The Barber of Seville*) (Rossini), 146
Il maiale nero: rivelazioni e documenti (*The Black Pig: Revelations and Documents*) (Notari), 35–36
"In Another Country" (Hemingway, short story), 13, 44, 93; marriage in, 56, 319–20; mechanotherapy in, 113
"Indian Camp" (Hemingway, short story), 23, 311; Nick Adams in, 103, 106; suicide in, 103
In Our Time (Hemingway, short story collection), 13; cover art, 3; dedication, 4; faith in, 71, 319; Nick Adams, 42, 249; Rinaldi, 42
Inquisition, 314, 315
In Search of Lost Time (Proust), 81, 88
Ireland, John, 79
Islands in the Stream (film), 11
Islands in the Stream (Hemingway, novel), Thomas Hudson, 11, 83
Isle of Capri, 37–38, 47, 79, 155, 172
Isonzo front (Italy), 20, 22, 73, 88, 143; deaths from cholera, 28
Italian Army and the First World War, The (Gooch), 27
Italian Fourth Army, 260
Italian Second Army, 77–78, 191, 208
Italian Socialist Party, 220, 229
Italian Third Army, 77, 78, 191, 213, 232, 260

Italo-Turkish War, 90
Italy (Baedecker), 26, 30, 44, 66–67, 115–16, 127, 138, 171, 174, 184–85, 190, 212, 220, 225, 249, 250

Jackson, L. E., 108
James, Henry, 12–13, 81–82, 205, 252
Jessup, Elsie, 55
Jew of Malta (Marlowe), 310
JFK Library, 13, 98, 214
Joseph, Franz (Emperor of Austria-Hungary), 35
Joseph Andrews (Fielding), 12, 83
Josephs, Allen, 96, 99
Journeys Out of the Body (Monroe), 99
Joyce, James, 9, 94, 214
Julius Caesar (Shakespeare), 167–68

Kahle, Hans, 8
Kansas City Research Hospital, 305
Kansas City Star, The, 159
Keegan, John, 77
Keeler, Clinton, 15
Ken (magazine), 93
Key West (Florida), 4, 7, 181, 297
"Killers, The" (Hemingway, short story), 8
King James Bible, 24
King Vittorio Emanuele II Galleria, 115–16, 121, 145
Knights of Malta, 251
Knowles, John, 249
Kory, Fern, 136
Kümmel, 172

La Bohème (Puccini), 146, 148
La coscienza di Zeno (Svevo), 94
Lago Maggiore (Italy), 171
Lamentation for the Dead Christ (Mantegna), 277
Lancet, 105–6
Lanfranchi, Ubaldo, 66
La Scala opera house, 43–44, 116, 121, 145, 146
"Last Good Country, The" (Hemingway, short story), 228
Lausanne (Switzerland), 289, 300–302, 304–6, 309, 313
Lausanne Cantonal Hospital, 305
Lausanne Peace Conference, 301, 302
Lausanne University Hospital, 305
Lee, Henry, 14
Le Feu (*Under Fire*) (Barbusse), 83, 265
Letters (Hemingway, collection), 4, 5, 83, 87, 92, 107, 146, 163, 170, 175, 181, 197, 215, 259, 260, 283, 287, 292, 296, 301, 304, 314

Light for Me, 157–58
"Light of the World, The" (Hemingway, short story), 13
Lincoln, Abraham, 114
Little, Brown, 74
Lives of the Saints, The (Fell), 24
Lockridge, Ernest, 263
Lockwood, Preston, 12–13
London Times, The, 232
Look Homeward, Angel (Wolfe), 9
Luschnig, C. A. E., 12

MacDonald, Elsie, 136
Macdonald, John, 199
Macedonias, 91
Machine in the Garden (Marx), 51
Magic Mountain, The (Mann), 183
Major, in *FTA*, 42, 53, 81, 90, 94, 190; faith, lack of, 50; visit with Frederic in hospital, 104
Malatesta, Sigismondo, 83
Mandel, Miriam, 35, 136, 148, 153, 154, 156, 158, 236, 247, 254, 264
Mann, Thomas, 183
Manning, Frederic, 81
Mantegna, Andrea, 277
Man with hernia, in *FTA*, 74–75
Manzoni, Alessandro, 145
Margaux, 139
Marlowe, Christopher, 310
Marryat, Frederick, 81
Marsala, 146, 171, 172
Marvell, Andrew, 181–82, 184, 215, 303
Marx, Leo, 22, 51
Max Perkins (Berg), 7
May offensive of 1917, 89
Mazzini, Giuseppe, 117
McAdams, in *FTA*, 149, 157
McIlvaine, Robert M., 313–15
McKinley, William, 79
MeasuringWorth.com, 46, 250
Mechanotherapy, 113
Medea (Euripides), 12
Mefistofele (*Mephistopheles*) (Boito), 146
Memoirs of an Infantry Officer (Sassoon), 224
Men at War (Hemingway, anthology), 4, 78, 81; dedication, 4; introduction, 93, 167–68, 265; mechanotherapy in, 113
Menocal, Mayito, 4
Men without Women (Hemingway, short story collection), 233
"Mercenaries, The" (Hemingway, short story), 25, 42; Rinaldi Renaldo, 42
Meriwether, James, 193

Metropolitan Museum of Art, 11
Meyerbeer, Giacomo, 247
Meyers (Mr. & Mrs.), in *FTA*, 146, 150, 153, 157–58
Middle Parts of Fortune, The (Manning), 81
Midwife's Pocket Companion, The, 24
Milan (Italy), 43–44, 49, 55, 102, 104, 113–22, 125, 127–28, 130, 136, 144–48, 153, 159–60, 162, 164, 166, 170–72, 174–76, 180, 184–85, 189, 195, 207, 216, 218, 240, 243, 245–46, 248, 250, 257–59, 277, 307; bombing of, 44; canals, 79; International Exposition, 138; Piazza alla Scala, 116, 145, 178; Piazza Cavour, 178; Piazza del Duomo, 154; Piazza Quindici Martiri, 9; Via Alessandro Manzoni, 145; Via Dante, 154–55
Milan Aquarium, 138
Milan Cathedral, 79
Moddelmog, Debra, 180, 254
Monfalcone (Italy), 19; capture of, 93–94
Monroe, Robert A., 99
Monte Kuk (Italy), 62, 144
Monte Sabotino (Italy), 22–23, 29, 30
Monte San Gabriele (Italy), 22, 25, 53, 70, 105, 143, 144, 159, 189, 199, 203
Monteiro, George, 82
Montreux (Switzerland), 278–80, 283–84, 286–87, 289, 291, 300–301
Mont-Saint-Michel and Chartres (Adams), 47, 83
Moore, Walter, 10
Moretti, Ettore, in *FTA*, 39, 117, 157, 149–50, 246; source for, 146, 149
Mosè in Egitto (*Moses in Egypt*) (Rossini), 146
Moveable Feast, A (Hemingway, memoir), 150, 154, 155, 158, 197, 210, 283–85; Ford Madox Ford characterization in, 11, 80; Restored Edition, 9
"Mr. and Mrs. Elliot" (Hemingway, short story), 254
Mr. Britling Sees It Through (Wells), 265–66
Mürren (Switzerland), 176, 279
Mussolini, Benito, 9, 20, 25, 28, 39, 79, 88; wounding, 88–89
Mutinies, 78, 92
"My Old Man" (Hemingway, short story), 153; crooked racing in, 156; Joe Butler, 153, 154

Nagel, James, 98, 102, 156, 164, 257
Napoli (Italy), 49
National Book Award, 7
National Enquirer, 99
National League, 162

"Natural History of the Dead, A" (Hemingway, short story), 182, 224
Near-death experience (NDE), 96–97, 103
Nerone, Antonio, 149
Nerone, Beato Nicola (Nick), 38–39, 46, 112, 146–47, 149, 175
New Orleans Charity Hospital, 311
New Slain Knight (Hemingway, abandoned novel), 83, 130, 215; Jimmy Breen, 130
New York Giants, 162
New York Times, 12–13, 162, 261
New York Yankees, 163
"next to of course god America i" (Cummings), 207
Nice (France), 114–15
"Night Watch, The" (Rembrandt), 315
Ninth Health Company of the Italian Army, 37
Nobel Prize in Medicine, 10, 196
Notari, Umberto, 35
Nothing Ever Happens to the Brave (Rollyson), 167
Notturne (D'Annunzio), 25, 205
"Now I Lay Me" (Hemingway, short story), 98; insomnia in, 123; Nick Adams, 215, 225

Oak Park High School, 97, 147, 159
Och Brothers, 279
Of Time and the River (Wolfe), 9
Oldsey, Bernard, 14
One Man's Initiation (Dos Passos), 33–34
Only Thing That Counts, The (Bruccoli), 74
"On the Quay at Smyrna" (Hemingway, short story), 23
Orr, Mary, 87
Ospedale Maggiore, 127–28, 143, 161, 176
Otello (Verdi), 145
Othello (Shakespeare), 262–64
"*Othello* as a Key to Hemingway" (Lockridge), 263
Ottoman Empire, 90
Out-of-body experience (OBE), 96–100
"Out-of-Body Experience, An" (Blackmore), 99
"Out of Season" (Hemingway, short story), 146, 166; Peduzzi in, 197
Oxford Book of English Verses, 14, 215
Oxford English Dictionary, 24, 43, 107
Oxford University, 44
Owens, Wilfred, 206

Palermo (Sicily), 37
Pallanza (Italy), 171, 271, 273–74
Parade's End (Ford), 11, 80

"Passing of Pickles McCarty or The Woppian Way, The" (Hemingway, short story), 263; Nick Neroni, 25
Passini, in *FTA*, 91, 92, 93, 94; death, 134, 135
Patton (film), 11
Patton, George S., Jr., 11
Paxton, Joseph, 115
Peele, George, 14–15, 206, 263
Perkins, Maxwell, 3, 4, 7, 9, 73–74, 172, 233, 259
Perret, P., 107
Persistence of Memory, The (Dali), 135
Petacci, Clara, 9
Peter Simple (Marryat), 81
Pfeiffer, Gustavus Adolphus, 4, 116
Pfeiffer, Paul, 4
Phelan, James, 156
Philosophical Dictionary (Voltaire), 167
Piani, Luigi, in *FTA*, 210, 220, 223, 227, 229–31, 239, 240
Piermarini, Giuseppe, 245
Pinacoteca di Brera, 277
Pisa (Italy), 36, 66–67
Pivano, Fernanda, 243
Plimpton, George, 220
"Polyhymnia" (Peele), 14
Pordenone (Italy), 209, 212, 232, 236
Porta Nuova Arch (Italy), 145, 178
"Portrait of a Lady" (Eliot), 310
Portrait of the Artist as a Young Man (Joyce), 9
Pound, Ezra, 9, 25, 82, 83, 87, 181
Pride of the Yankees, The (film), 164
Priest, in *FTA*, 33, 97, 142; faith, 10, 35–36, 40, 42, 50, 70, 110, 181, 198–201; hometown, 43; innocence of, 34; inspiration for, 37; love, 57, 111, 181, 257; relationship with Frederic, 45–46, 48, 50, 100, 107, 192, 198–201, 240; relationship with Rinaldi, 42, 194; as role model, 162; sexuality, thoughts on, 112, 197; shortcomings, 79–80; visit with Frederic in hospital, 104, 109–12; war, perceptions of, 110, 144, 200–201, 230
"Prisoner of Chillon, The" (Byron), 278
Privileges, The (Stendhal), 81
Proust, Marcel, 81, 88, 257
Puccini, Giacomo, 145
Purple Land, The (Hudson), 83

Rasmussen, Daniel, 6
Reading Hemingway's Across the River and into the Trees (Cirino), 11, 25, 168, 205, 225
Reading Hemingway's The Sun Also Rises (Stoneback), 154

Red and the Black, The (Stendhal), 316
Red Badge of Courage, The (Crane), 82
Remarque, Erich Maria, 3, 73
Rembrandt, 315
Remembrance of Things Past. See *In Search of Lost Time* (Proust)
Renoir, Pierre-Auguste, 7
Reparti d'assalto (shock troops), 92–93
"Revolutionist, The" (Hemingway, short story), 277
Reynolds, Michael, 4, 12, 24, 41, 43, 54, 81, 82, 85, 99, 113–14, 121, 127, 143, 145, 153, 165, 196, 209, 223, 232, 236, 237, 306, 311
Richardson, Hadley. *See* Hemingway, Hadley
Rinaldi, in *FTA*, 78, 97, 101, 142, 192, 195, 318; attraction to Catherine, 56, 107, 129; faith, lack of, 10, 34, 35–36, 55, 106, 194–95; hometown, 47; identity and, 54; language proficiency, 53, 60, 65; love, 44, 84, 106–7, 194; name, source of, 42; as rationalist/voice of reason, 45, 54, 55, 70, 80, 106, 193, 196–97, 211; relationship with Frederic, 42–43, 45–46, 65, 71, 84, 100, 106–8, 240, 253–54, 269; relationship with priest, 80, 106, 194; as role model, 162; sexuality, thoughts on, 33, 43, 44, 106–7, 192–93; sexually transmitted diseases, 45, 69, 192, 196–97, 240; skill as a surgeon, 105; source material for, 194; visit with Frederic in hospital, 104–8, 115–18
Risorgimento (Italian Unification), 154
Rocca, in *FTA*, 80
Rodgers, Crowell, in *FTA*, 153, 154, 157
Rollyson, Carl, 167
Rome (Italy), 34, 42, 43, 148, 153, 246; legend regarding the founding of, 115; Piazza Vittorio Emanuele, 225
Romeo and Juliet (Shakespeare), 185
Rommel, Erwin, 207, 222
Roosevelt, Theodore, 79
Ross, Lilian, 8
Rossini, Gioachino, 146
Rubens, Peter Paul, 277
Russo, John Paul, 25, 94
Ruth, Babe, 156, 163–64, 168

Saint Anthony of Egypt, 85, 86–87
Saint Anthony of Padua, 85–86, 87, 140; death, 166–67; Miracle of the Mule, 88
Saint Valentine, 128
Salvarsan, 196–97
Sancarlone, 250

Sanford, Marcelline Hemingway, 172, 261
San Siro, 153–58
Sassoon, Siegfried, 224
Saunders, Edgar, in *FTA*, 40, 145
Save Me the Waltz (Fitzgerald), 3
Savoia (France), 95, 114–15
Savoia Cavalleria, 95
Scanlan, Anna, 121–22
Scenes from Italy's War (Trevelyan), 22, 51, 89, 159, 204, 214, 216, 230
Schmitz, Ettore. *See* Svevo, Italo
Schneider, Daniel, 133
Schneider, Isidore, 83, 87
Schrödinger, Erwin, 10
Scott, George C., 11
Scribner, Charles, 6, 11
Scribner's Magazine, 7, 74, 172, 261
Second Battle of the Aisne, 78
Sempione Park (Parco Sempione), 138, 154–55
Sentimental Education (Flaubert), 82
"separate peace," 42, 155, 249, 254, 262, 263
Separate Peace, A (Knowles), 249
Serena, Enrico, 42–43
"Sexual Identity in *A Farewell to Arms*" (Solotaroff), 263
Sexually transmitted diseases, 32, 69; gonorrhea, 197; syphilis, 45, 196–97, 240
Sforza, Francesco, 154
Shakespeare, William, 64, 73, 131, 167–68, 185, 262–64
"Short Happy Life of Francis Macomber, The" (Hemingway, short story), 168
Short Stories, The (Hemingway, collection), 9; foreword, 83; Nick Adams, 83
Shroud of Turin, 174
Simmons, Ralph, in *FTA*, 40, 145, 245–46, 250, 253, 269; source for, 147
Simplon Pass (Switzerland), 155
Smith, Bill, 7
Smith, Kate, 283
Smith, Y. K., 38
"Soldier's Home" (Hemingway, short story), Harold Krebs, 98
Solotaroff, Robert, 263
Sonnet 138 (Shakespeare), 131
Spanier, Sandra, 133, 253, 305
Spanish Civil War, 7–8
Sportsman's Sketches, A (Turgenev), 112
Stein, Gertrude, 8, 12
Stendhal, 81, 82, 316–17
St. Estephe, 179
Stigler Company, 138

Stoneback, H. R., 82, 83, 85, 145, 154–56, 166, 236, 250, 251, 261, 270, 306
Story of the American Red Cross in Italy, The (Bakewell), 228, 231, 232
Straf expedition, 147, 161
Strega, 47, 53
Stresa (Italy), 171, 175, 245–46, 248–51, 254, 258, 260–61, 269–74
"Summer People" (Hemingway, short story), 8; Nick, 228; Kate, 8, 228
Sun Also Rises, The (Hemingway, novel), 6, 7, 89, 210, 257; Bill Gordon, 103, 194, 244; Braddocks, 11, 80; Brett Ashley, 43, 63, 179, 304, 305; Count Mippipopolous, 262; cover art, 3; dedication, 4; epigraphs, 12, 13; faith in, 63; foreword, 9; insomnia in, 123; Jake Barnes, 43, 59, 63, 83, 112, 179, 183, 194, 200, 228, 244, 304, 316; Mike Campbell, 240; Pedro Romero, 43, 304; Robert Cohn, 83; sexuality in, 63
Sun Valley (Idaho), 8
Svevo, Italo, 94
Swierczewski, Karol, 8
Switzerland (Baedecker), 176, 278, 280, 301
Sylvester, Bickford, 263

Tableaux Vivants (Perret), 107
Tagliamento River (Italy), 62, 102, 118, 208, 209, 212, 229; bridge over, 213, 216, 230–32, 240, 259; Frederic's trip down, 234–38
Taormina (Sicily), 38, 43, 175
Taranto (Italy), 204
Teatro Lirico, 245
"Temptation of Anthony, The" (Schneider), 87
Temptation of Saint Anthony, The (Flaubert), 87, 88
Tender Is the Night (Fitzgerald), 9
"Ten Indians" (Hemingway, short story), 228
Third Battle of Ypres, 160
Thompson, Mark, 22, 28, 31, 52, 58, 73, 77, 94–95, 159–60, 168, 191, 199, 232
Thought in Action (Cirino), 135, 168, 239, 247
"Three-Day Blow, The" (Hemingway, short story), 271
Three Soldiers (Dos Passos), 88, 234
Thurston, Herbert, 128
"Today Is Friday" (Hemingway, short story), 233
To Have and Have Not (Hemingway, novel), 74; Harry Morgan, 184
"To His Coy Mistress" (Marvell), 181–82, 184, 215, 303
Tolstoy, Leo, 36, 204

Tomb of Alexander (Hemingway), 11
Toronto Star: "Fishing the Rhône Canal," 285; "A Veteran Visits the Old Front," 21
Torrents of Spring, The (Hemingway, novel), 6, 7, 13; epigraph, 12, 83
Tosca (Puccini), 145, 147–48, 245, 247; "*Vissi d'arte*" ("I Lived for Art"), 148
Toscanini, Arturo, 145
Toulouse-Lautrec, Henri de, 7
Tour de France, 210
"Train Trip, A" (Hemingway, short story), 130
transatlantic review (journal), 11, 80
Treaty of Campo Formio, 226
Trentino (Italy), 29
Trentino front, 73, 164
Trevelyan, G. M., 22, 27, 30–31, 51, 62, 72, 89, 104, 159, 190, 202–3, 204, 209, 213, 214, 216, 230, 231–32
Trieste (Italy), 53, 93–94, 191, 237
Triple Entente, 20, 34
Triumph Over Death, The, 66
Turati, Filippo, 229
Turgenev, Ivan, 73, 112
Turin (Italy), 72, 159, 174–75
"Twa Corbies," 215
Twain, Mark, 215
Twenty-seventh Corps of the Italian Army, 207
Tyler, Lisa, 63, 141

Udine (Italy), 31, 118, 125, 189, 208–9, 211, 213–14, 216–18, 222–27, 229, 237, 239; capture by Germans, 231; description of, 26–27
Ulysses (Joyce), 9
Umberto I, 32, 94
Unbelievable Happiness and Final Sorrow (Hawkins), 10
University of Buffalo Library, 214
"Up in Michigan" (Hemingway, short story), 228
US Customs, 74
US Seventh Army, 11

Valentini (Dr.), in *FTA*, 128–29, 239
Van Campen, in *FTA*, 102, 137, 171, 172–73; source of, 122
Vatican, 34–35
Vecelli, Tiziano, 260
Verdi, Giuseppe, 116, 145
Vermouth, 110, 123, 171, 172
Vernon, Alex, 129
"Very Short Story, A" (Hemingway, short story), 93, 131, 176; Luz in, 137, 209–10
V.E. soldiers, 92–93

Vesuvius (Italy), 37
Vicenza (Italy), 118, 160–61
Villard, Henry, 42, 43, 55, 98, 102, 130, 170–71
Voltaire, 46, 167, 220
Voluntary Aid Detachments (VAD), 41, 63
von Berrer, Albert, 223–24, 230, 237
von Hutier, Oskar, 207
von Kurowsky, Agnes, 42–43, 55, 63, 70, 130, 136, 153, 154; diary, 146
von Martini, Friedrich, 82
von Metternich, Klemens, 261

Wagner-Martin, Linda, 42
Walker (Mrs.), in *FTA*, 121–22
Walsh, Ernest, 215
War and Peace (Tolstoy), 36, 204; Pierre Bezukhov, 36
War and the Future (Wells), 31, 32, 266–67
Warren, Robert Penn, 11
Waste Land, The (Eliot), 64, 127
Watch and Ward Society, 74
Watson, James, 10
Way of All Flesh, The (Butler), 87
"Way You'll Never Be, A" (Hemingway, short story): Nick Adams, 95, 191–92; Paravicini, 247
Weapons and armaments: Astra 7.65 caliber pistol, 67; battery, 51; gas masks, 67; helmets, 73; Italian field artillery in WWI, 51; Martini Rifle, 82; potato mashers, 149; Skoda 305-millimeter gun, 96; stick bombs, 225
"We Live in a Country Where Nothing Makes Any Difference" (Moddelmog), 254
Wells, H. G., 31, 32, 265–67
Wengen (Switzerland), 278

"Western Wind," 215
West front, 144
Wexler, Joyce, 50, 133
What Is Life? (Schrödinger), 10
White War, The (Thompson), 22, 28, 52, 77, 94–95, 159, 232
Whitlow, Roger, 126
Whitney, Gertrude Vanderbilt, 44
Wilcox, Vanda, 118
Wilhelm II, Kaiser, 160
Wilkins, Cleonike Damianakes. *See* Cleon
Williams, Taylor, 8
Williamson, Samuel, 46, 250
Wilson, Andrew J., 263
Wilson, Edmund, 132
Wilson, Robert, 168
Wilson, Woodrow, 101, 114
Winner Take Nothing (Hemingway, short story collection), 224
Winter Olympics, 279
"Wish I were at Fiume" (Hemingway, letter), 25
With British Guns in Italy (Dalton), 21, 42, 54, 78, 92, 194, 213
Wolfe, Thomas, 7, 9
"Woppian Way, The" (Hemingway, short story), 263
Wuthering Heights (Brontë), 63, 140–41
Wyatt, David, 215, 228

"You Don't Know the Italian Language Well Enough" (Cirino), 39, 61, 81, 138, 149, 210
Young, John Harley, 311
Young, Philip, 14, 132

Zbyszko, Wladek, 3
Zona di Guerra post cards, 76